Southeast Asia
People, land and economy

Ronald Hill

ALLEN&UNWIN

To Roger, Lucia and Roderick William, to Ngaire, Mark and Maximillian Ivan and to Alexandra

This edition published in 2002

Allen & Unwin
83 Alexander Street
Crows Nest NSW 2065
Australia
Phone: (61 2) 8425 0100
Fax: (61 2) 9906 2218
Email: info@allenandunwin.com
Web: www.allenandunwin.com

National Library of Australia
Cataloguing-in-Publication entry:

Hill, R. D. (Ronald David), 1935– .
Southeast Asia: people, land and economy

Bibliography.
Includes index.
ISBN 1 86508 517 0.

1. Asia, Southeastern—Geography. 2. Asia, Southeastern—Historical geography. I. Title.

915.9

Set in 10/11pt Times Roman by DOCUPRO, Canberra
Printed by South Wind Production (Singapore) Private Limited

10 9 8 7 6 5 4 3 2 1

Contents

Figures

TABLES

ACKNOWLEDGEMENTS

A quarter of a century ago I observed—in a preface to another geography of Southeast Asia—that, 'The time when one person could hope to write a fully satisfactory book about such a large and varied region as South-East Asia has probably passed.' Milton Osborne, the eminent Australian historian of the region, challenged me to prove myself wrong. Whether I have succeeded the reader must judge but by supporting—even cajoling—Osborne has materially aided the work. My historian colleague Norman Owen has repeatedly disproved his rash statement that I know more about the region than any two people alive by answering my many importunate queries with unfailing precision and good humour. Ronald Skeldon, a former colleague in the Department of Geography, has been a meticulous critic from whose suggestions I have greatly benefited. By gently reminding me that there are yet other things to be done my room-mate Sanjay Nagarkar has bestirred me to continual effort. I am also especially grateful to colleagues in the Department of Ecology and Biodiversity who gave a wandering geographer 'a place, a habitation and a name' at a crucial time, especially to John Hodgkiss and David Dudgeon, respectively past and present Head of Department. Richard Corlett has been a mine of information in natural history. Colleagues in History have also been supportive—Kerrie MacPherson, Tom Stanley and the Head, Chan Lau Kit Ching. In particular, Michelle K.F. Wong worked wonders in transforming my steam-age manuscript into typescript.

R.D Hill
Late Professor of Geography,
Honorary Professor in Ecology and Biodiversity and in History,
The University of Hong Kong
5 March 2000
(birthday of Mercator, geographer and cartographer, 1512)

A NOTE ON PLACE-NAMES AND STATISTICS

First-time acquaintances of the region are often perplexed by its toponyms. Following international agreement, names are supposed to be rendered into the Roman alphabet according to the official system of each country concerned—thus Myanmar, not Burma, Yangon not Rangoon. Unfortunately, this principle has not been universally adopted. Many compilers of atlases take the view that common place-names have been assimilated to English and are thus retained—thus Malacca not Melaka, Sumatra not Sumatera. Furthermore, some official names are extraordinarily long, to the extent that they are not used—for Bangkok, 'Krungthepmahanarkorn' (and that is just the beginning). There is an element of politics in this too. Many people refused to use 'Kampuchea', the official name for Cambodia under the Khmer Rouge, and some refuse to use official names in Myanmar as a mark of disapproval of the present regime.

A number of changes in Malay/Indonesian orthography are worth noting. The Dutch-influenced 'dj' is now 'j', thus Jakarta, not Djakarta; 'j' is 'y', thus Yogyakarta not Jogjakarta; while the English-influenced 'sh' is now 'sy'. Another major change is 'ch' to 'c' (but pronounced 'ch'), so that 'Cat Town', Kuching, capital of Sarawak, is now officially 'Kucing', though many Sarawakians prefer the older spelling.

There are other complications, especially in insular Southeast Asia. The island of Borneo is known as Kalimantan in Indonesian, though strictly that term applies only to the southern two-thirds. 'North Borneo'—strictly 'British North Borneo'—was a separate state until after the Pacific War and the formation of Malaysia in 1962. Sarawak likewise. Brunei alone has remained independent. 'West Irian', known to its inhabitants, confusingly, as 'Papua' and as Irian Jaya, remained Dutch on the formation of Indonesia, only later being ceded. 'Timor' refers to the whole island. The Indonesians referred to East Timor as 'Timor Timur'. It has now been reconstituted, with the west Timor enclave of Okussi (Ocussi, Oecussi), as an independent state having the same boundaries as the once-Portuguese colony.

The 'Malay Peninsula' is a geographical, not a political entity for it includes the southern linguistically Malay-dominant provinces of Thailand, once mostly independent states like those that now make up Peninsular Malaysia. Pulau Pinang (Penang) and Malacca (Melaka) were exceptional, formerly comprising, with Singapore, the British Colony of the Straits Settlements. These, but not Singapore, joined 'Malaya' following the Pacific War. Singapore, member of the Malaysian Federation from 1962, became independent upon leaving it in 1965.

'Mainland Southeast Asia' is used here to refer to the band of countries from Myanmar to Viet Nam. Occasionally the term 'Indochina' is used for this group, especially from Thailand eastwards, but here it refers only to the former French possessions of Cambodia, Laos and Viet Nam. There is no official spelling for either Indochina or Southeast Asia. Indo-China (Indo-Chine) and South-East Asia or South-east Asia are as correct as Southeast Asia. Scholars searching library catalogues may wish to know that the Library of Congress listing, also widely used outside the US, uses the rubric 'Asia—Southeastern'.

Every attempt has been made to use the most recently available sources but for some countries these are not only out of date but quite rough estimates. In some tables, single sources have been preferred for the sake of consistency though the data they contain may not match exactly with those from other sources.

ONE
INTRODUCING THE REGION: UNITY AND DIVERSITY

Does Southeast Asia really exist? Many scholars, in many disciplines, writing since the 1960s have been so certain that the region is a distinctive and coherent entity that they have not bothered to define it. A few, the historians Chandler and Steinberg for instance, are careful to delimit the region, while recognising that at different times its boundaries might be placed other than where they are now generally considered to be. In political terms the land boundaries are clear enough, encompassing the swathe of mainland countries east from Myanmar (Burma) to Viet Nam and the great 'Indian Archipelago', as it once was termed, extending from Sumatera's western islands east to the entirely arbitrary boundary of Indonesia's West Irian with Papua New Guinea. (The maritime boundaries are still to some degree a matter of dispute, especially in the South China Sea.) But most of the land boundaries have been inherited from colonial times as foreign administrators, adopting what was for the region the then novel concept of fixed, delimited boundaries, sought to impose that notion, probably on the basis that good 'fences' (i.e. defined boundaries) make good neighbours.

Such boundaries, as in Africa, cut across cultural and linguistic zones leaving similar peoples on opposite sides of new national fences. The Shan of northeastern Myanmar are essentially 'Thai', using that term in a broad sense. The Mon (Talaing) of southern Myanmar spill over into Thailand, while along China's southwestern borders lives a multitude of ethnic minority peoples whose affinities in the past, and still to some degree today, are with Southeast Asians rather than with Han Chinese. Language, music, the once-prevalent custom of body tattooing, chewing *betel* and the technique of *batik* cloth manufacture are just a few basically Southeast Asian characteristics that have survived there.

The land boundaries of mainland Southeast Asia, except politically, are best regarded as transition zones or 'clines'—in far northern Burma from clearly 'Southeast Asian' Kachin people to Tibetans, in the provinces along the Chinese border from similarly 'Southeast Asian' peoples to Han Chinese. Along both sides of the region's land border with India and Bangladesh are to be found peoples of broadly similar cultural affinities—Nagas, Chins and a host of others distinct from majority lowland Indians and Bengalis. To the south the island Andamanese and Nicobarese, though lying around the same longitude as western Myanmar, 92°E, are culturally rather unlike most Southeast Asian peoples, except perhaps remnants of so-called 'Negrito' groups in the Malay Peninsula. They have long been part of India politically.

The only really clear boundary is that to the southwest and south where the great emptiness of the Indian Ocean extends to Madagascar (which, however, has Malay affinities dating back to the sixth century AD), to the eastern coast of Africa and to Antarctica. To the southeast exists a great transition or cline, from equatorial Asian flora and fauna (the latter especially) to Australian. In human terms the eastern archipelagic languages and physical types grade from 'Indonesian', in a wide sense, to broadly 'Papuan' characteristic of, for instance, many Timorese and the multitude of linguistically-distinct peoples of West Irian.

Size

Southeast Asia is clearly distinct from the two neighbouring cultural poles—one to its west 'Indic' in South Asia and one 'Sinic' (Chinese) to its north, though arguably such marginal countries as Myanmar and Viet Nam share cultural elements with their western and northern neighbours. All three regions are subcontinental in size though only South Asia is usually referred to as a subcontinent.

The region shares physical size with both South Asia and China. It stretches from the margins of the Tibetan Plateau in northern Myanmar, roughly 28°N, to the remote island of Rote, about 11°S, a north–south distance of some 39 degrees of latitude, more than either China or the Indian subcontinent. West–east it cannot match China's 63 degrees, but, stretching from western Arakan (Myanmar), to the boundary with Papua New Guinea, a distance of some 49 degrees, it is far wider in extent than the Indian subcontinent. It is also much more tropical and equatorial. Only part of northern Myanmar lies beyond the Tropic of Cancer. But much of Southeast Asia is made up of enclosed seas with two major archipelagoes—the Indonesian and the Philippine—so that while the land areas of Southeast Asia and South Asia are similar at about 4.5 million km^2 the former is spread over a segment of the globe roughly two-fifths larger.

Southeast Asia's land area is almost exactly the same size as South Asia, about 46 per cent that of China and the US, and about 58 per cent of the size of Australia.

The theme of diversity in Southeast Asia begins with the extreme size range of the countries which comprise it, though other global regions—Oceania, Europe—also show such a range. Size is especially important because of its implications for natural resources endowments. Other things being equal, a large country will have a much more diverse stock of minerals, climate, vegetation and soils than a small one. Thus Singapore has no other land resources than its granite and other rocks and some water though not enough for its needs. Brunei, happily, sits over petroleum-rich geological structures which provide it with virtually all of its income, not needing to attack its forests which remain a scientific treasure-house. By contrast, Indonesia, whose land area makes up over two-fifths of the regional total, has a climate ranging from weakly monsoonal in the west to strongly so in the east, forests that thin out eastwards, a terrestrial fauna that has Asian affinities in the west and Australian affinities in the east, rocks and soils that include both rich, basic and poor acidic volcanics, plus vast areas of rather poor sedimentary and metamorphic rocks, many so long exposed that heat and moisture have robbed them of much of the potential plant nutrients they may once have had.

But large size, as well as the spatial distribution of land and sea, mountain and valley may impose penalties as well. The 'friction of distance', though diminishing with improvements in transportation technology, nevertheless remains, as for instance amongst the smaller islands of eastern Indonesia, southern Philippines, in West Irian, and especially in the great tract of mountains, hills and valleys extending from northern Myanmar east to the Chinese border and beyond.

Unity and diversity

The degree to which Southeast Asia's cultural diversity reflects the diversity of its terrain will forever be a matter of debate but it is difficult to deny some relationship. The region has no really large plains on which communication is relatively easy. The largest river, the Mekong, is interrupted in its middle course by rapids and only the Irrawaddy, the Menam Chao Phrya and the Hong (Red) rivers are navigable for any great distance, though the lower Mekong system gives access as far as Phnom Penh even to modern ocean-going ships. Valley systems are separated by often steep and sometimes high hills and mountains. Thus, for example, movement in any direction in the scenically spectacular mountains and gorges north, west and east of the northern valleys of the Irrawaddy basin is slow and difficult. Not coincidentally, these mountains are the home of a multitude

Table 1.1 Land area of Southeast Asian countries

Country	Area (km^2)	Proportion of region's total (%)
Brunei	5 765	0.13
Cambodia	181 035	4.04
Indonesia	1 904 443	42.52
Laos	236 800	5.29
Malaysia	329 758	7.36
Myanmar	676 552	15.1
Philippines	300 000	6.70
Singapore	648	0.01
Thailand	513 115	11.46
Viet Nam	331 114	7.39
Total	4 479 230	100.00

Source: *Europa World Year Book, 1997*

of linguistically diverse peoples amongst whom trade and other contacts are still quite limited. By contrast the major plains have seen the emergence of major unitary states such as Siam, now Thailand, in the Chao Phrya basin, Burman states in the Irrawaddy, Cambodia in the lower Mekong and Dai Viet centred in the Hong basin of northern Viet Nam. In contrast again, the usually calm waters of the Indonesia Archipelago, especially, have clearly facilitated the emergence of past maritime empires such as that of Sri Vijaya, centred on what is now Palembang. This may be a case of a necessary but not sufficient condition, for the Philippine Archipelago has not seen such empires, until Spanish times remaining a collection of tiny states or even smaller tribal units.

Unity in a shared prehistory

Using 'race' in its correct, biological sense, Southeast Asia's peoples are mostly descendants of Southern Mongoloids, sharing with Mongoloids generally such characteristics as a low incidence of the Rh positive blood-groups and a bluish patch at the base of the spine of new-borns. (It quickly fades.) Most have a vestigial eye-fold. Environmental exposure being equal, most have more melanin in the skin than northern Caucasoids (Europeans), but less than Negroid or Australoid peoples, the last forming a possibly 60 000-year-old substratum of people, mainly in insular Southeast Asia.

An ancient *Homo*, not *sapiens* like us, but *erectus*, certainly inhabited parts of our region—Java is one—half a million years ago. Whether this ancient form played any part in the biological ancestry of any of today's peoples is extremely doubtful. What is very likely is that early *Homo sapiens* was in the region, especially its insular parts, some 60 000–40 000 years ago, some people drifting eastwards to colonise Australia, others staying to become the ancestors of today's Negrito and Melanesian peoples. The former survive in tiny pockets in Peninsular Malaysia and in the Philippines, being known in the latter country as 'Aeta'. (There are communities in Luzon's Zambales mountains where one group makes a good living from eco-tourism to the Pinatubo area.) In the Eastern Archipelago and in West Irian, Melanesians form a basal population, one which is to varying degrees overlain by and intermixed with later southern Mongoloid peoples. One result is a range of physical types from west to east. In the west most people are brown-skinned, lightly-built, straight-haired. In the east the skin colour is much darker. People are more thick-set and to varying degrees have fuzzy hair.

Towards the end of the Pleistocene era—8000–10 000 years ago—much of the region, especially mainland Southeast Asia and, was thinly peopled by people of a broadly similar culture as evidenced by their stone tools and the practice of burying the dead in the floor of caves and rock shelters, often with a sprinkling of red clay around the body. This culture is called Hoabinhian after a key archaeological site at Hoa Binh in northern Viet Nam.

For the most part it is animal remains rather than plants that have been recorded by archaeologists. These indicate a wide range of diet including even such large and difficult-to-kill animals as wild oxen (*Bos* species). Notable, too, was the consumption of molluscs, especially those of estuaries. (A hundred years ago large mounds of discarded shells were fairly common along parts of the west coast of Peninsular Malaysia.)

Hoabinhian people may have used fire as an aid in hunting and employed it to convert some of all but the dampest forests to grass and woodland. What is certain is that these practices continued well into the twentieth century. Their economic basis is the fact that such savannas, as they are known, support far more herbivores than forest, ensuring a good supply of meat.

Beginnings of agriculture

There is no particular reason why agriculture—the purposive growing of crops or raising of animals—should be thought of as a once-for-all event. The region is the globe's richest biologically, providing an abundance of useful plants and animals to be protected, nurtured and raised. Hoabinhian peoples were not perpetually on the move, as archaeological evidence shows. Whether the later phases of the Hoabinhian culture, termed by some 'Bacsonian' for a type-site at Bac Son, Viet Nam, actually segued smoothly into agriculture is still debated, though increasingly opinion is that they did not. Certainly agriculture, based mainly on bananas, sugar-cane, and taro (*Colocasia* species), had evolved by around 4000 BC. But this evolution was marginal, amongst Melanesians of the New Guinea Highlands, from which these domestic crops initially seem to have diffused eastwards rather than westwards.

It seems possible that there may also have been another centre of early agriculture in the Eastern Archipelago of what is now Indonesia, for early botanists—notably Rumpf in the seventeenth century—noted the absence of rice in that region, the basic starchy staple being prepared from the sago palm, *Metroxylon sagu*. But this is highly speculative.

What is much less speculative is that by about 3000 BC mainland Southeast Asia saw farmers well established in areas such as Thailand's Korat Plateau, where a number of notable archaeological sites have been excavated to reveal the remains of rice—the earliest possibly collected rather than deliberately grown—several other crops, dog, chicken and pigs. Cattle bones have also been found but whether they were domesticated or not is less clear. Pottery and distinctive tools have also been found, suggesting the arrival of culturally distinct peoples, possibly speakers of Austro-Asiatic languages.

Further east other farming peoples, probably speaking Austronesian languages, seem to have moved from what is now southern China, via Taiwan and the Ryukyus, reaching the Philippines around 3000 BC and perhaps 500 years later arriving in parts of present-day Indonesia. Around 2000 to 1500 BC these folk reached the Malay Peninsula and southern Viet Nam. These 'Austronesian' peoples were once thought to have spread out in a series of migration waves but there is no evidence of this. Equally there is no evidence to suggest that those who arrived early in our region were physically different from those who came later. However, they were or became maritime, only slowly moving into the interiors of the larger islands.

Austronesian speakers developed considerable navigational skills, though the relative importance of purposive voyaging and of being 'cast-aways' as new lands were settled is still debated, especially in Oceania. The lands reached by these peoples cover two-thirds of the globe. Madagascar was reached from insular Southeast Asia by about 500 AD while other folk, members of the Polynesian branches of this language group, later reached New Zealand in the south and Easter Island in the east.

While farming was certainly part of Austronesian culture it was far from being exclusively so, for fishing and foraging must have provided most of the fats and proteins essential to life. The older view is that these peoples were shifting cultivators, clearing a patch of forest to grow crops for a year or two until proliferating weeds and regrowth made it more economical in labour to clear a new patch. Increasingly it seems likely that environmentally-favoured areas were selected for settlement—a mixture of forest and grassland (some of the latter deliberately created by burning), access to fishing grounds, clean water. Such areas were probably occupied semi-permanently. Rice may not have been the dominant crop, especially in the more equatorial parts of the region, for its earliest domestication, about 6000 BC, on present evidence seems to have been in the seasonal environment of the middle Yangzi, now China. Several millennia of plant selection may have been necessary to adapt this long (summer) day-length swamp plant to the rather different environments of relatively short days and/or dry hill-slopes. Nor did peoples of Austronesian descent universally grow rice. For some it was a crop grown by others even in modern times. For example, twentieth-century aboriginal groups in the Malay Peninsula considered rice a 'Malay thing', a commodity to be bought or exchanged rather than grown. A similar situation existed on the islands off western Sumatera.

Sedentary farming, based upon annual cropping of permanent rice-fields, appears in parts of the region towards the beginning of the second millennium BC. Some scholars have associated this with bronze metallurgy as practised by 'Dong-Son' peoples (Dong Son is yet another major Vietnamese archaeological site), though Dong-Son artifacts do not appear before about 700 BC in northern Viet Nam. Notable amongst the artifacts are strikingly beautiful bronze drums. Dong-Son farmers are said to have based their economy upon the growing of rice in permanent wet fields tilled with buffalo or cattle-drawn ploughs. This led to permanent village settlements. An alternative view is that Dong-Son drums were the work of itinerant artisans, also being important trade items. Certainly finds are widespread in both insular and mainland Southeast Asia. (There are superb examples in the Museum of History at Ha Noi.) Though some scholars have argued for a very early date for bronze metallurgy, around 3500 BC, the consensus is that it is much later, emerging in the borderlands of what is now southwestern China rather than in the heart of Southeast Asia. Certainly, there is no necessary link between bronzes and agriculture.

Unity and diversity in history

'History' in the sense of written records begins very variously in the region. Chinese accounts of what is now northern Viet Nam go back to the second century BC. Yet other places had no written or inscribed records until the arrival of colonial-era explorers, missionaries and administrators at the beginning of the twentieth century. (The last previously unknown groups to be contacted by administrators were in Myanmar and in West Irian in the early 1950s.) Chronicles or 'histories of events', usually written by rulers' officials, and stone inscriptions go back about a millennium and a half. These were the product of 'civilised' states which began to emerge at around that time as some chieftains became kings. This process is often thought to have taken place under the stimulus of cultural contacts with India, southern India especially. Thus was forwarded a process of cultural diversification that had clearly begun earlier, for it is marked by an increasing variety of archaeological artifacts, types of tools and pottery especially. States emerged. One such was 'Funan'—the name is that given it by the Chinese—in the lower Mekong valley. Haripunjaya and Dvaravati developed in the northernmost parts of what is now the Malay Peninsula. In insular Southeast Asia loosely confederated empires—Sri Vijaya and Mahapahit—incorporated smaller polities into larger.

But large parts of the region lay outside these developments, at least so far as the exercise of centralised political power was concerned. Borneo, interior Sumatera, the islands west of Sumatera and east of Bali, the Philippines, the uplands of mainland Southeast Asia, were and long remained the bailiwick of tribal peoples, subjects of no ruler. It was only at relatively few points that new, 'Indian' elements arrived to transform local cultures, though the precise mechanisms involved are to this day still a matter of scholarly debate.

'Indian' strands

Historically Southeast Asia, if it were recognised as a region at all, was known as 'Further India' or 'India beyond the Ganges [River]', a recognition of the pervasive influence of South Asian culture that began probably a millennium and a half ago and of the fact that westerners reached it via India. This influence is reflected in many aspects of language and life. It has been argued by scholars that the emergence of the state as a religious and political entity in which the king (*raja*) was a god (*deva*) and a god was the ruler goes back to Indian models. There is no doubt that even today surviving 'rajas', Sihanouk and his son Ranariddh in Cambodia, King Bhumibol in Thailand, are in the minds of the people endowed with mystical power and status. Even in Muslim Malaysia the rulers and their families enjoy a degree of respect that may include such an element. Certainly the Malay royal custom of a spiritually cleansing bathing with oil prior to marriage has a clear Indian model. In the Indonesian/Malay world the famous 'shadow puppets' (*wayang kulit*) retell stories from the classics of Hindu India, the *Mahabharata* and *Ramayana*. These tales form the basis of classical dance from Myanmar to Cambodia, in earlier times probably in Champa (a kingdom in what is now southern Viet Nam), as well as in Sumatera, Java and Bali. Aspects of them are immortalised in stone and brick in the region's great monuments, Khmer at Angkor and Phimai, Thai at Sukothai, Sawankhalok and dozens of other sites, Cham in southern and central Viet Nam, Javanese at Borobudur and Prambanan; as well as alive and flourishing throughout

Bali which has, almost alone in the region, retained a distinct culture that is partly indigenous and overtly Indian in origin. The retention of 'state Brahmins' at the Thai royal court is another ancient 'Indian' survival.

But it is in the language of the region that early Indian influences are quite clear, though these are not necessarily direct. Burmese, Thai and Khmer (Cambodian) are all written in Indic scripts though the two former are linguistically more akin to Chinese than to any Indian or other Southeast Asian languages for they are part of the Sino-Tibetan family. (This is despite the fact that Burmese does not have tones whereas Thai and Chinese do.) Certainly most of the major lowland languages of the region, except perhaps those of the Philippines, contain many words of Indic origin, ranging from a simple but not staple commodity like bread, in Malay, Indonesian and the old Indic language Sanscrit, *roti*, to a term in government such as *raja* (ruler), in religion, *dharma* (fate?), in culture *pustaka*, a library. For other cultural elements the Indian region was the direct but not the ultimate source. Islam, which entered the region at Aceh, northern, in the thirteenth century, seems to have been spread initially by 'Indian' rather than Arab missionaries. Thus Arabic influences in art, architecture and writing may have come first via South Asia, though it is difficult in specific cases to decide whether they are direct or indirect imports from the Arab world.

'Chinese' strands

By contrast Sinic influences are mostly later and sporadic except along China's borderlands, most notably in Viet Nam, where the whole structure of government, even the the architecture and layout of the nineteenth-century capital at Hué, were based upon Chinese models, not surprisingly since northern Viet Nam was essentially a colony of China from about the second century BC until AD 938. The Vietnamese language, though at its base somewhat similar to the languages of the Philippine and Indonesian archipelagoes, as some scholars argue, was written in Chinese characters until well into colonial times when the French, in order to reduce the power of the ruling mandarins, replaced Chinese writing with a specially devised Roman script called *quoc nu*.

Other Chinese influences entered elsewhere in the region at various times especially via Chinese colonies of settlement scattered from north-eastern Myanmar to Borneo, and through trade activities centred mainly on river ports in southern China but extending throughout much of Southeast Asia either directly or indirectly. Melaka, for example, was a major centre of trade, though not just Chinese. Like other languages, Chinese has donated words to local languages, often for things of Chinese origin; for example *loceng* is Malay/Indonesian for bell.

Another area of cultural borrowing is that of food. Every regional cuisine has incorporated noodles, with appropriate modifications to avoid pork amongst Muslims. Chopsticks have long replaced fingers as the traditional method of conveying food to the mouth in Viet Nam though not necessarily elsewhere, where western-style spoon and fork are now ubiquitous.

Other Chinese cultural elements, however, though widespread in the region, have not been taken into local cultures, remaining the 'property' of people of Chinese descent. Few people of indigenous origin speak any form of Chinese though a scattering of non-Chinese in Singapore speak a little Hokkien, that nation's commonest Chinese dialect. No non-Chinese have adopted traditional Chinese dress except in modified form in Viet Nam. Indeed few Chinese now wear it except on special occasions. Amongst communities originally Chinese, borrowings have tended to be the other way. Thus women amongst the 'Baba' Chinese of Melaka traditionally wear the Malay *sarung kebaya*, now rarely worn by Malays themselves, and have developed a distinctive *nonya* cuisine that blends Chinese and Malay styles of cooking. Many Babas speak as much or more Malay as Chinese but have generally not assimilated to Malay culture because they have not converted to Islam.

Some once-Chinese communities, though, have been assimilated to greater or less degree, in Thailand and the Philippines especially, where many old-established urban families are partly or entirely of Chinese origin though they have adopted Thai or Filipino names. The wealthy Cojuangco family in the Philippines was once known by the common Chinese patronym 'Ko', or 'Koh'. Other Chinese groups have disappeared as identifiable entities. In the eastern Peninsular Malaysian state of Terengganu, for example, where once two-thirds of the population was Chinese, Chinese farmers may scarcely be identified as such, so closely have they assimilated to the rural Malay way of life, eschewing the rearing of pigs and the consumption of pork out of deference to their Malay neighbours. In the once-Chinese city-state of Bantey Mas, now Ha Tien, close to the Cambodian border in southern Viet Nam, its founder—a Cantonese named Mak—survives as a temple deity, a remnant of Chinese things past.

'Western' influences

Though 'Indic' and 'Sinic' influences have in many cases penetrated deeply into languages and the very fabric of life and society, to the extent that the ordinary person in the street is unaware of their origins, 'western' influences are clear, obvious and mostly recent. Three phases of contact may be distinguished, though indigenous and immigrant peoples were very unevenly affected by them until recent decades.

Early contacts with the west basically began in the fifteenth century as Portuguese, Spanish, Dutch and British merchants began to compete with Indian, Chinese, Arab and indigenous traders, notably the Bugis from Sulawesi, and started to tap into existing seaborne trading networks. Cultural borrowing began but was focused at rather few points along the coasts, some of which were to develop into the metropolises of today—Batavia, now Jakarta, Ayuthia until it was sacked by the Burmese in 1767, then Bangkok, its successor, Manila, Yangon (Rangoon). Others did not so develop—Hoi An, near Da Nang, Patani, Melaka. From these points of contact 'western' goods spread out, though not all were in fact of western origin. Indian and British textiles, for example, were a major item of import, as were iron bars used by blacksmiths in many parts of the region, replacing hard-won locally smelted iron. It is to this early trading activity that borrowings from western languages may be traced—in Malay/Indonesian the words for butter, *mantega,* and cupboard, *almerah*, are directly taken from Portuguese. Other, later, borrowings included architectural elements. At Melaka, for example, some village houses were constructed with elaborately tiled staircases leading to the main entrance (*tangga*) and these are thought to be derived from early Iberian ideas of what was appropriate.

Perhaps the most ubiquitous 'western' borrowings are not really western at all but, from the perspective of Asia, 'eastern'. Though little is known of the details of their spread, tropical American crops are now to be found in most parts of Southeast Asia, some common like maize, manioc (cassava), sweet potato, chilli, tomato, tobacco, some less so, like the sweet and sour sops, the cherimoya fruits and the temperate 'Irish' potato which is not Irish at all. These accompanied priests, officials and merchants from the Spanish colony of Mexico to Manila and thence the commoner ones seem to have spread quite rapidly throughout the region, being botanically recorded in the region's earliest floras.

The second phase, that of 'territorial imperialism', when foreigners actually governed, is variously dated, from the Spanish conquest of Cebu in 1565, the Portuguese defeat of the Melaka sultanate in 1511, or Dutch control of Batavia and most of Java in the seventeenth century. But it was not until the late nineteenth century that western control became firmly established and even then there were areas beyond the control of colonial governments, such as parts of northern Burma, as it then was, or the uplands of the Viet Nam–Laos border regions. Thailand alone remained politically independent but like every other country in the region set about acquiring the apparatus of the modern state—a government bureaucracy, land registration, fixed rather than arbitrary taxes, customs dues, railways, steamships, roads, postal services, telegraphs, modern armed forces, police, towns and cities devoted to commerce and a modicum of government.

Agricultural economies were partially transformed. No more did the farmer produce for himself and his family with a little surplus to barter or trade for cotton thread or cloth, salt, ceramics, tools, jewellery and other 'positional goods' whose possession reflected social status. Rice, the very essence of food in most of the languages of the region, became an export commodity in Java, later in Lower Burma, then the Chao Phrya plain, then southern Viet Nam—cheap food for the industrial masses of Europe: 'Half a pound of tuppenny rice' as the English nursery rhyme has it. Sugar from cane, long known as a wonderful but expensive sweetener in the west, expanded, especially during the American Civil War when slave-produced sugar exports declined. Industrial expertise from the west vastly lowered sugar's cost and raised its quality. Exports, especially from the Philippines, expanded hugely, as did profits from them. Other crops were brought in: *Arabica* then *Robusta* coffee, rubber, and just before the Pacific War, oil palm, all produced in veritable 'factories-in-the field'. Local commerce expanded enormously but manufacturing only a little for the imperialist vision saw its Southeast Asian colonies as sources of food and raw materials and as markets for imperial manufactures which, too, expanded greatly.

These developments left a lasting impression on the region. Every country, except Thailand, is a successor to a colonial entity, and Thailand is basically what was left over by the British in the late nineteenth century pressing eastwards from Burma and by the French pressing westwards from its protectorate in Cambodia. The detail varies only a little. Neither Sarawak nor Sabah, now states in Malaysia, were part of a larger colonial entity but became independent of British control within the context of the federal state. With only minor post-colonial adjustments the land boundaries of the region's constituent parts are colonial-era and only Myanmar has sought to adjust its national boundary to reflect the fact that imperialist line-drawing split peoples who are otherwise culturally identical. It is true, of course, that many colonial states were based upon pre-existing political entities—Burma, Cambodia, Viet Nam—but these were not western-style units with defined territorial limits. On the other hand, Indonesia, Laos, Malaysia and the Philippines did not exist as identifiable units in pre-colonial times. Though in some cases developing from a pre-colonial core, present-day states substantially owe their territorial extent to the colonial period.

They are colonial creations in many other respects as well. As will be discussed in more detail in chapter 9, both the internal structure of cities and many of the towns themselves originated in colonial times or at least were hugely expanded from pre-colonial settlement nodes.

Their architecture reflects the absorption of western elements. For example, what is regarded as the 'traditional' Chinese shophouse in Malaysia, Singapore and Thailand, though built and owned by Chinese, has few obvious Chinese elements beyond a sign in Chinese, Chinese guardian dogs or lions at the decorated door which may contain Chinese motifs, and perhaps a Chinese-style tiled roof. Such elements as wooden louvres, balustrades of turned wood, false pillars, sometimes in classical Greek form, and plaster decoration are clearly of western origin. These elements are also to be found in the homes of wealthy Singaporeans—Chinese, Malay, Arab—built before the Pacific War, as Lee Kip Lin's book *The Singapore House* shows. Their combination resulted in a distinctive, eclectic style not wholly Chinese, Malay or western but truly Singaporean (and Malayan), and though colonial-period most definitely not inspired solely by the west.

This is a reminder, of course, that many other cultural elements began to be absorbed in colonial times. Western dress, for example, is adopted at least partly, by both men and women. Trousers replace the *sarung*, or the *longi*. The pith helmet or 'solar topee' (*topi* is of Hindi origin, as is 'bungalow'), became an article of male headwear, surviving to the present particularly amongst the Vietnamese military and trishaw riders. Women adopted the western blouse and skirt or even the frock.

Languages adopted thousands more terms, partly as a result of intensified contact, partly as a result of there being so many more things of western origin for which a name had to be made up (e.g. in Malay/Indonesian *keretapi*, literally 'cart fire', for railway) or an existing foreign name taken up (e.g. *teksi*, 'taxi'). New concepts and organisations too began to arrive with exposure to western-style education—democracy, trades unions and many others. Urban people, especially, were quite unlike their rural cousins and more in touch with the larger world outside via newspapers and, towards the end of the era, by public radio broadcasts.

Arguably, the colonial era saw the greatest influence of the west in the region, ranging as it did from creation of the very states themselves to class differentiation, to shifts in language, diet and dress. These influences were felt most directly in the urban areas. While cultivated areas in the countryside expanded greatly and many peasant producers were drawn into the global markets—with serious consequences when, as in the 1930s these contracted—it can be argued that in the rural areas the old ways mostly survived despite modern works of drainage and irrigation, roads and rail that improved market access and facilitated spatial mobility amongst the people. The peoples of the uplands were only marginally affected, though some were removed from traditional foraging grounds and clearings by plantation interests, as in the Malay Peninsula and in parts of Sumatera. In mainland Southeast Asia, particularly in the teak (*Tectona grandis*) forests of eastern Burma and northern Thailand active logging by western capitalists forced upland peoples to make new adjustments. But broadly such folk—hunters and gatherers, shifting cultivators—were left to their own devices, bothered only by missionaries, mostly Christian, and occasional colonial administrators 'showing the flag'.

The Pacific War and after saw further large changes. The Japanese threw out the western imperialists, replacing them with their own brand in the form of the Greater Japanese Co-Prosperity Sphere, in turn to be conquered. But in spite of imperialist efforts to re-establish their control, sometimes with the aid of the Japanese forces they had just defeated, these were ultimately unavailing though they continued, as in Indochina, into the 1970s. Nowhere was the transfer of power wholly without violence, ranging as it did from civil disorder in Singapore and Malaysia to full-scale wars in Indochina where the US saw itself as a bulwark against expansionist Communism. The region's split into Communist (or in Myanmar socialist) and capitalist blocs resulted not only in war and political isolation, it resulted, for Left-leaning countries, from Myanmar to Viet Nam but excluding Thailand, in a serious diversion of effort and income away from promoting the growth of the new nations' wealth.

At one level during the post Pacific War era the capitalist countries saw simply a continuation of social and economic trends established earlier. The colonial elite was replaced by a new one that included even more closely people of immigrant origins—Chinese and Indian—many of whom finally turned their backs on their countries of origin and became new citizens of new countries. After fits and starts in the 1950s and 1960s, partly caused by doubts about political stability, foreign capital flowed in, local capital was mobilised, especially for infrastructure, and rapid growth ensued. Western influence, broadened to include things Japanese, especially money, took the form of globalisation. Old colonial trade links fell away to be replaced by more diverse ones both as regards destinations and sources as well as regards commodities, for substantial industrialisation was part of a massive relative shift out of agriculture—relative because there are still today more farmers in the region than ever before (see chapter 6).

At other levels, however, by the 1980s and 1990s things were very different as compared to the colonial period. Virtually nowhere was outside the reach of the global economy, not even shifting cultivators in the hills of northern Thailand, now producing commodities for market—and not only illegal opium—now commuting seasonally to work for wages in Bangkok. Virtually nowhere is beyond the reach of manufactured goods, of the radio, of education, of civil administration. The result has been a great, though possibly superficial, cultural homogenisation of which blue jeans, T-shirts, soft drinks, pop music and, in urban areas, hamburgers are manifestations. Worlds beyond the local are there to be conquered and these are partly western. English has emerged as a regional *lingua franca*, mastered in part to give access to cyberspace, to acquire status or merely to explore foreign cultures which are less and less foreign as international contacts, at all levels, grow.

The socialist countries, except Myanmar which has chosen to remain in isolation, are rapidly opening to the outside world, slowly in Laos which currently has little to offer global capitalism or more rapidly in Viet Nam. As one northern Vietnamese friend remarked, 'We have wasted forty years'. Once current economic difficulties are resolved, assuming that they can be, westernisation in its new guise as globalisation will proceed apace.

Nowhere are these processes more clearly shown than in the region's languages, themselves become *lingua franca* for minority peoples. Thus a recent word count of Indonesian shows that there are more loan-words from English than from Arabic and Dutch combined. New words are in turn formed from these loans; thus *hoki*, the sport of hockey, and *pehoki*, a hockey player. Borrowing, especially where no exact equivalent exists, is common—thus *politik, ekonomi, demokrasi, kalibrasi* (calibration). Yet other words enter 'officially' as language authorities try to standardise scientific and technical terms. Some 100 000 such words have been standardised in the Malaysia–Brunei–Indonesia language region.

Social diversity?

The peoples and cultures of Southeast Asia's component countries comprise such an extraordinary variety that this cuts across both physical extent and size of population. While it is true that the larger the country the greater its resources and physical diversity, this idea does not necessarily apply with people, even using 'official' ethnic categories. True, most countries contain a major group identifiable by the language its members generally speak, by its traditional dress, cuisine, music, art, and especially, by the marriage preferences of its members. Thus the Burmans are the major group in Myanmar, the Thai in Thailand, the Khmer in Cambodia, Kinh (Viet) in Viet Nam. Small countries may show similar group dominance—Chinese in Singapore, albeit a heterogenous group, Brunei Malays in Brunei—or, as in Laos, they may not, for in that land there is no single dominant group.

But 'official' or generally accepted categories may hide a range of yet further categories. These may be defined by the sorts of cultural characteristics just mentioned or by group members themselves. Such 'self-definitions' are inconsistent, even contradictory, as for instance with one Javanese gentleman who explained that he was a Christian but also a Muslim. An official category such as Singapore's 'Indians' encompasses people of Tamil origin from south India, Malayalam folk originally from Kerala, Gujeratis from the Mumbai (Bombay) region, Bengalis whose ancestors came from pre-Partition Bengal in the east, Sikhs from undivided Punjab in the west. Some of these second-level categories are linguistic—Tamil, Malayalam. Some, such as Sikh, are religious. To complicate matters further, even these categories are cut across by yet other divisions.

Thus Singaporean Tamils may be Hindus, Roman Catholics or Methodists amongst whom it would be rare for members to marry outside their small group. Such divisions are not necessarily hard and fast and even official ones may change or be set firm. Thus the Melanau, a fishing and sago-producing group mainly of Sabah's west coast, has tended to diminish in size through time as some, presumably mainly Muslim Melanau, have identified themselves as Malays.

Cutting across such social boundaries, whether permeable or impervious, is a further set of universal class-based boundaries, porous but well-established. Wealth generally meets wealth and wealth generally marries wealth. Poverty likewise. At least five social classes may be recognised in the region: the elite, the peasantry, a rural proletariat, an urban middle class and the urban proletariat. The elite comprises not only the wealthy but also professionals, large landowners, bankers and merchants, members of the old aristocracy, who may also have successfully used their aristocratic status to join the new aristocracy based on wealth, power and influence.

This elite may be ethnically diverse as is seen in the now discredited Suharto clique in Indonesia. It usually shares a common language, not necessarily that customarily spoken at home, English in Singapore, Thai in Thailand, Bahasa Indonesia in Indonesia, Vietnamese in Viet Nam. Its members' educational level is similar, often tertiary. In most countries significant numbers have been partly educated abroad, usually in a western country, the USA, Britain or for Vietnamese a former Soviet bloc country. Above all the elite controls wealth and power. The Suharto clique is thought to have controlled 70 per cent of all business in Indonesia while a similar situation existed in Marcos-era Philippines, where wealth is still substantially in the hands of an intermarrying elite group which includes members of the Romualdez, Aquino, Cojuanco and Ayala families.

Traditionally, by far the largest class comprised the peasantry, people working the land on their own account rather than directly for others. During the colonial era, this group became more diversified. Some remained in this group. A few acquired more land than they themselves could cultivate and thus joined the traditional aristocrats as rural landowners. Some became tenants partly or wholly working the lands of others, paying rent for their use but still being peasants because they worked on their own account. Some became landless, forming a rural proletariat, selling their labour directly to capitalist employers—individuals and companies growing sugar in the Philippines or central Thailand, cultivating rice in southern Viet Nam, growing rubber in Malaya (now Peninsular Malaysia), or on the red basaltic upland soils of southern Viet Nam and Cambodia. Such peasants were, and are, generally members of large, often dominant, ethnic groups—Burmans, Thais, Khmer, Javanese, Sundanese. They still form a major component of the population, for except until very recently, the numbers, though not the proportion, of agriculturalists in the workforce has steadily increased. Economically and politically though, the peasantry and the rural proletariat have tended to become less and less 'visible' as towns and cities have grown.

The substantial growth of urban areas (chapter 9) has added another major element to the region's class structure. In most cities the extremes of wealth and poverty are there for all to see—Forbes Park and much of Tondo in Manila, for example. In cities live most of the elite but also a growing middle class—sales people, clerks, managers, teachers and a host of others involved in meeting the needs of others while producing nothing directly themselves. Below them in the social hierarchy is the true proletariat, industrial workers processing rice, wood, metals, fabrics, plastics and much else, mainly consumer goods. In most parts of the region the numbers in this group are growing as economies move from being largely agricultural to being more nearly balanced, with up to about a quarter of the workforce being involved in manufacturing, some of it financed from outside the region by capitalists taking advantage of the region's relatively low-cost industrial labour. While in Myanmar, Cambodia and Laos this industrial workforce has scarcely begun to emerge, in Singapore 'deindustrialisation' has advanced, with a decline in numbers of industrial workers and a change in the nature of their work. Firms involved in producing lower-order goods such as textiles and clothing have moved their operations to places with lower labour costs, have moved up the technological ladder to produce electronics, or have found specialised niches in older industries—producing clothing for surgical theatres instead of clothes for children, for example.

But industrial workers—the proletariat—by no means comprise the major part of the urban population. Cities, unlike the countryside, offer opportunities, possibly for wealth, certainly for survival, for work can be almost infinitely subdivided in the households of the wealthy—someone to cook, another to do the laundry, someone to keep the garden in order, another to drive the car, yet another to guard the gate. Outside the household the possibilities, both legal and illegal, are endless—begging, scavenging, prostitution, offering 'protection' to car-owners or business-people, hawking foodstuffs or knick-knacks, cigarettes and drinks. The urban economy offers a niche of some sort to all who come even if occupying it means sleeping on the street or crammed into a dormitory.

If we conceptualise these boundaries—variously porous, permitting social and 'ethnic' mobility, or impermeable, as for followers of the Hindu or Zoroastrian religions which cannot be joined by conversion—we come up with a picture of the region's societies that is best described as 'segmented'. Each society is to a greater or less degree split vertically by language, religion, by 'who marries whom' and by as many other characteristics as one may wish to identify as separating one person from another.

Each society is also split horizontally by differences of social and economic class, though just where these class boundaries occur or even whether they should be drawn at all will always be a matter of opinion.

The degree to which these boundaries are permeable clearly varies from country to country, though clearly language is quite impermeable. It is more than a little difficult for a young couple to be courting if they don't have a language in common. Thus in Malaysia Islam is no real barrier to marriage between those of Indian Muslim descent and Malays who by definition are Muslim. Such intermarriage has given rise to a distinct community, the Pekan Jawi (Prime Minister Mahathir is a member) who are nevertheless looked down upon by some Malays as not '*betul betul Melayu*' ('real Malays'). At the same time lack of a common religion makes non-Malay/Malay marriage impossible in Malaysia, though legal outside it. By contrast, in Thailand non-Thai/Thai marriage is possible, especially where the non-Thai party is Buddhist in religion. Far from being a barrier, membership of one of the great religious traditions—Buddhism, Christianity, Islam—may facilitate marriage, and other personal and business relationships. To all there are degrees of 'otherness' which may or may not constrain relationships though it is probably true to say that education, especially in a national language such as Bahasa Indonesia, is playing a major role in bridging barriers. Thus Javanese, Sundanese and Balinese are happy to interact through that medium, retaining some aspects of their individual cultures yet melding others to form something new and adding yet further strands of richness in diversity.

Cultural unity?

Despite these differences there remain also broad similarities, especially in insular Southeast Asia. 'Austronesian' or 'Malayo-Polynesian' languages such as Malay, Tagalog, Batak, Javanese, Balinese, Iban and a host of others share hundreds of words—especially for such basics as numerals and traditional foodstuffs—though individual tongues are not necessarily mutually intelligible. It is thus very easy, for example, for an Iban in Sarawak to learn Malay and many speak it as a matter of course. Only the Papuan and Melanesian languages, mainly in West Irian, are very different. In mainland Southeast Asia there is less linguistic unity. Malayo-Polynesian languages are represented by tiny survivals: Rhadé of Viet Nam's central highlands is one. But the languages of the Mon (pronounced 'Mone') of southern Burma and Thailand, and of Cambodia, fall into the Mon–Khmer group, this with a tiny outlier amongst aborigines of Peninsular Malaysia, and a much larger group of related languages in the uplands of Indochina (Laos, Cambodia and Viet Nam). Forms of 'Tai', the group into which modern Thai falls, are extensive in the central parts of mainland Southeast Asia, the Shan states of Myanmar, Thailand and Laos, spilling over the region's borders into southwestern China. Further west, Sino-Tibetan languages predominate, Burman being the major member of the group, though unlike another major member, Chinese, it is not tonal. As with the Tai group, these tongues are also to be found across the Chinese border, for history and politics have by no means followed cultural characteristics.

Traditional music is another area of broad similarity. Most instruments are of the percussion family, beaten to produce sound, some tuned—but not to the western scale—some not. Notable are the 'ideophones' including gongs and 'metallophones', bars struck with hammers or sticks of varying hardness. The tunings are often similar. For example both the Indonesian gamelans and Khmer gong ensembles use instruments tuned with five notes between notes that are an octave apart on the western musical scale. Vietnamese and Burmese musics also share these broad characteristics, along with the substantial use of bamboo to make instruments.

More mundane is food. Rice is the staple universally to the extent that in almost every language the word for rice is the word for food. All else is 'with food'. The range of indigenous foods is nowadays probably a good deal narrower than formerly, for collected foods once added protein and vitamins, texture, taste and colour to rice and other carbohydrate foods. Rice, coconuts, taro and yam and dozens of minor crops are either indigenous, growing wild in the region, or were introduced so long ago that they may be considered indigenous. (Rice may be one of the latter.) The methods by which these crops are cultivated were probably developed within the region. Though the Sinocentric would see China as the origin of such things as advanced methods of terracing and water-control, such is certainly not the case. There is no evidence whatever that the spectacular rice terraces of Torajaland (Sulawesi), Bali, Banaue or Bontoc owe anything at all to foreign models. Rather they are a response to the need to feed people from limited upland areas. Similar considerations apply to the building of large current-driven water-wheels until recently still in regular use in upland Sumatera, the Negeri Sembilan of Peninsular Malaysia, and northern Thailand, and still in use in parts of Cambodia and Viet Nam.

Indigenous domestic architecture is another area of broad similarity. The rectangular house on stilts is almost universal. Traditionally this was built of split bamboo woven into mat sidings with a woven bamboo floor and a steep palm-thatch roof, usually with deep eaves to provide some shade and to shed rain quickly. A verandah was a common component, providing a comfortable sitting out area. Raising the dwelling on stilts minimised the effects of flooding in lowland areas, raising the living area above the heat and wet-season dampness of the atmosphere near the ground. The under-floor space allowed the burning of smoky fires to keep unpleasant and dangerous insects at bay while providing a place to store agricultural implements, fishing gear and to house domestic animals, especially at night. Increasing wealth has seen modifications to this kind of dwelling, one of the first being the use of sawn timber for the floor. Corrugated iron or tiles replace thatch and sawn timber replaces bamboo sidings for the walls. These kinds of houses are to be found in both urban and rural contexts, in some cases reproduced in their essentials in permanent bricks and concrete. The major exception to the near-universality of these kinds of traditional houses are amongst some Vietnamese and the Cham, both of whom tend to build dwellings at ground level.

Some would argue that, with Indonesia whose national motto it is, 'Unity [lies] in diversity'. Clearly the region is culturally more diverse than China though whether it is more so than the Indian subcontinent is another matter. Perhaps the question is trivial. What is not trivial is that the class structures of Southeast Asian countries are broadly similar, that though each is at a very different point on the scale of national and personal wealth, each is committed to rapid economic growth, to the aim of eventual open markets in goods, services and capital both domestically and internationally. Myanmar continues to experience active though diminishing internal instability. East Timor has resolved its conflict, with international political and military aid, though its economy is a disaster area. Indonesia's recent civil instability has bases in class and relative deprivation as much as in ethnicity, language, religion and regional irridentism. For the region as a whole, ASEAN represents a unique venture into a regional grouping that so far has been largely political though having the long-term aim of forming a single trading bloc on the model of the European Community. That is in striking contrast to South Asia where India and Pakistan are at daggers drawn and Sri Lanka wastes its substance on a civil war that seems pointless and fruitless to all but its participants. Southeast Asia is extraordinarily diverse yet has an underlying unity. It is far more than a mere geographer's construct.

TWO
THE PEOPLE

Roughly two thousand years ago Southeast Asia, compared with what were then India and China, was an underpopulated backwater. Although Asia as a whole was by far the most populous part of the world, containing about three-quarters of its population, our region probably contained no more than some 4 per cent of the global total, compared with nearly 30 per cent each in India and China. This fact accounts for a great deal. Settlement even of the now-agricultural lowlands is mostly quite recent and so, of course, is the clearance of the natural vegetation, mostly equatorial or monsoonal rainforests. No large land-based empire compared with Han or Tang dynasty China or Mughal India could emerge, for there were not enough people. Indeed into the eighteenth century in Southeast Asia, waging war aimed at controlling people much more than occupying territory. Massive warfare involving transfers of tens of thousands of people, many of whom died as a consequence, as well as disease, especially cholera, smallpox and malaria, probably helped to keep Southeast Asia's population small until quite recently.

Around 1600 the population totalled approximately 22 million; in 1800 roughly 32 million. In the 1820s the Malay Peninsula probably contained no more than about a quarter of a million people. Now it has about fifty times more. Even densely populated Java, whose population is now about 110 million, is estimated to have contained only about four million in 1600 when, together with northern and central Viet Nam, these were the most densely peopled parts of the region. The region's crude population density was a sixth or a seventh that of India and China, only half that of Europe. Much of this sparse population was concentrated in trading cities and in areas of intensive rice cultivation in parts of the lowlands—

Table 2.1 Population estimates 1600 and 1998 (millions)

Country/region	1600	%	1998	%
Brunei	n.a.	–	0.3	0.06
Cambodia/Champa/ Mekong	1.2	5.4	n.a.	
Cambodia	n.a.		11.4	2.26
Indonesia	9.8	43.6	203.7	40.42
Laos	n.a.		5.0	1.00
Malaysia	n.a.		22.2	4.40
Malaya	0.5	2.2	n.a.	–
Myanmar	3.1	13.8	4.4	8.81
Philippines	1.0	4.4	75.1	14.90
Singapore	<0.01	–	3.2	0.63
Thailand (Siam)	2.2	9.8	61.1	12.12
Viet Nam	n.a.	–	77.6	15.40
Viet Nam, north and central	4.7	20.9	n.a.	–
Total	22.5	100.1	504.0	100.00

Sources: Estimates for 1600 (except for Singapore which is my own) from Reid, 1987; for 1998 from *World Development Report, 1999–2000, General Population Census of Cambodia, 1998*

the Hong River delta of northern Viet Nam, the upper Irrawaddy Basin in the Bagan region, central and eastern Java, Bali, southern Sulawesi.

The rest was virtually empty and this included the plains of lower Burma, Arakan, most of the lower Chao Phrya except around Ayuthaya, the plains of the Malay Peninsula, Luzon, the Visayas, Mindanao and western Java. In Sumatera the population was small, maybe 2.4 million in 1600, despite the earlier existence of a major urban centre at Sri Vijaya (Palembang). Most of the eastern plains of that large island were empty, as were the plains of Borneo—not surprisingly, for some were mangrove swamp and inland were peaty freshwater swamp forests, both wretchedly difficult to reclaim for agriculture. Upland areas were also sparsely populated, being occupied by groups of shifting cultivators and by hunting and gathering peoples, some of whom were also to be found in small bands along the coasts. In the uplands it seems likely that endemic malaria helped to keep populations low, though in the rice-growing lowlands its effects were probably relatively less severe.

Although the region now contains over 500 million people, this earlier pattern has not changed all that greatly. To be sure, the alluvial soils of the region's great deltas—the Irrawaddy, the Chao Phrya, the Mekong—are now occupied at rural densities of two or three hundred to the square kilometre, having been colonised since around 1850. Certainly earlier-occupied upper deltas of the same great rivers and smaller ones in northern and central Viet Nam, Java and Bali now have rural densities of 800–1000 per square kilometre, higher than most suburbs in western cities. In equatorial regions, sloping lands of low elevation are now occupied by growers of rubber, coconuts, cocoa and oil palm rather than by hunters, gatherers and shifting cultivators. The mangrove and highly acidic fresh-water swamps are still substantially unoccupied, except in central and northern Viet Nam. But it is a fair guess, though no one has ever actually measured it, that nine-tenths of the people still live below the 100-metre contour, with notable exceptions only on the rich, basic volcanic soils of Java and Bali much of which have long been spectacularly transformed into the 'vertical swamps' of terraced wet rice cultivation.

Outside the few regions of dense population in the early nineteenth century populations were small. So small was the population of Siam that John Crawfurd, writing early in the nineteenth century, could quote an earlier traveller as scathingly joking that the King of Siam might have a vast kingdom but that it was inhabited by monkeys rather than people. The same could have been said of many other parts of the region, for the population grew very slowly during the seventeenth and eighteenth centuries even compared with South Asia and China, not to mention Europe. Anthony Reid suggests hard physical labour by women in agriculture, the prevalence of infertility-causing venereal diseases, amongst some upland groups the use of abortifacients, and especially warfare were amongst the factors keeping the indigenous population low until comparatively recently.

As Table 2.1 shows, in general there has not been a large change in the country-by-country proportions of the region's population over the last 400 years. 'Indonesia', mainly Java, still has about two-fifths of Southeast Asia's people. Myanmar's proportion has fallen slightly though that of its Thai neighbour has increased a little. The largest change, remarkably, given continued rapid growth recently, is the fall in the proportion of people in the Indochinese Peninsula, now comprising Viet Nam, Cambodia and Laos. Whereas in 1600 this contained about 26 per cent of the region's people, by 1998 it made up only about 19 per cent.

Much more striking is the huge increase in the total population—by about 22 times. But four centuries, in demographic terms, is a very long time, given that a population increasing at 3 per cent a year will double in size in a little over 20 years. Very rapid growth in population occurred mainly in the nineteenth and twentieth centuries but the earlier phase of this expansion is probably not to be explained by any improvement in health brought about by Europeans, most of whom, in any case, lived in coastal cities. These, to say the least, were quite unhealthy even into the twentieth century, especially with respect to gastro-intestinal disorders such as cholera and typhoid, stemming from the use of unclean drinking water and failure to dispose of human wastes in a sanitary manner. Colonial Singapore is a case in point as Brenda Yeoh describes.

The rapid growth of population in the nineteenth century, earlier in Java and parts of the Philippines, may be attributed to the reduction in warfare, which previously aimed at acquiring semi-slave populations from defeated states, and to the spread of wet-rice cultivation. Although wet-rice areas were not devoid of malaria, a potent killer of young, non-immune children, there is little doubt that its incidence was relatively low, mosquito-breeding being controlled by ensuring a steady flow of water through the fields and by rice-field fish whose diet includes the larvae of malaria-carrying *Anopheles* mosquitoes.

Mortality

'Death control' is of overwhelming importance in affecting death rates. While it is true that warfare and genocide have caused millions of deaths—perhaps two million, mostly soldiers, during the Viet Nam War, anywhere between 400 000 and 3 million more, mainly civilians, in Pol Pot's Cambodia—such losses have been made up relatively quickly though they will continue to be reflected in each country's age/sex structure for several decades to come.

Just when death rates began to fall significantly in the region is difficult to determine but it was clearly earlier than the setting up of modern systems of birth and death registration which still today in countries like Laos and Cambodia are quite imperfect. Certainly it seems likely that falls in death rates began in cities during the nineteenth century as governments gradually provided clean drinking water and promoted the safe disposal of human waste, for cholera, typhoid and other 'diseases of dirt' were endemic, ever-present, periodically breaking out into epidemics. But in all except the most densely populated rural areas it seems likely that densities were too low for such diseases to be serious killers, though epidemics unquestionably occurred. Smallpox was a major killer everywhere and malaria, especially in rural areas in the highlands and during epidemics.

Whenever 'death control' really began to take hold it is likely that three major changes were responsible for roughly nine-tenths of the declines in death rates: provision of clean drinking water, improved personal hygiene (including proper disposal of human wastes and the use of soap), prophylaxis against major diseases, initially smallpox and subsequently malaria (use of nets and of quinine), as well as the triple antigen against common childhood diphtheria, whooping cough and measles. Treatment of actual illness probably accounted for only about a tenth of

Table 2.2 Crude death rates by country, 1950–53 and latest (per 1000 people)

Country	1952–53	Latest[1]	Latest rate as % of 1952–53 rate
Brunei	17.4	3.3	19
Cambodia (1993)	n.a.	14.1	n.a.
Indonesia	n.a.	8.9	n.a.
Laos (1993)	n.a.	15.2	n.a.
Malaya/Malaysia (1993)	12.0	5.1	43
Myanmar (1993)	34.2	10.9	32
Philippines (1993)	8.8	6.5	74
Singapore	10.3	4.1	40
Thailand	9.7	6.1	63
Viet Nam	n.a.	7.9	n.a.
Southeast Asia[2]	16.0	8.2	55

Notes: [1] For 1996, except where otherwise stated. [2] Means based only on countries for which data are available and weighted by population of each country.
Source: *UN Demographic Yearbooks*

death control and until the 1960s hospital facilities were inaccessible to most rural people. Since then, the use of antibiotics to control infections has also contributed to reduced death rates.

There is also little doubt that by the 1950s most people were better fed than before. Good diet improves fertility and reduces susceptibility to disease. Improvements in government administration and transportation also allowed food to be moved quickly to areas of shortage which in earlier centuries might have led to famine and more deaths because of increased liability to disease.

What is clear is that by the time comprehensive statistics for death rates are available, in some countries not until the 1970s, rates were much below what they were thought to have been in the last century when they were, in the long run, only a little below the birth rates. Of the countries for which data are available in the 1950s, only Myanmar (Burma) had rates remotely approaching the crude death rates of 40–45 per thousand that probably existed earlier (Table 2.2). Elsewhere, rates were already moderate to low. By 1993, even the country with the highest rate, Cambodia, probably had a rate only a third of that earlier and in most countries they were very low, with a regional average of only 8.2 per thousand. Interestingly, it is likely that in countries with low rates—Brunei, Malaysia, Singapore for example—death rates will rise as their populations age and an increasing proportion of the population begins to die of characteristic conditions of old age such as cancer and heart disease. Singapore's population is kept 'artificially young' by the presence of a high proportion of migrant workers, and it seems likely that the death rate for Singaporeans may be higher than that of the population as a whole.

Fertility

It was not until after the Pacific War that population growth in the region became really rapid. In most countries, once some degree of recovery from the traumas of the Japanese occupation and the turmoil of local independence struggles had been achieved, a combination of factors led to rapid natural growth, in some cases, for example the Philippines, approaching 4 per cent annually. While factors conducive to growth can easily be identified, it is very difficult to apportion 'responsibility' to them in specific places and at specific times.

Widespread public security, except in Indochina (Viet Nam, Cambodia and Laos) certainly seems to have been a factor, along with the rapid spread of clean drinking water and basic health education into the rural areas. In most countries the spread of mass prophylaxis against smallpox, tuberculosis, poliomyelitis and childhood diseases such as diphtheria, measles and whooping cough was rapid and included all but the remotest areas. Rural clinics became the norm and played a major role in improving maternal and child health. Consequently, where once families might have lost up to half of their neonates—children under the age of one year—such losses became quite exceptional, confined to the remotest parts of the uplands of mainland Southeast Asia and West Irian. There is little doubt that diets have generally improved. At the same time family planning knowledge and practice was limited so that total fertility (number of children born to women in the childbearing age-groups, usually taken as 15–40 years) was quite high. In 1975, for example, total fertility rates (TFR) ranged between 5.5 (several countries) and 6.6 (Viet Nam). Only in Singapore, almost entirely urban, was the rate low at 2.8. Earlier, in the 1950s, even Singapore had shared very high birth rates characteristic of the whole region (Table 2.3).

To these demographic factors may be added the fact that children in some number were seen as a positive good. In the general absence of social security provision, parents would ensure care by their children when they could no longer work by having a lot of them. But more importantly, children played an economic role from a young age—gathering fuel, carrying water, minding siblings while adults worked, guarding crops and livestock, weeding and other agricultural tasks—for the predominant mode

Table 2.3 Crude birth rates by country, 1950–54 and latest[1] (per 1000 people)

Country	1950–54	Latest	Latest rate as % of 1950–54 rate
Brunei	52.9	25.0	47
Cambodia (1993)	51.0	38.2	75
Indonesia	52.0	27.3	53
Laos (1993)	n.a.	45.2	n.a.
Malaya/Malaysia	44.1	25.5	58
Myanmar	43.0	28.8	67
Philippines	50.0	31.2	62
Singapore	45.5	13.4	29
Thailand	46.0	18.1	39
Viet Nam	38.0	28.9	76
Southeast Asia[2]	43.0	27.2	57

Notes: [1] For 1996, except where stated. [2] Mean weighted by population of each country.
Source: *UN Demographic Yearbooks*

of agricultural production, growing rice, is remarkably responsive, in terms of yields, to increases in labour inputs.

Since the mid-1960s crude birth rates have fallen by almost half along with total fertility rates, though some countries still have high values. Laos and Cambodia, the two poorest countries in the region, with Gross National Products per person of US$350 and $270 respectively, have TFRs of 6.6 and 5.2, suggesting a link between poverty and fertility. By 1996 Indonesia and Thailand had TFRs lower than largely urban Singapore in 1975, that is below 2.7, while by 1996 Singapore had moved lower still—to 1.7—below the level at which the population was replacing itself by 'natural means' rather than by migration. Other countries had TFRs of between 3.0 and 4.1 and these are clearly headed lower. All except Myanmar and Viet Nam have GNPs per person one, or in the case of Singapore two, orders of magnitude higher than Laos and Cambodia. In terms of crude birth rates (Table 2.3) the patterns are somewhat similar, with Singapore and Thailand showing rates below 20 per thousand and most of the other countries showing rates two-fifths to half those of 40 years earlier.

The fact that Singapore, which in the 1950s had crude birth rates about as high as those of other countries in the region, had by the 1970s dropped its fertility rates close to replacement gives a clue as to the reasons why, mostly, birth rates had fallen. Some may argue that Singapore's aggressive anti-natalist population policy, until the 1990s maintained by giving maternity and other benefits such as education and housing to families with no more than two children, penalising families with more, was responsible for the change in people's fertility behaviour. On the analogy of Hong Kong, which has no population policy at all, yet experienced a parallel change, it seems likely that Singapore's rapid decline in fertility would probably have happened anyway. One early straw in the wind indicating change lies in the fact that in 1955–59 Myanmar's urban birth rates were almost a third lower than the 50 per thousand of the country as a whole. Birth rates were probably quite generally lower in the cities and towns, for people migrating into them generally seem not to have retained the higher rates of reproduction characteristic of rural people after having moved to the cities, though it is generally agreed that in the early phases of urban population growth perhaps as much as two-thirds of growth comes by natural increase, not by migration.

Urban living has clearly resulted in lower fertility. Again it is relatively easy to identify probable factors in this process but very difficult to weigh one against the other. Rural to urban migration is age-selective, most migrants being young adults. Since they are generally in the reproductive age-groups moving is probably only a factor influencing fertility insofar as moving and resettling affect reproductive behaviour. Migration is also selective in terms of marital status. Many who move are single and marry much later than countryfolk. Those long resident in towns do likewise. Townsfolk have easier access to contraceptive knowledge. They also have different life-styles and objectives. Slum-dwellers in particular see their environment as definitely not the place in which to raise a family—a reason why some who do have children may send them back to the home village to be raised. A nice house, a motorcycle or even a car, home appliances, entertainment, all are seen as objectives at least as desirable as children. Since agriculture is no longer the source of livelihood the imperative to gain income by gaining children falls away as educated children are seen to be the key to upward social mobility and one or two will do at least as well as many, for education requires 'deferred gratification' and investment for the future.

From the cities it seems likely that 'urban' fertility behaviours have spread into the countryside but at varying rates depending in part upon the degree to which family-planning has been promoted. The case of Thailand is notable in that while around two-thirds of the population may still be largely engaged in rural pursuits, its people's fertility patterns have become notably 'urban' in character, to the extent that around 1990–93 the total fertility rate fell to about or below replacement, that is to say, the average number of children born to women of reproductive age fell below 2.2. Thailand is the first predominantly rural country in the region of which this is true. Singapore reached this level much earlier. Despite its government's reversal of its earlier strongly anti-natalist policy—'Stop at two!'—Singapore's TFR is still well below replacement. In the region generally it is likely that the fertility behaviour of most urban residents, especially of those born in cities, leads to births being below replacement levels amongst such folk.

One intriguing question is the degree to which the emerging pattern of personal mobility between work on the family farm and work elsewhere affects fertility. Since men are more likely to be involved than women—though far from invariably—their absence tends to reduce fertility. In some areas, such male workers have a higher risk of contracting sexually transmitted diseases. Gonorrhoea, transmitted to women, may cause serious infertility.

Overall then, every country has seen a fall in birth rates and fertility since the 1950s, very rapid in Singapore, and probably amongst most longstanding urban residents, quite rapid in Thailand, less so but still fairly fast in Indonesia and Brunei—which may suggest that the Muslim religion is no significant barrier to fertility decline. Catholicism in the Philippines seems to be likewise. At the other end of the scale it is notable that the poor countries of the mainland—Myanmar, Cambodia, Laos and Viet Nam—still have moderately high birth rates, Viet Nam in particular showing the region's lowest rates in the early 1950s but those dropped by only a fifth 40 years later. By the late 1990s, however, these too were rapidly falling.

The demographic transition

A person born in the 1950s has seen the region's population more than doubled just as the death rates have fallen to a third of those when he or she was born, even though birth rates have fallen as well. In fact, both rates have fallen, death rates mostly more slowly than birth rates but beginning much earlier. This shift from a situation in which both birth and death rates are high—the former slightly higher than the latter and both fluctuating from year to year—to the present situation in North America, most of Europe, Japan, Hong Kong, Thailand and Singapore, where both rates are low—is described as the demographic transition. This is illustrated diagramatically in Figure 2.1. The slopes of the curves obviously vary from country to country. In some the death rates decline more slowly than the birth rates and the converse may be also true. (Unfortunately data for our region do not permit the tracing of the transition in a rigorous way.) But what is universal is that the fall in birth rates is later than the decline in death rates, though again the period of time between the two is variable and of course in reality the curves are not so smooth. The result of this time lag is a population explosion with

Figure 2.1 Generalised diagram illustrating the demographic transition

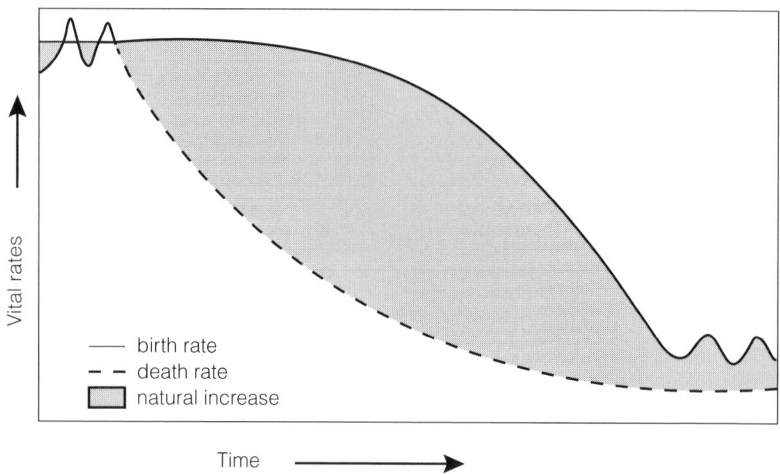

Figure 2.2 The real situation—birth and death rates for Thailand

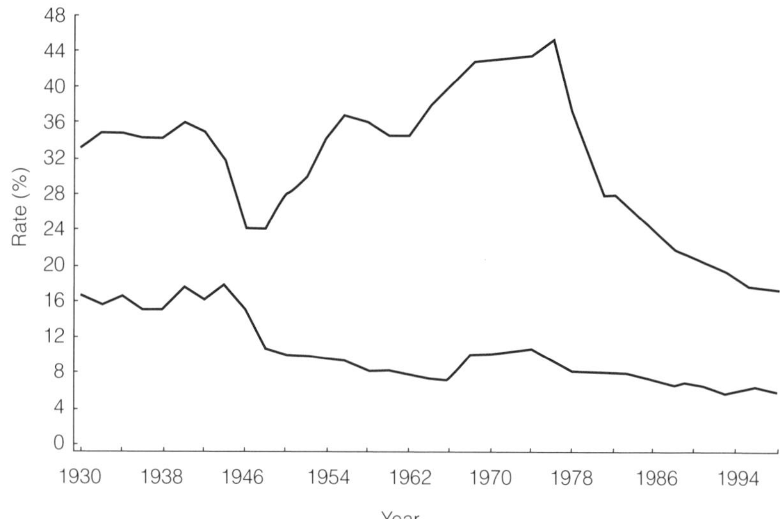

annual growth rates, excluding migration, ranging up to about 3.8 per cent, a figure approached by the Philippines in the 1960s.

Thailand, the first moderately large country in Southeast Asia to reach a situation in which the TFR is below replacement level, has reasonably good population data, though the figures for both births and deaths are probably understated in rural areas prior to the 1970s. Figure 2.2 shows the change in rates since 1930 when death rates, in this case probably urban death rates for the most part, had already fallen from the higher levels thought to have existed earlier. At the same time, birth rates, again probably urban, were about 50 per cent more than the death rates, the latter showing a small rise during the early 1940s even though Thailand was not a wartime combatant. Death rates continued to fall steadily, the small rise in the late 1960s probably representing improved registration. By the 1970s birth rates were almost four times higher than death rates but from that time they have continued to fall, not least through the family-planning efforts of Dr Meechai and his many associates. (Such were these efforts that a condom is known in Thai as a '*meechai*'.) In fact birth rates would probably have fallen anyway, as explained earlier, though doubtless not so fast.

The major consequence of falling death rates, followed by a fall in birth rates only after a gap of a decade or more, has been substantial population growth. In the case of Thailand this resulted in the population doubling between 1930 and 1959 and this was followed by a further doubling by 1982. Present indications are that it will not double again, though if the high forecast made by the United Nations in 1996 were to come to pass it would do so some time between 2030 and 2040.

To greater or less degree all the countries of the region have shared in this kind of growth and for much the same reasons, though rates have varied amongst them. This is reflected in the mid-year population estimates as shown in Table 2.4.

In the lifetime of a middle-aged person, born in 1957, the region's population has grown by 2.7 times. Malaysia, the Philippines, Thailand, Viet Nam and minuscule Brunei have grown faster than this, all except Viet Nam showing increases by over three times. Indonesia, comprising two-fifths of the region's population, has an overall increase just below the regional average, as do Laos and Myanmar, both still in the earlier stages of the demographic transition, while Cambodia, despite relatively large losses during its civil war, and Singapore, despite its long-continued anti-natalist population policies, exactly share the regional average. As will be seen later, a small country's population may be significantly affected by international migration. That has clearly been the case in Laos, where there has been significant outwards migration, or in Singapore and Brunei where inwards migration has been important.

Paradoxically, while the region has steadily added more and more

Figure 2.3 Population growth in Thailand

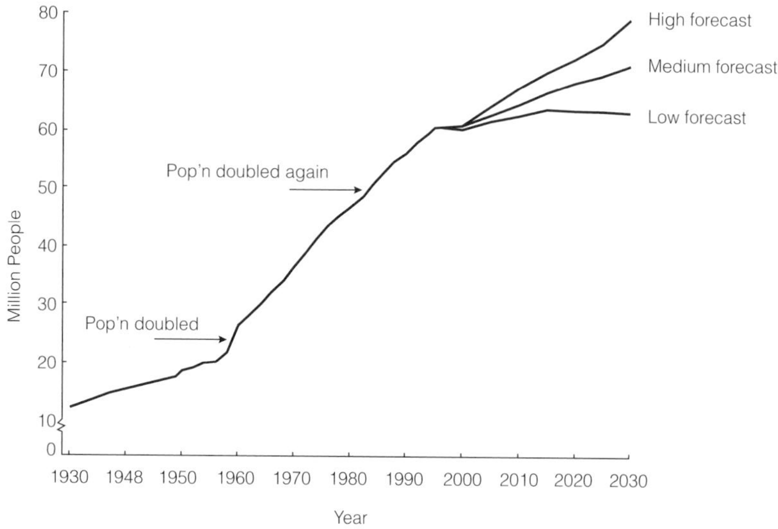

Figure 2.4 Birth rates plotted against death rates for all Southeast Asian countries (mid-1990s)

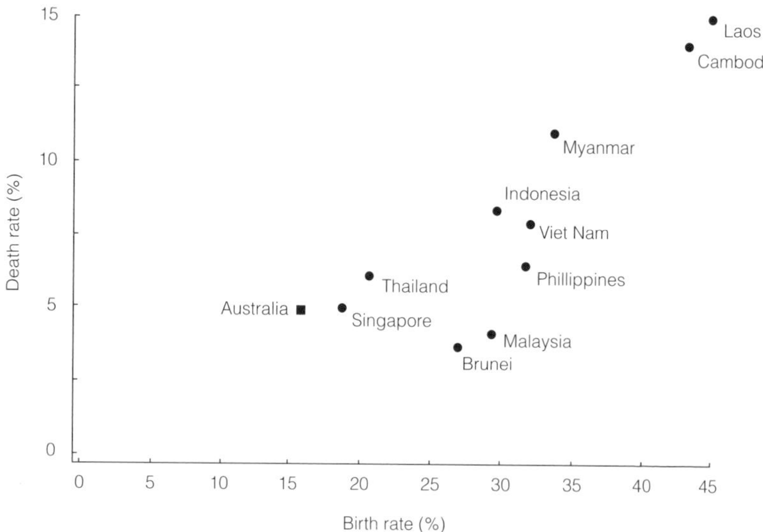

Table 2.4 Mid-year population estimates, 1953–2030 (millions)[1]

Country	1953	1965	1975	1985	1996	2030	Annual growth 1953–96 (%)
Brunei	0.1	0.2	0.3	0.3	0.3	0.4	5.0
Cambodia	3.9	6.1	7.1	7.5	10.3	16.7	2.7
Indonesia	79.5	105.7	132.0	164.6	197.6	254.1	2.5
Laos	2.0	2.6	3.4	3.6	5.0	9.7	2.5
Malaysia	6.7	9.4	12.3	15.7	20.6	30.0	3.1
Myanmar	19.1	24.7	29.9	37.1	45.9	64.7	2.4
Philippines	21.4	32.4	42.1	54.7	71.9	101.3	3.4
Singapore	1.1	1.9	2.3	2.5	3.0	3.9	2.7
Thailand	19.6	30.7	41.4	51.7	60.0	63.3	3.1
Viet Nam	25.9	35.1	47.7	59.9	75.2	102.8	2.9
Total	179.3	248.8	318.5	397.6	489.8	646.9	2.7

Note: [1] Figures rounded. Percentage increase calculated from unrounded data. Figures for 2030 are the low estimate.
Source: *UN Demographic Yearbooks*

people, the rate at which it has been doing this has steadily fallen (Table 2.5).

However, while every country has seen a slowing in growth rates, the speed at which they have changed and the initial growth rates in the period to about 1965 are very different. There is a world of difference between a growth rate of 4 per cent a year, at which a population will double in about 18 years, and a growth of 0.6 per cent per year at which rate it will take 115 years for the same thing to happen. Thus in the period 1953–65 four countries—Cambodia, the Philippines, Thailand and Singapore —experienced extremely rapid growth, ranging from 4.3 per cent (Philippines) to 6.1 per cent annually (Singapore), the last quite beyond achievable rates of natural increase, implying migration and/or improvement in enumerating people. Such rates imply doubling of the population in 12 to 18 years, so, especially in the case of Singapore, it was not surprising that steps were taken by governments to limit both migration and reproduction.

By contrast all the other countries had growth rates between 2.5 per cent (doubling every 28 years) and 3.5 per cent (doubling every 21 years), still much higher than the period of maximum growth during Europe's Industrial Revolution—roughly 1 per cent—which implies a doubling of population over about 70 years. Interestingly, between 1975 and 1985

Table 2.5 Number and annual rate of population increase

Period	Number (million)	Rate (%)[1]
1953–65	5.8	3.2
1965–75	7.0	2.8
1975–85	7.9	2.0
1985–96	8.4	1.7

Note: [1] Simple mean, not geometric.
Source: Derived from Table 2.4

Singapore, Cambodia and Laos experienced comparable low growth rates though by 1985–96 large countries—Indonesia and Thailand—have joined Singapore with rates below 2 per cent a year. In fact growth rates in Laos, Cambodia and, surprisingly, Singapore have increased in the last decade as compared with the previous decade, in the two former by sustained natural growth, 3.7 and 3.5 per cent respectively, or in the case of Singapore by renewed natural growth—though still at a rate below replacement—and by migration, an issue to be considered shortly.

Overall, then, such has been the speed of growth that our middle-aged person born in 1957 has seen Viet Nam's population grow to roughly the size of Indonesia's when he or she was born, while the Philippines and Thailand are not all that far below the same level. Malaysia in 1996 had about as many people as Myanmar, a much larger country, had in 1953. Singapore now has half as many people again as Laos then had. Myanmar has nearly twice as many people as Viet Nam had in 1953.

One clear result of differences in rates of growth has been to change the share each country has of the region's total population, a matter that may have political and strategic overtones. For example, though now growing less rapidly than in the 1950s and 1960s, Malaysia still has rapid growth, both naturally and by migration from Indonesia and the southern Philippines. Yet its Prime Minister, Dr Mahathir, has declared that the country could, and should, easily support a population of 80 million, achievable in half a century at the (simple) average rate of the period 1985–96, 2.8 per cent a year. The overall rankings, from Indonesia at number one to Brunei, have not changed though the gaps between them have (Table 2.6). However, by 2030 Myanmar may supplant its old enemy Thailand as number four in the rankings.

Most striking are the drop in Indonesia's share and the proportionately large rise in that of the Philippines, reflecting the fact that for Indonesia in 1953–65 growth was already moderate at 2.7 per cent a year, compared with 4.3 per cent in the Philippines. By 1985–96 the Indonesian rate had fallen to 1.8 per cent yet the Philippines' was still just under 3 per cent.

Table 2.6 Share of total population 1953, 1997–98 and 2030 (low estimate), by country (per cent)

Country	Rank	1953	1997–98	2030
Brunei	10	0.06	0.06	0.06
Cambodia	7	2.18	2.26	2.58
Indonesia	1	44.34	40.47	39.28
Laos	8	1.12	1.02	1.50
Malaysia	6	3.74	4.40	4.64
Myanmar	5	10.65	8.81	10.00
Philippines	3	11.94	14.90	15.66
Singapore	9	0.61	0.63	0.60
Thailand	4	10.93	12.12	9.79
Viet Nam	2	14.45	15.40	15.89
Total		100.02	100.00	100.00

Source: Calculated from Table 2.1 and *UN Demographic Yearbooks*

Relatively slow declines in growth rates have also resulted in Viet Nam and Malaysia enhancing their shares.

Consequences of population growth

Though intimately related, the consequences of growth are both direct and demographic and indirect, economic and social, the latter to be considered in chapter 6. The large and rapid increase of population induced by high birth rates and falling death rates resulted in greater youthfulness of the population as a whole. In 1947 for example, 62 per cent of Thailand's population was under the age of 25 years. By 1995, as a result of falling growth rates, just over half of the people were below that age. This high degree of youthfulness is, to greater or less degree, characteristic of most countries in the region and implies severe pressures upon health and education services as well as employment. Since people now live much longer than formerly those pressures will continue for decades as 'baby-boomers' grow older and, especially, as the survivors leave the workforce and require support from those still in it. Thai people, for example, born in 1947 on average could expect to live to 49 if male or 52 if female, whereas by 1985–86 the corresponding figures were 64 and 69 years respectively. Recent data show that in every country, except Laos, Cambodia and Myanmar where the expectation of life at birth was to an age of 50–58 years, children born in the mid-1980s could expect to survive into their 60s and in Brunei and Singapore into their 70s.

Dependency is a major economic aspect of the population. This is rather arbitrarily defined as people under 15 years and over 60 or 64 years.

Rapidly growing populations such as most in the region have a large proportion of children and few elderly dependants. Thus in 1995 Indonesia had about 73 million dependants, children outnumbering the aged ten to one. In 1992 Viet Nam's population included 45 per cent dependants, 40 per cent of the total being children. A rapid slowing of growth rates does not improve the dependency situation. In Thailand in 1947, for example, there were about 7.8 million dependants, 45 per cent of the total population, 7.4 million of them children. By 1995 there were 19.5 million dependants but these made up only 33 per cent of the population, children making up 85 per cent of the dependants, compared with 96 per cent in 1947. If, as seems likely, the population grows slowly or not at all, by the year 2030 just over 30 per cent of the population will still be dependants but more than half of these will be aged 65 or over. The kind of dependency will have changed but the level of dependency hardly at all.

The other side of the equation is the workforce. All countries have had and many will continue to have a major task in finding jobs for all. Thus Thailand in 1947–52 had to find work for roughly 450 000 new workers every year. By 1995–2000 that figure has more than doubled. Over the same period Indonesia will have about 4.5 million joining the workforce but only a million a year leaving it. In Viet Nam the situation is even more difficult with five times as many entrants as leavers. The point is that these people are alive and mostly well right now, so the magnitude of dealing with the economic implications is also known. On the other hand, Singapore, Malaysia and now, increasingly, Thailand are labour-deficit countries though only partly for demographic reasons.

As populations age so do their age/sex structures, often shown as pyramids in which each bar corresponds to the proportion of people in each age/sex group (Figure 2.5). Youthful populations—Thailand in 1947, Viet Nam in 1992—have a broad base, a relatively slender middle and apex, the latter dominated by women who, for biological reasons, live longer than men on average. Ageing population pyramids are relatively uniform from the base to about age 70—Thailand's 'slow growth projection' for 2030. The 'youthful' pyramid is characteristic of the early stage of the demographic transition—Thailand 1947—as the 'aged' pyramid is of the final stage—Thailand 2030. In the region most countries are ranged between these extremes—mostly nearer the early rather than the later stages.

In addition pyramids reflect demographic history. Thus for Viet Nam there is a clear relative deficit of men over 35 years, reflecting wartime losses. But there is also a relative deficit in the 20–34 age groups and this probably reflects the 'boat people' migration which followed the war. These deficits will have had knock-on effects such as not all women of reproductive age and wishing to marry being able to find husbands and

Figure 2.5 Age–sex pyramids for Thailand, 1947, 1994 and projected for 2030

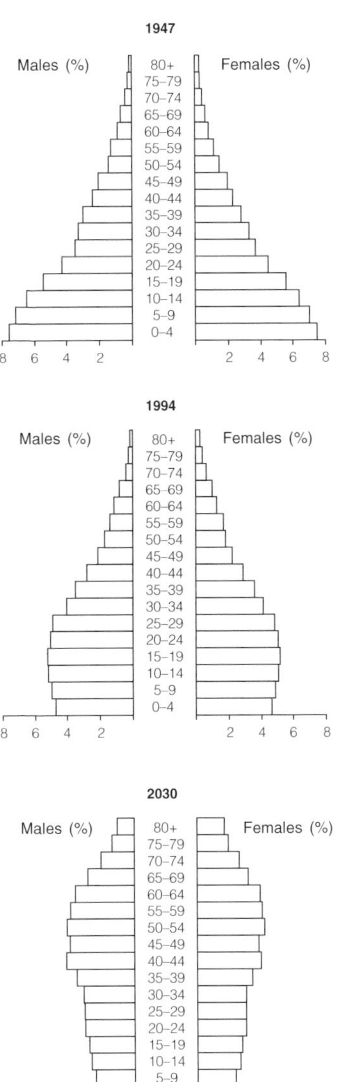

thus reproducing. As these groups age there will be an abnormally large preponderance of elderly women.

Given low death rates and despite falling birth rates, every country will continue for some time yet to experience natural growth of its population even if fertility falls below replacement. The reason is that as each youthful cohort moves up the pyramid most of its members will marry and reproduce.

Most countries have some distance to go before the expectation of life at birth is similar to that of economically developed countries—Singapore is nearest with means of 74 years for males and 79 years for females. (Compare this with Australia's figures of 75 and 81 years.) When they reach a similar level, death rates will rise slightly and if fertility is at or below replacement, unless there is significant in-migration of potentially reproducing people, the population will stabilise or fall. Just how far off that event may be can be judged from recent estimates for the region's population in 2030 (Table 2.4). Three estimates have been made by the United Nations: low 647 million, medium 722 million, high 798 million.

Either way these totals are expected to comprise about the same proportion of the world's population as at present, about 8.6 per cent, and the share of each country is expected to be much the same as now though slightly higher for countries still early in the demographic transition. Examples are Myanmar, Cambodia and Laos. Singapore and Thailand, in which the transition is well advanced, will have slightly lower shares. Our person born in 1957 is now 44 years old. If he is a Thai male he can expect to live on average another 27 years; if female another 31. If he makes it to the year 2030—aged 73—he or she will still have another six or seven years to live. By that date—in a single lifetime—Thailand's population will have grown naturally by somewhere between 3½ and 4½ times and the region's people will have increased from about 180 million to between about 650 and 800 million.

International migration

The contribution of migration from outside the region to this very large increase has been and is likely to be minuscule. Doubtless there are still small groups drifting into the region across the land borders with China, a process that has been going on for centuries, and the same may be true of the border with Papua New Guinea.

Emigration from the region has been more important—'boat people' from Viet Nam to Hong Kong, Malaysia, Thailand and Indonesia from which temporary havens some were returned, some few remain and others have moved to destinations outside the region, especially to Canada, Australia and the US. In addition there has been a fairly steady trickle of permanent migrants from other sources: Malaysian and Singaporean Chinese and Eurasians to Canada, the US and Australia; Singaporean Jews to various destinations; Filipinos likewise, some moving as family groups, some for employment, some upon marriage. But the total numbers are small both in relation to the region's population and to the population of the receiving countries. Skeldon, for instance, gives data for migration from Singapore, a major regional source, to Canada, Australia and the US, the major destinations outside the region. In the decade from the mid-1980s those countries received a total of 9.4 million migrants of which Singaporeans comprised about 35 000, a mere 0.4 per cent of their migration streams, though representing about 1 per cent of Singapore's population at the time.

Temporary migration outside the region, mainly as contract workers, is another matter though good data are scarce and there is a major difficulty in determining what is 'temporary' especially amongst split families in which the wife and children may be resident in one country, with the husband (usually) resident in the country of origin becoming an 'astronaut' flying between the two. The major sources of contract migrant workers are the Philippines, Indonesia and Thailand, which in the 1990s together supplied between half a million and a million workers a year to overseas destinations both within and outside Southeast Asia. These include the Middle East (mainly males), and Hong Kong (mainly females). Just how many of these are experienced migrant workers who have returned home to renew contracts and how many are first-time migrants is difficult to say but in either case the numbers are large enough to have significant demographic effects in the usually fairly restricted source areas of the migrants (more than half of Filipino workers come from Manila and nearby provinces). Amongst these are a relatively lower proportion in the working age groups and a lower incidence of marriage and reproduction. It has been estimated that in the early 1980s the growth of the Philippine population was depressed by about 140 000 a year, representing about 12 per cent of the total growth.

Regionally, the heyday of international migration was during the late nineteenth century until the 1930s when governments began to control it. This, of course, was the period when Myanmar acquired its Indian minority population, now largely repatriated, when Malaysia and Singapore also added significant, largely south Indian, minorities to their large Chinese minorities and Indonesia its Overseas Chinese.

Since that time two significant migration streams developed. One was at the time when the Pol Pot regime supplanted the Lon Nol government in Phnom Penh. This resulted in a considerable exodus westwards into refuges on the Thai side of the border and a movement of Vietnamese resident in Cambodia eastwards into Vietnamese sanctuaries. By the 1990s most of these seem to have returned to Cambodia.

The other major stream was of Vietnamese from the south around the time of the fall of Saigon in 1974. This mostly comprised urban people both ethnic Vietnamese, especially those employed by the southern government, and Sino-Vietnamese who feared persecution and loss of livelihood, the Sino-Vietnamese moving first. Later, however, the stream was joined by fisherfolk and farmers even from the north. Most—the 'boat people'—went by sea south and east to the South China Sea and the countries fringing it while others moved overland, some to China, others reaching Thailand where a few remain. The effects upon Viet Nam's population were significant, since there was a predominance of young men amongst the refugees. The effects upon the population of other Southeast Asian countries was negligible since they were put into camps and most were resettled outside the region or, more recently, with their children, have been returned to Viet Nam after sometimes extended stays in the camps. Small numbers of regional ethnic minority peoples were resettled as a result of conflict, a few hundred Muslim Chams from southern Viet Nam settling in Peninsular Malaysia and a few thousand Hmong in the US.

It is not known exactly how many moved but three million is probably a good round figure though possibly an underestimate as those who moved from Laos especially were never really counted. Of that number, just under half came within the purview of the United Nations High Commission for Refugees so that these are the people about whom most is known. Most of the migrants ended up in other countries—some 1.3 million in the US, 260 000 in China, 202 000 in Canada, 186 000 in Australia, 119 000 in France. Well over half a million have returned home, amongst them some 400 000 Cambodians who had fled the genocidal Pol Pot regime. Not all of these people were refugees in the sense that they actually fled their homelands during the conflicts. Some 600 000 Vietnamese and 15 000 Cambodians moved to the US under the post-1976 Orderly Departure Program which included some 40 000 'Amerasians' fathered by US servicemen and 141 000 prisoners in Vietnamese re-education camps whose previous association with the Republic of Vietnam government in the south of the country made it desirable for them to leave.

Much more important to the region have been migration streams resulting from the search for economic opportunity rather than from wars and their aftermath. Just how large these may be is not easy to establish, for the actions of the recipient countries have varied from encouragement of legal migration to toleration of illegal migration and settlement. Partly as a result of its anti-natalist policies combined with a rapidly growing economy, Singapore saw a considerable expansion of migrant labour in the 1970s, mainly of construction workers and domestic servants, most from Peninsular Malaysia, working on short-term permits. By the mid-1990s it is suggested that permit-holders numbered about 300 000, a tenth of the population and a quarter of the workforce. Since this group consists of both men and women living apart and legally unable to marry—either each other or Singaporeans—on pain of immediate deportation, it makes no contribution to natural growth in the republic. Its members can be sent home at short notice according to changes in labour demand. Participants include Malaysians, Thai, Indonesians, Bangladeshis and Filipinos employed as domestics.

Such people are, of course, legal migrants, but other countries may contain significant numbers of technically illegal migrants whose presence is tolerated as a source of cheap labour and for lack of the will and practical means to send them back to their countries of origin. It has been suggested, for instance, that Malaysia contains about a million of such migrants, mainly of Indonesian origin, as workers on plantations, in the timber industry especially. Many are from Sumatera, though in Malaysia's Sabah state there are significant numbers from Indonesia's eastern archipelago, including Timor, and from the largely Muslim islands of the Sulu Sea. Periodical amnesties have legalised the presence of some such migrants, though others, notably in Peninsular Malaysia, are being rounded up and sent home.

In mainland Southeast Asia another large group is Lao who fled their country in the 1960s and 1970s, settling mainly in the adjoining Isan region of Thailand which is ethnically essentially Lao. Their numbers are not known exactly, but together with their offspring there are probably between one and two hundred thousand. Thailand has also received large numbers of refugees from Myanmar, perhaps 1.2 million of them. Many are Karen and Shan (the latter linguistically Thai), who have fled in the face of forcible attempts by the central government to bring semi-independent regions and peoples under its control. While some refugees are in camps along the northern Myanmar/Thai border, others have moved further into Thailand, certainly as far as Bangkok. This city is also the destination of women smuggled into the country for prostitution from as far afield as the southwestern provinces of China as well as intervening areas.

Overall, in terms of numbers, the scale of international migration within the region is rather less significant than internal migration. Borders are relatively porous and a good deal of international movement is unrecorded despite the difficulties illegal migrants may have in settling permanently, obtaining employment and access to health care and education. Where policing is effective, as in Singapore, migrants form a temporarily resident underclass, to a degree excluded from normal social activities such as marriage and liable to be sent home at short notice. Elsewhere many succeed in settling, leading a more or less normal life as labourers or farmers and likely to be assimilated eventually into the broad mass of the people.

INTERNAL MIGRATION AND MOBILITY

Migration is basically a subset of mobility. Mobility involves two major variables—space and time. Thus migration, as distinct from, say, commuting, involves a greater time settled in more or less one place, though in these days of rapid, relatively cheap transportation, distance is less of a factor. What constitutes a transfer of residence is quite arbitrary and though census enumerations try to distinguish between 'residents' and 'transients' such enumerations are by no means wholly to be relied upon, especially as some censuses in the region record people where they usually are rather than where they are at the actual time of counting. Thus village people doing a couple of months' work in a city may be counted as villagers not as city folk.

Migration within countries is of various kinds—rural to rural, rural to urban, urban to rural, urban to urban, intra-urban—though these categories imply the drawing of a distinction that is increasingly fuzzy, especially around the region's great cities. Rural to rural migration characterised the period from about the middle of the last century until the 1950s, though it existed much earlier as witnessed by the southwards drift of Dai Viet (Vietnamese) from their homeland in the Tonkin delta region. This was the time when southern Burma and southern Viet Nam were developed for commercial rice production, as too was the Chao Phrya delta of Thailand. Settlers from Java and Bali began to settle, both spontaneously and under government auspices, in southern Kalimantan, Sulawesi and, some as rice-growing peasants, others on estates and smallholdings growing tobacco, coconuts, pepper, rubber and, in Peninsular Malaysia, oil palm. That movement continued after 1950 only in fairly limited areas: land development schemes in upland Viet Nam, many of which encountered serious difficulties, in Peninsular Malaysia and Sabah, in the same general areas of Indonesia which had earlier received migrants, and in upland areas of northeastern Thailand where commercial manioc (tapioca) and fibre (*Hibiscus*) production became important. Just how many have been involved is difficult to say for much depends on who is identified as a settler, but the country-by-country figures would reach the millions, especially if settlers' descendants are counted.

But such movements were and are by no means one way. In Indonesia, for example, it seems that the migration of settlers to the Outer Islands (i.e. excepting Java and Bali) has been pretty much balanced by return migration, much of it rural to urban. Rural to rural migration and other kinds are not necessarily detected by censuses in the region. In Indonesia, for example, only permanent movement from one province to another is recorded. One estimate, for the Philippines, suggests that between 1948 and 1988 about 10 million people migrated to upland areas, mostly in Mindanao. Another, for Thailand, suggests that about 1.23 million families moved onto new agricultural lands from the mid-1960s to the mid-1980s. Large though these streams are, they represent only a very small fraction of overall population growth though significantly changing the population distribution since the areas cleared for cultivation were previously inhabited at low densities.

Rural to urban migration is by far the most important form of movement though it is very difficult to document. Censuses, while detecting urban growth, do not necessarily pick up the migrant component. In Malaysia, for example, the proportion of the population classed as urban rose from about 3.2 million in 1971, representing 27 per cent of the total, to just over 9 million by 1991 when urban people comprised 50.6 per cent of the population—a threefold increase. Indonesia's urban growth has been rather less spectacular. Whereas in 1980 there were 30 towns with a population of over 100 000 and a total of 21.1 million people, by 1995 there were 45 such towns with 33.5 million people, an increase by about half in 15 years compared with an increase of the whole population of about a third over the same time-span. This is a steady rather than a spectacular growth since the population in cities of over 100 000 rose from 14.2 per cent of the total in 1980 to 17.2 per cent in 1995. But just what proportion of this came by natural growth and what by rural–urban migration, by small town to large town movement, not to mention 'growth' because urban boundaries have been extended is hard to say. The last factor is not trivial. It may account for close to a quarter of Peninsular Malaysia's urban growth, for instance. While agriculture may survive in such urban peripheral zones it often becomes a part-time activity as long-time residents, together with new arrivals housed in 'green-field' dormitory suburbs, are drawn into the urban economy.

Just how they get there is not at all clear. Some are clearly rural–urban migrants: others come in a stepwise movement via small towns to larger ones, especially to the capital cities. Other urban peripheral dwellers may have been decanted from crowded slums in the inner city, a process of some significance in Marcos-era Manila. What is clear is that with general increases in wealth, personal mobility has increased, allowing the partial, sometimes complete transformation of once-rural villages within commuting distances of large cities into dormitory suburbs still inhabited by people who are to some degree involved in farming, joined by migrants from a number of sources.

Circular migration

Urban peripheries are far from being the only zone affected by newcomers from village and small town. Transportation by motor vehicle now penetrates all but the remotest lowland areas and even in many of them, canoes propelled by outboard motors permit quick and relatively cheap access.

In most of the region the result has been the development of networks of temporary migration from rural areas to towns and cities, especially in the dry season. Thus Bangkok's dry-season population is about 9 per cent higher than its wet-season population, when male workers leave temporary jobs in construction, as hawkers, trishaw riders and much else to become farmers again. That city and most others in Thailand also contain significant numbers of sex workers, some full-time, some not, totalling perhaps half a million around 1980, representing about a tenth of all women in the 14–24 age group, a proportion not necessarily larger than that in other parts of the region. Whatever the sources of income, it is clear that involvement in such circular migration is substantial in most countries, excepting perhaps Myanmar, Laos, Cambodia and Viet Nam, though in the latter two it is clearly beginning. Residence in the city has become another subsistence strategy for many 'rural' families and many have one or more 'detached' members.

Whether permanent or temporary, the major reasons for migration are universal though varying somewhat between men and women and especially in access to and ownership of farm land. Rural conditions push. Perceived urban conditions pull. The landless and near-landless move. Those with land move also, but to a lesser degree. A 'better life' is usually given as a major reason for both women and men moving. Women may also say they follow parents, a spouse, a brother to the bright lights. At the very worst it is possible to pick up some sort of a living in the economic interstices of the city—'guarding' cars in carparks, hawking cigarettes, chewing gum or snacks, begging, scavenging and recycling rubbish, taking in laundry, a multitude of marginal occupations, always with the chance of striking it lucky.

Language, religion and ethnicity

Given that the region's population has grown and will continue to grow hugely, it seems reasonable to ask whether the same has happened to the diversity of the region's peoples. It could be argued that diversity is becoming less following the cessation of substantial migration of 'outsiders' such as that of southern Chinese or southern Indians. Certainly the setting up of truly national systems of education in the post-colonial era, marked by the use of a dominant or sole national language, has tended to reduce differences between one person and another. How can you 'love your neighbour as yourself' if you cannot communicate? Thus Indonesians under the age of 40 speak the national language. Indonesian, based upon Malay, long the *lingua franca* of coastal trading peoples from Aceh in Sumatera to the 'Bird's Head' in West Irian, is universal in the country. At home, though, they usually speak one of a host of local languages—

Minangkabau and Batak in the north Sumatran highlands, Sundanese in west Java, Javanese in the centre and east, in Sulawesi Tongja and Menadonese, in Makassar the Bugis version of Malay—and scores of others. Especially is this so in linguistically fragmented West Irian where 'Papuan' languages are very different from those of the dominant Austronesian group of the rest of maritime Southeast Asia, including the Philippines. There a diversity of home languages survives—Ilocano in the north of Luzon, a range of related tongues in the mountains, Tagalog, the official common language having its homeland in the central Luzon plain, Visayan dialects in the centre and another host of local languages in Mindanao and Sulu. Only in West Irian are Austronesian home languages replaced by other groups: in the north Papuan, in the centre and south Melanesian.

On the mainland languages form several large groups, Burmese being just one major member of the Tibeto–Burman group. In southern Myanmar and Thailand the Mon language, a major member of the Austroasiatic Mon–Khmer group survives. This group also has a remarkable outlier as Temiar in the Malay Peninsula though the dominant language in the group is Khmer, the language of Cambodia. The Tai group of languages spills over from Thailand into much of upland Myanmar, as Shan, to Laos and even into southwest China. The status of Vietnamese is sometimes argued about, some writers even classing it as 'Tai'. Certainly it has a significant Sinitic component, a result of nearly a millennium under Chinese imperial control. Until the colonial period when the French substituted a form of Roman script, with diacriticals to mark tones (which also exist in Tai and Chinese), Vietnamese was written in Chinese characters. In the rest of mainland Southeast Asia scripts of Indic (Indian) origin are used, remarkably for tonal Tai, reflecting ancient Sanscrit and Pali influence. In insular regions Indic scripts barely survive in Javanese and Balinese. Most languages now use Roman letters though with an Arabic alternative for some forms of Malay, especially Bahasa Malaysia. Ancient indigenous scripts have been relegated to museums.

While Malay/Indonesian languages—there are some differences in vocabulary and expression—extend as a *lingua franca* from Aceh to Mindanao, other local common languages exist. Thus Hokkien is a *lingua franca* for many Singapore Chinese, but then so is English and, as a result of official policy, Mandarin. Hakka dialect is a Chinese *lingua franca* in Malaysia's Sabah state as Tai is amongst non-native Tai speakers in northern Thailand. But by far the most important *lingua franca* is English, almost universally taught at university level, and widely at secondary level or even at primary school, as in Singapore. It is the official means of communication in intergovernmental relations and often also in trade and telecommunications. Such is the demand for English instruction that Vietnamese students, for example, will pay for it even though French instruction is available free. By contrast, there is little local demand for instruction in regional languages. A Tagalog-speaking Vietnamese, for instance would be a rare bird indeed. British and American universities offer courses in a far wider range of Southeast Asian languages than any Southeast Asian country. In the region generally multilingualism has probably increased with the spread of near-universal primary education that is often not in the language spoken at home. This process has probably served to blur ethnic distinctions to some degree so that in Malaysia, for example, Javanese, Sundanese, Bugis, Boyanese, Minangkabau or Banjarese linguistic and 'ethnic' antecedents play little part in who marries whom, differences being subsumed in a wider, legally defined Malay grouping that has Islam as a major component.

Religion, next to language, is a significant determinant of ethnicity for, to varying degrees, religion may be a barrier to marriage and to some extent has been incorporated into legal codes. Thus under Islamic law Muslim women may only marry Muslim men though such men can marry Jewish or Christian women. Women cannot inherit property equally with men. These laws are incorporated into the general body of law in Malaysia, for example, and serve to reinforce religious and ethnic differences while simultaneously facilitating marriage within religion despite ethnic differences, for example between Malays and Indian Muslims or Arabs. In the Philippines inter-religious marriage, for example between the dominant Roman Catholics and other Christian groups such as the Episcopalians or the indigenous Iglesia ni Cristo may be quite firmly discouraged. But even Islam should not be thought of as monolithic. In Indonesia, for example, the Acehnese of northern Sumatera, as befits the descendants of the country's first Muslim converts, are regarded as strictly orthodox Believers. But others are more relaxed. Thus while the broad swathe of indigenous peoples from Aceh to Sulu and Mindanao is substantially Muslim, within it there is a wide range of practice, some women, for example, wearing the recently introduced *chador tudung* to 'protect their modesty', others happily bathing naked in local rivers and streams.

Within this broad belt of Muslims, however, enclaves of other religions exist, some ancient, such as the broadly Hindu Balinese religion or the animism of so-called 'pagans' such as the Punan (Penan) of Borneo. Others are recent, the result of missionary activity and colonisation—Protestant Christian Bataks in north central Sumatera, Christians of various kinds in Sabah, Sarawak and parts of Kalimantan, Roman Catholic settlers in once-Muslim Mindanao. Similar enclaves exist amongst the matrices of other dominant religions. While Myanmar and Thailand follow the Way of Theravada Buddhism, along with Laos and Cambodia, significant patches of other religions exist, Karen Christians in eastern Myanmar being just one. In Viet Nam, where the Mahayana tradition of Buddhism prevails, having been part of intense contact with China, Christian groups exist amongst the so-called Montagnard peoples of the central uplands where ancient indigenous beliefs still also survive. Mainly Roman Catholic groups continue in southern Viet Nam to which at least a million fled on the partition of the country in 1957. In the centre and south, spilling over marginally into Cambodia, many once Hinduistic Chams are now Muslim, like some Roman Catholics, often settled in their own rural villages.

Religious diversity is also partly a consequence of the colonial-era introduction of immigrant communities. Thus there exist communities of Hindus who, while sharing the same basic religious beliefs, worship in temples set up by linguistically distinct communities, Tamils, Gujeratis, Bengalis. The Sikh religion is well represented in towns of Peninsular Malaysia and in Singapore. 'Chinese religion', an eclectic mix of Taoism, Confucianism, ancestor worship, sometimes with Buddhist overtones—the goddess Kwan Yin (alias Avalokitesvarà) is popular—is to be found wherever Chinese are settled. In social terms, though, religion is not necessarily a unifying factor, not merely because most Chinese encompass a considerable range of belief and practice but because unity of belief and practice may have linguistic diversity superimposed upon it. Thus Tamil Methodists form a distinct and endogamous group. Chinese Episcopalians don't necessarily mix with other Episcopalians. Thai Buddhists found temples in other lands and like followers of Christianity happily proselytise amongst co-religionists of only marginally different persuasions.

Religion also has both overt and covert roles in the state. In Myanmar and Thailand no government can afford to ignore the *Sangha*, the supreme Buddhist council, while in Myanmar some see present government efforts to exercise control over the Karen as an attempt to wipe out Christianity. Islam is the state religion in Malaysia. Heads of state must be Muslims, and proselytisation of Muslims is forbidden. In Singapore the Seventh-day Adventist Church is officially proscribed. There are also strong religious components in various 'freedom movements' in the region, as in Mindanao and Sulu (the Abu Sayyaf movement) against a dominating Christian government. The Pattani Liberation Front's struggle in southern Thailand pitted Muslims against a Buddhist government, while in Sabah, Malaysia, there is a considerable body of opinion that sees the state as subject to Malay, thus Muslim dominance and would prefer greater autonomy, even independence, though no armed struggle has yet emerged.

Language and religion thus may divide or unite, though there is little doubt that secularism continues to make great strides, with religion especially becoming for many, mostly urban, people a peripheral rather than a central concern. However, as major determinants of ethnicity these are still important. Thus until comparatively recently non-Tai peoples in northern Thailand were not Thai citizens and speaking Tai is still a condition of citizenship, as is speaking Bahasa Malaysia in Malaysia. Status as a *bumiputera*, a Malay or other 'indigenous person', allows access to a whole slew of benefits denied to citizens who are descended from 'immigrant races'—Chinese and Indians. Universities and many businesses have ethnic quotas, for example. Ethnicity is also bureaucratically entrenched in Singapore where every citizen is allocated to a category—Chinese, Indian, Malay or 'Other'—such ethnicity descending in the male line so that, for example, the children of a European father and a Chinese mother are not 'Eurasian', a population census sub-category of 'Other', but 'European', another sub-category of 'Other'.

Nowhere are these official categories actually uniform. Chinese are very much divided linguistically, though all who are literate in Chinese can communicate in writing. The ancestors of most came originally from Guangdong and Fujian provinces and still often speak a dialect of that area at home—Hokkien, Cantonese, Hakka, Teochiu (Chiu Chow). Others came from Hainan, speaking the Hailam dialect, or from Shanghai with its distinctive manner of speech and regional cuisine. To these may be added a round dozen other, minor Chinese dialects, most of them southern. In Indonesia and Malaysia, people of Chinese ancestry may speak little or no Chinese, using Indonesian/Malay, even in the case of the Baba Chinese community of, Penang and Singapore, wearing a form of Malay dress on special occasions.

The Indian community is similarly split. In Malaysia and Singapore most Indians are Tamil-speaking at home but there is a long list of other languages. Amongst south and central Indians are Malayalam speakers from Kerala and speakers of Telegu from Gujerati, while Punjabis and Sindhis originate from the northwest of the old undivided India and Bengalis from the east.

Wherever they live—Indonesia, Malaysia, southern Thailand, Singapore or the Philippines—people of broadly Malay linguistic and cultural affinities are divided by religion and language. 'Malay' has specific legal, religious—Islamic—and linguistic connotations in Malaysia and Singapore, where an apostate is no longer considered to be Malay. Elsewhere a 'Malay'-speaker may be a Christian, a Muslim or have no religion at all. Some will use Malay/Indonesian as a home language. Some do not, preferring a local tongue—Acehnese, Lampung, Javanese, Sundanese, Madurese, Balinese, Bugis (Makassarese) or a hundred others.

Ethnicity is still an issue in many parts of the region. The Karen–Burman conflict has already been mentioned. Anti-Chinese feeling is unquestionably latent in both Malaysia and Indonesia, and periodically breaks out into rioting. In the riots of 1969, for example, largely confined to Kuala Lumpur, some four-fifths of the casualties were Chinese; whilst in the 1998 Jakarta riots Chinese businesses were put to the torch, some not for the first time, and over 75 Chinese women are reported to have been raped. 'Ethnic cleansing' is a matter of the recent past. The removal of Indians from Burma in the 1960s is one case. During the Pol Pot era in Cambodia some hundreds of thousands of Vietnamese were either killed or fled their homes. Likewise thousands of Sino-Vietnamese, especially from the south, fled in the face of what was seen as ethnic oppression.

It might be argued that these allegedly wealthy and exploitative minorities were mistreated because they were wealthy and exploitative, but the fact remains that they are easily identified by their ethnicity and civil authority has, in some instances, not merely been unwilling or unable to protect them but has taken an active role in persecuting them. But, and this is important, in day-to-day living, ethnicity is not a matter of conflict. Within some groups ethnic divisions are becoming blurred even to the extent that people identify themselves with one group rather than another. That, of course, is only one reason, for changing ethnic group dynamics is another. This is a political issue in Singapore where the dominant Chinese population has been growing more slowly than the Malay and Indian populations, leading Singapore to promote Chinese immigration in an attempt to retain the same ethnic balance as in the 1960s. Recently, the falling proportion of Chinese in the population has also become a political issue in Malaysia. Elsewhere, this is not an issue and ethnicity is usually a matter of which everyone is aware but few allow to dominate behaviour except, to a degree, when marriage is in question.

Conclusion

Demographically, patterns are similar throughout the region, differing mainly in timing. Every country has either passed through the demographic transition—Singapore, Thailand—or is at some point along the way. Myanmar, Laos and Cambodia are still at the stage of rapid population growth. Birth rates, though falling, are still relatively high. Death rates are lower but still have some distance to go before reaching the low levels of other countries. Birth rates in Viet Nam have begun to fall rapidly only within the last five years, while rates are lower in the Philippines, Malaysia and Indonesia. Their populations, like Singapore and Thailand, are beginning to age, moving, especially in Malaysia, towards a labour-deficit situation. (This, of course, is only partly demographic, for economic expansion contributes by influencing the labour market.) Ageing will lead to new economic demands, especially the support of the elderly by a smaller workforce.

One response to this situation, already visible in late-60s Singapore, is to employ migrant labour and this is now also characteristic of Malaysia as well as beginning to emerge in Thailand. Such importation tends to push down the cost of labour generally, helping to keep receiver countries economically competitive. In principle these migrants can be sent home in the event of a downturn in business, though the practicalities of doing this are doubtful, as the Thai authorities have recently discovered in respect of migrant workers from Myanmar. Keeping labour costs down, however, tends to delay the substitution of capital for labour, thus keeping the sectors that employ cheap labour at a technologically simple level.

Migration from the countryside to the towns and cities is far larger in scale, involving tens of millions of people and being substantially responsible for their rapid growth (chapter 9). Whether moves are permanent or temporary—with people moving between agriculture in the villages and short-term jobs in cities—the demographic consequences are considerable. People newly arrived in the city are often single. It takes time to forge new relationships, including marriage. Married couples usually adopt urban patterns of reproduction quite quickly, mostly having fewer children than couples who remain in the villages.

City life, and the occupational diversity that accompanies it, leads to quite new ways of life for it promotes the emergence of new social classes based upon wealth. Class lines thus cut across the linguistic and other cultural divisions that divide person from person. Some of these divisions are clearly fading, a process much aided by adherence to one or other of the great religious traditions and by the growing universality of national languages within countries, even, to some degree, by the emergence of a common international tongue—English. If anything, the region's population is even more diverse than it was half a century ago, in part as a result of major structural change in its economies (chapter 6). This human diversity is paralleled by the extraordinary physical diversity of the very land itself.

THREE
THE LAND

Diverse peoples, diverse terrains are keynotes of the region: tropical atolls, sand cays, tangled mangroves, volcanic islands, limestone towers set in clear seas, iridescent blackwater swamps so acid that tools rust immediately and boots rot in a few days, rice-fields swirling with dust in the dry season and virtual inland seas in the wet, dusty plateaux, plains, deep gorges, raging rapids, on the China border and in West Irian snow-capped mountains. The marine environments are rather less diverse for the seas are ever-warm, roughly 24–28°C, most very well provided with nutrients from adjoining land masses, some excessively so. Truly oceanic water impinges on the region only along the southern coasts with their fringing islands and the eastern coasts from Luzon to northern West Irian. These waters are rather less provided with nutrients than the seas which range from the rather open Andaman Sea in the west through a series of virtual maritime lakes such as the South China, Sulu and Celebes seas which have notably narrow entrances—including the strategically important Strait of —to rather more open seas such as the Seram, Banda, Arafura and Timor seas. Other than the Celebes and Banda seas, all are remarkably shallow and, south of the southern limit of typhoons—roughly 8°N—are quite calm compared with the powerful swells of the Pacific and Indian oceans. The seas thus unite while the oceans divide.

LAND AND SEA

The distribution of land and sea is of considerable significance. It clearly influences the climate. Mainland Southeast Asia, a broad-based peninsula, has considerable areas far from the sea whereas in insular Southeast Asia

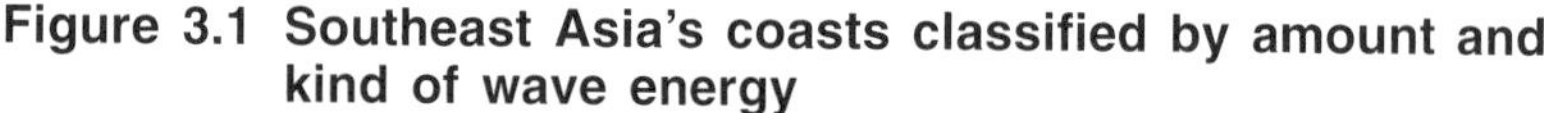

Figure 3.1 Southeast Asia's coasts classified by amount and kind of wave energy

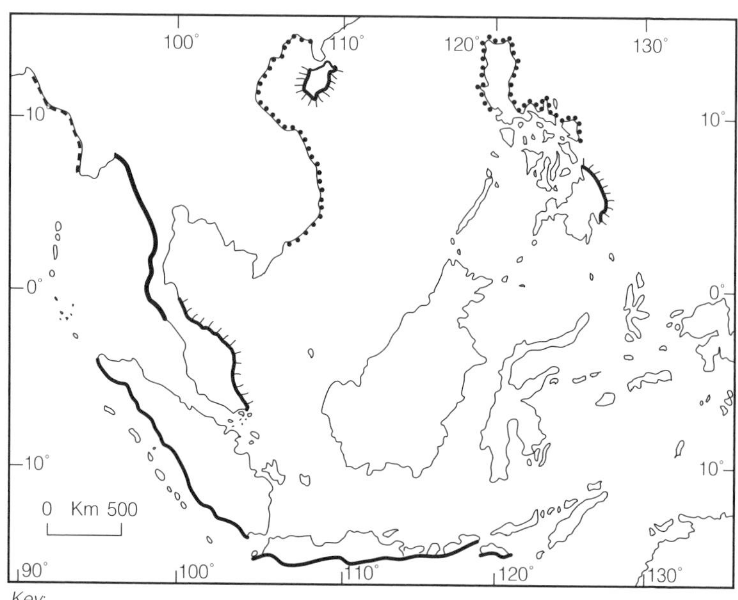

Key:

Seasonally high wave-energy coasts:

Northerly to easterly component

As above, typhoon waves also

Southerly to westerly component

As above, cyclone waves also

No symbol: Low wave-energy coasts

only interior Borneo is distant. Consequently the mainland portion, roughly a quarter of the region as a whole, tends to be drier and to have a greater temperature range than the three-quarters comprising insular Southeast Asia, in part because it is more distant from the source of moisture and the sea's moderating effects.

Seas, unless perpetually stormy, allow accessibility though movement on them is a matter of technology. The 'friction of distance' by water is substantially less than by land. Thus inter-island travel is simple, especially south of about 8°N, where the larger islands and peninsulas daily generate alternating land and sea breezes superimposed upon the prevailing monsoons. Even beach coasts open to the winds are accessible to small

Table 3.1 Length of coastlines, area of land

Country	Length of coast km	Area of land km²	Ratio: km² of land per km of coast
Brunei	161	5 765	36
Cambodia	443	181 035	409
Indonesia	54 716	1 904 569	35
Laos	Nil	236 800	Nil
Malaysia	4 675	329 758	71
Myanmar	1 930	676 578	351
Philippines	36 289	300 000	8
Singapore	193	618	3
Thailand	3 219	513 115	159
Viet Nam	3 444	331 689	96
Total	105 070	4 479 927	Average 43

Note: The source does not give the scale at which lengths of coastlines were measured.

Sources: Coast: http://www.odcc.gov/cia/publication/factbook (accessed 25–5–2000). Area: United Nations *Demographic Yearbook, 1996*

craft for at least part of the year as is the multitude of rivers, though entry to some may be hindered by sand-bars. This applies along the east coast of the Malay Peninsula or much of the coast of Viet Nam between major natural havens such as Nha Trang, Cam Ranh Bay or Da Nang, even though these are high wave-energy coasts, at least seasonally (see Figure 3.1).

In earlier times the unifying influence of the sea was reflected in the emergence of extensive maritime empires such as those of Majapahit, centred in Java (1294–1478), Sri Vijaya, whose capital was at Palembang, southern Sumatera (seventh to fourteenth centuries), and the Melaka sultanate founded around 1400. By contrast, in mainland Southeast Asia, east–west communication was difficult by reason of topography and its great kingdoms were confined largely to a single major river basin, except for Viet Nam which spread south from its core in the Red River valley to incorporate the small valleys and narrow coastal plains of the centre, reaching the marshy Mekong Delta only in comparatively recent times.

With one notable exception all these great civilisations were oriented to the land. The exception was Champa in what is now southern Viet Nam, a maritime trading kingdom that existed between the second and the thirteenth centuries. Its land resources seem to have been quite limited, certainly in comparison with its western neighbours. Overall, there is still a broad correspondence between these old empires and modern states. Thus Myanmar, Thailand, Cambodia, and to some degree Viet Nam, are

Figure 3.2 Block diagram showing the ratio of land to sea

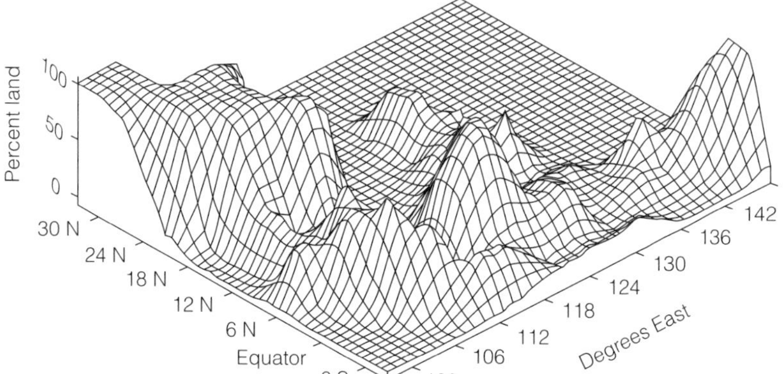

land-based whereas Indonesia and the Philippines are clearly archipelagic states.

In very remote times, though, things were different. Our kind of people, *Homo sapiens*, not to mention earlier, primitive hominids, seems to have been present several hundred thousand years ago. But early *Homo sapiens* spread quite slowly eastwards and south through what is now the eastern Indonesian Archipelago, succeeding in traversing deep straits such as the Makassar Straits, but not reaching Australia until somewhere between 40 000 and 60 000 years ago. On the way they passed through a major zone of transition between largely 'Asian' flora and especially fauna to the west and 'Australian' species to the east.

The relationship of land and sea properly should be measured by examining the areas enclosed by each country's maritime boundary and comparing the ratio of land to sea in each. Unfortunately, few countries have formally and fully delineated their maritime boundaries on a consistent basis such as the principles set out by UNCLOS III—the third UN Conference on the Law of the Sea. Territorial waters and economic zones of countries in the region overlap, sometimes involving several claimants. Thus no attempt has been made to look at ratios country by country. Instead an arbitrary boundary has been drawn between the mainland and insular parts of the region and ratios calculated for each. Ratios have also been computed on the basis of an arbitrary grid. Mainland Southeast Asia and its maritime fringe, thus determined, comprises 26 per cent of the whole region and is 61 per cent land. By contrast, maritime Southeast Asia is only 22 per cent land, almost exactly the global average. This points up the very real contrast between the two segments (see Figure 3.2).

Figure 3.3 Mainland Southeast Asia showing distance from the sea

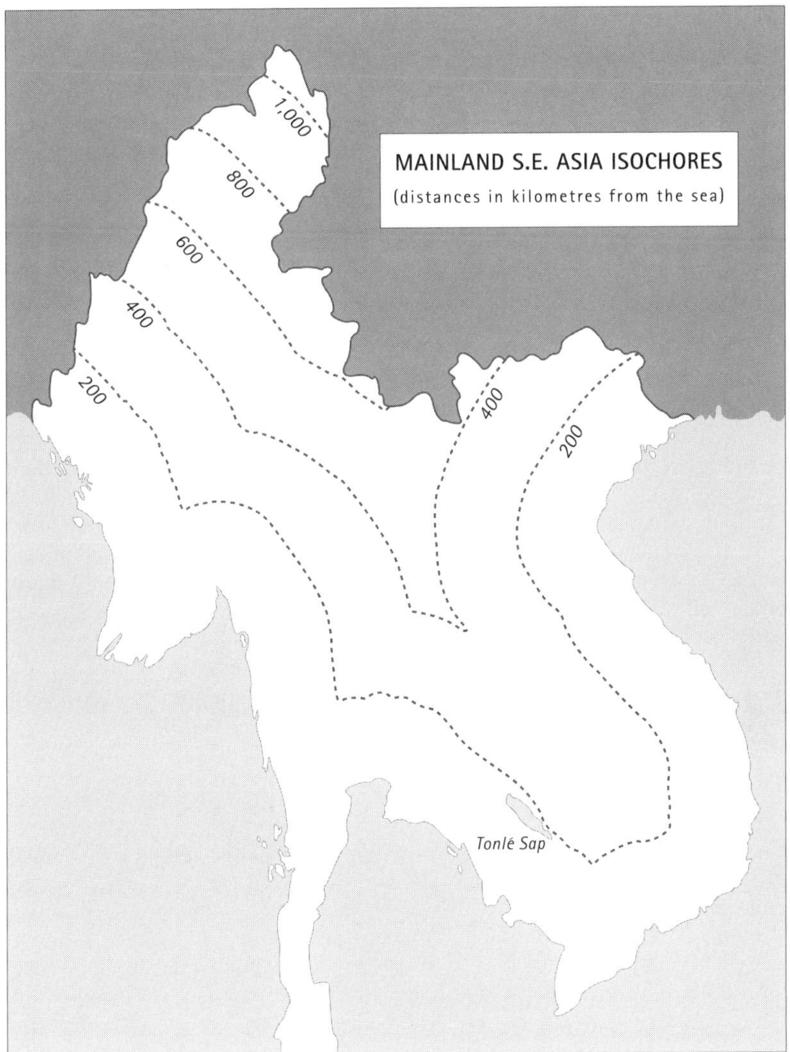

Another aspect is the land–sea relationship of length of coast to the area of land. A long coastline in comparison with the land area, other things being equal, has advantages in accessibility to the sea, not only in terms of transportation and trade but also of marine resources such as fisheries and salt, an element essential to life and health. It is not a coincidence, for example, that many areas of the mainland far from the sea, for example northern and northeastern Myanmar, have quite a high level of endemic goitre, an iodine trace-element deficiency disorder that can lead to cretinism. This condition is much less prevalent, indeed often unknown, in insular Southeast Asia where access to seafood, fresh or dried, and to sea salt is easy and sufficient to supply the very few parts per million of iodine required for human health. Only in parts of interior Borneo does goitre sometimes occur. Table 3.1 gives data for length of coastline, in comparison with land area.

The contrast between mainland and insular Southeast Asian countries is very clear. Laos, of course, is totally landlocked. Cambodia and Myanmar have rather a lot of land in relation to their coasts. Myanmar, like neighbouring Thailand, would have a much lower ratio of coastline to land but for the sections of peninsula and fringing islands of their southern tracts. By contrast, the extreme archipelagic character of the Philippines is reflected in a very low ratio of land to coast. In Indonesia only the existence of two of the globe's largest islands, Sumatera and Borneo, pushes up the ratio. Within insular Southeast Asia the only major unit at all similar to the mainland is the highly compact island of Borneo, which contrasts with the sprawling 'quadripode' of Sulawesi. Discussion of the reasons for these varied and contrasting patterns is included in the next section where the shape of the land and its evolution are examined.

The shape of the land and its evolution

Perhaps surprisingly, no one can answer the question 'What is the shape of the land?' in any detail—because no one has measured it. There are no data for height categories, for slope orientation or steepness, so that it is simply not known how much flat land there is or what kind—swamps, rice-fields and so forth. Nor is it known how much plateau or sloping land there may be, though it is likely that these together are the predominant landforms in the region. There are no data on average elevation though it seems likely that Myanmar, for example, because it includes high mountains along its northern border as well as great masses of hill country both east and west of the great Irrawaddy valley, is much higher on average than, say, Cambodia which contains only one major range, the Cardamom Mountains. There are, though, data for the highest points in the countries of the region (Table 3.2), a poor substitute but instructive

Table 3.2 Highest points by country or region

Country	Highest point	Height (m)
Brunei	Gunung Pagon	1 850
Cambodia	Cardamon Mts.	1 814
Indonesia	Gunung Jaya	5 030
Laos	Bia	2 820
Malaysia		
Peninsular	Gunung Tahan	2 189
Eastern	Gunung Kinabalu	4 094
Myanmar	Hkakabo Razi	5 967
Philippines	Apo	2 954
Singapore	Bukit Timah	161
Thailand	Doi Inthanon	2 585
Viet Nam	Fan Si Pan	3 142

Sources: *The Times Atlas of the World*; *Britannica Online*. The height given in these sources for Bukit Timah is incorrect having been based on a misread figure in a survey of 1898.

nevertheless, if only to show the falseness of the common claim that Malaysia's Gunung (Mount) Kinabalu is 'the highest peak in Southeast Asia'—or in insular Southeast Asia. West Irian has a whole range a thousand metres higher while peaks along the edge of the Tibetan Plateau in northern Burma are higher still and are perennially snow-clad, as are the tops of the range flanking Gunung Jaya, despite its low latitude (4°S). These montane, indeed alpine fragments are climatically and biogeographically quite unlike the adjoining uplands.

Despite their limitations, the data in Figure 3.2 give some clues about landforms and their evolution. The Indochinese Peninsula, except for a band comprising Myanmar, together with the Malay Peninsula, most of the South China Sea and the western third of Borneo, represents the furthest outlier of the Himalayan mountain system. The eastern Himalayan region is made up of a great knot of mountains at the southeastern margin of the Tibetan Plateau. These mountains, made up mostly of sedimentary and intrusive rocks of Mesozoic age, fan out eastwards, southwards and all directions between. With increasing distance from the base of the 'fan' the mountains become lower and lower, ultimately being represented by some tiny islands, many superficially coated with coral, in the South China Sea. Flowing through this knot of high mountains, which form the base of the fan of lower mountains, are the headwaters of several of Asia's greatest rivers, China's Chang Jiang (Yangzi), the Mekong, Salween and Irrawaddy, all in stupendous narrow gorges 1500–2000 m deep. All flow parallel to each other and fan out into a series of basins that are partly structural in geological origin. Seismically, this zone is reasonably stable, forming part of the Indo-Sinian tectonic plate. This means that earthquakes are infrequent and mountain-building, having taken place mainly in the Mesozoic era, roughly 250–65 million years ago, is now inactive except towards the great knot of mountains of the eastern Himalayan margin—where, of course, mainland Southeast Asia's highest peaks are to be found.

This region has been subjected to erosion for several hundred million years with two major effects. First, it has stripped away its cover of early to mid-Mesozoic sediments to expose igneous rocks put in place slightly earlier. Thus, for example, the granitic spine of the Malay Peninsula is largely exposed, flanked by limestone and other sedimentary remnants of the once more extensive cover. Second, the stripped-off materials were deposited in shallow seas and estuaries from which some have been subsequently raised to form sandstone plateaux such as the Shan Plateau, now well dissected by rivers, and the relatively young Korat Plateau, which was sea in the Tertiary era no more than a few million years ago, accounting for the fact that some soils in the region are saline to this day. Here erosion has had time to do little more than to create a landscape of gently rounded swales and hollows with here and there more upstanding hills, once islands in the Tertiary sea.

Flanking this tectonically stable zone is another, partly stable at best, much of it unstable. Here are earthquakes, active volcanism and in West Irian, as eastwards in Papua New Guinea, the continued building of great ranges such as those flanking Gunung Jaya. The cause of this tectonic turmoil is the grinding together of four more plates. These are large slabs of light crustal material called 'Sial' after its two main components, *Si*licon and *Al*uminium, floating on a red-hot crustal 'sea' of 'Sima' so-named after two of its main constituents, *Si*licon and *Ma*gnesium. These slabs move about, propelled by deep convection currents. In the west the Indian Oceanic Plate is pushing north against the relatively stable Indo-Sinian Plate just described. To the east the Australian Continental Plate (which also includes the southern half of New Guinea) is moving north and impinging on a corner of the globe's largest plate, the Pacific Plate. This plate is rotating clockwise about as fast as your toenails grow—though a bit faster in some parts. This corner catches the southern margin of the small Philippine Sea Plate which in turn impinges on the eastern side of the relatively stable Indo-Sinian Plate. In between is a great 'crush belt' marked by arcs of largely volcanic islands in the Indonesian Archipelago, intervening chunks of sedimentary rocks, such as the limestones of southern Java and the Mesozoic sedimentary and plutonic rocks (like granite) of central and eastern Borneo, as well as the more irregularly shaped volcanic zones of the Philippines.

Most of the volcanoes have been active in historic times, some disastrously so, as with Tambora on the Indonesian island of Sumbawa, which

Figure 3.4 Tectonic sketch-map of Southeast Asia

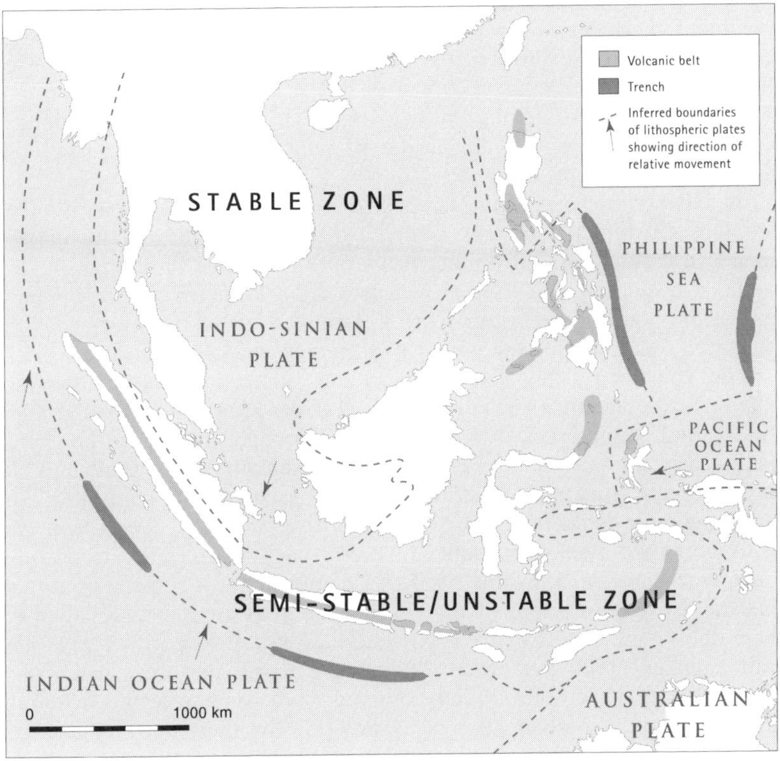

exploded in 1815 killing many tens of thousands of people, ejecting 30 cubic kilometres of material and, it is thought, initiating a global year with no summer. The peaks formed by active volcanism are generally not particularly high. Most do not exceed much more than 3000 m. Some, notably Taal on the island of Luzon, less than 100 km south of Manila, and Krakatoa in the Sunda Strait between Java and Sumatera, are notably low. These are the particularly dangerous ones, for the protracted emission of lava and ash can lead to collapse of the cone and an immediate inrush of water, at Taal from the lake, at Krakatoa from the sea, followed by a catastrophic series of explosions. It was just such a sequence of events at Krakatoa in 1883 that resulted in tens of thousands of lives being lost, many more from the tsunami (tidal wave), estimated at 30 m high, along the nearby coast of Sumatera. The eruption is estimated to have hurled about 18 cubic kilometres of material into the earth's atmosphere.

Although many volcanoes are inactive at the moment, none can be considered truly extinct, as the case of Mount Pinatubo, in the Zambales mountains northwest of Manila, illustrates. This erupted in 1991 causing some loss of life, severe damage to crops and forcing the evacuation of thousands of people, mainly as a result of lahars—volcanic mud-flows—flowing down its eastern and southern slopes. Its eruption, like Tambora's, also resulted in a global depression of temperature resulting from the clouds of ash and gas emitted.

In the period from January 1980 to September 1995 some 857 000 people worldwide had to be evacuated because of volcanic activity, mainly lahars, three-quarters of them in Indonesia or the Philippines. This included a quarter of a million evacuees from Pintatubo in 1991 where half of the region's fatalities occurred. Deaths from such activity, though, were just 5 per cent of the global total caused by natural disasters.

But volcanicity may also be beneficial. While the ejected materials may be acidic and thus virtually valueless as the source of soil nutrients—the floating pumice rock of Krakatoa is an example—they may be chemically basic and rich in minerals for plant growth when weathered. In moist tropical climates weathering processes, especially on permeable ash, are remarkably rapid so that within a year or two plants, even crops, can again be grown after an eruption. Java, Bali and the volcanic areas of the Philippines have soils notable for their richness and it is sometimes argued that the dense populations of the two former areas are to be explained by their rich volcanic soils. (Rural population densities in parts of Java and Bali approach 1000 per square kilometre.) Significant areas that themselves do not have soils directly derived from basic volcanic materials have probably benefited from ash showers, for these may extend for several hundred kilometres downwind of their source. The nature and extent of such showers is not well studied in the region but it seems likely that most of insular Southeast Asia has benefited from occasional 'aerial topdressing' by ash.

In contrast the uplands of mainland Southeast Asia, like those comprising the fragments of Mesozoic rocks of the southern archipelagoes, have been subjected to aeon-long chemical weathering, severe in hot, moist equatorial regions, less so in higher latitudes and at higher elevations, where, however, greater physical weathering may compensate for the lower rates at which rocks chemically rot away. The result is that sedentary soils—that is, those not developed on recently transported materials such as marine or alluvial sediments—are generally low to very low in plant nutrients even if the unweathered rock is relatively rich in them. Often it is not and in moist equatorial regions such unweathered materials may lie 30 m below the soil surface, far out of the reach of plant roots. In some places, though, highly depleted weathered materials are actually of economic value: bauxite, the ore of aluminium; kaolinite, the source of kaolin (China clay); laterite, an iron-rich clay, brick-hard when dry and thus of use as a building material, especially for road foundations.

Erosion

Erosion and sediment transportation continue, rapidly on unconsolidated ash, anywhere slopes are tilled, but much more slowly where a good vegetative cover, not necessarily primary forest, is maintained. People play a major role here, often unwittingly and it seems likely that in many parts of the region the rate at which soil is removed from sloping land is substantially faster than the rate at which it forms. The respective quantities of sediment reaching rivers, being deposited along banks, in channels, in inter-montane basins or ultimately reaching the sea are not well known. It is likely that they are highly variable through time, with major rainstorms mobilising sediments throughout the hydrological system while lesser events affect only part of it.

A great deal of variability also occurs in space, partly because of uneven human impacts. Some rivers have large average yields of sediment, others small, reflecting not only cultivation, clearance and vegetative cover, though these are very important, but also hardness of weathered rock, its cohesiveness, its behaviour when saturated and the characteristics of rainfall. In large catchments spatial variation, and to some degree temporal variation, are evened out so that the region's largest catchment, that of the Mekong, with an area of 810 000 km^{-2}, not all of it in our region, has a relatively low average sediment yield of 154 t km^{-2} yr (tonnes per square kilometre per year). Much of the catchment is reasonably well vegetated and comprises resistant rocks. By contrast the Irrawaddy's 367 000 km^2 catchment has a great deal of active shifting cultivation in its headwaters and in some places is actively eroding the older plains and terraces through which it runs. Its annual sediment yield is 830 t km^{-2}.

Values for small catchments are much greater and directly reflect land use. This is shown by data for Sarawak, where climate and slope angle are more or less the same (Table 3.3).

These data show that primary forest does not necessarily have lower sediment yields than secondary forest. Characteristically, there is a sudden burst of erosion when forest is logged, much of the sediment coming from roughly bulldozed roads and tracks on benches cut into hill slopes. The material cut away is loose and in addition the bench wall is unsupported so that the slope above it readily fails. Along drag paths and on log-stacking areas heavy machines compress the soil leading to reduced infiltration of water into the soil, increased run-off and concentration of flow. But if the land is left to recover, rates of erosion fall again, especially

Table 3.3 Erosion rates under forest and shifting cultivation, Sarawak

Land use	Location	Slope (degrees)	Period (years)	Soil loss ($t\ km^{-2}\ year^{-1}$) mean
Primary forest	Niah F.R.	25–30	4	19
	Semongkok	25–30	11	24
Secondary forest				
(a) logged 10 years previously	Niah F.R.	25–30	4	23
(b) with hill padi	Semongkok	25–30	11	10
(c) 2 month old	Semongkok	25–30	11	10
lallang and scrub	Niah F.R.	33	3	100
Hill padi/shifting cultivation				
(a) terraced with cover	Semongkok	20	11	120
(b) bush fallow	Semongkok	16–26	3	23.3
(c) bush fallow	Tebedau	25	2	34
Traditional pepper	Semongkok	25–30	11	8 944

Sources: Ng and Teck (1992), Teck (1992)

as woody vegetation re-establishes itself. If it does not, the land being used for cultivation or as pasture (the latter generally requiring annual burning to promote young palatable growth), then rates of erosion remain high. Should the land be tilled or clean-weeded then rates rocket, commonly being three orders of magnitude higher than under a dense closed cover of vegetation. The data for traditional clean-weeded pepper reflect this. By contrast, the growing of hill padi, in which the patches cleared by fire are small—one or two hectares—and the seeds are dibbled into the ground with a stick, raises sediment yields only slightly. These measurements have been made on actual slopes where, other things being equal, sediment yields are generally higher than those measured in nearby streams since not all eroded materials find their way into streams.

Why, then, are the yields for large catchments given earlier so much higher? The answer probably lies in the fact that measurements made in the lower courses of large rivers include quantities of sediment deposited in and near river channels which are mobilised by floodwaters. Little is known of how long such temporarily deposited materials, already in the drainage systems of Southeast Asian rivers, may take to reach the coast but it probably takes tens or hundreds of years, fine sediments moving faster and coarse ones slower. One implication of this is that even if the amount of sediment generated declines—by the cessation of logging, by stopping tillage on steep slopes, by introducing soil conservation measures—floods and abnormally large quantities of sediment in the rivers will continue for substantial periods.

Sedimentation

Where do the sediments go? Obviously they build plains and deltas and have done so through geological time so that many such lowlands are flanked by terraces and rolling hills cut into older alluvium, some of it laid down in the Tertiary era, 2–4 million years ago. The soils developed in such localities, such as along the middle course of the Irrawaddy, may be almost as much leached of their original nutrients as soils developed on weathered bedrock. Indeed, in some older terrace lands, especially those nearer the upper courses of the rivers where the old alluvium is coarser, soils may be extremely poor because they are porous, free-draining and easily leached of nutrients.

Mostly, the soils of plains and deltas are still undergoing occasional replenishment at flood times and are thus rich in nutrients. Because they contain a great deal of clay laid down in the geologically recent past and because they are lowlying and not free-draining, the bulk of their nutrients has not been leached out. These soils are now mostly developed into the classical rice soils. All such soils contain a fair amount of organic matter and have done so since their alluvial parent materials were first laid down, for being more or less constantly wet, organic matter decays slowly. In very lowlying parts of the plains and deltas, such as back-swamps away from river courses and along coasts where sand-ridges thrown up by present or past wave action block off sections of deltas from the sea, organic matter accumulates. This process has continued for some tens of thousands of years, certainly occurring when the region's sea levels were lower as a result of the global Ice Ages that ended roughly 10 000 years ago. The result is that the base of such 'organic swamps' may be well below current sea level. Such swamps, where peaty organic matter may be 15–20 m deep, are exceedingly difficult to reclaim for agriculture, pineapples being one of the very few crops able to tolerate the extreme acidity that results from the decay of the plant materials forming such peats. These swamps have a highly distinctive flora and fauna partly in response to acid but freshwater conditions. Freshwater swamps cover many thousands of square kilometres, especially in eastern Sumatera and the lowlands of Borneo.

Where sea-water actually covers the land at least part of the time, another kind of swamp exists. This is the mangrove, marked by specialised trees and other plants, such as the Nipa palm (botanically *Nypa*), that to greater or less degree tolerate salt or brackish water. Characteristically, the soils they grow in are heavy clays with some organic matter but are not as peaty as many freshwater swamps. Protected from tidal flooding and flushed with fresh water to remove the salt, they make excellent soils for rice, though because of their lowlying locations, they suffer from flooding and waterlogging. Along the coast of the Hong (Red) River delta, northern Viet Nam, for example, farmers are so quick to colonise the delta margins that mangrove scarcely has time to become established before the newly formed land is embanked and turned to agricultural use. Elsewhere mangrove swamps may be very extensive, occurring as far as 100 km inland on such rivers as the Musi in southern Sumatera, along the great rivers of Borneo and on the southern coast of West Irian.

Not all the sediments arriving at the coast are fine clays and silts. Sands may also be included especially at flood times. These may be sorted by wave action and form extensive sand-ridges, even dunes reworked by wind where not colonised by vegetation. Long beaches form, as along the east coast of the Malay Peninsula and especially the coast of Viet Nam away from major deltas such as those of the Mekong and Hong rivers. In Viet Nam, for example, dune systems, interspersed with lagoons formed by blocking off many of the smaller rivers, may extend several kilometres inland from the beaches. Soils formed on these virtually sterile, free-draining sands are of little use agriculturally, even the hardy coconut often failing to thrive in areas of seasonal climate. The sands themselves, mainly silica, may be of use in glass-making where not contaminated with iron compounds. Perhaps the greatest attractions are the beaches as tourist resorts and those developed include the famous China Beach at Da Nang and various resorts along the coasts of the Malay Peninsula and its offshore islands.

Given the substantial amounts of sediment transported by the rivers and arriving at the region's coasts it is not surprising that the deltas are growing, though just how fast is not known in detail. Parts of the Hong River delta seem to be pushing seaward at rates up to 1 km a year, but people are clearly aiding that. A more usual rate is about 60 m a year.

The growth of deltas has been and in some cases still is affected by regional geological processes. Thus the Irrawaddy has a notably large and classically D-shaped delta. (Delta is the Greek letter D.) By contrast that of the nearby Sittang is much smaller, clearly the result of the capture by the early Irrawaddy drainage system of most of the ancient Sittang's drainage at a point near Mandalay. By contrast again, the Chao Phrya, not by any means as large as the Irrawaddy but still a big river, also has a relatively small delta. The reason here is that the Chao Phrya occupies a 'structural trough', an elongated basin extending into the Bight of Bangkok whose floor is slowly warping downwards even as sediments spill into it.

But far and away the largest single expanse of plain and delta is that of the mighty Mekong. Its delta is fed by a number of major distributaries splitting the delta into a series of elongated triangular islands, facilitating water-borne transportation and hindering road travel, for bridges are very few. Much of this delta, like all the others in mainland Southeast Asia, has been reclaimed for agriculture, in this instance mainly since the last decade of the nineteenth century. As with the Chao Phrya, especially, it is criss-crossed with artificial canals constructed primarily to facilitate transportation and to drain the land rather than to provide irrigation water for crops. Such is the size of the Mekong that ocean-going vessels up to about 6000 tonnes can penetrate upstream as far as Phnom Penh. This is close to one of the world's most remarkable hydrological phenomena, a branch of the Mekong that flows northwestwards into the Tonlé Sap (Great Lake) as the Tibetan snows melt in spring and the rainy season sets in. As flow in the Mekong decreases with the onset of the dry season the flow reverses, sustaining discharge downstream. As the water rises it expands the area of the Tonlé Sap by a third to two-thirds, providing the basis of one of the world's largest and most highly productive freshwater fisheries.

Another major geological process that has affected the growth of deltas, and probably still is doing so, is the general rise in sea levels throughout the region since the end of the Pleistocene Ice Age about 10 000 years ago. Since that time levels have risen in fits and starts by perhaps as much as 100 m. This rise has had a number of important effects besides slowly drowning the outer margins of deltas even as they have grown—usually fast enough to more than keep pace with the sea's encroachment. Insular Southeast Asia, especially, bears all the marks of a drowned landscape—highly convoluted coastlines, especially in the Philippines, Sulawesi, the islands of Nusantara and the rest of the eastern Indonesian Archipelago—many steep slopes down to the sea, as well as relatively small deltas and coastal plains though these also reflect the small size of most rivers, except in eastern Sumatera, Borneo and West Irian.

The period of lower sea level unquestionably facilitated the spread of animals, including people, and plants as well, though to a lesser degree because they are less mobile. At the end of the Pleistocene, mainland Southeast Asia, the Malay Peninsula, Sumatera, Java, Borneo and islands east to the Makassar Strait sat on a great plateau known as the Sunda Shelf. West Irian and its fringing islands, possibly including Halmahera, sat on another great shelf, the Sahel, joined to Australia across the Arafura Sea. Separating the two shelves were a series of deep straits and basins—the Makassar Strait, the Sulu, Celebes and Banda seas. These formed substantial barriers to the spread of plants and animals so that those of the Sunda region, sometimes called Sundaland, have affinities with mainland Southeast Asia and with continental Asia as a whole. To the east the biological affinities of the Sahel Shelf are with Australia, though there is some degree of overlap between the two, especially with respect to plants, many of whose ancestors probably straddled the modern biogeographical boundary during the Pleistocene or earlier.

Riches under the land?

Riches under the land and under the land under the sea are by no means evenly or randomly distributed. Indeed it is not at all clear what the riches are. A century ago petroleum was just becoming something more than a cheap replacement for whale oil or a substance long used for waterproofing the hulls of boats or as a medicine. Just 25 years ago tin was a major resource in Peninsular Malaysia, in the Indonesian islands of Bangka and Belitung, both onshore and offshore in southern Thailand. Yet today mining is very limited, for tin-coated steel-plate is no longer a major part of the packaging industry, having given way to plastic coatings and aluminium cans.

What lies under the land is obviously related to geological history. Whether it is used is a matter of economics—market demand and technology. It will be recalled that a major geological feature is the relatively stable Indo-Sinian plate, comprising most of mainland Southeast Asia and the southwestern third of Borneo. Here the rocks are mainly of Mesozoic age, in some few places older—roughly 250 million to 65 million years. In these rocks are to be found minerals such as tin ore, copper, lead, zinc, titanium, gold, wolfram, coal, and in some places gemstones, such as rubies in northern Burma, around Pailin in western Cambodia, and the semi-precious jadeite so beloved of Chinese and Vietnamese who make jade jewellery of it. Important mines are located northwest of Myitkyina in the far north of Myanmar. However, none of these minerals is of global significance. The Malay Peninsula may once have been so rich in gold, mainly found in alluvial deposits, that it truly deserved its ancient Greek name of 'Golden Chersonese' and its reputation as one of the possible locations of King Solomon's fabled mines. Gone too are the diamonds of the region inland of Pontianak, western Borneo, where Chinese miners sought them, and gold, in the late eighteenth and nineteenth centuries.

The current situation sees Indonesia, Malaysia and Thailand as major producers of tin, ranked respectively as second, third and fifth globally. But production is declining with the near-demise of the tin-plate industry though the demand for tin to be used in solders, especially in electronics, remains. So far as other metals are concerned Indonesia ranks fairly high as a producer of nickel, used for electroplating and hardening steel. So do Malaysia for titanium, also used to harden steel and its oxide as a white pigment in paint, and Thailand in respect of tungsten, another hardening agent for specialised steels. The sedimentary rocks of the region abound in limonite, an ore of iron, but the actual iron content is too low to be extracted economically. Another iron ore, hematite, is richer and at times has been used, for example at Bukit Ibam, inland from the tiny East Coast Malaysian port of Dungun. Bauxite, an aluminium-rich product of the weathering of some sedimentary rocks, is also quite widespread, sometimes being exported. A major user is the aluminium smelter in Sumatera near the Asahan river. Indonesia, outside the volcanic zone of southern Sumatera, Java and Nusatenggara, is likely to be rich in metallic ores, West Irian especially. There exploitation has only recently begun, mainly using foreign capital and expertise.

Along the borders of the Indo-Sinian Plate, and beyond on the other plates, earth movements, warping sedimentary rocks upwards and downwards, have continued since the Tertiary era, roughly the last 4 million years. The structures thus formed trap oil and gas. These are exploited not only in a broad arc following the boundary of the Indo-Sinian Plate from central Myanmar, eastern Sumatera, northern Java, but are also likely to exist under the politically contested waters of the South China Sea where both oil and gas are exploited by Viet Nam and by the People's Republic of China. One important offshore petroleum field appears to be in a Tertiary inlier on the Indo-Sinian Plate, lying east of the Malay Peninsula and just inside Malaysia's maritime economic zone. Others also lie away from plate boundaries where earth movements and volcanism are too active for petroleum fields to form. Notable are those around the coast of Borneo from Sarawak through Brunei, whose economy is almost entirely based upon the export of oil and gas, to the southern fields around Balikpapan. The Philippines, with the exception of a small field off the island of Palawan, does not (yet?) share in this natural bonanza. Further afield there is the strong possibility of petroleum offshore on the Sahel Shelf where, as with the Sunda Shelf, the submarine topography, especially the shallowness of the seas, makes exploitation technically feasible with modern drilling technology though much more expensive than onshore. Petroleum is likely to become the mainstay of East Timor, though the large cost of getting at it will probably have to be met from abroad. Just how many fields there may be and how much petroleum they may contain are secrets, probably at least partly known to international oil companies—but they are not saying!

Governments are at least partly privy to such secrets. Such is the economic importance of petroleum that the delimitation of offshore 'Economic Exploitation Zones' is a significant political issue, one resolved only to a limited degree by bilateral agreements. One such, between Malaysia and Thailand, in respect of areas in the western part of the South China Sea has agreed that some areas are exploited by one country or the other and some by both. In much of the rest of the South China Sea matters are complicated by overlapping claims by various countries, surmounted by a blanket claim over the whole sea by both varieties of

Chinese government, the PRC in Beijing and the ROC in Taipei. Active though limited conflicts have already occurred, focused mainly around the Spratley and Paracel islands.

Petroleum apart, most of the unstable zone's rocks do not contain much by way of minerals of direct use other than hard rocks, of use as construction aggregate and limestone for cement. There is a little gold in western Sumatera, some manganese in Java and the Visayas, central Philippines. The most important is an area of mineralisation associated mainly with the emplacement of granites near Baguio, north-central Luzon. Here significant deposits of copper together with some gold, zinc, lead and chromium have been worked commercially for many decades. Indeed in other parts of Ifugao, gold is to be found in small quantities in placer (alluvial) deposits. Some of the bedrock sources of this gold are known but the people of the region are happy to leave it there, contrary to the wishes of big business.

Energy supplies

Big business and all countries in the region are very much interested in energy, for modern economies are highly energy-dependent. Generally energy demand is outpacing population growth and even economic growth in general. In Indonesia, for example, power demand grew by 20 per cent every year from 1969 to 1989. Only in the last two years has demand slackened, resulting in the probably temporary shelving of plans for major hydroelectricity schemes, such as at Bakun in Sarawak, and also in Laos. But it is not renewable energy that is of major interest in the region except to rural people amongst whom wood fuel probably accounts for four-fifths of their requirements.

Petroleum and natural gas are far and away the most important commercial energy sources in the region. Though published data are incomplete, roughly 82 per cent comes from these sources. Amongst the countries there is an enormous range, from Brunei, 98 per cent of whose Gross Domestic Product comes from oil and gas production, to Singapore, which has no indigenous energy sources at all, to Laos where 95 per cent of all commercial energy comes from hydroelectricity. Substantial quantities of petroleum and, especially, natural gas, are exported, especially to Japan.

Overall the region is more than self-sufficient in these energy sources, though production may be levelling off. Indonesia, for example extracted only about 3 per cent more crude oil in the mid-1990s than in the mid-1980s, with a corresponding figure of 8 per cent for Brunei. Reserves are state and company secrets. However, it does seem likely that Cambodia has some as yet untapped reserves, mainly offshore where a French consortium was exploring and drilling more than 20 years ago. Viet Nam

Table 3.4 Primary indigenous energy production by country and type (10^{10} kJ) 1995

Country	Oil & gas	Coal	Hydro	Geothermal	Total
Brunei	71 917	–	–	–	71 917
Cambodia	–	–	33	–	33
Indonesia	514 047	101 827	4 748	7 934	628 556
Laos	–	–	402	–	402
Malaysia	286 201	356	2 240	–	288 797
Myanmar	2 177	176	695	–	3 048
Philippines	23 442	8 637	9 810	9 136	51 025
Thailand	51 845	23 128	2 416	–	77 389
Viet Nam	35 462	34 328	5 619	2 646	78 055
Total	985 091	168 452	25 963	19 716	1 199 222

Notes: Data exclude electricity generated using fossil fuels or geothermal energy, whether indigenous or imported. Some may be unreliable. All are converted to kJ.

Sources: UNESCAP, *Statistical Yearbook for Asia and the Pacific*, 1998; *APEC Energy Statistics 1995*

may well have more oil and gas offshore in the South China Sea. Other littoral states such as Indonesia, Malaysia and Brunei almost certainly do so, as well as the Philippines, which thus far is exploiting only a small field off Palawan. The actual ownership of the seabed remains unresolved, although China considers that it owns most of it.

So far as coal, the other major source of fossil energy (14 per cent of the region's current usage) is concerned, reserves are reasonably substantial, given current demand. Most is of Tertiary age and thus of sub-bituminous or even lower quality. The main exception is the Hon Gai coal-field, near Hai Phong in northeastern Viet Nam. Here the quality is excellent with fair reserves. Some of the lower-grade coals have been mined in the past, for example at Umbilin and Bukit Asam in Sumatera, Martapura and Kutei in Kalimantan.

Renewable energy sources, geothermal and hydroelectric power, are insignificant in the region's energy sources—just under 3 per cent. Geothermal sources are not infinitely renewable as most geothermal fields show declining production over decades. However, total production is sufficient to sustain electricity generation over the economic lifetime of wells and stations. An individual hydroelectric station may have a similar problem where generation is based on water storage behind a dam rather than the run of the river, since reservoirs silt up, sometimes rapidly. The Ambuklao dam, east of Baguio, Luzon, is a case in point.

In the region generally the potential for hydroelectricity is sometimes claimed to be large as befits an area with high rainfall and many mountains. The reality is quite otherwise, partly for economic reasons. Dams need good foundations, often lacking in areas of volcanic ash or soft Tertiary rocks. They must not silt up too rapidly as loss of storage means that power generation is subject to the vagaries of rainfall and run-off. Reservoirs may drown good agricultural land and long-established settlements whose inhabitants may strongly object to having to leave them for the dubious benefit of supplying power to distant cities. Such is the case with a number of potential sites on the Chico River, north-central Luzon, for example. Finally, hydroelectric stations must be reasonably close to major consumption centres since the cost of building transmission lines is very substantial and losses in sending power down them rise with increasing distance. In several areas, Peninsular Malaysia and Thailand are examples, all the water-power potential realisable under current pricing has already been used. In the Malaysian case, power from a large station at Bakun, in Sarawak, is planned to be sent by cable to the peninsula, perhaps with some being sold to Singapore on the way. In Thailand the state generating authority, EGAT, has plans for a substantial expansion of hydroelectric capacity in Laos from which it already draws substantial supplies. Some of this is to be from new stations within the Mekong catchment. In this, however, the most favourable sites are probably in China, where a 1000 km-long, steep, sparsely-inhabited gorge on the Upper Mekong (there termed the Lancang Jiang) has already begun to be developed almost entirely without consideration of the interests of downstream states, whether for power generation, irrigation, navigation or fisheries.

The rivers of mainland Southeast Asia invariably suffer from a great variability in flow, reflecting the rainfall regime. Moreover, the degree of seasonal variation increases in step with the size of the stream—the smaller the flow the greater the variation. Storage is thus essential. In addition, many potential sites are either already well populated, are far from consuming centres, or the regions are not yet sufficiently developed economically to have both a large market for power and the means of investing to satisfy it. Thus Myanmar has considerable hydro potential in the Irrawaddy, Salween and Sittang catchments but little means of realising it. Much the same is true in respect of Borneo's large rivers and in West Irian, areas far too remote to permit more than limited development.

Nevertheless, there are still unexplored avenues for hydroelectric development though small rivers, especially in insular Southeast Asia outside the two largest islands, mean small generation facilities and higher unit costs. One neglected area, in which Chinese technology excels, is in low-head (0.5–5.0 m) run-of-the-river generation. Its application in the lowlands and hill country near consuming centres would assist the long-term sustainability of supply with minimal environmental impact.

In the even longer term arises the question of what happens when the oil runs out. While globally there is no prospect of this within the next several decades, a scenario in which the region's producers and consumers are faced with this question is one to be dealt with. Vehicles and much else do not run on electricity. Here the region generally is well placed. With abundant solar radiation, plenty of water, though seasonally not well distributed in mainland Southeast Asia and the Eastern Archipelago, there is obvious potential for biofuels, though the areas required to grow them would be very large. The day when they will be essential are far off. Warmth and wetness, though, promote the growth of plants of many kinds, probably more kinds than anywhere else in the world. On these many kinds of animals, including humankind, still depend.

FOUR
WARMTH AND WETNESS

There is little doubt that Southeast Asia has been warm and, mostly, wet for very long periods. To be sure its land area expanded and contracted as sea levels rose and fell during the Ice Ages which ended only about 10 000 years ago. These changes unquestionably allowed plants slowly, animals and people more quickly, to move from what is now one island to another. Mean temperatures probably fell four to six degrees during the glacial periods, during the last allowing substantial glaciers to form on the mountains of northern Myanmar, West Irian, even on Gunung Kinabalu close to the equator. At that time, conditions were somewhat drier and it seems likely that mixed trees and grassland vegetation—savanna—occupied significant areas in mainland Southeast Asia and the eastern Indonesian archipelago. Our human race, *Homo sapiens*, was also around and may have had fire for 40 000–60 000 years. Whether these hunter-gatherers used fire to modify and maintain the grassy vegetation preferred by animals favoured in the hunt—such as pigs and deer—is not known for certain but it seems likely that they did. Whatever the case may be, the forests survived the glaciations in pretty much the form they were in 400 years ago outside the major centres of population—northern and central Viet Nam, the Angkor region of Cambodia, Myanmar's Dry Zone, Java and a few scattered centres elsewhere. Only at high altitudes and possibly a few particularly dry spots was the unmodified vegetation anything other than forest.

SOLAR RADIATION AND TEMPERATURE

Plants, animals and people ultimately derive life from the sun and the region is well placed to benefit from its radiation, its light and heat, for its lands and seas straddle the equator and extend to about 28°N in northern Myanmar. According to the Russian physicist Budyko, were the earth's atmosphere completely transparent, which it is not, the amount of solar radiation annually received at the surface at the equator would average 321 kcal cm^{-2} (kilocalories per centimetre) [1344 kJ cm^{-2} (kilojoules per square centimetre)]. At 10°N this falls only marginally, to 317 kcal [1327 kJ] cm^{-2}, dropping to 304 [1273] at 20°N and only 282 [1181] at 30°N. (These figures compare with 254 kcal [1063 kJ] cm^{-2} at 40°S, roughly the latitude of Sydney, and 183 kcal [766 kJ] cm^{-2} at 50°N, roughly the south coast of England. A person consumes roughly 2300 –3000 kcal [9630–12560 kJ] of food each day.)

Under this unrealistic assumption, the region would be very hot, the heat being greater nearer the equator. In reality, the amount of radiation actually reaching the surface is much affected by the amount of cloud through which it passes, for it is scattered on the way. It is also influenced by the presence of water, in the sea and other water-bodies as well as in the soil, because a great deal of the incoming energy is used by evaporation. Even though only a small proportion (globally about 0.3 per cent) is used to drive photosynthesis, there is little doubt that a reduction in photosynthesis, as when forests are felled, leads to more energy being available to evaporate water and locally to heat the atmosphere.

The total incoming radiation arriving at the surface of land and sea is thus about a third less in Southeast Asia than in clear-sky desert regions, even though the amount of energy at the top of the atmosphere is greater. The region probably averages 145–160 kcal [607–670 kJ] cm^{-2} per year, possibly marginally higher in the Dry Zone of Myanmar. It is almost certainly much lower in the condensation zone of high mountains—very roughly 1500 to 3000 m above sea level—but probably more than this at higher levels where cloud cover is less, though for lack of observations no one really knows.

Another effect of latitude is to create variations in solar radiation from season to season. In part these reflect day-length. (This is also a factor in the growth of plants which are sensitive to such variations—rice is an example.) At the equator all days are 12 hours long but the difference between longest and shortest days increases by about seven minutes for each degree of latitude. Thus the difference is only nine minutes at Singapore but more than three hours in northern Myanmar. The intensity of solar radiation, other things being equal, is largely controlled by the altitude of the sun above the horizon. Near the equator this varies little over a year. At Singapore the difference between maximum and minimum elevations of the sun at noon meridional time is 25 degrees of angle. But at Bhamo, 24°N, the difference is 48 degrees. And the lower the sun's angle the lower the radiation—other things being equal. Thus on midwinter's

Table 4.1 Average monthly temperatures in January and June and annual range for coastal stations

Station	Latitude (°N)	January (°C)	July (°C)	Range (°C)
Singapore	1°21'	25.6	27.3	1.7
Merising	2°27'	25.5	25.8	0.3
Kuala Terengganu	5°20'	25.3	27.2	1.9
Kota Baharu	6°10'	25.3	26.7	1.4
Songkhla	7°09'	26.8	28.0	1.2
Surat Thani (Bandon)	9°07'	25.9	27.8	1.9
Qui Nhon	13°45'	22.8	30.0	7.2
Da Nang	16°05'	21.2	28.5	7.3
Thanh Hoa	19°48'	15.9	28.5	12.6

Source: Partly after Nieuwolt, 1981

day (22 December) at 30°N the amount of radiation arriving at the top of the atmosphere is 0.48 kcal [2.01 kJ] cm^{-2}, compared with 0.87 kcal [3.64 kJ] cm^{-2} at the equator, so it would be cooler solely for 'astronomical' reasons. In December the region's surface receives 8–12 kcal [33.5–50 kJ] cm^{-2}, 14 [58.6] in southern Myanmar. In June the range is only marginally higher—10–12 kcal [41.7–50 kJ] cm^{-2}—in the equatorial regions, a little higher again—12–14 kcal [50–58.6 kJ] cm^{-2} in mainland Southeast Asia but much higher at the surface of the Western Pacific Ocean. It is no coincidence that this is where tropical cyclones are spawned, as radiation heats water and warm water drives the cyclones.

Air temperatures at low altitudes generally match solar radiation. The quite uniform mean temperatures over insular Southeast Asia reflect the uniform amounts of radiation arriving at the surface, buffered by the sea, which is slow to heat and slow to cool. As has just been noted, the receipts of solar radiation are much the same at 10°N and S as at the equator but drop rapidly with increasing latitude. By choosing stations at low elevations near the sea the effects of altitude and continentality can be filtered out, leaving those of latitude alone. Average temperatures in January and July march hand-in-hand with latitude. At the same time annual ranges become greater, reflecting the greater range of solar radiation.

Solar radiation is much influenced by cloudiness and in turn this is affected by dominant air masses and the atmospheric circulation. At low latitudes these effects are small but become noticeable north of latitude 15°N. Here the absence of cloud in the inter-monsoon period of April and May leads to intense radiation, in turn resulting in high temperatures during the early afternoon heat-peak, often exceeding 35°C and sometimes reaching 40°C. This may lead to physiological stress in animals and people in the absence of abundant water, as in plants. It is, perhaps, no co-

Table 4.2 'Traverse' data: distance from the sea and temperature ranges

Station	Long. (°E)	Distance from sea (km)	Average daily range (°C)	
Equatorial ~ 3°N			*Jan*	*Jul*
Kuala Selangor	101° 15'	0	8.5	8.5
Bentong	101° 55'	77(W)160(E)	10.0	11.9
Temerloh	102° 26'	105(W)124(E)	7.9	9.9
Kuala Pahang	103° 28'	0	4.7	7.1
Continental ~ 20°N				
Sittwe (Akyab)	92° 55'	0	12.5	4.4
Minbu	94° 53'	155	14.7	7.3
Yamethin	96° 09'	295	16.1	7.9
Luang Prabang	102° 08'	290	14.0	8.8
Thanh Hoa	105° 47'	15	6.9	8.3

Source: Nieuwolt, 1981

incidence that in Thailand the Songkran water festival is celebrated at this time of the year. Not only is it a chance to cool off but by sympathetic magic the rains may be brought. By July, though, with the establishment of the southwest monsoon, cloudiness increases while radiation levels and temperatures fall though the humidity rises.

But variation in solar radiation is not the only major cause of variations of temperature from place to place. Another factor is continentality, that is, distance from the sea. This is usually reflected in a relatively low temperature range near the sea, which acts as a heat sink, warming by day and giving up heat to the atmosphere at night. This process accounts for the alternating day and night breezes found in all the region's coastal zones, a phenomenon still of some significance to local sailing vessels. Greater diurnal ranges of temperature reflect increasing distance from the coast despite overall air-mass characteristics being similar over long distances. Continentality shows up even on the scale of some tens of kilometres so that in the Malay Peninsula and on the larger islands of insular Southeast Asia daily temperature ranges inland are greater than near the sea, though the ranges are greater still on the mainland where distances from the sea are also greater. In the mainland part of the region ranges are much larger in winter than in summer, mainly because skies are usually clear, promoting heating of the air by solar radiation during the day, low absorption of energy in evaporation because it is dry, and vigorous outgoing long-wave radiation at night. Dew and, at elevation, frost may result though the frequency of neither is well known. Continentality on different scales is illustrated in data for two 'traverses'—west to east—across the Malay Peninsula and Myanmar to Viet Nam (Table 4.2).

Table 4.3 Vertical temperature profile on Gunung Kinabalu, March 1978

Station	Altitude (m)	Mean daily temperature (°C)	Extremes (°C) lowest	highest	range
Park HQ	1 620	18.3	11.7	25.1	13.4
Kambarongoh	1 890	16.5	11.3	26.1	14.8
Carson's Camp	2 730	12.0	8.3	19.4	11.1
Panar Laban	3 270	10.6	5.0	21.7	16.7
Sayat Sayat	3 820	9.2	4.7	16.9	12.2

Source: Unpublished data, Hong Kong University expedition, 1978

A further major factor influencing temperature is elevation. In the region generally, temperatures fall by around 0.6°C with each rise in elevation of 100 m, though the rates at which they decrease vary from day to night (the latter usually lower), from summer to winter as well as with altitude. (How large the variability of the last may be can be judged by results of observations on Gunung Kinabalu where lapse rates varied from 0.2°C per 100 m at 3 p.m. to 1.0°C per 100 m in the evening at two stations only a kilometre apart horizontally and 270 m vertically.) Other things being equal, radiation incoming from the sun and outgoing from the earth increases with altitude, in part because the air is clearer there. Incoming radiation is also less scattered because it has less atmosphere to travel through—one reason why a stay in the mountains often results in a suntan. Highlands thus have much greater temperature ranges than lowlands nearby. The differences are small during the day when intense insolation rapidly heats uplands but at night cooling is rapid. The usual condensation layer that forms on isolated mountains often dissipates, especially above about 3000 m, with strong cooling and low temperatures. This is illustrated by data from Kinabalu obtained during a week in March, 1978 (Table 4.3).

Where mountains are usually clouded, and this is generally true in continental Southeast Asia, the pattern of temperatures is rather different. As a result of uplift and condensation, clouds form over mountains much earlier in the mornings than over the adjoining lowland. Their formation slows the usual daily temperature rise in the uplands while the rise continues over the lowlands. The result is a large temperature difference during the day. At night, should cloud remain, cooling in the mountains is slower than in the lowlands, where clear nights are more frequent. Thus in most parts of mainland Southeast Asia the daily ranges of temperature diminish with increasing altitude.

Both in the mainland and insular uplands freezing temperatures may occur, in the mainland especially during the winter monsoon, but only if skies are clear, leading to strong outgoing radiation at night and consequently to frosts. Even in Java, close to the equator, tea plantations at altitudes of only 1600 to 1650 m are annually visited by frost at least once. Under clear, still conditions cold air drainage downslope occurs—because cool air is heavier than warm—so that in locations where high-level valleys and basins are surrounded by mountains, night-time temperatures are often lower than they otherwise would be given their elevation.

RESPONSES TO RADIATION AND TEMPERATURE

Solar radiation is a major 'driver' of plant growth, both directly in photosynthesis and indirectly via temperature. Just what the responses of plants, animals and people to their variations may be are not altogether clear, largely for lack of detailed scientific investigation. So far as plants are concerned it can be confidently asserted that at all levels below the snowline—that is, virtually everywhere—there is enough light and heat for plants of some kind to grow. Less radiation may accompany more cloud without significant depression of temperatures, as is the case in most parts of the region during the southwest monsoon.

Temperatures can also be low yet accompanied by high daytime radiation when skies are clear. This happens in continental Southeast Asia when the northeast monsoon prevails. It seems likely that rice, for example, and possibly most other light-loving plants (heliophytes), grow better at high light intensities, for in regions of double-cropped rice the necessarily-irrigated dry-season yields are invariably higher than those of the often gloomy wet season. (There are additional reasons for these higher dry-season rice yields, including better water control, fewer pests, better care of crops.)

One major response to lower temperatures, and possibly to lower solar radiation though no one really knows, is slower growth, reduced stature or, in crops, reduced yields. Thus in upland areas there is a general reduction in total phytomass with increasing altitude and the species present are usually quite unlike those of the lowlands. Amongst crops it is clear that yields in some cases are reduced. For example, the yield of latex from the rubber tree, *Hevea brasiliensis*, in Malaysia are so reduced above about 300 m that it is not economic to plant it. On the other hand, temperate crops can often be successfully grown at altitude such as at Cameron Highlands in Peninsular Malaysia or northeast of Baguio in Luzon. This is, of course, subject to the proviso that such temperate crops are not sensitive to day-length, for tropical highlands are by no means an exact analogue of temperate climes.

So far as animals are concerned, very little is known of the effects of variation in light, heat and temperature. Obviously all animals lacking mammalian heat-regulating mechanisms are likely to be less active when it is cool. Most mammals may suffer heat-stress though this is often compounded by insufficient water intake. Wild mammals and many other animals of the forest and savanna seek shade and rest during the early afternoon heat-peak. Such is the case with tree-dwelling gibbons (*Hylobates* spp.) and macaques (*Macacus* spp.), for example, and it seems likely that many birds forage mostly when it is a little cooler, during the morning and late afternoon. Night-time temperatures are lower than day-time, in the winter substantially so. What effect this may have upon nocturnal foragers is largely unknown.

People also respond to temperature variation in the region. In the days before air-conditioning an afternoon siesta was common. Hard field labour, tillage and transplanting rice especially, are avoided during the heat of the day, the former not just because of human discomfort but also because of the risk of draught animals, especially buffaloes, suffering heat-stroke. But a major human behavioural response, particularly in colonial times, was the seeking out of accessible mountain areas for the construction of sanitoria and resorts. Since the blood parasite responsible for malaria, *Plasmodium*, dies at temperatures below 20°C, cool upland areas were free of this disease, one to which non-immune foreigners were, in the absence of prophylaxis, particularly prone.

This feature and the desire for relief from what was regarded as the oppressive moist heat of the lowlands led to the establishment and expansion of numerous small towns in the uplands. Examples include Maymyo in Myanmar, Dalat and Tam Dao respectively in southern and northern Viet Nam, the Cameron Highlands of Peninsular Malaysia, Puncak, near Jakarta, and Baguio, north of Manila. Around each of these and other similar settlements have developed areas for the production of temperate crops now supplying markets in general rather than merely meeting the needs of Western expatriates.

Rainfall

Precipitation as anything other than rain is rare. Snow certainly falls on the high mountains of northern Myanmar and the central range of West Irian, where enough remains to form permanent snow-fields and glacial tongues. It does not now fall on Gunung Kinabalu, which nevertheless bears the scars of glaciation in the geologically recent past. Low's Gully, on the flank of the peak, is clearly of glacial origin as also in all likelihood are the great boulders with which the gully is choked.

Vigorous convection in cumulonimbus clouds may occur at any latitude carrying moisture to heights at which it freezes into hail. Usually this melts as it falls through lower, warmer layers but sometimes it does not,

Figure 4.1 Mean annual rainfall

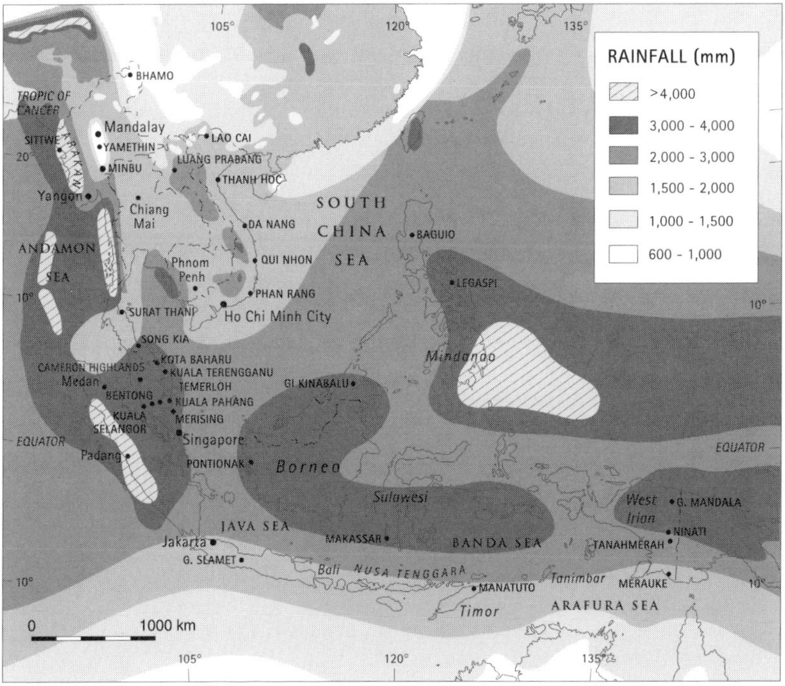

resulting in ground-level hail-storms. Freezing rain—sleet—also occasionally occurs in the mountains of northern Viet Nam and westwards to Myanmar.

Rain is far and away the most important form of precipitation and Southeast Asia as a whole is unquestionably the world's wettest major region though smaller regions—windward slopes of the eastern Himalaya, the western slopes of New Zealand's Southern Alps—may be wetter.

Over most of the Andaman Sea and adjoining parts of the Indian Ocean the annual average rainfall is over 3000 millimetres (mm), rising to over 5000 mm on the Arakan coast of southern Myanmar and well over 4000 mm along the western mountain margins of Sumatera. Most of Borneo, Sulawesi, Mindanao and northern West Irian receive over 3000 mm. Half of Indonesia is thought to receive over 3000 mm. Of all the seas and islands only the western part of the South China Sea generally gets less than 2000 mm each year. Locally, annual rainfall can reach even higher totals. Where high relief is combined with exposure to rain-bearing winds totals may exceed 6000 mm. Thus in Java two stations on the southern flank of the volcano Slamet, Baturaden (650 m) and Tenjo (700 m) show large totals, the former a record 8837 mm and the latter an average of 7168 mm. Other remarkably wet localities in Indonesia include Ninati in West Irian with a mean of 6343 mm and Muarasako on the west coast of Sumatera with 6416 mm. Regionally, one of the best-instrumented upland areas is Java. Out of 261 rain-gauges located between elevations of 900 and 1700 m, nearly three-fifths receive more than 3000 mm, a quarter of them more than 4000 mm. Stations above 1700 m are somewhat drier, as is usual on tropical mountains generally.

Most of mainland Southeast Asia gets 1000–2000 mm, except for the Dry Zone of Myanmar which is shielded from westerly rain-bearing winds by moderately high mountains. Its core averages less than 1000 mm a year. The central plains and plateaux of Thailand and Cambodia are also comparatively dry for the same reason, although this area, which receives 1000–1500 mm is not as dry as the Dry Zone. Small areas of coastal southern Viet Nam, roughly Phan Rang Bay to Qui Nhon, are also protected from the southwesterlies in summer, while the winter north-easterlies have travelled too little distance over the northern part of the South China Sea to have picked up much moisture. In all these areas dryness limits most plant growth in winter and many annual crops require irrigation either from large rivers—the small ones dry up—or from storage in reservoirs or natural underground aquifers. Trees survive of course but deciduous species shed their leaves.

Another, less well-known region of dryness is the eastern island chains extending through Nusatenggara, Indonesia. Here rainfall is less than 1000 mm annually and, as in mainland Southeast Asia, this mostly falls in only a few months. Manatuto, on the island of Timor, for example, has an average rainfall of only 565 mm, with rain falling on only 45 days each year, 78 per cent of it in the wet season from December to April. The islands of this chain suffer severe water shortages. Since they are small, there are no big rivers. Those that are low—many of them atolls or raised atolls—fail to push moist maritime air upwards orographically sufficiently far to cool it and cause condensation into rain. Many also have free- draining soils and poor stocks of groundwater. Environmentally they are truly inhospitable.

Rainfall variability

Variability of rainfall from year to year is generally claimed to increase as the annual means decrease. For Southeast Asia, unfortunately, published data are rather too scanty in both time and space to be sure that this inverse relationship exists. For Indonesia the French climatologists Fontanel and Chanteforte claim that there is considerable variability even at some high-rainfall stations such as Jakarta, Pontianak, Makassar and Bali. In only nine years in the period 1962–71 the range of annual rainfall varied from a low of 1492 mm to a high of 6948 mm, against a 23-year mean of 2697 mm. An analysis of 26 sets of data ranging north–south from Lao Kay in northern Viet Nam to Jakarta and east–west from that city to Bali shows that for only five, Vientiane, Phitsanulok, Da Nang, Nakhon Ratchasima and Bangkok, was the range about the mean less than half of the annual mean. Thus Bangkok's range, 679 mm, is 46 per cent of that city's average total, 1492 mm. By contrast, two cities, Luang Prabang in Laos and Makassar in Sulawesi, had ranges greater than the mean.

Unfortunately the range of rainfall from year to year is time-dependent. This means that the longer the period over which records are kept the more likely is it that exceptionally high or low totals will be recorded, so that comparisons amongst stations for differing periods are not valid. Nonetheless they are suggestive of a positive relationship between year-to-year range and the average total—the more it rains the greater is the variation. But the scatter is considerable and three stations with relatively low annual totals nevertheless show a large range—Luang Prabang, Chiang Mai and Phnom Penh.

Certainly, variability is important. Heavy falls usually bring floods, increased risk of landslides, crop damage, or good crops if the falls are not excessive. Droughts bring lowered crop yields, and problems in irrigating farms and generating hydroelectricity.

There can be little doubt that irrigation is a response to the need to ensure reliable crops in the face of unreliable rainfall. Even normal patterns of distribution are reflected in crop yields. In Indonesia, for example, annual rainfall decreases from west to east and this decline is broadly related to rice yields. In Java some 4.1 million hectares (ha) is harvested each year from 3 million ha of wet-rice land, a ratio of 1.37. In Sulawesi the ratio is 1.44 but eastwards it falls to 0.97 in Kalimantan and only 0.42 in eastern Nusatenggara where, on average, only two-fifths of the wet-rice land is cultivated in any year.

For Malaysia, Nieuwolt's agroclimatic studies have demonstrated the importance of climatic factors in a rather uniform environment in which rainfall, both its total and its seasonal distribution, is the dominant controlling factor below an elevation of about 500 m. Working on major upland crops—rubber, oil palm, cocoa, coconut, coffee, cashew, mango, citrus, durian, plus herbs such as manioc, pepper, pineapple, banana, papaya—he found a rather complex pattern. The first three listed were confined to regions below 300 m elevation with the others ranging up to a maximum of 1800 m, for citrus. For some—rubber, oil palm, coconuts—drought beyond one or two months depressed yields. For others—coffee, mango, citrus, sugar-cane—two to four months dryness increased yields. The response of cacao was more precise: one month's low rainfall was advantageous but two months was the reverse. In addition, for most crops, saturated soils and strong wind gusts were disadvantageous.

Maize, sugar-cane, *kenaf* (*Hibiscus* fibre) and manioc are entirely rain-fed, as is much of the rice. The consequence is a wide range of yields from year to year, drought years causing substantial falls in yields—rather less on lowland rice-growing soils where residual moisture may be sufficient to keep crops growing if not flourishing, rather more on upland soils, especially those growing shallow-rooted annual crops such as dry rice, maize and many others.

When it rains it rains really hard except in spring in northern Viet Nam when drizzle may be prolonged for weeks at a time. This results in the paradoxical situation of a great deal of rain in most places but not so many rainy days. As an example, for 29 stations from Bhamo and Lao Kay in the north, south along both coasts to Singapore, plus another 10 in the Philippines, the average number of rain-days is only 143 each year, with a low at Mandalay in Myanmar's Dry Zone (mean rainfall 871 mm a year) with 53 rain-days and a high of 223 rain-days at Legaspi, central Philippines, where the annual fall averages 3371 mm. The standard deviation, which measures spread around this regional mean, is only 37 days. On average then, there are twice as many days without rain as with it though there is a broad contrast between continental and insular parts of the region. Taking 24 stations on the mainland with at least 30 years of records, the average number of rain-days is only 123 (standard deviation 25), that is 39 per cent of days have rain. By contrast, for 16 stations in the Malay Peninsula and the Philippines, the average number of rain-days is 174 (standard deviation 27), or close to half of the days in a year.

Dryness

These data give some clues as to dryness in the region as a whole, dryness rather than excessive moisture being particularly significant to plants and thus to farmers and those dependent upon them. For most farmers throughout the region it is the seasonality of rainfall that brings many questions. When will it rain? Will the rains be sustained? How deep will it flood? Will it be dry enough to ripen and to harvest the crops?

They are, on the whole, unlikely to receive precise answers and not just because forecasting anywhere is as much an art as a science. Meteorological services are poorly developed and even after the weather has happened published data are scanty. One thing is certain: seasonal variation of rainfall is greater than the statistics show. In meteorological records generally, these variations tend not to show up clearly for several reasons.

First is that mean data are given month-by-month. A month without rain except for 100 mm on the last day comes out as a wet month. Thus the archetypical humid tropical station, Singapore, is said to have no seasons by reason of the apparently even distribution of rainfall through the year. It actually experiences dry spells, commonly in February. Though these are rarely more than six weeks long, they are enough to trigger greater rates of leaf-fall in many trees, to initiate breeding behaviour in some species of birds and, when the 'drought' breaks to promote a flush of fungal growth.

The second reason why dry periods do not necessarily show up fully in meteorological records is that their length may vary quite substantially from year to year just as the total rainfall often does. In biological terms and in terms of soil water which is, after all, what plants depend upon, the occurrence of a few short, sharp showers during a dry period probably makes little difference, for most of what does not quickly evaporate runs off and is thus unavailable to recharge soil water reserves.

Finally, dry spells do not necessarily occur every year and this fact may be partly or entirely hidden by averages. The effects of a single sustained drought may continue for many years. For example it seems likely that parts of the region may very occasionally experience upwards of a year without significant rain. One late nineteenth-century explorer of southeast Borneo, Carl Bock, for example, reported a drought so prolonged that great forest trees were defoliated and dying. It is possible that during such rare droughts even the humid rainforest can carry fire. What else explains charcoal widely diffused through soil in an area not known ever to have been inhabited in the Danum valley, Sabah? Certainly, the monsoonal forests of mainland Southeast Asia are adapted to seasonal dryness as perhaps a third of the species are deciduous and some (the teak tree *Tectona grandis* is an example) are adapted to low-intensity ground fires.

What then are the patterns? Taking the region of the Sunda and Singapore straits as a baseline region where dry spells are relatively short, not occurring every year, two 'climatological traverses' can be made, one from the north, the other to the east. Seasonal dryness increases from south to north and from west to east. Along the northern traverse dryness is accompanied by winter-time depression of temperature, whereas traversing to the east lower temperatures do not accompany the dry season.

The pattern of variation in rainfall is not entirely regular from south to north. South of around 6°N there is no longer any month, on the average, with less than 50 mm rain. Alur Setar, nevertheless, still has a dry season with less than 10 per cent of the total falling in the winter months December to February, the same dry months as further north. By contrast, for Kota Bharu, at much the same latitude, these are the wet months when the northeast monsoon picks up moisture in its passage across the South China Sea and dumps much of it along the east coast of the Malay Peninsula south of the Isthmus of Kra. Kota Bharu receives 77 per cent of its rain from November to January.

Table 4.4 A north–south climatological traverse: Bhamo to Singapore

Station	Lat. (°N)	No. of dry months*	Av. total rainfall 3 driest months* (mm)	Proportion av. ann. rainfall in 3 driest months*(%)	Av. temp. 3 coolest months (°C)
Bhamo	24	6	38	2.0	17.8
Mandalay	22	5	11	1.3	21.1
Sittwe	20	4	18	0.3	21.9
Chiang Mai	19	5	28	2.2	21.9
Toungoo	18	5	18	0.9	22.9
Yangon	17	4	15	0.6	25.9
Nakhon R'sima	15	5	14	1.2	23.5
Bangkok	14	4	45	3.0	26.1
Battambang	13	4	48	3.5	25.1
Mergui	12	2	96	<0.1	25.7
Saigon	11	4	32	1.6	26.0
Ha Tien	10	4	73	3.8	26.0
Bandon	9	2	121	6.5	25.9
Phuket	8	2	147	6.7	27.2
Alur Setar	6	0	230	9.8	25.8
Kuala Lumpur	3	0	570	23.7	25.8
Singapore	1	0	514	21.2	25.8

Note: * A dry month is one with less than 50 mm.
Source: Based mainly on Nieuwolt, 1981

Location with respect to rain-bearing winds is crucial as the case of Mergui shows. Like stations further south it receives a reasonable amount of rain in the three driest months, but because it receives an annual total of more than 4 m of rain, especially from the southwest monsoon, the proportion falling in those months is minuscule. Overall, though, there is a clear increase in the length of the dry season from south to north. Generally this is accompanied by cooler, less humid conditions though with some slight variations, such as for Saigon and Yangon where swampy locations no great distance from the sea tend to buffer temperature changes.

A west–east traverse

A traverse eastwards from Jakarta shows a similar increase in the length of the dry season, though unlike Singapore its driest month is August rather than February. Indeed throughout the great arc of islands 6°–8° south of the equator the southern spring is the dry season, which in some

Table 4.5 A west–east climatological traverse: Jakarta to Merauke (all stations are between 6° and 10°S)

Station	Long. (°E)	No. of dry months*	Av. total rainfall in 3 driest months* (mm)	Ann. rainfall (mm)	Prop'n in 3 driest months (%)
Jakarta	107	0	191	1 798	10.6
Cilacap	109	0	823	3 857	21.3
Pati	111	3	130	1 676	7.5
Surabaya	113	4	121	1 518	8.0
Kalianget	114	3	65	1 519	4.3
Waingapu (Sumba)	120	7	10	757	1.3
Maumere (Flores)	122	5	97	970	10.0
Kupang (Timor)	123½	6	10	1 140	0.9
Manatuto (Timor)	126	6	10	565	1.7
Tepa (Babar)	129½	3	36	1 767	2.0
Saumlaki (Tanimbar)	131	3	26	2 228	1.2
Merauke (S. West Irian)	140	5	119	1 366	8.7

Note: * A dry month is one with less than 50 mm.
Source: Compiled mainly from Fontanel and Chanteforte, 1978

of the islands extends to as early as May and as late as November. The wet season occurs from November to February, when rain-bearing winds are more or less northerly. At its eastern extremity the traverse shows shorter dry seasons as in Timor and the Tanimbar islands which are open to the southern monsoon. (This is essentially the same maritime airstream as the southwest—northern summer—monsoon.)

The data given in Table 4.5 were deliberately chosen to emphasise the seasonal dryness in parts of the eastern archipelago and many stations are on the leeward side of the islands concerned. Regions on the northern side of the Java, Banda and Arafura seas still have a dry season centred on August and September but it is neither as long nor as intense as in Nusatenggara. Much the same is true for islands in the Arafura Sea and the southern part of West Irian. Here the width of the sea is very important, allowing initially dry air moving north from the Australian continent to pick up moisture and to dump it further north.

The result is steep south–north rainfall gradients. For example, Merauke, Tanahmerah and Ninati lie within half a degree of longitude 140°E. Merauke (8°28'S) receives an average annual rainfall of 1366 mm, Tanahmerah (6°05'S) gets 4577 mm. Ninati (5°30'S), at an elevation of 250 m, receives a remarkable 6343 mm, amongst the highest in the whole region, attesting to the strong influence of mountains (rising to 4700 m at Gunung Mandala, no great distance away).

Evaporation

Before looking at the reasons for these regional patterns of temperature and rainfall it is necessary to look at evaporation, for this is of fundamental significance to crops and plants generally. As already noted, it is soil moisture not rainfall that is crucial. Unfortunately not much can be said about evaporation, as it is measured by different methods in different places. The best that can be stated is that the annual evaporation in the humid equatorial areas is about 1600 mm annually, enough to cause seasonal soil water deficits in some areas. In mainland Southeast Asia evaporation is about 1000 mm each year, though the difference in published figures for the two regions seems rather too large to be explained by differences in temperature, cloudiness, relative humidity and amount of sunshine. Soil moisture levels generally lag six to eight weeks behind rainfall, so that there is usually a diminishing water deficit early in the rainy season with a corresponding diminishing water surplus as the dry season sets in. The result is that many plants, except very shallow-rooted ones, do not respond immediately to the rains. Similarly, growth does not necessarily stop with the onset of the dry season as plants continue to draw on stored soil water. However, it is likely that plants' responses to the rainfall regime, as to other meteorological phenomena, vary from species to species and, even for the same species, from time to time and place to place. The scientific discipline of phenology, which studies the life cycles of plants and animals, is very weakly developed in the region, so that there is much that is unknown.

Atmospheric circulation

This is what causes the weather and, of course, climate is pretty much average weather. The region as a whole is under the influence of systems at various scales from a major portion of the globe down to very local phenomena reflecting differences within cities even between indoors and outdoors, inside a rainforest and outside it. At the largest scale, the circulation of Southeast Asia, as of the tropical zone generally, is dominated by what is called Hadley Cell circulation. Because of strong heating near the equator, warm air rises up to an altitude of about 12 km. This air then moves poleward in the upper atmosphere, falling to lower levels in the subtropical atmosphere and finally returning equatorwards as the trade wind flow, northeasterly north of the equator and southwesterly south of it. The geographical position of this circulation shifts north and south accompanying the apparent height of the sun and its consequential heat equator. The Hadley Cell circulation thus moves back and forward across the geographical equator. In the southern summer the rising air is located around 10 to 20°S while in the northern summer, rising ar reaches its maximum speed at around 5°N latitude.

A significant part of this pattern of atmospheric circulation in the region is represented by the monsoons, a word perhaps ultimately derived from the Sanscrit *mausim* 'a season'. The general pattern is illustrated in Figure 4.2.

Northerly monsoon

In January atmospheric pressure is high over eastern Siberia and northern China, the edge of the system being marked by the polar front. The air mass associated with this semi-permanent high is very cold and dry. It travels south, warming as it goes by contact with the land that still retains some heat from the preceding summer. It does not move directly south because of the effects of the earth's rotation. These are at a maximum around the equator and thus tend to drag the air masses westwards so that in the northern hemisphere the prevailing wind direction is northeasterly, becoming northwesterly south of the equator, there to reach a low pressure zone or front of convergence where the air is sucked in and whirled aloft. By the time it reaches this zone, what started out as cool, dry air is warm and damp, having passed over warm seas from which it has drawn up enormous quantities of water. The pressure gradient gives rise to steady winds of around 4–6 metres per second (14.4–21.6 km/h). This air mass has the shape of a great wedge thinning to the south. Thus over southern China it is about 3000 m thick but only about 1350 m thick over Singapore.

At the same time, there is another very different air mass lurking in the wings. This has its origin over the Pacific north of the equator and is consequently relatively warm, moist and stable. The boundary between these two air masses forms part of the polar front, on Figure 4.2 shown to the east of the Philippines, though its position actually may move, at sea level, from 25°N as far south as 10°N. Along or near this front disturbances occur as the two different air masses come into contact. These bring heavy cloud and light, drizzly rain to northern Viet Nam and to eastern parts of the Philippines. In mainland Southeast Asia this warmer, moist air rarely penetrates west of the mountains of Viet Nam so that most of the region is dry, comparatively cool and sunny. The boundary between air masses continues southwestwards across the South China Sea. Disturbances along it and convergence of streams of air warming and moistening as they travel across the sea bring rain to the east coast of the Malay Peninsula south of about 10°N and to north- and west-facing coasts generally. Though these air masses lose some moisture over the chain of islands fromeast to West Irian, beyond them open seas permit the air to

Figure 4.2 Atmospheric circulation and pressure

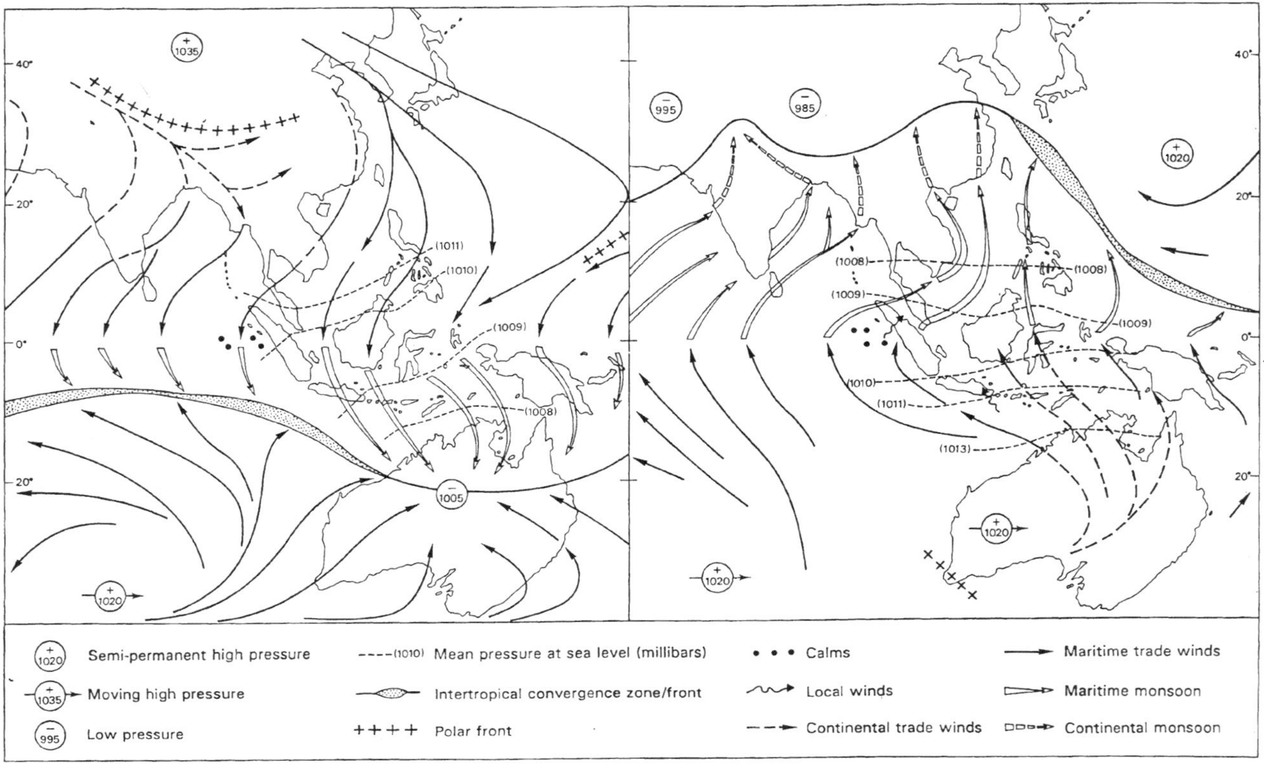

Symbol	Meaning	Symbol	Meaning	Symbol	Meaning	Symbol	Meaning
(+ 1020)	Semi-permanent high pressure	----(1010)	Mean pressure at sea level (millibars)	• • •	Calms	→	Maritime trade winds
(+ 1035) →	Moving high pressure		Intertropical convergence zone/front		Local winds		Maritime monsoon
(– 995)	Low pressure	+ + + +	Polar front		Continental trade winds		Continental monsoon

gather moisture once again to supply the southern chain of islands. Even areas which might be expected to be in the rain-shadow of the north-easterlies, such as the west coast of Sumatera, in the shadow of the Barisan Range, or northeast Sumatera, in the shadow of the hills and mountains of the Malay Peninsula, do not have a dry season at this time. In fact stations like Padang and Medan are wet from September to January.

By February and March the speed of the northeast monsoon diminishes as the high pressure cell over northern Asia weakens. As it does so, the warm, stable air associated with the Pacific trade winds gradually takes over, though in fits and starts. Rain generally diminishes. At the same time, temperatures in the inland areas of the mainland start to rise as a result of increased insolation, in turn a reflection of longer days and a higher altitude of the sun. Higher daytime temperatures increase convection and thunderstorms result, marking the end of the dry season and creating the early 'mango rains'. They also create low pressure cells so that the air over the South China Sea tends to diverge rather than converging. It is thus less likely to rain, as the air is stable.

Intermonsoon

The next act in the region's dramatic battle of the air masses is something of a hiatus. During April and May there is a transition between the retreating northeast monsoon, now no longer supported by high pressure over northern Asia, and the advancing southwest monsoon, supported by semi-permanent high pressure cells following the sun north to around 20°S. Slowly, with rapid advances and retreats on the way, this transition moves north. General circulation is weak, with light and variable winds. Inland there is strong heating, resulting in fierce heat and low atmospheric pressure over Myanmar and Thailand. Air streams are weak. They include an extension of the northeasterly trade winds from the North Pacific, southeasterly trade winds from Australia and the South Pacific, barely reaching the equator, strengthening westerlies from the Indian Ocean and some penetration into the northwestern part of mainland Southeast Asia of the gathering Indian southwest monsoon. The weak regional circulation results in local winds—land and sea breezes, valley and mountain winds—becoming predominant. Convection is often strong, with thunderstorms during the day though they do not usually bring much rain. Unlike India, where the southwest monsoon bursts on the scene, in Southeast Asia its entry is gradual, with advances and retreats related to changing positions of the jet stream high in the atmosphere at around 15 000 m.

Southwest monsoon

The southwest monsoon sets in from about June, advancing across the whole region so that by July the intertropical convergence zone is usually far to the north, lying across central China and the Himalayas. Pressures are low north of this zone, drawing warm air from the south, though because the gradient is not as strong as during the northeast monsoon, wind-speeds are only 1–3 metres per second (3.6–10.8 km/h). Across much of the region this air is moist, especially that travelling across the Indian Ocean. To the east the air is initially less warm, heading north from the southern winter. But unlike the major air mass to the west this one is dry, coming off the deserts of Australia's 'dead heart'. As it crosses the fringing seas it gains only a little moisture so that many of the islands of Nusatenggara are dry at this time. However, the Arafura Sea and the Gulf of Carpentaria are wider stretches of water so the northwards-moving air picks up some moisture. Thus southern West Irian receives quite a lot of rain at this time. Ninati, for instance, receives more than 500 mm in every month but August from April to September, helping to maintain the great freshwater swamps of that region. Between the thick (9000 m) moist air mass in the west and the shallower (3000 m) mostly drier air mass in the east lies another zone of convergence, another air mass boundary. Along this, mixing of the air gives rise to light, extensive rains, for example in the Malay Peninsula. But much of the region—mainland Southeast Asia, Sumatera, even the Philippines—to some degree falls under the influence of the moist southwest monsoonal flow and its convergence with somewhat drier 'Australian' air is only one of the major sources of rain.

North of about 10°N tropical depressions form over warm seas in the Bay of Bengal, in the South China Sea and in the Pacific Ocean east of the Philippines, the last being much the most important breeding-ground for tropical depressions affecting Southeast Asia. From this area, roughly half approach the east coast of the Philippines but then recurve away to the northeast towards Taiwan and Japan. The other half continue west, often crossing the Visayas, occasionally crossing Luzon without their circulation being disrupted enough to cause them to disintegrate, sometimes heading across the northern tip of Luzon. These all commonly continue west or northwest across the northern part of the South China Sea to hit land in central and northern Viet Nam. Occasionally, usually as tropical depressions rather than full-scale typhoons, they may affect Mindanao, northern Borneo, southern Thailand and northern Peninsular Malaysia, sometimes reconstituting themselves in the Andaman Sea. Heavy to very heavy rains usually accompany these revolving storms, half a metre in a couple of days being not uncommon. Rain and wind may cause serious damage to crops, forests, housing and communications as well as loss of life, typhoons being second only to volcanic eruptions and mud-slides in this regard. In the Philippines the annual cost of all natural disasters is estimated at around 1 per cent of Gross Domestic Product annually.

South of about 10°N conventional thunderstorms are common during the southwest monsoon, sometimes forming a 'line squall' as is common across the Straits of Melaka at this season. Rain is intense but shorter-lived than that from tropical depressions and much more localised. The other main cause of rain at this time of the year is orographic lifting, the pushing of air upwards by mountain barriers. These are naturally most effective where they lie more or less at right angles to the air-streams as along the Arakan Yoma, Myanmar, the Barisan range, Sumatera, the central mountains of Java or the Zambales mountains west of the central Luzon plain. Once the air-streams have crossed the mountain barriers and in doing so have given up much of their moisture, the air descends, becoming warmer and drier as a result. This is the well-known *föhn* effect and it has the result of making many of the region's plains much drier than they otherwise would be. Examples are the Dry Zone of northern Myanmar, the Chao Phrya plain north of Bangkok, northeast Thailand, the central Mekong plain in Cambodia, the central plain of Luzon and dozens of other smaller plains throughout the region. Where plains lie directly open to the prevailing moist air, orographic lifting is much less important over it but mountains at the head of the plains or even plateaux will still intercept the moisture. Such is the case with Myanmar's northern mountains for example, or at the opposite side of the region the Sudirman and Jayawijaya ranges of West Irian.

Intermonsoon

Tropical cyclones reach their greatest frequency in September but in this and the following month the southwesterly flow weakens and starts to retreat, leaving very weak circulation behind it. The Asian continent starts to cool in September and the northeast monsoon, represented mainly by trade winds from the northern Pacific, begins to appear in the northeast part of the region. By October cool, dry air from northern China and eastern Siberia begins to make its presence felt as the semi-permanent high-pressure system there intensifies. An air mass boundary between cool, dry air from this high and the somewhat warmer and much moister air from the northern Pacific appears in September, intensifying and moving south during October. Disturbances along this boundary bring significant rainfall in the more easterly parts of mainland Southeast Asia, where October may be the wettest month of the year as far west as Phnom Penh. Tropical depressions are still quite frequent but track further south to affect the whole of Viet Nam. By November the northeast monsoon is re-established and the cycle repeats, usually with considerable variation from one year to the next.

Tropical disturbances

These occur as a result of regional or local disturbances in the atmosphere. Most last only a short time, a few days in the case of tropical cyclones (typhoons) or just a few minutes or hours in the case of line squalls, thunderstorms and cold surges.

In the northwest Pacific, 26 tropical cyclones form in an average year, making up almost a third of the global total. Since most cyclones track westwards for at least part of their journey, many affect the eastern parts of Southeast Asia, especially polewards of about 8–10 degrees of latitude. Heat from warm seas is the essential driver of tropical cyclones. This comes from the evaporation of water followed by the release of energy by condensation. A small area of low pressure may be enough to trigger cyclonic development but only if it is located far enough polewards for Coriolis Force to set the air spinning. This force is zero at the equator and very weak to about 5–8 degrees polewards.

Once spinning, the cyclone's trajectory is steered by the particular characteristics of the regional pressure systems. Thus in the northern winter, high pressure (and cold air) heading southwestwards from the Asian continent tends to put late season cyclones well to the south of their earlier tracks with many entering the South China Sea to affect the coastal regions of Viet Nam especially. Tropical cyclones may also form in the South China Sea itself, generally tracking westwards sometimes to affect the Gulf of Thailand and the Kra Isthmus. While most tropical cyclones peter out as they cross land, being deprived of their source of energy, some may succeed in southern Thailand to be reconstituted in the Bay of Bengal and affecting southern Myanmar. To the east the complex alternation of islands and warm sea in the Visayas often poses little barrier to cyclones though just to the north Luzon's highlands usually do.

The effects of tropical cyclones may be very severe, especially where buildings are made of wood and thatch. Crop damage, directly by wind and indirectly by rain and flood, may also be considerable. On vulnerable slopes catastrophic erosion and deposition may occur, especially where materials such as volcanic ejecta are weakly consolidated. Even mature forest can be seriously damaged especially where cyclonic winds penetrate further equatorwards than usual. To this day the forests of Kelantan, northeast Peninsular Malaysia, bear signs of damage that occurred nearly 120 years ago.

Line squalls are essentially lines of thunderstorms and the two can thus be considered together. Thunderstorms occur largely as a result of local convection, the heat island effect of cities probably being sufficient materially to increase their incidence in and around cities. They are local, rarely extend over a diameter of more than 10 km and rarely do they last more than an hour or two. Such storms are particularly characteristic of the equatorial zone where regional circulation at the surface is weak, allowing local circulation to predominate. In Singapore, for example, mid to late afternoon thunderstorms occur at most times of the year.

Singapore and the Malay Peninsula generally are on the receiving end of rather large thunderstorm systems, especially during the southwest monsoon. Lines of thunderheads form over the mountains of Sumatera during the night and then drift eastwards across the Straits of Melaka and the peninsula usually arrriving in the morning or early afternoon, bringing heavy rain and, briefly, strong swirling winds that may cause damage to lightly built structures on the ground and pose some risk to aerial navigation.

Cold surges do affect most of insular Southeast Asia with a strengthening of the northeast monsoon flow, strong winds and below normal temperatures. As cold air from the mainland parts of the region passes over the warm seas, it is quickly warmed and becomes laden with moisture. The resulting heavy rains and strong winds impede fishing and agriculture along the more exposed parts of the east coast of Peninsular Malaysia and northern Borneo. Movement of small craft along the coast may have to stop entirely for the four to six days such surges last.

By contrast, in mainland Southeast Asia the land surface cools much more rapidly than the sea so that cold air from the northeast is heated only a little as it passes. When the winter anticyclone is strong, cold winds may cause damage to agricultural crops, notably rubber, and at higher elevation frosts may occur.

Conclusion

The region is one of the warmest and wettest on the globe, providing sufficient warmth at all but the very highest elevations for plants to grow. Plants of some kind also receive enough moisture to grow, in western equatorial parts of the region and on mountains facing moisture-bearing winds, superabundantly. Only in rain-shadow locations, where initially moist air masses have given up their moisture to fringing highlands, and in parts of the Eastern Archipelago, which come under the climatic influence of Australia, does dryness prevail. Both mainland and insular parts of the region experience seasonal dryness, often unpredictably in terms of timing and intensity. But mostly there is enough rain to support forest, evergreen in the western and central parts of insular Southeast Asia, deciduous in the east and through much of the seasonally drier and cooler mainland.

And if there is enough to grow trees there is more than enough to grow crops though these—especially rice—benefit from irrigation for this reduces the uncertainties inherent in the sometimes capricious interplay of the region's air masses. Compared with northern temperate lands especially, the region's climate has long been relatively stable—with important consequences for its plants, animals and people.

FIVE
PLANTS, ANIMALS AND PEOPLE

By about 10 000 years ago, most of the major groups of plants and animals had already been in the region for ages. So had people. Long-lasting, relatively stable conditions had permitted the evolution of thousands of species—possibly around 10 000 species of flowering plants alone—allowing a great deal of specialisation and filling every conceivable ecological niche. Some reach back several hundred million years: the cycads, the horse-tails (*Equisetium* spp.), the club-mosses, Lycopodiaceae, the spectacular tree-ferns (mainly *Cyathea* spp.) of the sub-montane forests. More primitive still are the blue-green algae, to be found everywhere on otherwise bare surfaces but not by any means confined to Southeast Asia, dating back at least 3000 million years. This enormously long period has allowed them to fill every conceivable ecological niche from the vicinity of volcanic hot springs to rocks near perennial snow.

The region is the home of plants and animals found nowhere else. The camphor tree *Dryobalanops*, the mighty *Koompassia* tree—80 m high when full-grown—and two species of wild cattle, the *mithan* (*Bos frontalis*) and the *banteng* (*B. sondaicus*) are examples. Some consider it to be the home of certain groups of plants more often considered to belong in temperate climes. The oaks (*Quercus* spp.) and chestnuts (*Castanopsis* spp.) both found close to the equator, are examples for the northern hemisphere. Three groups of trees found on the region's tropical mountains may be similar examples for the southern hemisphere—*Agathis* spp., the kauri, the podocarps (especially *Podocarpus* spp.), both primitive conifers, and the scrubby *Leptospermum*, the tea-tree.

One notable group of plants that belongs mainly in the region is the palms. About 80 per cent of those studied in detail since the 1970s are found only in Southeast Asia. Some may have been present on the ancient supercontinent called Laurasia before it split into its smaller components as a result of plate tectonics.

About the middle of the Miocene geological era, roughly 14 million years ago, Laurasia began to collide with another supercontinent called Gondwanaland, which includes New Guinea and Australia. On this landmass had evolved a distinctive flora and fauna, the latter being marked by marsupial mammals in contrast to the placental mammals characteristic of Eurasia. By about 5 million years ago this collison of continents had resulted in a land migration route from Sulawesi to Australia via New Guinea. The result was a mingling of Southeast Asian and Australian elements. This process was probably enhanced in the mid-Pleistocene, 1¼ million years ago, by lower sea levels and continuous dry land from mainland Southeast Asia at least as far east as Timor. Only a narrow strait would have separated this land from a then much larger Australian continent.

Types of vegetation

Forest is naturally the overwhelmingly common type of vegetation—for climatic reasons. Over the last 400 years, and especially over the last 50, two major processes have been at work. One is the entire removal of forest and its replacement by such managed ecosystems as those of tree-crop plantations and rice-fields, even the artificial 'savannas' and 'deserts' of urban areas though these probably account for no more than a few per cent of the land area. Shifting cultivators also attacked primary forest though nowadays they rarely do so, now clearing vegetation previously cut and burnt for the growing of crops. The other major process is logging. Where cultivators do not then move in, the result is modification of the forest rather than its complete destruction, for only commercially valuable species are removed, though many others are damaged and die in the process. Forest, of a kind, remains.

One consequence is a major change in the forest cover. Large expanses still exist only in remote areas such as parts of West Irian. Elsewhere the cover is extremely patchy, as is clear in Figure 5.1. Such fragmentation has important implications for forest survival since, for complex reasons, small patches, even if not continuing to be affected by foraging for food and fuel, may not survive. Fragmentation also has major effects upon the larger animals such as elephants, especially top predators, such as tigers, as their feeding range is constricted.

These impacts have resulted in a huge range of vegetation types superimposed upon what was already a fairly complex situation before people really got to work to modify the distribution and characteristics of once omnipresent forest. Although the different vegetations have been

Figure 5.1 Forest types, 1990

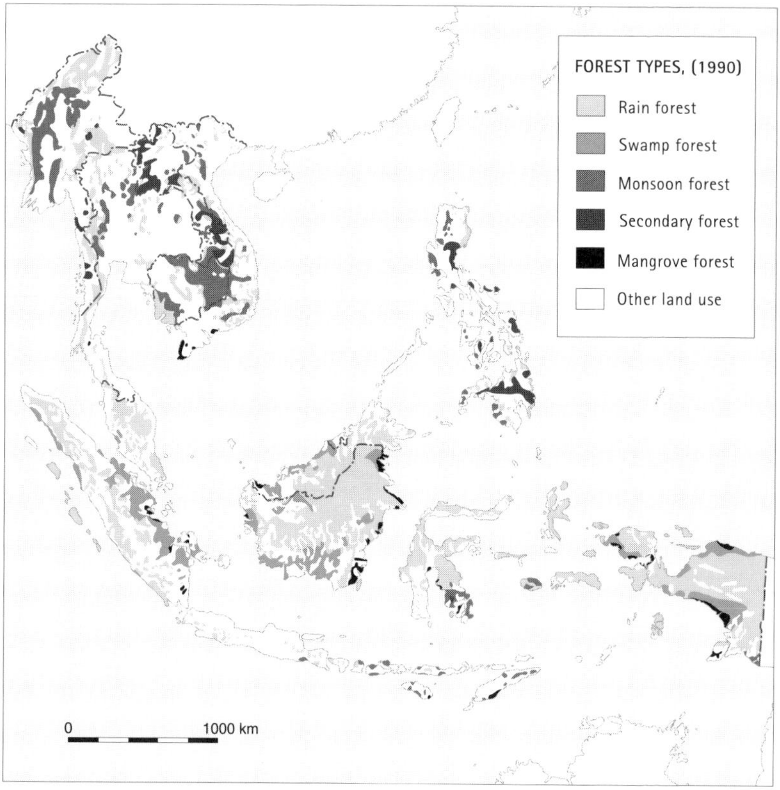

substantially modified by human activities it is still worth describing the 'modal'—or average—types as baselines with which to compare the others. Van Steenis, a famous Dutch biogeographer, recognised two major modal types: equatorial rainforest, otherwise known as humid tropical evergreen forest, and monsoonal forest, alias seasonally humid tropical (evergreen) forest. These occupy average free-draining soils, up to an elevation of about 500 m, given the lowland climates described earlier. To these some might add savanna, a mixture of grass and semi-deciduous trees, in areas with a marked dry season. Though such a naturally occurring type unquestionably existed in the past, any such surviving savanna is, on current knowledge, indistinguishable from that created by human activities.

Vegetations that diverge from these 'ideal types' do so for two main groups of reasons. First are the 'edaphic' reasons (from the Greek word *edaphos*, the ground). The basic reasons for differences from a modal type include slope angle (thus soil thickness and stability), drainage, soil structure, its chemical composition as this reflects rock decomposition (weathering) and the particular minerals present in the original rock.

On very steep slopes soils are thin, even absent. Trees are reduced in stature and only those with tough, wide-spreading roots survive. Many species of fig (genus *Ficus*) are examples. Where much water accumulates, dead plant material decays very slowly, in very wet montane environments forming a blanket of peat that may be a metre or two thick. Here *Sphagnum* moss thrives. Should water accumulate in lowland depressions to form swamps, peat may also form, sometimes 20 m thick and extending below present-day sea level. Such 'blackwater swamps'—so named because, like tea, the water is darkened by dissolved tannins—are highly acid and are occupied by distinctive plant and animal communities.

Where soils are very free-draining and poor in nutrients, as on old beach-ridges marking the former position of the shore on accreting coasts, other distinctive plant communities grow. The chemical composition of the soil is also influential. Limestone, as much as 98 per cent pure calcium carbonate, is a fairly common sedimentary rock in the region, sometimes weathering into fantastic peaks and towers clad in low forest with ramifying roots helping the very rock to hold together. Another well-known local example is the area of ultrabasic—highly alkaline—rocks on the tourist track to the summit of Kinabalu. This is dominated by tall *Leptospermum* scrub which probably would otherwise not exist at this location.

The second group of reasons concerns elevation. As was seen earlier, increasing elevation results in lower temperatures. In turn this reduces evaporation. Cloudiness increases. So does rainfall, at least up to a height of 3500 m or so. Slopes are steep. Soils are thin. Erosion may be greater than lower down and surely must be where the vegetation is cleared. Differences in elevation give rise to a zonation of the vegetation. This is reflected in two ways. With increasing elevation the vegetation becomes lower in stature. At next-to-highest levels grasses and herbaceous plants replace shrubs—such as *Rhododendron*—and trees. The phytomass falls from around 500–600 t ha^{-1} (tonnes per hectare) in lowland rainforests to perhaps just a few tens of kilograms where 'alpine' tundra and bare rock are intermingled. At the same time both the number and the kinds of species present is lower. Thus in the rainforests of the Malay Peninsula roughly 7600 species of flowering plants are present, with trees of the fairly large family called Dipterocarpaceae being dominant. Some of these may be 45 m tall. By contrast, no great distance away at 2000 m above sea level, the vegetation structure is quite different—basically a single layer of low trees of the heather family (Ericaceae) especially *Rhododendron* and *Vaccinium* species, only 10–12 m tall.

Finally, a third set of factors influencing the vegetation is that of human activities. There is scarcely any kind of vegetation that has not, somewhere in the region, been to some degree affected. Collectors gather plants for ornamental purposes. The British collector Kingdon Ward, for example, introduced scores of rhododendrons from the mountains of northern Myanmar to Britain, whence growers have spread them very widely. Other people gather orchids from the wild, for there is a lively trade in rarities, some of it illegal.

For many centuries fire has been set to clear forest for temporary or permanent cultivation and to encourage the growth of grasses to feed desirable wild game, in whose meat there is now also some trade. Tropical hardwoods are almost universally admired for their beauty as timber, but also for their relative cheapness when extracted using highly damaging mechanical methods.

It is doubtful whether many of the logged-over forests left to regenerate will ever become as they were previously, at least in terms of species composition, even though they may appear to be similar to unlogged forests. Where clear-felled, and if cutting and burning cease, forests may re-emerge, though quite unlike what was there before. Where cutting and burning continue any one of many other kinds of secondary vegetation follows, ranging from grassland to scrub and low forest, depending upon the intensity and kind of human impacts.

Multiply each modal type, each edaphic variant, and most montane types by human impacts of different kinds and intensities, including those of towns and cities, and the result is an almost bewildering array of different kinds of vegetation.

Major lowland vegetations

Though some writers identify many more, here only two broad modal types are recognised, though neither is by any means exactly the same throughout its extent. With each of them are six edaphic variants. Most occur at scales from roughly a few square kilometres up to some hundreds or even thousands. (An area of less than a few square kilometres could hardly be said to be unmodified, because the environmental effects of changes along a vegetation boundary penetrate some distance beyond the actual boundary. Singapore's tiny rainforest remnant at Bukit Timah is a case in point.) Rheophytic vegetation is rather different. This comprises the very distinctive communities in the usually ever-wet environment of the shores of lakes, the banks of streams and rivers and in the water-bodies themselves. The characteristics of these types are set out in Table 5.1, though unfortunately it is not possible to give data on the extent of each.

Rainforest

Rainforest is found in the wetter parts of the region where there is little seasonal drought. It was once thought that the periods during which individual trees flowered, set fruit, put out new leaves or shed them bore no relation to climate, which was assumed to be ever-wet. This lack of seasonal response was thought to be typified by the not-uncommon sight of one branch of a tree shedding leaves while another was putting out new growth. In fact there is a definite tendency for plants of the same species at the same location to do the same thing at the same time even though it is not always clear what triggers, for example, flowering of the prominent species of the Dipterocarp genus *Shorea*. Deciduousness, the shedding of leaves at about the same time, scarcely exists. The tree species are virtually all evergreen broadleafs.

Structurally the rainforest is complex. To look upwards from its floor is to see many different kinds of leaves and of branching patterns overlapping at various levels up to the topmost crowns (leaves and branches) of the highest trees, dividing the sky into a myriad irregularly shaped patches. Often these bits of clear sky are quite small, flecking the forest floor, moving with the sun but providing, overall, as little as 1/100th or 1/1000th of the amount of light compared with that arriving at the top of the forest canopy. This probably is why rather few plants occupy the floor. Those that do may be juveniles of potentially great trees growing extraordinarily slowly until perchance an old tree falls— opening a gap in the canopy, multiplying light intensities and promoting rapid plant growth. Others, thorny *Pandanus* species and *Calamus* palms, herbaceous plants—some species of swollen-stemmed Araceae, wild gingers, Zingiberaceae—see out their lives in the gloom of the forest floor.

The roof of the forest is irregular. Tall emergents, often species of Dipterocarpaceae such as *Shorea*, *Dryobalanops* and *Dipterocarpus*, rise above the general level, occasionally reaching 65 m, more usually about 45 m. Their crowns may be rounded or umbrella-shaped. Seen from above this leafy canopy looks to be substantially unbroken, for all the world like a layer of green cumulus clouds. Between the emergents and the ground layer all appears confusion and it is only by carefully measuring the trees that order emerges. Distinct layers can be observed, sometimes two or three, sometimes four or five. While each may contain a few 'youths' that will grow into a higher layer as they reach adulthood, mostly each layer contains a fairly distinct assemblage of species.

Thus the gutta percha tree, *Palaquium gutta*—famous because its dried latex was used to waterproof submarine cables and in golf balls—wild relatives of the nutmeg (*Myristica* spp.), of the rose-apple (*Eugenia* and *Zizyphus*), of figs (*Ficus*), of breadfruit (*Artocarpus*), of persimmon (*Diospyros*), some of the wild durians (*Durio*), wild mango (*Mangifera*),

Table 5.1 Major lowland vegetation types (not drastically modified)

	Rainfall distribution	Drainage	Other soil conditions	Topography
Modal types				
Rainforest	ever-wet	well-drained	diverse soils	flat or sloping
Monsoon	seasonal	well-drained	diverse soils	flat or sloping
Edaphic variants				
Beach vegetations	both	well-drained to very well-drained	sand or rock	on or behind beach
Mangrove	both	submerged	salt/brackish	tidal
Swamp forest	seasonal or ever-wet	submerged	fresh, eutrophic[1]	flat
Peat forest	ever-wet	submerged	fresh, oligotrophic[2]	flat, on peat
Heath forest	ever-wet	well-drained	acid podzols	flat, on sand
Rheophytic	mainly irrelevant	ever-wet	sand, gravel, rock	channels

Notes: [1] Eutrophic—rich in nutrients, weakly acid to basic in reaction.
[2] Oligotrophic—low in nutrients, highly acid.
Source: Partly after van Steenis

wild mangosteen (*Garcinia*), are all to be found in the intermediate layers of the rainforest. So too are tall palms such as the ferociously spiny *Oncosperma*.

Linking the various levels, from floor to roof are lianas, some as thick as ships' cables. These usually grow up with their host trees and may be 50 m or more long, linking several trees. When an old tree falls or if any are felled, it is common that others, linked by lianas, fall as well, so strong are these woody ties. Some lianas are the economically valuable rattans, especially the spiny palms *Calamus* and *Daemonorops*.

Another structural feature, found at all levels, are the stranglers, many of them *Ficus* species, partially or completely enveloping their hosts, and sometimes surviving them as independent trees as the host dies and rots away.

At every level too are to be found epiphytes—plants that grow on other plants—even epiphytes growing on other epiphytes. Many are light-seeded or propagated by spores, dispersed by wind. Some make their home on branches high in the canopy. Such include a host of orchids (Orchidae) and some ferns, such as the bird's-nest fern *Asplenium nidus* and the beautiful stag's-horn fern (*Platycerium* spp.). Less prominent are the shade epiphytes, mainly mosses and lichens; while on virtually every older leaf, on trunks and branches, there is a vigorous growth of fungi, yeasts and algae, especially blue-green ones (Cyanobacteria). Some of these are host-specific, growing only on one or a few species. The fungus *Nipicola* species, for instance, is confined to the common brackish-water palm *Nypa fruticans*.

Monsoonal forest

Monsoonal forest seen at the height of the wet season looks remarkably like equatorial rainforest. Look again in the dry season and its aspect is quite different. Yellows and browns of dying leaves are common and some trees may have no leaves at all. This is deciduousness and is what largely distinguishes the two modal types. With increasing length of the dry season the proportion of deciduous trees grows. The main deciduous genus *Kylia* is prominent. As might be expected, soil texture, and thus its moisture-holding characteristics, also influences which trees grow where. Thus in its natural home in mainland Southeast Asia teak (*Tectona grandis*), highly valued for furniture and flooring—once also for ship-building—is a more prominent forest component where the rainfall is in the 1000–2000 mm range. On free-draining sands dry teak forest occurs in areas with around 1900 mm annually, normally the home of moist teak forest. On clayey soils dry teak forest survives on around 1000 mm a year but not on sandy soils, where it is replaced by dry deciduous forest.

In terms of species composition the monsoonal forest is less rich than the equatorial rainforest, mostly averaging 40–60 species per hectare, slightly more on the wetter margins, slightly fewer on the dry side. This compares with 100–200 species per hectare in the wet rainforest. Dipterocarpaceae are still present though represented by fewer species; thus in Thai monsoonal forests there are only 30 and in Java only 10. With teak, they are important timber trees, but whereas in the equatorial rainforest there is no tendency for one or two species to predominate, in the monsoonal forest they tend to do so. At Korat, for example, 40 per cent of the forest trees are either *Memecylon* species (family Melastomaceae) or *Hopea ferrea*, a Dipterocarp. Bamboos, absent from the rainforest, are common and where fire burns the undergrowth, grasses, a rare occurrence in rainforest, may be prominent, probably in part because light intensities are higher under the more open canopy of monsoonal forest.

Structurally, monsoonal forests are also different. Total phytomass is about half that of equatorial forest. Trees are not quite so high and their trunks are more slender (see Table 5.2). Two or three layers rather than up to five are characteristic, the upper canopy being markedly discontin-uous except in wetter areas. The ground layer is usually very dense, though

Table 5.2 Comparison of tree heights and girths, Singapore (equatorial) and Korat (monsoonal) (per cent)

Height (m) class	Singapore	Korat	Girth (cm) class	Singapore	Korat
<10	67	42	<10	44	54
10–15	15	42	10–20	29	31
16–23	5	10	21–50	14	10
24–35	9	7	51–100	9	5
>35	5	–	>100	4	–
	101	101		100	100

Source: Data from surveys by Hill, Tem Smitinand and others

in silviculturally managed forests it is kept fairly clear. Epiphytes are still abundant, as are lianas, but trees with buttress roots are rare.

Like equatorial forest, monsoonal lowland forest is by no means the same everywhere. On the mainland teak is a major component in Myanmar and northern Thailand, with a minor extension into Cambodia. Further east teak drops out of the species list and two Dipterocarps, *Hopea pierri* and *Parashorea stellata* become prominent. North of about 13°N winter cold begins to take effect and mid-latitude trees such as pines begin to intrude, especially at some elevation and after disturbance. Forest still is predominantly broadleaf in the lowlands, still tall—up to 30 m—still tropical in appearance, with many lianas and epiphytes. At altitude native pines come in, *Pinus merkusii, P. khaysia* in the west and *Pinus massoniana* in the east.

The monsoonal forest in the eastern islands of the Indonesian archipelago is little known. Parts of it may have been subject to human impact for upwards of 60 000 years. Archaeological evidence suggests that some of these islands were stepping stones settled by the ancestors of today's Australian Aborigines. It seems unlikely that they left the vegetation entirely untouched, possibly setting fire to forest to open it out in favour of grazing animals which they then hunted.

Certainly from east Java eastwards, where rainfall is only moderate and there are at least three dry months, the Dipterocarps characteristic of the forests further west give way to deciduous trees of the Leguminoseae—the pea and bean family—together with teak. (In the twentieth century the area occupied by teak has been extended by afforestation.) Thus of the 26 species of major dominant trees said by Whitmore to be typical of the eastern monsoon forest, 11 are leguminous. Australian species are also present, most strongly represented south of the central ranges of West Irian. *Eucalyptus alba* reaches central Flores. *Casuarina junghuniana* grows as far west as east Java, though this is a montane or submontane species rather than a lowland one, as well as being characteristic of burnt-over lands above 1400 m.

Other 'Australians' include *Banksia* and *Eucalyptus* species. Some kinds of drought-adapted trees occur only in this region, while yet others have close relatives in mainland Southeast Asia though separated from them by the true rainforest. Some writers suggest that both such groups may be remnants from the Pleistocene era when climates were drier, split apart by expanding rainforests.

Spatially, the patterns of 'modal' lowland forests are complex, not least because of sustained human impacts. Mainland Southeast Asia is basically monsoonal forest with some ever-wet rainforest (not really 'equatorial') along the very wet Arakan coast. Around the Isthmus of Kra there is a transition southwards to truly equatorial rainforest marked by more species and by more Dipterocarps, the genera *Shorea* and *Parashorea* especially. In the western Philippines another similar transition occurs: in the west of Luzon and Mindanao, monsoonal forest; in the wetter east, rainforest. Rainforest once occupied the lowlands of the whole of Sumatera, the Malay Peninsula south of the Isthmus of Kra, the island of Borneo except for a small drier area around Banjermasin in the southeast, and much of West Irian. The islands of Nusatenggara form the core of the eastern limb of monsoonal forest. Between this and the equatorial rainforest is a highly complex interfingering of both types, reflecting local rainfall regimes, often on a scale of a few tens of kilometres, if that.

Lowland edaphic variants

These may be distinguished from modal types by the overwhelming importance of soil factors—very wet, highly organic, very free-draining, strongly acidic, salty or brackish. These are quite distinct from montane vegetations, for they occur in the lowlands. The differences among them are not to be explained by increasing elevation and decreasing temperature but by what they grow in.

Mangroves

Mangroves grow in salty and brackish water where mud rather than sand is the usual substrate. Mangrove zones vary in extent from a belt a few metres wide to great forests tens of kilometres across, flanking the estuaries and coasts of most prograding low-energy coasts except where people get in first and develop them for agriculture. Since the degree of salt-tolerance varies amongst the component species, there is usually some degree of zonation reflecting this. Each zone is usually dominated by a single species. Thus on the west coast of Peninsular Malaysia for example,

Avicennia species occupy the saltiest outermost zone, actively colonising newly deposited mud. Inland from this are the slightly less salt-tolerant *Rhizophora* species, easily identified by their stilt roots, coping with daily submergence at high tide. Inland again lies *Bruguiera cylindrica*, with very slight buttresses at the base of the trunk, its roots and lower trunk capable of surviving monthly submergence at high water. Inland again the mud is to some degree consolidated, brackish rather than salty. Here are trees such as *Intsia* and *Xylocarpus* and the stemless palm *Nypa frutescens* whose fronds make durable thatch and whose preserved fruits form part of the famous ice 'kacang' dessert. Here too is the undergrowth fern *Acrosticum* whose young leaves make a tasty green vegetable. Further towards freshwater conditions rainforest occurs where the alluvial soils are reasonably well drained or freshwater swamp forest where they are not, the transition in this case often being marked by an abundance of the horribly spiny *Oncosperma* palm, often cut to make piles for fish-traps in coastal waters.

Beach vegetations

Beach vegetations are found on high-energy coasts throughout the region. They may be divided into two basic kinds: those growing on sandy substrates and those on rocks. Both environments are affected by sea salt blown inland from breaking waves and during storms by waves themselves. Further inland from active beaches other types may be distinguished.

Above the high tide mark creeping plants such the leguminous beach morning glory, *Ipomoea pes-caprae*, and spinifex grass, *Spinifex littoreus*, quickly colonise the hostile environment of bare, unstable sand. Within a few metres landward this may give way to broadleaf shrubs such as *Vitex* and *Hibiscus* species, *Barringtonia* trees and the ever-useful screw-pine *Pandanus* whose pineapple-like fruits and very young leaves may be eaten and its gently fragrant older leaves used for matting. Where sandy shores are rapidly prograding seaward, the pioneer plant is often the beefwood tree, *Casuarina equisetifolia* growing in almost-pure stands, a feature highly unusual in tropic climes. On rocky shores shrubs and screw-pines (*Pandanus* spp.) also grow, sometimes with scattered casuarinas as well but since such shores are steep they usually quickly give way to more or less modal forest. Unlike the modal types, though, the structure and composition of the beach vegetation is broadly similar throughout the region. Where cleared the characteristic 'tree' is the salt-tolerant coconut palm, joined in recent decades by the similarly tolerant cashew-nut tree *Anacardium occidentale*, an introduction from America.

Beaches are not necessarily active. In many lowland parts of the region sand-ridges and sand-flats mark old shorelines, some reflecting a higher sea level several thousand years ago. Their soils are notably free-draining and very poor in nutrients. Consequently, like modern beaches, they carry a distinctive tree vegetation. Where the soils are not totally impoverished broadleafed forest 10–25 m tall with three distinct layers is usual though in equatorial regions representing far fewer species, around 50 per hectare, compared with around 100–200 per hectare in rainforest nearby. Particular *Shorea* species are notable. Where the soil is extremely deficient in nutrients trees are stunted and spindly. Those of Sarawak are notable floristically in being primitive conifers, *Agathis alba* and *Dacrydium elatum*, prominent components in a vegetation containing notably few species. A similar but more seasonal environment occurs in the sand-hill complex of coastal Viet Nam. There the beefwood, *Casuarina equisetifolia*, is prominent along with patches of broadleaf scrub.

Swamp forests

Swamp forests form another distinctive habitat, one confined entirely to equatorial areas with impeded drainage and at least 2000 mm of rain yearly. Most are peaty. Peat characteristically forms inland from the mangrove under completely waterlogged but fresh rather than salty or brackish conditions. The water is low in nutrients, rich in tannins dissolved from the slowly rotting forest litter, and extremely acid (pH about 1.5 to 3.0). A steel tool put into peat and withdrawn rusts in about 20 seconds. Cloth or leather boots may last a week. The island of Borneo, West Irian and eastern Sumatera have many tens of thousands of square kilometres of this type of land. This may be occupied by mixed species forest rather like the heath forests or by forests with a single dominant species. The former are rather distinct but in Sarawak *Shorea albida* occurs in both peat and heath forests. Undergrowth may be extremely dense and where dominated by the stemless palm *Calamus*, which is well equipped with vicious recurved barbs, is penetrable with great difficulty.

Swamps are not necessarily salty or peaty and nutrient-deficient. Some are nutrient-rich (eutrophic) supporting forest 30–50 m tall, though there is some tendency for the trunks of its component trees to be more slender than in modal rainforest. In seasonally dry swamps, as around the Tonlé Sap in Cambodia, stature is less and the number of species much fewer, as submergence may be both deep and prolonged. The species composition in eutrophic swamps varies considerably from place to place, probably reflecting variation in the depth, duration and frequency of flooding. Dipterocarps are still dominant but not necessarily the same ones as in modal rainforests, most *Shorea* species, for example, being absent, along with most species of *Hopea* and *Vatica*. Palms often predominate in the ground layer: *Licuala, Livistona, Pinanga* and the ferociously-hooked *Calamus*. Grasses, sedges and herbaceous plants may also occur in some eutrophic swamps, as around the Tonlé Sap. But overall the number of species is substantially fewer than in the modal types. In many parts of the region the extent of eutrophic swamps is now much less than formerly because they make good rice land except where deeply flooded for long periods.

Rheophytes

Rheophytes are plants that grow in or near running water. They thus reflect a highly specialised environment, one in which periodical flooding, certainly wetness, is ever-present. They do not grow in soil but on sand, gravel, boulders, or in crevices. Plants are low shrubs or herbs. Many are not flowering plants at all but algae, lichens and other lower forms of plant life. Some, relieved of the force of gravity by living in water, are delicately membranous or filamentous. Many of the higher plants have wide-spreading root networks to seek out nutrients and to anchor them in place. Many are locally endemic, found nowhere else, because dryness is anathema and dry habitats hinder spread from one catchment to another. One family, the Podostemaceae, is found only in this tropical habitat. This vegetation type is very distinctive, containing no conifers, no bamboos, no lianas, no tree-ferns but many other ferns, a few screw-pines (*Pandanus*) and a few palms.

Plants in the mountains

In the lowlands the effects of climatic variation upon the vegetation are by no means easily discerned. Variation in moisture explains much of the variation in mature vegetation with latitude. Temperature comes into play to a limited degree. On mountains it is very much the other way around. They are much cooler, usually cloudier, thus reducing evaporation and increasing wetness. They are also wetter anyway as mountains cause humid air to rise, condense, and fall as rain. They are often the home of highly distinctive plant species, for they are continuous only over relatively short distances. In a sense they form isolated 'islands' from which plant dispersal is difficult because the intervening lowland is environmentally unsuitable. For example, on Gunung Kinabalu nearly 4000 species of flowering plants have been found in an area of only 700 km^2. This extraordinary diversity probably results from a combination of factors: great temperature range (33°C during the heat of the day in the lowlands, sometimes freezing at night on the summit), steep topography that may isolate species over short distances, locally diverse geology, and considerable year-to-year climatic variation, especially in rainfall.

Not all mountains are so high or so isolated, of course, so that major ranges have greater uniformity over longer distances. Nevertheless, all have considerable diversity, possibly as a result of rapid speciation. All show zonation of species and of structure, and all have reduced phytomass and stature with greater elevation. Not all vertical zonation, though, can be easily explained by reduction of temperature with height, especially when particular plant families and species are concerned. For example recent work on Dipterocarps in Sumatera shows that some are strictly confined to areas below 150–200 m, while others extend up to around 400 m. This is well known within the lowland forest of course and just why such overlapping zonation occurs is simply unknown.

Submontane forest

Lowland forest is generally considered to give way to submontane forest at about 800–900 m, lower on isolated hills, in humid rainforest areas. Further north, possibly as a result of lower winter-time temperatures, this transition zone—it is certainly not a sharp boundary—occurs rather lower. In the equatorial parts of the region submontane forest continues upwards to about 1300–1400 m where another transition—to montane forest—occurs.

In the equatorial submontane zone, trees are less tall and slimmer than in the lowlands, the tallest rarely being more than about 25 m high. Structurally, though, there are considerable similarities, with four distinct layers: 20–30 m, 15–20 m, 8–15 m and a ground layer up to about 2 m, often with many climbing rattans and stemless palms, especially *Arenga* and *Licuala* species. Floristically there are fewer species. A few Dipterocarp species may still be present, notably *Shorea platyclados*, which in Sumatera grows from a low of 400 or 500 m above sea level up to 1400 m. Towards the upper transition zone of the submontane forest a few so-called 'temperate' genera may appear—oaks and chestnuts, the family Fagaceae, the primitive conifers *Agathis* and *Dacrydium*. In the western and central parts of mainland Southeast Asia true pines, *Pinus merkusii* and *P. khaysia* mark submontane forest which still contains broadleafs such as *Quercus* and *Castanopsis* (Fagaceae) and beautiful *Magnolia* and *Gardenia* species. Further east, where the mountains are cooler for longer and are drier, the forests above 700–800 m are rather different. As at higher altitudes nearer the equator, they contain distant relatives of conifers, but different ones—*Podocarpus cupressina* and *Fokienia hodginsii*. These are mixed with genuinely temperate trees—alder (*Alnus*), ash (*Fraxinus*), maple (*Acer*)—as well as truly temperate oaks (*Quercus*) and chestnuts (*Castanopsis*).

Montane forests

Montane forests in the equatorial parts of the region begin at around 1400 m and extend up to about 1800 or 1900 m. Stature of the tallest trees reaches 20–30 m and these form a continuous upper layer. This and the intermediate layer below it at 8–15 m, are made up mainly of tropical oaks and chestnuts with many species of laurels (Lauraceae) and some myrtles (Myrtaceae). This is a very damp and cloudy zone and the ground, tree trunks and branches are smothered with a great variety of ferns, orchids and other herbaceous plants. Tree-ferns, especially *Cyathea* and *Dicksonia* species, are common, particularly where there has been some disturbance. Where the soil is free-draining or low in nutrients, primitive conifers—*Agathis alba*, the same as in lowland heath forests, *Dacrydium* and *Podocarpus* species—occur, the same genera as in far-away New Zealand's rainforests.

Above 1800–2000 m the character of the equatorial forests changes again. Few trees grow above 10 m in stature and 5 m is more usual. Below the trees grow shrubs and the ground, trunks and branches are carpeted and festooned with mosses and herbaceous plants. The tree layer contains rather few species, some of them of the heather family (Ericaceae), such as *Vaccinium* and *Rhododendron*. Myrtles also occur, including mountain *Syzygium* species and, especially on difficult substrates, *Leptospermum*, the aromatic tea-tree, another plant with close kin in Australia and New Zealand where its leaves were once brewed into a substitute for real tea.

Higher zones

Above 2400–2500 m the equatorial vegetation changes yet again. (Some writers call this the 'tropical subalpine' zone, a term best avoided since only Europe really has 'alps' and the grasslands that begin to appear at this height are not like those of Europe.) Plants of the Erica family thin out though some Rhododendrons survive. Grasses and low herbaceous plants become important, being most extensive in the mountains of northern Myanmar, where they may be grazed by herds of yak, and in the mountains of West Irian where they are not used at all. Even higher up, at around 4500 m, the snowline occurs—rather lower in northern Myanmar—and only a few species of hardy snow-patch plants, lichens and algae survive.

Variation

Variation in altitudinal zonation is very considerable, even within the equatorial parts of Southeast Asia. The descriptions just given would apply generally in the wetter parts, on large islands and ranges. In particular the species composition varies significantly from place to place, a reflection not only of a great variety of habitats but also of the fact that mountains in many ways resemble islands separated from each other not by salt water but by a 'sea' of environmentally hostile lowland across which seed dispersal can take place only with difficulty, for instance by birds. This is illustrated by the cases of two nearby mountains, Gunung Kobipoto and Gunung Binaia in the Manusela National Park, Seram. On the former, at 1000 m *Lithocarpus* (oak family—Fagaceae) and *Weinmannia* species make up 43 and 11 per cent respectively (by basal area) of the trees. On Gunung Binaia, at 1060 m *Aglaia gongo* accounts for 28 per cent, with *Syzygium* (myrtle family, Myrtaceae) species totalling another 21 per cent.

Nevertheless, some generalisations can be made. As on difficult substrates in the lowlands—acid, nutrient-depleted—tree height and total phytomass are reduced with increasing elevation. So are the numbers of tree species and probably other plant species as well. On the other hand, because of the great variety of environmental niches over short distances in the mountains and because of the 'island effect' just described, when measured at the scale of hundreds of square kilometres, mountain vegetations are very rich in species. How rich is not really known, because on few—Kinabalu is one—has collecting been sustained and wide-ranging. There is certainly much yet to be discovered.

Animals in the forest

William Blake's 'tiger, tiger burning bright' could have wandered anywhere in the forests of a large region that includes India, the whole of mainland Southeast Asia, southern China, the Malay peninsula and the large western islands of the archipelago. This is the Oriental or Indomalayan zoogeographical region. To camp in a forest in Peninsular Malaysia might be to hear the spine-tingling night-time cough of a hunting tiger, an elephant's trumpet, the squeak of bats. One might see wild cats, dogs, pigs, cattle, porcupines, civets, monkeys, gibbons, tree shrews, lorises; a wide variety of snakes—including cobras, king cobras, pythons; and of amphibians and other reptiles—crocodiles, lizards large (the monitors, *Varanus* spp.) and lizards small, like the cosmopolitan geckos, inhabitants of every dwelling. Every one of these might equally be encountered in forest remnants in India, though most have long since disappeared from southern China.

Just a few of these kinds of animals are found exclusively in this Malayan region. One is the extraordinary flying lemur (colugo), notable not so much because it can 'fly'—it can only glide—but because its genus, *Cynocephalus*, forms, on its own, the family Cynocephalidae which in turn forms, on its own, the order Dermoptera. In a word, it is way out on its own, very slender evolutionary branch. Another interesting mammal is the large, mostly mangrove-dwelling proboscis monkey, *Presbytes nasalis*, which looks exactly as its name, 'old man with the nose', suggests.

Australian animals are represented in the eastern part of insular Southeast Asia. Here, notably, are marsupial rather than placental mammals, including kangaroos and a number of opossums, cuscus and phalangers. Here too are typically Australian groups of birds: cockatoos, parakeets and birds of paradise of plumage so gorgeous that they were once notable trade items. (They were also thought by reputable European scientists never to stop flying, for they had no feet! In fact traders cut them off before sale and the scientists for long saw only dead birds.) Very widespread are the honey-suckers which live in area extending from Sulawesi and Lombok through Australia and out into the Pacific as far as the Marquesas and New Zealand.

Zoogeographical boundaries

Traditionally, zoogeographers, starting with Alfred Russell Wallace in 1863, have tried to draw boundaries between the Oriental fauna in mainland Southeast Asia and the western islands of the archipelago and the Australian fauna of New Guinea and the eastern islands of the archipelago (Figure 5.2). Wallace himself was astonished by the differences in the bird faunas of Bali and nearby Lombok. Subsequent collecting, mainly of birds, and further research led him to separate Oriental and Australian faunas with a line, now called after him, running between those two islands, between Borneo and Sulawesi and south of Mindanao. Later another line, Weber's, was drawn, mainly on the basis of molluscan and mammalian faunas, to delimit Australian elements. This skirted Halmahera and the Moluccas on the west, separating the Kei islands and Timor. Thus was left a sort of zoogeographical 'no-man's-land' between the two.

Perhaps coincidentally, these two lines more or less mark off Sundaland in the west and the Sahel Shelf in the east, both dry land during the Pleistocene Ice Ages. Java, Sumatera and Borneo, once contiguous with the mainland, thus have a mainly Oriental fauna—though Borneo lacks elephants of indigenous origin. New Guinea, the Moluccas, the Kei and Aru islands have a mainly Australian fauna. The bits in between include some fairly large islands—Sulawesi, Flores, Lombok, Timor. Many may have been under the sea for some of the Tertiary and Pleistocene eras, emerging as independent land masses not previously connected to either zoogeographical realm. They therefore have highly distinctive faunas. Sulawesi has few indigenous mammals, few amphibians and remarkably few freshwater fish. Notable are a dwarf buffalo and a now-extinct dwarf elephant.

But the islands between Wallace's and Weber's Lines, a transitional region sometimes called Wallacea after the great 'A.R.', is not the only part of Southeast Asia to have distinctive assemblages of animals. During the last Ice Age the Philippines were joined to Sundaland only by a narrow land bridge running through the island of Palawan to Borneo. Everywhere else was deep water. Probably for this reason many groups of Oriental

Figure 5.2 Wallace's and Weber's lines

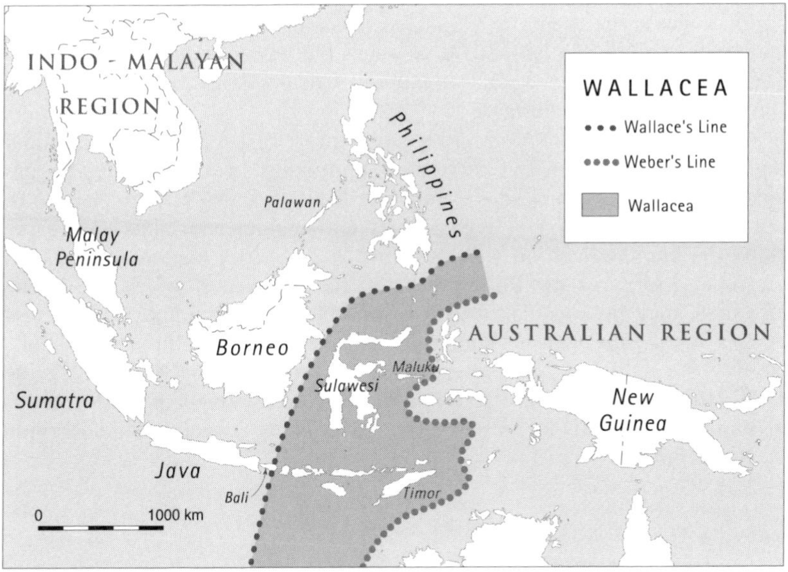

animals were filtered out, never reaching the Philippines archipelago, so, as Wallace himself noted, this island group is truly insular whereas Java and Borneo are really continental. He recorded just 13 or 14 species of mammals, probably just one monkey, a macaque, one tarsier, two shrews, two carnivores (and no big ones like tiger or leopard), five ungulates, three of them deer (*Cervus*), and two species of rodents. By contrast he recorded 24 species of bats in 17 genera. Clearly the fliers outpaced the walkers. There would thus be good grounds for regarding the Philippines, if not as a part of Wallacea then as a distinctive impoverished part of the Indomalayan zoogeographical region, at least as far as mammals are concerned.

Mammals

Mammals and their distribution are fairly well known though new discoveries occasionally occur. In the 1990s, for example, five 'new' species were discovered or rediscovered in Viet Nam: three deer, an ox (*Pseudoryx* sp.) and a pig (*Sus bucculentas*). Mainland Southeast Asia forms a single sub-unit within Indomalaya but contains rather few distinctive endemic species. Its western boundary extends beyond Myanmar to the Brahmaputra River while its narrow southern boundary, the Kra Isthmus, coincides with distinct climatic and vegetational limits. Northwards is a broad transition, in the west to the distinctive animals of the Himalayan region—one is the domestic yak—and in the east to temperate Palaearctic mammals such as the badger (*Meles*) and the mouse (*Apodemus*), though Southeast Asian species such as the *muncak* deer (*Muntiacus*) and the civet (*Vivervia*) are fairly common.

Insular Southeast Asia comprises three distinct zoogeographical regions, each of which can be further subdivided. In the west lies Sundaland. All of its major units—Peninsular Malaysia, the Mentawei islands, Sumatera, Java, Borneo—have distinctive assemblages of mammals, especially the Mentawei group west of Sumatera, probably longer isolated than the others. Most of the Philippines, except Palawan which has Bornean affinities, may be considered as a distinctive, faunally-impoverished part of the Wallacean region. Wallacea includes some Australian elements, notably the phalanger *Ailurops* and cuscus *Stigocuscus*. To the east, the small islands of Weigeo, Misool and the Aru Archipelago, at least in terms of mammals, belong to the strongly 'Australian' zoogeographical region of New Guinea.

Conclusion

But what of other animal groups, the Insecta, for example? The region is home to an enormous array, as yet very imperfectly known, outside perhaps the moths and butterflies. Many of these are spectacularly beautiful and the group as a whole is moderately well known. Not so most other groups—the flies (Diptera), the springtails (Colembola), the wasps (Vespidae), the ants (Formicidae) and scores of others. Do they, like mammals and birds, fall into distinct Oriental and Australian assemblages?

No one really knows much about the distribution of animals in relation to plants. Obviously honey-sucking birds are adapted to the many species of plants, mainly Australian, upon which they feed. The fact that a number of forest trees—the genus *Durio* is one—depend upon fruit-bats to fertilise their flowers suggests a long mutual relationship.

It is, perhaps, only in extreme environments that clear relationships can be seen between vegetation (and soil) on one hand and animals on the other. Earlier it was suggested that peat swamps are one such habitat. The water is dark with dissolved tannins from the wood, highly acid, rich in sulphate, very low in primary producers. In it live distinctive fish communities, each being characteristic of more or less acid water in much the same way as distinctive kinds of mangrove live in water to greater or less degree salty. Many members of these communities live nowhere else. Some are highly specialised. A survey of fish in a blackwater swamp in western Peninsular Malaysia showed that 22 out of 47 species were air breathers, a clearly advantageous adaptation to this extreme habitat.

What can certainly be said of animals and plants is that in all kinds of tropical forests the zoomass—the mass of animals—at least of the higher animals such as mammals, reptiles, amphibians and so forth, is very much lower than the phytomass. The main reason for this is that most of the phytomass is wood, an admirable food for the great abundance of termites and wood-borers, but highly indigestible to others. By contrast, savanna and grassland provide digestible food for many grazing animals, the ungulates especially deer (*Cervus, Muntiacus* spp.), pigs (*Sus* spp.) and cattle (*Bos* spp.). Consequently such areas carry more animals. As was noted earlier, people have long exploited this fact, using clearance and fire to reduce the proportion of woody vegetation, to increase the grasses and herbaceous plants and thus also the animal population whether wild or domesticated.

Secondary vegetations, deforestation, timber

Secondary vegetations come into existence when people modify a 'natural' vegetation by clearing, by burning or, to a lesser degree, by collecting. Just what a 'natural' vegetation might be is a matter of some debate since in some parts of the region people have lived for tens of thousands of years, attacking local vegetation with axe and fire. One particular area of debate is the degree to which prehistoric peoples used fire to create and maintain grasslands which supported grazing animals in greater number and quantity than forest. It is fairly clear that during the last Ice Age the climate was cooler and drier than it is now, especially in the monsoonal parts of the region. In such places grass and scattered woodland probably arose naturally in response to these climatic conditions, with the woodland occupying damper sites such as backswamps and other areas with heavy soils.

It is also possible that during severe droughts standing forest dried out sufficiently to carry fire. Whether this actually resulted in a change from forest to grassland is not known but it seems likely that in some places it did although continued burning would probably have been necessary to maintain it. Where lands were 'sterilised' by volcanic ash and lava, ferns and grasses—being light-seeded—would have been early colonisers. Some of today's grasslands and savannas may thus owe their existence to past climatic change, to volcanic eruptions and to deliberate burning.

Clearing and burning for agriculture came later, perhaps 6000 years ago, though the areas initially affected would have been very small. Growing food crops on sloping land, an activity in which clearing and burning occur in a more or less regular cycle, probably came somewhat later than the earliest semi-permanent forms of cultivation. But this shifting cultivation steadily increased the areas of secondary vegetation at the expense of primary types.

But which types and where? Forests along inhabited coasts—mostly sandy ones—along major rivers and on well-drained lowland soils where there was a reliable supply of clean water were probably prime candidates for initial clearance. In the lowlands neither swamp forests nor the mangrove would have been cleared and burnt in early times, being both difficult to burn and lacking clean, fresh water for settlers. Indeed it was only in the colonial era that many of the heavily forested, low-lying parts of the major deltas were cleared and settled, and some, notably in Borneo and West Irian, still have not been. The great civilisations—Burman, Mon, Thai, Khmer, Vietnamese, Javanese—arose in the upper deltas and basins, not in lower deltas and swamps though small ports, involving limited forest clearance, certainly existed. Oc-Eo on the lower Mekong is one; Kuala Kedah in western Peninsular Malaysia is another. Montane forests, equally, have generally been little modified.

These speculations are not entirely unsupported, for profiles of pollens trapped in swamps and lakes show changes from tree pollens to grass pollens and sometimes back again. What is clear is that vegetation change is extremely uneven in space and time. The submergence of the remains of whole civilisations in regrown forest, the existence of 'lost cities' complete with now-forested rice-fields are not myths. Considerable regions not known to have been inhabited may bear evidence of past fires, perhaps set deliberately as few fires are known to originate naturally (for instance as a result of lightning strikes).

Clearance, burning, regeneration

In turning to the processes of clearance, burning and regeneration more solid ground is reached. Large-scale clearance is clearly a matter of the last 150 years or so in most of the region, in some parts earlier, in others later as Peter Boomgard's data show (Table 5.3).

As was noted in chapter 2, the population 400 years ago was generally small, though where there were concentrations based upon rice cultivation it was moderately dense. Even in and around such concentrations it seems likely that patches of forest and savanna were maintained. Rulers kept large areas for royal hunts. Villagers kept reserves of land for future cultivation and for foraging. Forests were the source of useful commodities—timber for houses, fungi for food and medicine, sweet-smelling woods, gums and resins, poisons, a host of 'medicinal' substances. Some were of plant origin—camphor, dragon's blood (*Daemonorops, Dracaena*), benzoin (*Styrax*), sandalwood (*Santalum*), eagle-wood (*Aquilaria*), *Derris* for stunning fish, *Antiaris* for killing mammals, including people. Others came from forest and savanna-dwelling animals—tiger bones, tiger whis-

Table 5.3 Estimated proportion of forest cover by region, selected years

Region	Year	Cover (%)
Indonesia outside Java	1941	69
Java	1985	27
Philippines	1900	65–70
	1937	58
Peninsular Malaysia	1960	85
Myanmar	1940	56
Indochina	1950	47
Thailand	1930	70
SE Asia	*c.*1940	62

Source: P. Boomgard, 1996

kers, snake and bear gall. Some were consumed locally. Others were traded locally and abroad especially to China which imported scores of substances for its extensive pharmacopoeia. Forests prevailed. Even at the beginning of the twentieth century Thailand, for example, is thought to have been more than 90 per cent forest-covered.

Clearance without burning is a very recent phenomenon and is confined to limited areas in which secondary forest is totally harvested for wood-chips used in pulp and paper manufacture. Burning without clearance is generally confined to already-existing secondary grass, scrub and savanna woodland. Since most indigenous grasses, such as the widespread *Imperata* species, are rather unpalatable to grazing animals when mature, the deliberate late dry-season burning of grasslands and savannas in order to promote fresh young growth for cattle is widespread. At this time of the year fire can easily escape from controlled burns aimed at clearing vegetation for subsistence shifting cultivation or at the extension of tree-crop plantations, but usually only where the nearby lands are already in secondary vegetation.

Most secondary vegetations arise from cutting followed by burning. What happens over the next few years is crucial to the kind of vegetation that regenerates. Where a couple of annual crops are taken from a small forest clearing, quick-growing trees and herbaceous plants combine with vigorous regrowth from stumps to form dense scrub or low forest two or three metres high within a year or two. The particular regenerating and colonising plants depend in part on what was there before—many species coppice freely—upon seed-sources nearby and on the regional vegetation type. In Peninsular Malaysia, for example, common components of secondary forest—true jungle—include species of *Macaranga, Trema, Melastoma*, the prickly climber *Smilax*, the wild banana, *Musa*. Open patches, especially where the soil is poor, are colonised by grass, especially *Imperata*, fern, creepers such as *Mikania* and the daisy *Eupatorium odoratum*, the last a relative newcomer from mainland Southeast Asia. But where such patches are small and provided that there is no further disturbance, such herbaceous plants are eventually supplanted by woody species.

Woody colonisers are not necessarily components of a mature broad-leafed vegetation. For example, in the uplands of central Luzon, past clearance has been so extensive that the main forest tree is a pine—*Pinus insularis*—and it is this that occupies cleared areas rather than the broad-leaved submontane forest which was clearly the original type. Where cleared and burnt land is left to itself for long periods, a more or less stable forest probably re-establishes itself, though in terms of its species composition it is doubtful if it ever becomes what was there before, if that were primary forest.

When, as is usual these days, further cycles of clearance and burning follow the initial onslaught, major, more or less permanent changes take place, mostly away from woody species, though a few such—*Macaranga* and *Melastoma* are examples—can, seemingly, survive many cycles. This is especially true where forest remnants are far distant from secondary vegetations, because substantial numbers of the seeds of forest species are dispersed by gravity or by animals. Moreover, very few true forest species can survive and compete successfully with the plants of the open, sunny, drier environment of cleared land. There grasses dominate: 'cogon' (*Imperata* spp.), *Arundinella*, *Arundo* and many others; bracken fern, in mainland Southeast Asia mainly *Dicranopteris* species; a wide range of herbaceous plants; and a few hardy scrub species such as *Melastoma* just mentioned. These are highly inflammable during the dry season but grow quickly after rain, some (such as *Dicranopteris* and *Imperata*) drawing upon their own carbohydrates stored in underground organs to make a quick recovery.

But clearance and burning are only part of human impacts upon the various kinds of vegetation. Viet Nam, for example, had defoliants sprayed over a tenth of its inland forests and a third of its mangroves in the late 1960s. The effects on inland forests were similar to repeated timber harvesting and cycles of shifting cultivation, while mangrove areas remained bare for years and recovery has been slow.

Logging

Logging has been of far greater importance. Not only have the areas logged increased very rapidly, but so has the intensity of logging. In addition, the replacement of traditional methods of timber extraction, which employed human and animal labour—elephants and buffaloes—by

Table 5.4 Thailand: changes in forest area, selected years, 1900–98

Year	Forests (million ha)	% of the total land area	Deforestation rate (% yr)
1900	46+	90+	–0.73
1948	32.43	63.2	–0.19
1953	32.13	63.6	–1.99
1961	27.36	53.3	–1.74
1973	22.17	43.2	–3.63
1976	19.84	38.7	–6.03
1978	17.52	34.1	–2.77
1982	15.66	30.5	–1.24
1985	15.09	29.4	–1.59
1989	14.34	27.9	–2.37
1991	13.67	26.6	–1.16
1993	13.36	26.0	–0.77
1995	13.15	25.6	–0.77
1996	13.05	25.4	–0.77
1998	12.85	25.0	–0.77

Source: UN, *Common Country Assessment of Thailand, 1999*

heavy machinery has vastly increased collateral damage. In the years before the Second World War logging was highly selective. In equatorial forests only one or two trees per hectare were extracted as only a few species, mainly Dipterocarps such as *Shorea,* were valuable. Very large specimens were often left standing because of the difficulty of moving them. Teak forests had a rather higher proportion of extractable logs but by the 1930s these were generally harvested on a managed, sustainable basis. Since the 1960s the global demand for tropical hardwoods has increased substantially, resulting in an increase in the number of millable species as well as large increases in the areas logged. The result was declining forest, as Table 5.4 shows for Thailand.

As Table 5.5 for the whole region shows, the amount of forest remaining in 1980 further decreased rapidly by 1995, especially in the Philippines and Thailand where less than a quarter of their total area is now forested. Much of what remains is poor quality forest in areas too remote to log economically, though it remains as valuable protection for catchment areas. Much also, though technically 'forest', has been logged at least once. Since the most valuable timber trees have gone, it is doubtful that these can ever regenerate naturally as no attempts were made to retain at least some of them as seed sources. The extraction of wood for direct consumption as fuel or for conversion into charcoal does not yet seem to be levelling off even though continued urbanisation has seen the substantial replacement of wood fuels by electricity, gas and kerosene. Data for

Table 5.5 Forest areas in 1980, 1995, decrease 1980–95, and proportion of total land area in forest, 1995

Country	Area 1980 (mill. ha)	Area 1995 (mill. ha)	Decrease 1980–95 (%)	Proportion forested 1995 (%)
Cambodia	13.5	9.8	27	54
Indonesia	124.5	109.8	12	58
Laos	14.5	12.4	14	53
Malaysia	21.6	15.5	28	47
Myanmar	32.9	27.2	17	40
Philippines	11.2	6.8	39	23
Thailand	18.1	11.6	36	23
Viet Nam	10.7	9.1	15	27
Total	247.0	202.2	Av. 18	Av. 45

Note: Singapore has about 4000 ha of forest, none logged.
Source: *World Resources 1998–99*

Singapore in 1996 show a consumption of only 25 m^3 of wood per 1000 people, compared with 760 m^3 in Indonesia, 480 m^3 in Malaysia—where just over half the population is urban—or a formidable 922 m^3 in Laos where the move away from wood fuels has scarcely begun.

In fact the attack upon the remaining forests has two major prongs quite apart from clearance, for the production of fuelwood and charcoal is almost as important as the production of timber, as Table 5.6 shows. (These data do not distinguish between production from land cleared of forest and planted to something else and forest land that is harvested again and again. Virtually all fuelwood comes from the latter, whereas a significant proportion of timber comes from forest not previously harvested.)

Table 5.6 Production of timber and fuelwood (million m^3), 1996

Country	Timber	Fuelwood	Total	Timber as % total
Cambodia	7.9	6.9	14.8	53
Indonesia	200.8	153.5	354.3	57
Laos	5.4	4.6	10.0	54
Malaysia	45.8	10.0	55.8	82
Myanmar	23.6	20.6	44.2	53
Philippines	40.7	37.3	78.0	52
Thailand	39.7	36.9	76.6	52
Viet Nam	35.7	31.3	67.0	53
Total	399.6	301.1	700.7	Av. 57

Source: *FAO Yearbook of Forest Products, 1996*

DEFORESTATION AND CONSERVATION

Forests are very much like money in the bank. If harvested wisely, production is much like interest, providing a perennial income. In Southeast Asia, however, it is still an open question as to whether natural forests can ever be managed on a truly sustainable long-term basis. For teak the answer, after more than a century of silviculture in Java, Myanmar and parts of northern Thailand, is probably that it can. But for other types things are more problematic, mainly because full regeneration is thought to take 200–300 years, a very long time to wait for an economic return, one not justified either by current or projected timber prices. 'Full regeneration' would certainly mean fully grown forest. However, since logging is selective, potential seed sources for the selected trees will have been reduced by removing the mature trees. Trees of different species probably also respond differently to the pressure upon their habitat that logging represents. Climatic change may also be a factor in influencing the nature of regenerating forests. They are thus unlikely ever to be just like what was there previously.

If forests are harvested unwisely conventional wisdom holds that a whole series of adverse environmental changes follow—increased run-off, greater erosion on slopes and increased sedimentation in the lowlands, reduced capacity to absorb atmospheric carbon dioxide, climatic change, loss of biodiversity and amenity value of forests. Much turns on just what harvested unwisely may mean. Thus there can be little doubt that on sloping land the replacement of forest, scrub or grassland by tillage greatly increases run-off and erosion, as for example in the Shan highlands of Myanmar or in regions of intensive vegetable production. The less phytomass there is on the land the less rain is intercepted and evaporated, the less is taken up from the soil and transpired. More runs off, carrying sediment with it. Just where, in detail, this additional material goes is simply not known, though throughout the region unexpectedly rapid sedimentation of reservoirs is common.

But increased run-off may be a benefit. Certainly water-users would argue so. Shifting cultivation is often held to be very environmentally damaging. Yet, long-term studies in Sarawak (Table 3.3) suggest that provided the vegetation is allowed to regenerate, erosion is no greater than under forest. Whether this holds true throughout the region is, for lack of comparable studies, scarcely known. Certainly, on loose, friable soils characteristic of volcanic areas, cultivation, whether involving tillage or not, even tree-cropping, does lead to the greater generation of sediment on slopes. How long this continues is not clear because most erosion studies last only a few years when decades are needed. In fact slopes eventually come into equilibrium with new conditions. Thus during and immediately after logging erosion increases rapidly, mainly from roughly bulldozed roads and tracks, and from drag paths and storage areas where compression of the soil and removal of the litter reduce infiltration of rain and increase run-off. But four or five years later these scars have healed and erosion is reduced to normal.

Where clearance of forest is total, where forest is replaced by tree-crops or pasture, the phase of greater erosion lasts longer, perhaps 20 years, eventually reducing to stable levels somewhat above those of forest. As the roots of forest trees decay and loosen their grip so the incidence of landslides increases, but, as evidence from outside the region indicates, probably not forever. In Southeast Asia there has been very little controlled experimentation linking deforestation and changing land use with erosion. As elsewhere, it remains difficult to distinguish between what occurs as a result of vegetation change and what would happen anyway. The latter can occasionally be catastrophic, as for example in the Philippines where slopes may be saturated by cyclonic rains and shaken by earthquakes.

Reduction of ability to absorb carbon dioxide is a global issue. Since Southeast Asia accounts for about 12 per cent of the world's forests, this is not a trivial matter. Generally, the less phytomass there is the less carbon dioxide can be taken up in photosynthesis. But things are not quite as simple as that. Enhanced levels of carbon dioxide may result in faster growth, especially of young plants. The degree to which this is so for the thousands of species making up the region's forests is simply not known and may never be, given the formidable technical and financial difficulties in measuring their carbon dioxide response. Even if global carbon dioxide production were stable instead of rising as it is, deforestation in Southeast Asia would make a significant contribution to its levels in the atmosphere both directly by burning and indirectly by reduced uptake.

The question of whether loss of forests actually changes climate has been inconclusively debated for two centuries. At the regional level it is probably impossible to separate vegetation change from other factors leading to climatic change. At individual locations matters are quite otherwise. Clearing vegetation leads to warmer, drier conditions near the ground and in the soil. Since less incoming energy is used to evaporate water in cleared, especially bare areas, more is available to heat the atmosphere and the upper layers of the soil. At Singapore, for example, during the daily heat-peak bare soil at a depth of 2 mm rises to temperatures above 45°C whereas under forest they are very stable at about 24°C. Even at a depth of 50 cm the soil is about 4°C warmer than under forest. A grass cover drastically reduces these extremes. Ecologically these local effects are quite important. It seems likely that the seeds of many forest species cannot survive the high temperatures and dryness of sunny, open sites, thus hindering regeneration. On the other hand, the seeds of grasses and spores of some ferns seemingly tolerate extreme conditions. In some parts of the region, especially in mainland Southeast Asia, iron-rich sedentary soils may be baked hard to form laterite (from the Latin *latus*, a brick) should the protecting vegetation be removed. On this material vegetation regeneration is extremely slow, because the change is irreversible.

Loss of forest biodiversity is a further serious issue. Science has barely begun to understand the potential uses of Southeast Asia's forest plants and animals, whether for new drugs, as sources for the breeding of new and better varieties of crops and domestic animals, or for new materials. The medicinal use of the region's plants has been known to western science for more than a century. Though thousands have long been used in indigenous medicine, scientific screening is in its infancy. The discovery, for instance, of a drug to control cancer would pay for all the biological science of the last several centuries. In breeding disease-resistance into animals, indigenous animals may have a part to play. Swine fever, rinderpest, foot-and-mouth disease, Newcastle disease, are serious epidemic diseases of pigs, cattle and poultry. Might Southeast Asia's wild populations bear genes that resist these economically important disorders? Extinction of a species results in the loss forever of a distinct assemblage of genes. Given the yet to be fully studied extent of the region's gene pool, preservation must make excellent economic sense.

Economic sense is also contained in the amenity value of forests and all that they contain. A forested river, a lake, a seashore has aesthetic as well as economic value. Carefully managed tourism to places of natural beauty and interest is a sustainable use provided that tourist impacts are minimised. As wealth in the region increases so will the demand for access to pristine landscapes. These thus have an increased amenity value making conservation a desirable end for sound economic reasons as well as for reasons of science and aesthetics.

SIX
ECONOMIC SYSTEMS AND SHIFTS: GLOBALISATION, WEALTH AND POVERTY

Not just trees but plants of many kinds still form the direct basis of daily life in Southeast Asia. Despite significant economic growth, burgeoning cities and a major shift away from agriculture as the predominant source of the region's income, the majority of people are still dependent upon agriculture. According to FAO estimates there were in 1997 more farmers and dependants than ever before—256 million of them, 51.3 per cent of the population, though a year later these values had dropped marginally. Farmers certainly do not produce anything like half of the region's income, though for lack of comprehensive data it is difficult to be sure just what proportion they do produce. Somewhere between a quarter and a fifth would probably be about right. The rest comes from the manufacture of goods and the provision of services, a very new situation.

STRUCTURAL SHIFTS

The structural shift out of agriculture into manufacturing and services began at different countries at different times. Singapore never had a significant primary sector though the early to mid-nineteenth century saw massive forest clearance for crops such as pepper, gambier, nutmegs and coconuts. Its transformation into an industrial centre began in the mid-1960s as a result of deliberate government policy. But over the last decade its income from this source has steadily declined as its economy has swung back to its earlier functions as an entrepot and a provider of services, especially in finance. Brunei, too, was long an entrepot, becoming a specialist petroleum exporter from about a century ago. Since the

Figure 6.1 The structural shift out of agriculture

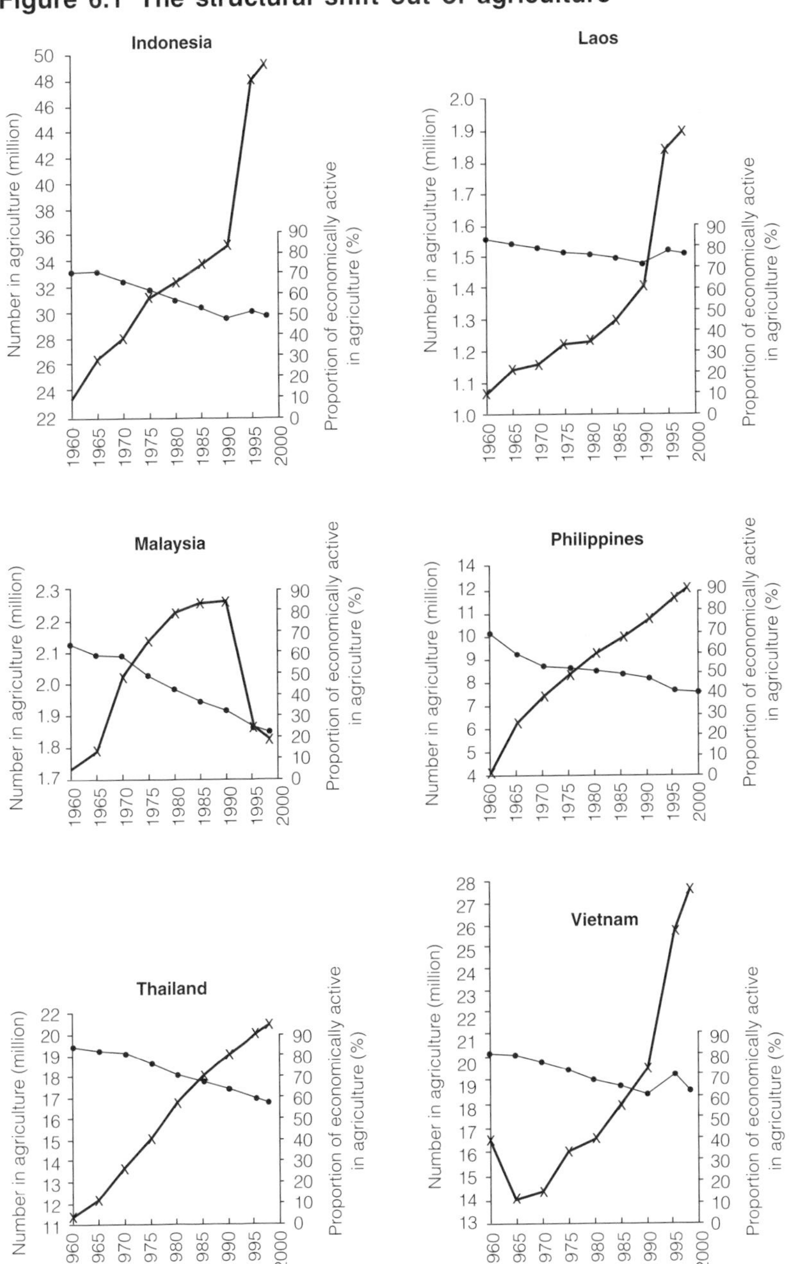

Source: Compiled from *FAO Production Yearbooks*

Table 6.1 Gross Domestic Product by sector, 1988 and 1998 (%)

	Brunei		Cambodia	
	1988	1998	1988	1998
Primary				
Agriculture etc.	2.2	2.8	50.5	38.3
Extractive	47.0	31.6	1.0	0.2
Secondary				
Manufacturing	(1)	(1)	6.8	16.1
Other	4.3	7.5	7.9	4.4
Tertiary	46.5	58.1	33.9	41.1
	100.0	100.0	100.1	100.1

	Indonesia		Laos	
	1988	1998	1988	1998
Primary				
Agriculture etc.	22.2	17.2	61.5	52.1
Extractive	10.5	9.8	0.2	0.4
Secondary				
Manufacturing[1]	19.7	25.3	7.4	16.5
Other	6.0	7.2	3.5	2.7
Tertiary	41.7	40.5	27.4	28.3
	100.1	100.0	100.0	100.0

	Malaysia		Myanmar		Philippines	
	1988	1998	1988	1998	1988	1998
Primary						
Agriculture etc	20.7	9.0	57.4	57.9	23.6	19.4
Other	10.2	7.7	0.7	0.9	1.8	1.2
Secondary						
Manufacturing	24.1	26.6	7.5	7.7	25.7	24.9
Other	5.0	7.1	1.5	2.5	7.7	8.2
Tertiary	40.0	49.6	32.9	31.0	41.2	46.3
	100.0	100.0	100.0	100.0	100.0	100.0

	Singapore		Thailand		Viet Nam	
	1988	1998	1988	1998	1988	1998
Primary						
Agriculture etc	0.4	0.1	16.2	14.2	46.3	25.7
Other	0.1	–	1.7	1.8 }	}	}
Secondary				24.0 }	24.0 }	26.8 }
Manufacturing	27.0	23.4	25.8	28.3 }	}	}
Other	8.1	10.9	7.0	7.5 }	}	5.7
Tertiary	64.4	65.6	49.2	48.3	29.7	41.7
	100.0	100.0	99.9	100.1	100.0	99.9

Note: [1] Manufacturing included in 'Extractive' sector.

Source: *UNESCAP Statistical Yearbook for Asia and the Pacific, 1999*

1960s, and especially in the last decade, Malaysia, Indonesia, the Philippines and Thailand have become significant producers of manufactures, all now deriving more income from their factories than from their fields. Viet Nam will probably join them before long. By contrast, Cambodia, Laos and Myanmar are still basically agricultural though the two former have recently seen rapid growth in manufacturing (Table 6.1).

The economies with significant manufacturing sectors are, of course, those longest integrated into the global capitalist system. There are still significant areas and numbers of people quite marginal to the global economy. East Timor's labour-force structure shows clearly its very limited integration, because most people are farmers and subsistence producers, growing and consuming their own food with only a small surplus getting to limited markets. Were data available, large areas would show a similar pattern—for example the uplands of mainland Southeast Asia, interior Borneo, and many of the region's smaller islands.

But the structural shift is not a simple matter of rising shares of manufacturing and services in national economies. At the level of the region as a whole that is certainly happening whether measured by the share of primary industries in total production or by the proportion of workers in those industries. Through time the shift shows up first in production, later in the labour-force, for people usually need to move not merely from one economic sector to another but from one place to another, from country to towns and cities. This takes time. However, as these proportions have been falling, populations have still been growing, particularly in rural areas. Thus the number of people in the primary sector, especially in agriculture, has continued to grow even as the sector's share of production and in some countries of the workforce has fallen.

Agricultural workforce

In much of the region, leaving aside the non-agricultural 'specialist countries', the agricultural workforce continued to expand into the early 1990s. Only in Malaysia was there earlier evidence of a fall in the actual number of agriculturalists. By the late 1990s Thailand also showed a fall, in part probably as a result of lower rural population growth rates as well as continued rural to urban migration. Indonesia, too, showed only a small growth in the agricultural labour-force. But while every country has lower rates of growth in its agricultural workforce, some clearly continue to show a piling up of people in this sector. Notable are Cambodia and Laos, followed by East Timor, Viet Nam and Myanmar, all of them still strongly agricultural and still significantly subsistence (see Table 6.2).

The economic crisis of the late 1990s may have influenced this picture, to some degree, by driving some marginal urban workers back to their villages of origin. But the consensus amongst experts is that a flow back

Table 6.2 Estimated numbers (000s) and proportions, total population and in agriculture, 1990 and 1998, and growth of agricultural population, 1990–98

	1990			1998			Av. growth in agric. pop'n, 1990–98
Country	**Total**	**agric.**	**%**	**Total**	**agric.**	**%**	**% p.a.**
Brunei	257	5	1.9	315	3	1.0	–5.7
Cambodia	8 652	6 388	73.8	10 716	7 589	70.8	2.4
East Timor	740	619	83.6	857	706	82.3	1.8
Indonesia	182 812	93 085	50.9	206 338	93 679	45.4	0.0
Laos	4 152	3 242	78.1	5 163	3 964	76.8	2.8
Malaysia	17 845	4 646	26.0	21 410	4 089	19.1	–1.5
Myanmar	40 520	29 688	73.3	44 497	31 520	70.8	0.8
Philippines	60 687	27 687	45.6	72 944	29 577	41.2	0.7
Singapore	3 016	11	0.4	3 476	6	0.2	–5.7
Thailand	55 595	31 622	56.9	60 300	30 428	50.5	–0.5
Viet Nam	66 689	47 546	71.3	77 562	52 869	68.2	1.4
	440 965	244 539	Av. 55.4	503 578	254 430	Av. 50.5	Av. 0.5

Source: FAO Production Yearbook, 1998

to the land has not been significant. Any perceived economic improvement will see a shift of such workers back to manufacturing and services with a continued slowing, even reversal, of growth of the agricultural populations. This is confirmed by latest FAO data. These show just a slowing in growth of the agricultural population. For Indonesia, for instance, the agricultural population grew by only 594 000 between 1990 and 1998—less than 0.01 per cent a year.

Participation

Another structural shift in the workforce has been in participation, though it is not possible to document this as closely as for changes in the agricultural sector. Overall it seems that a higher proportion of people are in employment. This stems from changes in age structure especially, though some of this change may merely reflect better enumeration. (It is usually easier to count people in cities and towns.) As populations age there is a reduction in the proportion of dependants under the age of 15. This frees women, especially, from household duties. So do later marriage and childbearing, while family-planning enables couples to reduce the period spent in childcare. These processes, when coupled with expanding employment opportunities, result in greater participation in the workforce

Table 6.3 Total and female labour-force participation rates, 1990s

Country		Total labour-force		Female participation rates (%)
		Number (000s)	Proportion (%)	
Brunei	(1991)	171	65.6	46.4
Cambodia	(1996)	4 904	47.4	48.2
Indonesia	(1990)	74 395	63.3	44.6
	(1998)	92 734	65.3	49.9
Malaysia	(1998)	8 884	60.7	41.6
Philippines	(1990)	21 106	57.7	39.2
	(1998)	31 275	66.0	49.3
Singapore	(1990)	1 516	64.9	50.3
	(1997)	1 932	63.9	51.3
Thailand	(1996)	32 749	54.5	49.2
	(1998)	33 140	73.6	65.8
Viet Nam	(1989)	30 521	77.2	73.6

Note: The figures given here include only actual workers, whereas those in Table 6.2 include dependants as well.

Source: *ILO Yearbooks of Labour Statistics*, 1998, 1999

both generally and specifically by women, except where religion or custom interfere. Table 6.3 sets out the situation as nearly as sources allow.

Clearly there is a great deal of variation in labour-force structure from country to country though some of this is probably the result of different views as to what constitutes participation. (It is a bit hard to accept that Cambodia and Viet Nam, with fairly similar, poor economies and recent economic histories, have such divergent structures.) In fact overall participation rates lie between these extremes. What is significant, for those countries for which data through time are available, is the general rise in the proportion of the population at work—almost certainly because of changes in the demographic structure discussed earlier. Interestingly, Thailand shows a drop in the total labour-force between 1997 and 1998, by some 400 000 workers, possibly reflecting an economic downturn.

Women's participation rates are significantly lower than for men, except in Viet Nam. This pattern is usual because of the numbers of women involved in child-rearing and household duties. (Some may, in fact, be part-time workers at home as 'out-working'—contracting out simple industrial tasks such as assembling artificial flowers—is fairly common.) The Malaysian data might suggest a slight reluctance for women to work (or their fathers to let them) for reasons of religion, in this case Islam. But this can hardly be true generally, for Indonesia and Brunei—both Islamic—have female participation rates only marginally below those of non-Islamic countries such as Cambodia, Philippines and Thailand. As with general participation rates, female rates have clearly risen through time.

The significance of these changes is considerable. Work creates wealth so that, other things being equal, a country with a higher proportion of people working is better off than one with a lower proportion, for those working must support those who are not. By this reckoning Viet Nam might appear to be best off, which it clearly is not. The proviso is important and poverty may force some into employment that they might prefer not to have to undertake. Singapore, a wealthy labour-deficit country with an ageing population and access to migrant workers to make good its deficit, has about as high a participation rate as might be expected where it is not an absolute imperative for everyone old enough, especially women, to work. The rise in the proportion of working women is a measure of their enhanced economic independence, derived in part from improved education and some relaxation of traditional male attitudes. Nevertheless, while female participation in the workforce has risen, women generally still suffer from lower wages than men doing the same job. They are less likely to be promoted in most large organisations and are more likely to be put off when there is an economic downturn. Such has certainly been the case since the beginning of the so-called 'Asian Crisis'.

Shift into manufacturing and services

The relative shift out of agriculture has, of course, been paralleled by movement into manufacturing and services of various kinds. Here two broad processes may be distinguished. One is global. The move into services and out of manufacturing is characteristic of all developed economies. Singapore, notably, shares in this. The day when 30 per cent of its workers were in a manufacturing sector that owed its expansion to government intervention and initiatives in the face of 6 per cent unemployment has long gone. The manufacturing that remains is mostly 'high-tech', because a rise in the cost of labour, brought about partly by the very success of those initiatives, has resulted in the disappearance of relatively low-skill labour-intensive industries such as clothing. Singapore is also rapidly reclaiming its traditional entrepot role as well as becoming the region's entrepreneur and provider of services, especially those in the financial sector.

The other shift, into manufacturing, is more local and characteristic of developing economies. In part this has come about as entrepreneurs in developed countries have sought to lower the costs of production by moving some or all of the manufacturing process offshore where wages are lower. This has been aided by lower costs of transportation—by container on land, sea and in the air—relative to the total costs of production. It has also been helped by governments providing basic economic and social infrastructure, the latter including quite good levels of education and, in some cases, notably in Malaysia, Indonesia and the Philippines, by partially lifting tariff barriers and other forms of economic protection and by setting up tariff-free export-processing zones. Consequently the proportion of workers in manufacturing has tended to rise, albeit steadily rather than spectacularly. In no country do they yet comprise a third of the labour-force, the proportion characteristic of countries at the peak of industrialisation. It is a moot question whether any will actually reach that level given the contrary processes of deindustrialisation, rising capital intensity in manufacturing and the shift towards services, processes already evident in Singapore.

Other sectoral shifts

Structural change involves a good deal more than a simple shift from primary activities like farming, forestry and fisheries to secondary occupations, such as manufacturing and construction or to tertiary 'industries' such as trade, transportation, financial, business, community and personal services. Other sectors, such as mining (including petroleum extraction), transportation, electricity, gas and water production are relatively unimportant in terms of employment, but are economically crucial. Their shares tend not to change much through time.

On the other hand the share of other important sectors does change. Very generally manufacturing has expanded, for reasons just given and because the growth of population and increase in its purchasing power have made production for local markets more attractive. This expansion has been fairly steady, for time is needed to build factories, to equip them and to construct infrastructure to support them.

The construction sector, however, tends to fluctuate over short periods, expanding when times are good and contracting when they are not. This sector is also very much involved with migrant labour, sometimes international as in Singapore, sometimes drawing labour from rural areas on a temporary or permanent basis.

Data to illustrate these inter-sectoral shifts are not available for the whole region. Table 6.4 gives examples of relatively poor, middling and rich countries. Interestingly the data for 'socialist' Myanmar show a pattern of change quite similar to that of its 'capitalist' neighbour Thailand, though one that is substantially slower. By 1988 Malaysia had already experienced a relative decline in agriculture, adding workers in manufacturing and construction but not, proportionately, in the service sectors. The pattern of change for Singapore is probably not characteristic of primate cities in the region generally, though for lack of data there is no knowing

Table 6.4 Employment (%) by sector, 1988 and 1997, selected countries

	Myanmar		Thailand		Malaysia		Singapore	
Sector	**1988**	**1997**	**1988**	**1997**	**1988**	**1997**	**1988**	**1997**
1	65.0	63.4	66.5	50.3	30.9	17.3	0.4	0.3
2	0.6	0.7	0.1	0.1	0.5	0.5	0.1	–
3	8.7	8.8	8.4	12.9	16.1	23.4	28.5	22.6
4	0.1	0.1	0.4	0.5	0.7	0.6	0.6	0.7
5	1.7	2.1	2.4	6.1	5.6	9.3	6.7	6.9
6	9.8	9.7	9.8	13.9	18.3	18.4	22.9	21.8
7	3.3	2.6	2.2	3.0	4.3	4.9	9.7	11.5
8	6.6	3.2	10.2	13.1	3.8	5.2	9.6	14.9
9	4.2	9.4	10.2	13.1	19.9	20.5	21.2	21.2
0	–	–	–	–	–	–	0.3	0.1
Total	100.0	100.0	100.0	99.9	100.1	100.1	100.0	100.0

Key to sectors: 1 agriculture, forestry, fisheries; 2 mining & quarrying; 3 manufacturing; 4 electricity; gas, water; 5 construction; 6 wholesale & retail trade; 7 transport, communication, storage; 8 finance, real estate, business services; 9 community, social, personal services; 0 other

Source: *Yearbook of Labour Statistics, 1998*

if this is so. Deindustrialisation, in relative terms, has clearly begun, industrial employment having expanded since the early 1960s. Also notable is a slight drop in wholesale and retail trade—perhaps because Singapore is no longer a 'shopper's paradise' but possibly also because neighbouring Malaysia no longer needs to use Singapore as a wholesaler. Transport, communication, finance and business service functions have clearly expanded in step with its expanding entrepreneurial and service role.

Globalisation

Why have these structural shifts taken place? Fundamentally, other than in Singapore which was part of the global economy from the outset, governments have decided that economic autarky does not promote rapid economic growth. They feel it is not a sin to become rich. Nor is it a sin to allow foreign investors to help them. To be sure protectionism remains, though under the aegis of the Association of Southeast Asian Nations (ASEAN) controls are slowly being dismantled. They were regarded as a necessary temporary measure to encourage initial industrialisation. A major shift has taken place from import substitution to export-driven manufacturing. This is part of the globalisation process.

Narrowly defined, globalisation means no more than the emergence of markets for particular commodities in which prices are set by international competition so that the only major differences in price from place to place are those arising from transportation costs. An example would be woodchips. More broadly, globalisation refers to the emergence of single global markets not only for commodities but also for the basic factors of production—land, labour and capital. This applies particularly because labour and especially capital are to some degree mobile. Labour and capital move not only from sector to sector but also from country to country and from region to region. One of the longest standing private capital flows in Southeast Asia is almost certainly that from country to town, though such flows are intrinsically hard to measure. One estimate for the Philippines is that four-fifths of the wealth generated in the countryside flows to urban areas, especially Manila. At the same time, since the 1950s there has been a significant public capital flow to rural areas—in the form of improved agricultural infrastructure, for instance—though this is beginning to tail off for deliberate policy reasons and because urban investments give superior returns to public investment.

Measuring the degree to which countries and regions are integrated into the global economy is a matter of considerable difficulty. Financial reporting often does not distinguish between capital outflows and repatriated profits and takes little account of how long capital has remained in a country and what it has done while it was there. Increased trade is a clear indicator of increased economic integration but its expression in money terms immediately encounters severe problems of comparability from one time to another as terms of trade, prices and rates of exchange vary. The last is a particular problem for Myanmar, whose official rate is some 30 times that of the unofficial rate. Trade statistics may not help much. Except for primary commodities like rice, rubber, or crude oil, they do not necessarily distinguish between local production and re-exports. In addition, who owns what is a commercial secret. Although public-company shareholder lists are public documents, these are little help because major shareholders often hide their holdings behind nominee companies and many substantial businesses are privately owned. How great is the lack of knowledge about financial matters may be judged by the fact that with the onset of the Asian financial crisis in 1997, several governments in the region—the Indonesian is one—had little idea of levels of private offshore debt.

Investment flows

Two levels of economic integration can be distinguished. First is integration between Southeast Asian countries with others outside the region. Second is integration amongst the countries within the region. Both reflect

Table 6.5 Foreign direct investment, 1998 (million US$)

Country	Inflow	Outflow
Brunei	4	10
Cambodia	140	–
Indonesia	–356	44
Laos	45	–
Malaysia	3 727	1 921
Myanmar	40	–
Philippines	1 713	160
Singapore	7 218	3 108
Thailand	6 969	122
Viet Nam	1 900	–

Source: UNCTAD *World Investment Report 1999*

globalisation, for a significant flow of investment comes into the region from outside, especially to Singapore and Malaysia, yet both are also major investors, especially within the region as a whole. At the same time investment flows from outside—known as FDI, foreign direct investment—together with locally formed capital (savings), push structural change in particular directions. These are basically out of agriculture and into light industries, mostly producing consumer goods such as clothing, footwear, food, simple pharmaceuticals and much else.

More recently it is clear that the 'wave' of industrialisation is passing through Southeast Asia as Singapore and outside the region, Hong Kong, are deindustrialising, largely as a result of the rising costs of labour. The industry that survives is relatively capital-intensive (for instance Singapore's petrochemicals industry), is 'high-tech', or is government-supported (e.g. Singapore's arms industry). Investments then flow to the tertiary sector, a process well under way in Singapore but in its early stages elsewhere in the region.

FDI patterns vary strikingly from country to country. Only one, Brunei, invests more abroad than it receives, though the aggregate amounts are small (Table 6.5). Singapore is the largest importer of capital and also the largest exporter, with the outward flow representing 43 per cent of the inward flow. Thailand is the second-largest importer but virtually all is retained, unlike Malaysia where just over half flows out again. Indonesia began losing capital following the 1997 Asian economic crisis.

The region's poorest countries are obviously rather differently perceived by foreign investors. Myanmar, with a population almost ten times that of Laos, has received somewhat less FDI, much of that reportedly from Singapore, for few Western investors are willing to risk their money there. Viet Nam has attracted more than the Philippines—their populations are comparable—despite its currently inferior infrastructure.

Table 6.6 Ratio (%) of trade to Gross Domestic Product (selected countries)

Country	1980	1990	1997
Indonesia	47	45	48
Malaysia	95	129	192
Philippines	42	46	99
Thailand	46	61	91

Sources: C.W. Paderanga, 1996; *World Economic Factbook, 1998/99*

Overall, however, Southeast Asia has not received a particularly large amount of FDI—in 1998 around 22 billion US dollars, compared with China's 45 billion. Inflows also respond very quickly to perceptions of political and economic instability, with 1998 levels having been lower by around a quarter than in 1997.

Trade and GDP

One well-established way of measuring economic integration is by the ratio of total commodity trade to Gross Domestic Product. (This sort of measure avoids problems of monetary inflation through time, though not the problem of obtaining data in a single currency, so that Table 6.6 covers only a handful of countries.) These latest-available data show a considerable variation from one country to another in levels of commodity trade integration, with overall levels substantially greater by 1997 than in 1980 except in Indonesia.

The two specialist economies—Singapore a trading post and producer of manufactures, Brunei of crude petroleum and natural gas—have long had very high levels of economic integration, the former since its founding as a free port in 1819, the latter since the discovery and exploitation of its only major natural resource since early in the twentieth century.

At the other end of the 'integration scale' all the other countries in the region were once only marginally integrated into world trade, producing only precious stones, woods and drugs. With the colonial era, Java emerged as an exporter of sugar and rice, Sumatera as a producer of pepper, later tobacco, later still rubber. By the late nineteenth century Burma, Siam and Cochinchina (southern Viet Nam) emerged as major exporters of rice and the Philippines of sugar. To this list in the twentieth century can be added natural rubber and tin, later palm oil, from Malaya (Peninsular Malaysia), largely as a result of very substantial foreign investment. The colonial economy, however, was arguably a form of enclave production, only marginally linked with the fishing, farming and foraging that had existed for millennia. Whole regions within countries and indeed one whole country, Laos, were scarcely linked to the global and regional economies at all.

Since the Pacific War widely varying levels of integration persisted at the country-to-country level. The concept of autarkic development ('pull yourself up by your own boot-straps') was by no means confined to the socialist bloc—Burma, Cambodia, Laos and Viet Nam—whose trade, directed largely to other socialist countries, was minuscule. Most other countries, notably the Philippines and Indonesia, tried to shelter nascent industries by various protectionist measures, aiming to supply their own rapidly growing markets with manufactures that previously were imported. Especially after the formation of ASEAN in 1967, there was a steady shift in policy towards export-based manufacturing and freer trade and investment, especially within the original ASEAN group of Thailand, Malaysia, Singapore, the Philippines and Indonesia.

The result was increasing economic integration even though country-to-country trade within this bloc has not expanded much beyond the 18 per cent of total trade of a decade and more ago. As Table 6.6 suggests, Malaysia, as a country already well integrated into the global economy, has continued the integration process. Thailand has been less concerned than the Philippines to protect its own economy and so shows increasing trade integration. Indonesia's policy-makers, perhaps harking back to the old mercantilist (protectionist) notions of their former Dutch masters, have not been so forthcoming and since 1980, levels of trade integration have actually decreased. With its very large population (some 200 million), Indonesia may be better placed than other countries in the region to go it alone and, following recent events, may be forced to.

It certainly sees itself as the possessor of surplus labour. As an Indonesian minister is said to have remarked, 'Malaysia and Singapore are always urging us to open our markets to their products but when I suggest that they open their doors to our labour they are not so keen.' Economic integration may mean mobility of capital. It does not yet mean more than limited labour mobility, though it is no coincidence that Thailand, Singapore and Malaysia—all well integrated into the global economy—contain significant numbers of foreign migrant workers, whose remittances form another strand in the cable of integrative linkages.

Service-sector integration

One important and growing area of linkages is the service sector, particularly banking, other financial services, transportation and communications, which comprise the infrastructural core of economic development. In contrast to the manufacturing sector, which in most Southeast Asian countries is substantially open to foreign investment and thus control, the service sector is generally closed, though not entirely. Major international oil companies, for example, and Japanese retailers have to some degree penetrated the merchandising sector, though in reality the sale of a great many commonly used international brand-names is the subject of licensing agreements with local businesses rather than goods being sold directly by multinational corporations.

Given the crucial role of producer services in economic growth and thus the need for investment it might be expected that foreign investment, and thus international linkages, would be actively fostered. This has not so far been so. The Filipino economist Mario Lamberte, for instance, states boldly that in his country the service sector remains closed. Singapore, which derives two-thirds of its GDP from services, is probably the most open and has the highest degree of service-sector integration into the global economy.

Retail banking is perhaps one sub-sector by which to measure levels of integration, though it may be objected that it is 'only natural' that countries should wish to retain a high degree of control over a commodity as important as money. Only in Singapore and Malaysia do foreign banks own extensive retail networks, including not only Standard and Chartered and HSBC, established in colonial times, but also relative newcomers like the Bank of America and Citicorp, though their market share is much less.

The other side of service-sector integration in the global economy is the degree to which enterprises based in the region have become the providers of services for others. None can be regarded as being of more than local or regional significance. One measure is the degree to which firms generally, not just service providers, are cross-listed on stock markets. Within the region the strongest links are between the Singapore and Kuala Lumpur markets, where a large number of local companies are listed in both places. Listings outside the region are notably few, especially in major centres such as Tokyo, London and New York.

Probably in part because of Overseas Chinese connections, Hong Kong's stock market lists half a score of Southeast Asian companies, some directly, Berjaya Holdings, C.P. Phokphand, some via subsidiaries, Lam Soon, Sime Darby, San Miguel. (Hong Kong, for the same reason, is a significant source of Southeast Asia's investment capital, especially that seeking a quick return. Much of the region's timber industry, for instance, is financed from the Hong Kong Special Administrative Region.)

National-level analysis tends to leave a quite false impression of levels of integration. As was mentioned previously, there are whole regions which are at best marginally connected to the global economy, perhaps furnishing a market for cloth, pots and pans, matches, kerosene, soap and other simple requirements. In return they supply a few widely traded commodities. Rattans collected from the forest, destined for furniture manufacture, are an example, but many goods—a bag of rice, some leaves of tobacco—are exchanged only locally. Basic foodstuffs may not be traded at all. In Viet Nam, for example, it is estimated that two-fifths of rice-farmers have no surplus for sale.

Subsistence farming—and consequent minimal involvement in the larger economy—is alive and well in many of Southeast Asia's uplands, especially on the mainland. Other areas would include most of eastern Indonesia and East Timor.

Even in cities there are groups—scavengers for example—whose existence is marginal to the broader economy. For such folk and their rural counterparts, globalisation is more likely to be represented by an occasional tourist handout, a gift of small change or perhaps visions of other ways and other worlds via someone else's transistor radio or television set.

Ethnic dimensions

Arguably, some parts of Southeast Asia have been part of the economy of the world, or at least of major parts of it, for a long time. The colonial period added commercial agriculture but not manufacturing other than a few commodities for local consumption—beer and soft drinks initially for resident foreigners, matches, soap and other simple daily necessities for the locals. Colonial manufactures, natural silk is an example, were deliberately excluded from metropolitan markets or found no market other than as exotica. Colonies were seen as outlets for the manufactures of the imperial powers. Yet their marketing was just as much part of an international, or more accurately, a series of national economic systems linking Europe and the region. These links were not necessarily direct. It was not British moneylenders and shopkeepers who gave Burmese farmers advances on their rice-crop but Indians. It was generally not French, Dutch, Spanish, American or British merchants who dealt with Vietnamese, Indonesian, Filipino or others of the region's peasantry and townsfolk but the Chinese. Chinese and Indians, joined by Vietnamese in Cambodia and Laos, were the headlink with the developing global system of trade. From humble beginnings as labourers or shopkeepers, a major 'compradore' or middle-man class emerged—and it was almost entirely male. Outside those countries which decided to pursue an autarkic socialist path of development, this class has family and clan roots often reaching back to the nineteenth century.

No one knows what proportion of private wealth and the business that provides it is in the hands of the descendants of Overseas Chinese whose ownership far, far outweighs that of Overseas Indians in the region. (Most of the latter, merchants or labourers, were kicked out of Burma in the 1960s, as the Vietnamese were from Cambodia in the 1970s, if they were not slaughtered as 'counter-revolutionaries'.) In the 1930s it was estimated that Chinese owned a third to two-thirds of the modern, commercial sector in agriculture, fisheries and trade. They 'knew money'. They supported each other economically and socially. They were supported by the colonial powers.

With independence after the Pacific War, government support was removed and outside Burma and Indochina the Chinese quickly came to political accommodations with governments dominated by 'indigenous' interests. At the same time those governments, especially in Thailand and Malaysia, saw 'state capitalism' as a necessary counterweight to a situation in which, it was held, 'migrant races' had come to own and to control the modern sector of the economy—plantation agriculture, trade and services—as 'western' capital was expropriated (as in Indonesia), fled, or reduced its financial exposure. State capitalism was initiated in Malaysia through the medium of the New Economic Policy of 1971. This aimed to create an indigenous capitalist class, in reality mostly a Malay capitalist class, for rather few non-Malay *bumiputera* in Sabah and Sarawak have shared in the wealth this policy created. The result has been the emergence of large corporations—such as Petronas, Pernas, Antah and Bank Bumiputera—capable of competing successfully with long-established Chinese firms and fostering the 'repatriation' of major British-owned firms such as Guthries or Harrisons and Crosfield, major players in the plantation sector. Capital from outside the region is still very important, though its nature has changed. US and Japanese multinational involvement has grown substantially, mainly via joint ventures. Malaysian examples include Esso in petrochemicals, Matsushita in electronics and Mitsubishi in motor vehicles.

But in 'capitalist' Southeast Asia, small 'Overseas Chinese' businesses have remained. Some have grown into medium or large corporations, at least judged by regional standards. The list is a long one. In Thailand are the 'big four' banks (actually conglomerates with many interests outside banking): the Bangkok Bank, Thai Farmers Bank, Bangkok Metropolitan Bank and Bank Ayuthia. In Indonesia are, or were, Liem Sioe Liong's Salim group, long associated with ex-President Suharto and his family, Mochtar Riady's Lippo group and many others. In Malaysia and Singapore 'old Chinese money' is represented by the Kwok and Kwek brothers' interests, 'new' Chinese money by Loh Boon Siew's Oriental Group, Vincent Tan's Berjaya group and many others.

One common theme amongst these corporations, all of which can be regarded as regional-level multinationals, is linkage with the political leadership in particular and government in general, often via directorships. The Liem–Suharto link has already been mentioned. Goh Swie Kie's Gunung Sewu group had strong links with BULOG, the government purchasing agency. In Malaysia the Kwok brothers and the Kwek brothers (Hong Leong group) have links with the United Malays National Organisation, part of the ruling Alliance. In the Philippines, links between the Marcos regime and the 'ruling families'—Aquino, Cojuanco, Romualdez, Ayala—were strong, and some critics assert that President Estrada, for all his populism, was a mere creature of their business and political interests. All have 'Chinese' and 'European' as well as Filipino family links. This longstanding pattern of family links is almost universal because even quite large businesses are family-run, though the companies themselves may be public.

Business networking, whether based on family links, overlapping membership on boards of directors, cross-holdings of shares or, increasingly, through formal management and other contracts, extends widely within the region and beyond. Thus Chinese-owned banks in Malaysia and Singapore, such as the United Overseas Bank, Yat Lee Bank, and Overseas Chinese Banking Corporation—major players locally—have forged global links beyond the region to China, Japan, the US and Britain. They are, nevertheless, still pretty small beer compared with the multinational HSBC, Standard and Chartered, or any of the major Japanese banks. Indeed, there is little doubt that Chinese companies in the service sector have lost ground relative to other multinational enterprises. In Singapore, for instance the banking sector is dominated by large international firms. While Chinese remain an important agency in the economic globalisation of national economies, very large numbers of others are now employed in the hugely expanded manufacturing and service sectors.

Wealth and poverty

Few other major world regions have such extremes of wealth and poverty as Southeast Asia. In part this is a statistical aberration, because in few other regions are a single city or a small petroleum-producer separate countries as Singapore and Brunei are. But the extremes would probably exist even if those countries had significant rural, agricultural hinterlands. This immediately alerts us to the fact that countries in the region with a large agricultural sector are poor. Countries that opted for autarkic development after the Pacific War, severing their links with the emerging global economy, are doubly poor—being predominantly agricultural. In global terms the region shares barely 2 per cent of gross world product, so in economic terms it amounts to very little.

The sizes of the region's economies, as measured by Gross National Product, range from that of Laos, with US$1.6 billion—less than the turnover of a major supermarket chain—to about $138 billion, that of Indonesia. When population is factored in, the range increases enormously. Singapore with 3.3 million people has an economy larger than that of neighbouring Malaysia with seven times as many people. Indonesia, whose population is now over 200 million, has an economy worth just 31 per cent more than that of Singapore (Table 6.7).

Table 6.7 Size of economies, GNP, 1997–98 (billion US$)

Country	GNP	Proportion (%)
Brunei	7.1	1.3
Cambodia	3.0	0.5
Indonesia	138.5	24.6
Laos	1.6	0.3
Malaysia	79.8	14.1
Philippines	78.9	14.0
Singapore	95.1	16.9
Thailand	134.4	23.8
Viet Nam	25.6	4.5
Total	546.0	100.0

Note: There are no data for Myanmar, probably because of the difficulty of using an appropriate exchange rate.
Source: *World Development Report, 1999–2000*

These relativities have been maintained into the period of the still ongoing Asian financial crisis, though from 1997 to 1998 Viet Nam's economy, alone in the region, grew both absolutely and relatively. Between these years Southeast Asia's economies contracted sharply, with total GNP falling from US$718 billion in 1997 to 546 billion, i.e. by almost a quarter. Most of this was accounted for by Indonesia, whose GNP fell by almost 38 per cent in a single year, though all countries except Viet Nam suffered some contraction.

Measuring wealth

Measuring wealth from one country to another is a tricky business, not least because the only true economic wealth is goods rather than money. When money is exchanged for money the exchange-rate demon rears its head and rates may influence the figures more than somewhat. The conventional approach in comparing wealth is to take GNP (at a chosen rate to the US dollar) and divide it by the number of people to obtain a GNP figure per person. This tends to ignore often-significant variations in the cost of living. Recently economists have devised an alternative way of getting at 'real' wealth by using the Purchasing Power Parity (PPP) basis for their calculations. This tends to reduce per person GNP in wealthy countries where goods (and most services) are expensive and to increase it in poorer economies where they are cheap. Consequently it may give a truer picture of variations from one country to another. (Table 6.8 gives both sets of data.)

Whichever way wealth per person is measured the range is truly

Table 6.8 Per person wealth and poverty by country, 1997–98

Country	GNP per person (US$)	
	Conventional basis	PPP basis
Brunei	25 090	n.a.
Cambodia	280	1 240
Indonesia	680	2 790
Laos	330	1 300
Malaysia	3 600	6 990
Philippines	1 050	3 540
Singapore	30 060	28 620
Thailand	2 200	5 840
Viet Nam	330	1 690

Note: No data for Myanmar.
Source: *World Development Report, 1999–2000*

enormous. The 'average Cambodian'—a convenient fiction like all such averages—'possesses' just the cost of a couple of nights in a modest hotel to see him or her through a year. She or he has just under one-hundredth of an 'average Singaporean', whose wealth ranks fourth in the world, substantially above Australia for instance. On a PPP basis, the region's 'middle-income' countries—Malaysia, Thailand, the Philippines and Indonesia—come out of it fairly well.

The groupings are clear. The specialist producers Brunei and Singapore are extraordinarily wealthy. One has oil and gas, plus some forests which it chooses not to exploit, plus substantial investment income; the other has no significant resource other than the skills of its people. Both are small and easily administered. Both have authoritarian governments, excellent education systems and strong links to the global economic system. Neither has a national debt but are substantial creditor nations. Neither has a peasantry. Neither has a large territory in which decision-making and development effort are diluted and slowed by sheer space or the friction of distance. Each has found a specialised niche in the increasingly international division of labour.

The middle-income group is more diverse, containing varied natural resources though the Philippines and Thailand have limited indigenous sources of energy, especially petroleum. In this group only Indonesia still has significant, though rapidly-diminishing reserve forests, the others having largely converted theirs into cash. Each has a substantial peasantry, many of whose members are being displaced by the increasing commercialisation of agriculture or who are finding that work on the land must needs be supplemented by work off the farm, in the fields, factories and construction sites of others. Peninsular Malaysia, parts of Luzon and the Visayas especially, have a 'rural proletariat', wage-workers on large-scale agricultural enterprises such as rubber, oil palm, and in the Philippines sugar. Indonesia, Thailand and Malaysia have an important group of agricultural smallholders producing rubber, for which market demand is weak, a situation existing equally for Filipino coconut producers and Thai manioc growers. Agriculture is generally a relatively depressed economic sector while still employing the bulk of the people, except in Malaysia. Each country has a national territory that is extensive and/or spatially split so that face-to-face contact is more difficult and expensive. Local authorities may go their own way while the need to refer many matters to the 'head office' in the capital—a particular feature even in federal Malaysia—slows administration. Government is seen as far away and little concerned with marginal, poorer, areas.

While some economic specialisation exists—oil palm in Malaysia or high-quality rice in Thailand—it is commodity-based rather than reflecting a whole economic sector such as financial services. Some specialised activities, especially in agriculture, enjoy 'natural protection' because of environmental limitations but many—electronic components in Malaysia is an example—could be produced almost anywhere. Specialisation has its rewards but also its risks. Arguably, the middle-income countries now have economies that are much more balanced than in the days of the colonial economy. Their point of vulnerability is not so much specialised production as foreign-currency debt, both public and private, the extent of the latter being to a degree not known to economists and governments alike.

At the bottom of the region's economic heap lie all the countries of the mainland except Thailand. Each attempted to grow autonomously, with limited aid from the former Soviet bloc and China during the Cold War. They thus cut themselves off not only from sources of capital and expertise but also from the trade and personal contacts essential to the conduct of business in a capitalist world. They had little idea of international standards of quality for the goods they wished to sell. All are burdened with large peasantries, millions of farmers producing little more than enough for their own subsistence. Rates of internal saving and investment are desperately low. Singapore, by contrast, has experienced savings of up to 40 per cent of GDP. Physical infrastructure—roads, railways, harbours, airports—remains very weak. Education is limited, particularly for women. Even with foreign investment, growth is fairly slow, especially compared with Singapore where the latest annual growth rate is estimated at around 6 per cent. Problems are compounded by weak financial structures, for example in Myanmar an irrational exchange rate and a lack of free currency convertibility, The last is not something capable of being achieved overnight, for immediately floating the currency would further penalise savers and accelerate inflation.

Areal patterns

Extremes of wealth and poverty also exist within countries, from place to place, within and between economic sectors and from family to family. Obtaining data to show these is another matter. Few countries conduct regular income surveys or if they do they are confined to those who have most to spend—the urban elite.

Nevertheless, some broad observations can be made, first concerning spatial differences. There can be little doubt that most people in rural areas are poorer than most people in urban areas though the range of incomes is almost certainly greater in urban areas. Consider the income differences between a person living under a plastic sheet along the Manila Bay foreshore and one living in a Forbes Park mansion. To be sure there is wealth in the countryside—among owners and managers of large estates, for example—but they and their wealth tend to migrate to the cities, as that old Russian revolutionary Peter Kropotkin noted more than a century ago. The incomes of rural landlords may be secure but they can obtain much better returns on their money in the towns and cities.

But rural areas are far from being uniformly poor. In insular Southeast Asia, areas of permanent tree-crop production, of rubber, cocoa and coconut (rather than coconut monoculture), have long provided a modest but comfortable living though currently suffering from a 30-year low in rubber prices. In the same region, rural workers on rubber and oil-palm estates live reasonably comfortably, in part because labour unions have seen to it that this is so. On large-scale sugar plantations in the Philippines, by contrast, desperate poverty is commonplace, especially amongst migrant workers and at times when global sugar prices, always volatile, happen to be low. Growers of market-garden crops supplying cities may be poor but not seriously so. Raisers of freshwater pond fish or, along the coasts, of prawns, may be positively rich, because these are capital-intensive forms of production, mainly directed towards urban wealth or exports. Shifting cultivation remains a way of life for some, mostly minority peoples, in remote parts of Borneo and West Irian as well as many islands of the eastern Indonesian and southern Philippine archipelagoes.

Unlike some shifting cultivators in mainland Southeast Asia, especially those in the hills of eastern Myanmar, those in insular Southeast Asia have not added opium to their repertoire of crops. They thus remain poor. Growers of illegal opium in mainland Southeast Asia do not necessarily do particularly well out of the crop—processors into heroin and the middlemen do that—but opium provides a fair cash income, for it is one of the very few crops that bring a return sufficient to meet the large costs of transportation in steep, broken and remote terrain. (That is, since Air America, the Indochinese War-era offshoot of the CIA, no longer provides its services to the industry.) But most shifting cultivators on the mainland do not grow the crop and they are poor.

So too are most other farmers in the uplands, because only a few parts of the sub-region are climatically suited to rubber, probably none to cocoa and oil palm. Modest incomes can be gained from tea and coffee, or from lychee and other fruits, but problems of marketing limit their production. Short-term crops such as the fibre crop *kenaf* (*Hibiscus* spp.) and manioc (*Manihot esculenta*) are grown on more gently sloping uplands, notably in northeast Thailand, though returns are very variable in response to weather and to the considerable volatility of global market prices. But in relation to what urban employment can provide, at least in good times, incomes are low and uncertain.

Incomes are generally more stable for lowland rice-growers, as the crop is less subject to the vagaries of seasonal rainfall and irrigation ensures considerable uniformity of output compared with rain-fed production areas. Farmers producing two crops a year with irrigation, with sufficient land to keep family workers busy most of the time, can make a good living though not infrequently being victims of a 'cost–price squeeze' as the costs of farm inputs tend to rise faster than product prices.

Wealth and poverty by economic sector

One way of measuring the performance of an economic sector is to compare the proportion of people employed in it with the proportion of the value of goods and services that sector produces. While data are not available for all the countries in the region, those that are suggest that agriculture employs a fairly high proportion of the people but does not necessarily produce a major proportion of each country's wealth. In countries such as Cambodia and Laos, where manufacturing is little developed as yet, much of the production indeed comes from agriculture. But where economies are more diversified things are very different. In Thailand, for example, around half of the workers are in agriculture but produce only an eighth of the value of the kingdom's goods and services. Just under half of Indonesia's workers are cultivators but produce barely a fifth of the total value of production.

Under the capitalist form of development in the region there is a great piling up of people in the agricultural sector. They produce relatively little, some not even all their own food. Consequently most are relatively poor, though their poverty may be to some degree alleviated by periodical wage labour, especially in construction. Eventually, this imbalance between employment and production will probably disappear but only when agriculture ceases to be a major sector in employment—the situation in Australia, the US and western European countries. That time is probably still several decades away. For strongly agricultural countries it may be a century or more.

A similar approach can be used to find out which sectors of economies are relatively productive. The mining sector, which includes petroleum exploitation, is highly capitalised and productive though it is company shareholders rather than employees who benefit most. Thus in Indonesia the sector employs barely 1 per cent of the workforce but produces more than 10 per cent of the total value of production.

The service sectors generally produce about as much as their share in employment though much depends upon the extent to which business in these sectors is linked internationally and the degree to which their structure is dominated by large enterprises. Thus Indonesia's wholesale and retail trade sector employs about 18 per cent of workers and produces about 18 per cent of the value. The same sector in Thailand employs a lower proportion but produces a somewhat higher proportion.

Amongst the sectors, that making up finance, real estate and business services produces value twice or three times greater than the proportion of its workers. Again, this does not mean that all workers in the sector are better off than workers in other sectors but they certainly have a better chance of being so.

One sector that produces rather little directly, though obviously important in other ways, is public administration, defence, education, social work, health and other personal services. In a developed economy, this sector is rather large, Singapore's employing two out of five workers. It also produces, directly, rather little (in Singapore's case only a tenth of the value of goods and services, probably because of large expenditures on defence). Elsewhere employment and production in this sector are more nearly balanced though much smaller, around 17 per cent for Thailand and 12 per cent for Indonesia.

Sector-by-sector analysis clearly shows that, on average, 'modern' sectors such as manufacturing, trade, finance and similar services are more productive than agriculture though less so than 'mining', which, except for Brunei, is economically of less importance, especially in employment. To be sure each sector is to some degree linked to each other, even to agricultural subsistence production. Investment, in capitalist systems, tends to flow to the sectors where returns are seen to be greatest. These are generally not in agriculture. Consequently, rural areas tend to be relatively poor, urban areas relatively rich, for manufacturing and most services are usually urban rather than rural.

Income disparities

Just how much richer urban areas may be is not easy to establish, for lack of comprehensive surveys, not to mention the difficulties of establishing

Table 6.9 Urban incomes—lowest and highest incomes by quintiles, 1994

Country	Proportion of total income available to lowest 20% of population	Proportion of total income available to highest 20% of population
Indonesia	8.8	41.3
Malaysia	4.6	51.2
Philippines	5.5	48.0
Singapore	5.1	48.9

Source: Economist Intelligence Unit, 1994

what true wealth may be. What is certainly true is that the range of incomes is greater in towns and cities because few wealthy folk live permanently in the countryside, and those who do—in the Philippines mainly rural landlords, in Malaysia plantation managers—divert most of their income towards cities.

The range of incomes probably has little or nothing to do with average levels. Even in poor countries a few individuals may control much wealth. In Brunei, Malaysia and Cambodia some members of royalty may be included in this group though in Thailand the King has, it is said, no great personal fortune. The Suharto family in Indonesia is said to have controlled at least a third of the nation's wealth while in the Philippines the Lopez, Ayala, Aquino, Cojuanco, Romualdez and Marcos families, along with Lucio Tan, are claimed to be seriously wealthy.

Survey data confirm this impression of considerable wealth concentrated in rather few hands. A mid-1990s survey of urban income in four middle and upper income countries showed that a large proportion was concentrated in the highest 20 per cent of the population, with a very small fraction accruing to the bottom fifth (see Table 6.9).

Why do such discrepancies exist? Among many reasons the prime factor is the fact that the wealthy have their hands very firmly on the levers of political power, except in Viet Nam and Laos, and possibly also in Singapore. Power is exercised and consolidated by networks of patron–client relationships. The redistribution of wealth is not now a notable part of any country's policy though all governments are aware of the power of urban people to make or unmake governments whether though the ballot box or by direct action. A measure of redistribution is thus necessary, though in many countries—Cambodia, the Philippines and Indonesia are examples—governments are seriously constrained by their inability to collect the revenues due to them.

Such large disparities existed in colonial times and the wealth of some families was founded then. Examples of 'old money' include the Aquino family in the Philippines and the Lee Kong Chian family in Singapore.

Royal control of wealth goes back further still. But much is 'new money', deriving from rapid economic growth in the region's capitalist economies.

Socialist redistribution is perceived to have failed, resulting in slow growth and shared poverty. Increasing urbanisation and economic diversification have enormously broadened opportunities for 'ordinary folk' to make a living and possibly to strike it rich. That is a powerful perception. Dreams are realised often enough for many to continue to work towards them, in the meantime tolerating present irksomeness, delaying gratification, generally accepting large income disparities as means to greater ultimate wealth.

The consequences of income disparities are many-fold and can only be touched upon here. One of the most obvious is the often close juxtaposition of areas of poverty and wealth in the region's cities. A midnight walk in the Central Business District of Manila or Jakarta or many other cities is to encounter the urban underclass sleeping in doorways, on the footpath, under a mobile stall or a bridge, anywhere that offers shelter. The street is home. One step up may be a shanty along a drain, a railway, or in a more extensive settlement of self-built, minimally serviced houses complete with its own shops, simple workshops and brothels, even tiny gardens and farms. Such are or were Manila's Tondo, Bangkok's Klong Toey and Singapore's Potong Pasir. At the other end of the scale are Manila's Forbes Park, Kuala Lumpur's Damansara Heights or Singapore's Binjai Park. In between are middle-class suburbs, from Kuala Lumpur sprawling almost to Seremban and to Port Kelang. Only in Singapore is economic redistribution—mainly in the form of high-rise public housing—much in evidence.

The structure of retailing parallels the structure of housing and income. At one end is the village or shantytown shop or wayside stall selling simple necessities—salt, matches, cooking oil, canned meat for a special meal, cigarettes sold by the stick, sweets and biscuits to satisfy a habit or the need for a treat. At the other is the air-conditioned shopping arcade selling international brands of 'positional goods', designed to display wealth and status as much or more than for practical purposes. Whatever their origin such goods usually bear the 'magic' names of London, Paris, New York and Tokyo, bearing little or no relationship to the indigenous culture of the people who buy them.

One area that does not parallel income structure is that of savings and investment. Wealthy Singapore, despite substantial defence expenditure—a form of consumption—nevertheless saves 30–40 per cent of its income, investing both at home and abroad. By contrast, savings in the poorest countries are proportionately much lower and in absolute terms are minuscule. Virtually all of such revenue as governments succeed in capturing goes to support the government apparatus. Insofar as the poorer members of their communities have any savings at all these may be in non-liquid form—gold, jewellery, gongs, jars—and at best are so small and spatially dispersed that it does not pay banks to try to mobilise them for general benefit. The benefits from the private savings of the wealthy may also not be available for investment. Currencies such as the *kyat* (Myanmar), *riel* (Cambodia), *kip* (Laos), *dong* (Viet Nam), *rupiah* (Indonesia) are nobody's first choice as an investment home and it is clear that substantial amounts flow across borders to more reliable destinations such as the US dollar. The wealthy in poorer, less secure countries probably recycle their money in their own economies only to a limited degree, thereby helping to maintain income disparities.

SEVEN
PRIMARY ECONOMIC SYSTEMS

Primary economic systems combine natural resources with labour and capital in systems of direct exploitation. Their products may undergo processing, something that is more generally thought of as manufacturing, but such processing is usually simple—cleaning rattan collected from the forest, drying fish, husking rice—in order to preserve the product or to reduce its bulk for cheaper transportation. In the past, most people depended upon such systems for their livelihood, often in complex combinations, and even today many employ a combination of systems to survive, making use of 'free goods' such as fish in rice-fields as well as the rice they grow and the animals they hunt. Though work for cash in factories, on the streets, or on construction sites may be added to primary activities in a bewilderingly complex array of strategies for economic survival, the basic link is directly with land and sea.

Many different classifications of primary economic systems could be devised. Here several classes are distinguished, though in reality families may be simultaneously involved in two or more kinds of systems. First are systems that directly exploit 'free goods' such as fish in the water, animals in the forest, petroleum and other minerals in the ground. (There is, in fact, no such thing as a 'free good' for even catching a fish requires a labour input, but it is a convenient fiction.) Systems of hunting and gathering, fishing—but not aquaculture—and mining fall into this category. (So does capturing the energy of falling water in a hydroelectricity station but by convention this is either included as 'manufacturing' or put with other forms of electricity generation, gas and water to make up a small sector on its own.) Shifting cultivation forms a second category though it may also be combined with other, sedentary, forms of cultivation. Shifting cultivators usually produce a range of crops. Not so most sedentary cultivators, whether growers of wet rice, of rubber or small-scale raisers of animals, including fish. Such are peasants—small-scale, family producers, some only marginally integrated into the cash economy, most now largely or entirely so. These form another large group. Finally are the 'factories-in-the-fields', large-scale, wholly commercial enterprises with formal structures of ownership and management as well as considerable numbers of wage-labourers who form a rural proletariat that neither owns nor has access to land for independent, family cultivation.

Foraging—which broadly includes hunting, gathering and fishing—is as old as humankind in the region. With the spread of agriculture, perhaps 6000 years ago, its relative importance as a means of obtaining food declined. How early trade in foraged commodities such as dried fish, precious woods and gums collected from forests began is not known. Long-distance networks were probably in existence 2000 years ago, while trade between coastal and inland peoples in marine products and salt evaporated from the sea is likely to have been very early, not least because of humans' physiological needs for sodium and for trace amounts of iodine.

Fishing

Evolution

Little is known of the evolution of fishing in the region. The very wide range of methods used to catch fish, the many kinds of fish caught and the deep knowledge of their habits possessed by traditional fishermen suggest a long history. For example, though westerners once pooh-poohed the idea, Malay fishermen listening under water can identify kinds of fish and prawns by the sounds they make. Commercial exploitation by fishermen from outside the region has also existed for many centuries. Parties of Chinese once were left for months on remote shores to catch and dry fish, especially delicacies such as *bêche-de-mer* (Holothurians). Within the region, sea-nomads living aboard small outrigger canoes or in rough shelters on beaches, foraged far and wide in the archipelagoes, the Moken and like folk surviving still amongst the islands off the coast of Myanmar's southern panhandle and in parts of the Sulu, Timor and Arafura seas. Such peoples form tiny minority groups retaining many of their old ways. Rather larger is the Vietnamese fisher community on Cambodia's Tonlé Sap, said to number half a million.

Certainly fishing is a significant activity, because fish are a major source of fats and protein. This is reflected in the fact that the region produces about 12 per cent of the world's fish, though a proportion of this is raised by mariculture (in the sea) or by aquaculture (in fresh waters).

The region's contribution to global freshwater fisheries is about the same though a substantial fraction of that figure comes from pond culture rather than by captures from the wild. The Tonlé Sap is said to be the world's richest natural freshwater fishery.

All captures from the wild are dependent upon the richness of the bases of the fishes' food-chain, especially plant and animal plankton. At sea, daily production of plant plankton is rather variable though on average substantially below the levels of cold, nutrient-rich water in higher latitudes. In enclosed seas and particularly off the mouths of large rivers, production, especially of animal plankton, is much higher than in the almost desert-like oceanic water of the Indian and Pacific oceans. The average in Southeast Asian seas is mostly above 250 mg m^3 (milligrams per cubic metre) per day for plant plankton but ranges from 50–500 mg m^3 per day for animal plankton. The seas are thus moderately productive.

Organisation, techniques, products

Fishing has long existed with two distinct forms of economic organisation. On one hand it is part of a complex system of foraging by people who depend largely or entirely upon it for subsistence. Such may still exist in remote corners of the region. More commonly, farmers rely upon local fishing to supply some of their food needs though it may have as much a recreational function as being a serious food-getting activity. Only this kind of fishing is truly for subsistence.

On the other hand, fishing may be a specialised occupation. Specialised fishing, organised on a family basis, is widespread whether at sea, on lakes, or along major rivers. Though some writers refer to it as 'subsistence fishing' it is not so, for fishing alone cannot supply significant quantities of dietary carbohydrate. Necessarily, it has been always directed towards trade, at least in part.

Fishing techniques are extremely diverse, reflecting the long history of the activity and close observation of the quarry's habits. Some—casting nets, spears, portable traps, hook-and-line—are used by single individuals. Others require cooperation. The once-widespread use of an extract of 'tuba' root (*Derris* spp.) added to water to stun fish in a village 'fish-drive' has largely given way to other approaches, including the illegal use of cyanide and dynamite to stun or kill reef fish. Where once fishing was confined to near-shore waters about a day's sailing distance from the coast, now outboard motors or simple diesel engines have greatly extended vessels' range, even that of craft of traditional design. So too has the provision of ice at fishing ports, while larger vessels of modern design carry on-board refrigeration. The latter may range as far afield as the southern Indian Ocean on voyages of a month or more. As elsewhere in the world they use a range of trawls and long lines equipped with multiple hooks, locating fish using modern sonar methods. Trapping fish using large dip-nets or in the Malay world, *kelongs*, large structures of wooden piles in shallow offshore waters, is widespread, though diminishing.

Fish and fish products are very much part of the Southeast Asian diet, one of the reasons why such a high proportion of the global catch—about one-eighth—is landed in the region. Salting and drying was the traditional method of preserving the catch, one still widely practised in coastal villages where aromatic drying platforms are very much part of their layout. Both freshwater and marine fish, including crustacea and molluscs, are also transformed into a wide range of tasty condiments. From Myanmar to Viet Nam a fish sauce, *nam pla* in Thailand, *nuoc mam* in Viet Nam, is extracted by halic (salty) fermentation, a process that perfumes the air for kilometres around. This occupies much the same place in mainland Southeast Asian cuisine as soya sauce does in Chinese. Notable, especially in insular Southeast Asia, is the fish or prawn paste known as *belacan*, also a halic fermentation product. Canning is a modern development, of course, but it has not been widely adopted, except to some degree in Thailand. Smoking for preservation and quick-freezing are unknown except the latter in export prawn and high-value fish production. Most fish is sold dead, but iced, though increasingly there is a demand for live fish for the table even though these may cost three times as much as dead ones. Kudat, in Sabah, is one emerging centre in Malaysia for this luxury trade.

Fish culture

Catching fish from the wild has often been an uncertain affair so that both mariculture and aquaculture have steadily developed in the region, reducing some environmental uncertainties but introducing others, not least those of export markets. (Though not exploiting 'free goods', it is convenient to consider them here.) Both represent the 'domestication' of wild animals just as pigs or cattle once were, but production still relies to some degree upon the capture of live fish from the wild and raising in enclosures. Raising prawns in ponds constructed in former mangrove forest can be highly remunerative, so much so that in the 1970s such prawns formed two-fifths of Viet Nam's total exports. However, after some years pond production declines, mainly as a result of disease and toxicity problems. Ponds are abandoned as operators move on, leaving behind them a devastated ecosystem that takes decades to recover.

Aquaculture in fresh water is generally much more stable and ponds have run smoothly for generations as their inhabitants convert human and animal wastes and rough vegetation into edible products. A modest range of freshwater fish is employed—catfish (including highly valued air-breathers of the genus *Clarias*), carp, some kinds of goby, serpent-heads, milk-fish and, increasingly, the originally African species *Tilapia*. The last-named is regarded by ecologists as a matter of some concern as it escapes readily and tends to replace some species of native fish in natural habitats. In the region the cultivation of pond fish has been steadily expanding. Areas around cities once in rice are being converted into fish-ponds catering to the live-fish trade, because ponds give a much higher income despite the very substantial capital needs for construction.

Production

In the region as a whole, about a third of the fish production comes from fresh waters, a proportion that is steadily rising as marine catches decline. (In 1989 the regional marine catch was recorded as 9.9 million tonnes but only 9.1 million tonnes in 1997, the latest year for which figures are available.) One piscatorial area that has received very little attention (in contrast to Japan for instance) is the cultivation of molluscs—oysters and mussels especially—though people certainly esteem them. Perhaps the facts that coastal and estuarine waters near population centres are generally polluted and that people living where water is clear do not have the knowledge or the capital to break into a lucrative luxury market may explain the situation. A small Chinese-owned pearl oyster 'farm' manages to survive near Balambangan island, east Malaysia, but there are few of its kind.

Fisheries production is not fully reported, especially that of non-commercial producers, but sufficient data are available to discern regional patterns. As was noted earlier, the region produces substantially more fish than its population size might suggest. With only 8 per cent of the world's people it produces 12 per cent of its commercial catch, most of which, except for prawns, is consumed in the region. The two specialist economies, Singapore and Brunei, have notably small marine fisheries, relying upon Malaysia to supply their fish markets. Their freshwater fisheries scarcely exist, though Singapore's small industry is highly lucrative by being focused upon the supply of exotic aquarium fish. (Singapore plans to expand aquaculture substantially.)

The former command economies of mainland Southeast Asia also produce limited quantities of marine fish, partly because their fleets are small and mostly operate in near-shore waters. In all of them, freshwater fisheries are also important. The proportion of the total production ranges from about a third for Myanmar through four-fifths in Cambodia, where the Tonlé Sap fishery is dominant, to the entire production coming from fresh waters in Laos where, uniquely, pond culture may be combined with the shifting cultivation of cereals in the hills. Surprisingly, though Viet Nam has a long coast, more than half of its fish come from freshwater sources, but its marine industry has long been plagued by limited capital,

Table 7.1 Fisheries production, 1997

Country	Total production (000 tonnes)	Proportion from fresh waters (%)	Production per person (kg)
Brunei	4	1	15
Cambodia	106	79	10
Indonesia	3 682	17	18
Laos	40	100	8
Malaysia	936	3	42
Myanmar	892	27	20
Philippines	1 660	9	22
Singapore	8	1	2
Thailand	2 674	16	34
Viet Nam	1 077	38	14
Southeast Asia	11 079	Av. 18	Av. 22

Source: FAO, http://apps.fao.org, accessed 15-11-00

lack of fuel and spare parts as well as difficult environmental conditions, especially during the southwest monsoon. By contrast, Thailand has a more modern fleet, reflected in much larger catches. Freshwater production is also significant there and, perhaps surprisingly in view of their archipelagic character, also in Indonesia and the Philippines. The country-by-country situation is set out in Table 7.1.

The long-term trend of fisheries in the region is likely to be further in the direction of culture, because capture from the wild is already experiencing significant problems, reflected especially in falling catches of marine species despite increasing fishing effort. In none of the region's seas is there a management plan. While size quotas exist in a bid to conserve young fish, they are enforced only to a limited degree. Many species breed along mangrove coasts, or in forested freshwater environments around major lakes such as the Tonlé Sap. Others 'school' to breed, making capture and over-fishing a simple matter. Reef fish are especially vulnerable to illegal capture using cyanide or dynamite, while most kinds are vulnerable to the use of illegally small-meshed nets. River fisheries are also vulnerable to pollution and to physical barriers such as hydroelectric dams, which may cut off migratory species from their upstream breeding sites. The latter consideration, plus the prospective change in water flow as a result of dam-building, are particularly pertinent in the Mekong/Tonlé Sap system.

Foraging

The extent to which foraging survives, especially on land and in fresh waters, is not known. It is doubtful that any group of people now relies upon it entirely for food. (Indeed it is doubtful that foragers in deep unmodified forest have ever relied upon it exclusively, for accessible carbohydrate sources are limited.)

However, foraging as a supplementary source of food, especially sources of fats and proteins, is widespread amongst traditional cultivators. Forests contain significant quantities of meat in both their mammals and birds. Rivers, streams and lakes contain fish, small crustaceans and molluscs. Modification of forests towards grasslands, including the 'cultivated grasslands' represented by rice-fields, increases the biomass represented by mammals and, possibly, birds. Wet rice-fields are also occupied by a range of fish—serpent-heads, carp, gouramies, catfish—producing 30–120 kg per hectare a year, as well as molluscs and crustacea. This is particularly so where herbicides and insecticides are not used, for these seriously affect the edible rice-field fauna. Forests and waste places generally also furnish edible fungi and leaves, some used as flavourings. Even insects gathered from the wild add relish plus some fat and protein to the diet.

Foraging for food is still significant amongst hill farmers throughout the region, especially shifting cultivators, for regenerating clearings provide an array of foods, pigs and deer notably. Harold Conklin's classic 1950s study of the Hanunoo of Mindoro showed how important and varied collected foods may be, as does Ormeling's similar work on Timor and the large ethnographic literature by French and American scholars in the plateaux and mountains of Indochina. Most important are sources of fats, proteins and flavourings. While total animal biomass in the region's forests is thought to lie in the range of 150–200 kg/ha, much of this is insects, which are gathered for food only to a limited degree. Primates are the commonest large mammals, their live-weight biomass estimated to range from 5 to 30 kg/ha. How large the total mammalian and avian (bird) biomass in forests might be, and its annual production, are not accurately known but the values are likely to be higher where grasses and herbaceous plants exist to be grazed by bovids—wild cattle and buffaloes—as well as by deer and pigs.

In insular Southeast Asia, the Islamic religion is a barrier—not always observed—to the consumption of wild pork, but generally most mammals and birds are consumed, including rice-field rats, jungle cats—just about anything that moves. Traditional methods of capture—snares, pitfalls, blowpipes with poisoned darts, bows and arrows—have mostly given way to the shotgun. The consequent ease of hunting has tended to increase pressure upon game resources and this has been exacerbated by the emerging market for exotic meats where refrigeration and markets can be reached before serious putrefaction sets in. Large mammals such as elephant, rhinoceros, bears, in some areas wild cattle, are now rare or very rare, though wild pig and deer flourish in remoter areas. Under human attack are the primates—gibbons, orang utan and monkeys especially—major grazers of the rainforests. It is not known, however, how much of their decline is to be attributed to hunting for food or for sale as pets and how much to habitat destruction and modification.

Crops and animals

Fish and 'wild meat' are far from being the largest component of Southeast Asians' diet. Rice is almost everywhere the dominant source of carbohydrate and has been so for so long that in many of the region's vernacular languages 'rice' is 'food' and 'food' is 'rice'. Only in parts of the Visayas (central Philippines) and amongst the poorest segments of the rural population do maize and manioc replace rice. Rice is a lowland, swamp plant by origin (though not of acidic, blackwater morasses). Whether it was domesticated in the region, perhaps more than once, or along the middle Yangzi in China remains debated. Though archaeological sites in the latter region contain older remains of rice, dated to about 6000 BC, than in Southeast Asia, the existence of species of wild rice in our region would have allowed independent domestication. What is certain is that the crop's place of origin could not have been in the equatorial zone, for only further north (or south) is variation in the length of day sufficient to trigger flowering of the rice plant. Equally certain is the fact that rice—a swamp-dweller—could not have been an early component of the crop repertoire possessed by shifting cultivators using hill-slopes.

Though the evidence is very slim, it seems likely that the diet of early Southeast Asians was based upon carbohydrate from tubers such as taro (*Colocasia* spp.) and yam (*Dioscorea* spp.) perhaps also from bananas (*Musa* spp.), all of which have been in cultivation so long as to have lost the knack of sexual reproduction. In eastern Indonesia, perhaps elsewhere, sago starch from thick-stemmed palms such *Metroxylon sagu* may have been an early staple.

Crop plants

Until the sixteenth century people's diets must have been rather less varied than they are today. Common species, especially those of the ginger family such as cardamom, the galangals, ginger itself, coriander and cumin, the Asian parsleys as well as pepper (*Piper nigrum*) were widely used. There was also regional trade in such rarities as cloves (*Syzygium aromaticum*) and nutmegs (*Myristica fragrans*). But the chilli-pepper, now so characteristic of the region's cuisine, was missing. It is of American origin, like a long list of other crops all of which were probably introduced to the Philippines from Mexico via Spanish galleons. The list includes starchy staples such as the sweet potato, (*Ipomoea batatas*), though *Solanum* potatoes are later, almost certainly via Europe, and manioc (*Manihot esculenta*), as well as *Capsicum* peppers, maize (*Zea mays*), peanuts (*Arachis hypogaea*), the tomato (*Lycopersicon esculentum*) and the fruits papaya (*Carica papaya*) and pineapple (*Ananas comosus*).

Other common crops are also introductions, though no one knows when—from China: Chinese cabbage (*Brassica chinensis*), onions, (*Allium* spp.), soyabean (*Glycine max*), sweet mandarins; from South Asia: egg-plant (*Solanum melongena*), the mango (*Mangifera indica*) and possibly jackfruit (*Artocarpus heterophyllus*). Many fruits, however, are of truly Southeast Asian origin, including the masticatory nut of the *Areca* palm and the ever-useful coconut palm (*Cocos nucifera*), though possibly not *Borassus* and *Corypha* palms, once widely tapped as a source of toddy and, when boiled down, palm sugar. These may be of South Asian origin. The delectable durian (*Durio zibethinus*), mangosteen (*Garcinia mangostana*) and a close kin to the lychee, the rambutan (*Nephelium lappaceum*), are all natives whose distribution has been much extended from their home in the wetter parts of insular Southeast Asia.

Yet other introductions are important smallholder and plantation crops: the coffees (*Coffea* spp.) from Arabia and East Africa, oil palm (*Elaeis guineensis*) from West Africa, rubber (*Hevea brasiliensis*) from the Amazon via Kew Gardens, London, Sri Lanka and Singapore, cocoa (*Theobroma cacao*—literally 'the food of the gods') also from the Amazon basin via Mexico and the Spanish galleons. From the West Indies come the 'sops'—sweet and sour—as well as the custard-apple, not an apple at all but, like the sops, an *Annona*.

Animals

In contrast to many of the plants, most of the domestic animals are 'locals'—dog, pig, chicken, some breeds of cattle, buffaloes. Goats and sheep, the latter rather few in number, may have been introduced from about the thirteenth century by Arab or other Muslims as a substitute for the pig, like dog forbidden as food to the Faithful.

Cattle as herd animals were once much more common than they are today, especially in the less densely populated parts of mainland Southeast Asia. Local breeds are small in stature, though hardy, and may have been originally domesticated in parts of the region. By contrast, the tall white cattle are probably of fairly recent Indian origin. Prior to colonial times cattle were rare in the Philippines, the Spanish doing much to set up large-scale ranching. Cattle were also relatively uncommon in Sumatera, Sulawesi and the Sunda islands as far east as Timor. They were absent in Borneo as well as New Guinea, where numbers are still few. As draught animals for pulling a plough in heavy soils they are inferior to buffaloes but are effective as a pair on lighter soils, also withstanding hot conditions better than the buffalo. Until the advent of railways ox-drawn carts and pack-cattle were the main form of overland transport, their use surviving in Southeast Asia's borderlands with China to this day. Nowhere in the region are cattle milked for human consumption, except amongst recent migrants of South Asian origin. Curd, whey, cheese, butter were absent from traditional diets.

Buffaloes, still the tractive mainstay of wet-rice cultivation in much of the region, may have been originally domesticated in a large area encompassing northeast India and the more westerly parts of mainland Southeast Asia. Their spread eastwards cannot be well documented but that spread may have been at least partly in association with technically more advanced forms of wet-rice cultivation. The buffalo is still raised as a herd animal in less densely populated areas, grazing rice-stubble in the dry season and being driven into neighbouring forests and scrublands to fend for themselves during the wet season. Buffaloes seem to have spread rather unevenly, especially in insular Southeast Asia, where they were absent from northern Borneo and southern Philippines until after European contact. As draught animals their great strength and, when amongst people they know, their placid temperament, make them particularly desirable, though breeding slowly and readily suffering heat-stress. So crucial was the buffalo to rice cultivation that until recently epidemics amongst them triggered great hardship amongst peasant farmers who, in days of low-yielding traditional varieties, could not till enough land on their own to ensure their family's food supply.

Pigs are ubiquitous in much of mainland Southeast Asia, providing a significant proportion of dietary protein for special occasions amongst rural people and for better-off urbanites. Pigs are very efficient converters of what is often waste into meat and in intensive vegetable-producing systems found around most cities play an important role in recycling many kinds of waste. In insular Southeast Asia, except the largely Christian centre and north of the Philippines, pigs are limited by Islamic sanctions and in Singapore by the need to avoid pig-farm effluent flowing into sources of drinking water.

Chickens are also efficient converters of one kind of food into another and there can scarcely be a rural family, not to mention dwellers in informal housing in the cities, who do not keep some. Commercial production of both chickens and eggs is of some significance, especially near urban areas. This production depends partly upon imported feedstuffs such as low grades of wheat as well as locally produced maize and cassava (manioc) chips. A proportion of commercially produced chicken now finds its way into export markets in frozen form.

Land, crops and animals—some profiles

There are many ways in which profiles of agriculture could be constructed but the limitations of statistics and space basically require the construction of just two. One looks at kinds of agricultural land use country-by-country and the other what specific crops and animals are raised on these lands. Tables 7.2 and 7.3 show the former.

Population, agricultural population and land

What is particularly striking about the data in Table 7.2 is that each country's share of agricultural land in the region is very far from being in proportion to its population—leaving aside essentially non-agricultural Brunei and Singapore. (Arable and permanent crop lands do not produce all the crops, of course, only most of them, for people living in the hills and mountains rely upon shifting cultivation for both subsistence and for cash. But the area in this form of cultivation is anybody's guess.) Thus Cambodia, with just over 2 per cent of the region's people has almost 7 per cent of its agricultural land. More striking are Malaysia and Thailand, which have shares of agricultural land about double their share of the regional population. By contrast, Viet Nam's share of agricultural land is about half of its share of the regional population. Little wonder that most of its rice-land is cropped twice yearly. The shares of the other countries are more or less in line with their shares of the population.

Equally striking is the comparison between each country's share of the region's agricultural population and the share each has of agricultural land. Cambodia, Laos, Myanmar and Viet Nam—the region's poorest countries—all have a much higher share of the region's agricultural population than of the population as a whole. Taken together with agricultural land, the agricultural population shows up some interesting patterns. Some countries have rather few people working a lot of land—Cambodia, where most is in rice; Malaysia, where most is in rubber, oil palm, cocoa and coconut; Thailand, with much rice, some rubber. On the other hand, Viet Nam, mostly growing rice, has two-fifths of the region's agricultural population (compared with Indonesia's third) on just under 8 per cent of the land. Not surprisingly it is poor. Double-cropping is essential to survival and a significant proportion of people eat all they themselves produce. For the rest, the proportions of agricultural population and agricultural land are about the same.

Arable and perennial crops

Another set of comparisons is made in the country-by-country profile of arable and perennial crops shown in Table 7.3. Arable crops are dominated by rice (see Table 7.4 for more detail), while perennial crops include rubber, oil palm, cocoa and coconut. Unfortunately there are no regional data for the areas of each of these but taking perennial crops as a group some further striking contrasts emerge.

While comparisons of agricultural population and arable land show

Table 7.2 Population, agricultural population, area of agricultural land and regional proportions, 1997–98

	Population (1998)		Agric. pop'n (1998)		Arable & permanent crop land (1997)	
Country	**No. (mil.)**	**Prop'n (%)**	**No. (mil.)**	**Prop'n (%)**	**(mil. ha)**	**%**
Brunei	0.3	0.1	*	*	*	*
Cambodia	10.7	2.1	7.6	3.0	3.8	4.2
Indonesia	206.3	41.0	93.7	36.9	31.0	34.2
Laos	5.2	1.0	4.0	1.6	0.9	1.0
Malaysia	21.4	4.3	4.1	1.6	7.6	8.4
Myanmar	44.5	8.9	31.5	12.4	10.2	11.3
Philippines	72.9	14.5	29.6	11.7	9.5	10.5
Singapore	3.5	0.7	*	*	*	*
Thailand	60.3	12.0	30.4	12.0	20.4	22.5
Viet Nam	77.6	15.4	52.9	20.8	7.2	7.9
Total	502.7	100.0	278.9	100.0	90.6	100.0

Note: * negligible
Source: *FAO Production Yearbook 1998*

many similarities, as do comparisons between agricultural population and agricultural lands in general, the pattern for perennial crops is very different. Four-fifths of them are grown in the equatorial lands of Indonesia, Malaysia and the Philippines. In fact, were statistics available, they would show very little perennial cropping north of the latitude of Da Nang. True, coconuts may be found to the north, grown mainly around villages, but no rubber, oil palm or cocoa. (Rubber does grow, badly, on China's Hainan island and the adjoining mainland but could never compete on the global market.)

The reasons for this are partly climatic and partly historical. Both oil palm and cocoa prefer equable temperatures and an even distribution of rain. So does rubber. Its yield falls north of about 8°N latitude, though it is still grown by smallholders to a considerable extent along the 'panhandle' of southern Myanmar and Thailand. Small farmers dominate elsewhere as well but were not originally responsible for its introduction and establishment, capitalistic plantations being literally first in the field. In respect of oil palm they remain so, though the oil palm is a smallholder crop in its West African homeland.

History and climate converge in the Philippines, where rubber and oil palm scarcely exist. The early twentieth-century Homestead Acts made it difficult for enterprises to acquire blocks of land sufficiently large for plantations, which were discouraged by the American colonial government. Furthermore, rubber, unlike coconut, is notably prone to wind damage,

Table 7.3 Area and proportion under arable and perennial crops by country, 1997

Country	Arable		Perennial crops	
	Mill. ha	Prop'n (%)	Mill. ha	Prop'n (%)
Cambodia	3.7	6.0	0.1	0.3
Indonesia	17.9	29.0	13.0	45.1
Laos	0.8	1.3	*	
Malaysia	1.8	2.9	5.8	20.1
Myanmar	9.6	15.6	0.6	2.1
Philippines	5.1	8.3	4.4	15.3
Thailand	17.1	27.7	3.4	11.8
Viet Nam	5.7	9.2	1.5	5.2
Total	61.7	100.0	28.8	99.9

Note: * Less than 0.1 mill. ha
Source: *FAO Production Yearbook 1998*

effectively ruling it out as a crop appropriate to most of the country. The small areas of oil palm have been planted quite recently.

Agricultural land and total land area

A final set of country-by-country comparisons concerns agricultural land in relation to land in general. Were it not for the fact that politicians, and others, sometimes argue that there is plenty of potential agricultural land left in their country, some going further to suggest means of promoting rapid population growth to fill it up, this question would hardly be worth mentioning. In the region as a whole, only a fifth of the land area is permanently in agriculture—arable or perennial tree-crop. As with most other characteristics there is a considerable range from country to country. At one end of the spectrum is Laos—notably mountainous—with barely 4 per cent of its land permanently used for agriculture. At the other—again ignoring Brunei and Singapore—is Thailand, two-fifths of whose land is so used. Most of the rest range around the one-fifth level.

But for land not to be permanently used for agriculture does not mean that it is not used, even leaving aside the relatively small but rapidly growing fractions of the land area in urban uses. Shifting cultivation is a profligate user of land, though not as profligate as ultra-conservative 'greenies' may think. A family of shifting cultivators can live off one or two hectares of land in cultivation in any one year, but a field can be cultivated only one year—possibly two years—in ten, for weed problems and lowered soil fertility prevent more intensive use. Even gently sloping land must needs have a periodical fallow and most sloping land slopes steeply. Terracing is generally out of the question, because it is hopelessly uneconomic at current wage levels. Some lands terraced long ago—the famous Banaue rice terraces of north-central Luzon are an example—are going out of production or their owners are shifting to less-demanding sweet potatoes because it is barely economic to keep them going. In addition, of course, large areas are needed for forestry, water conservation and tourism. Large areas of swamp exist but these too are of extremely marginal value as agricultural land, except, as in Viet Nam, where people are living on the subsistence margin, costing their labour close to zero, reclaiming coastal land almost before it really forms.

Crops

Another way of looking at agricultural land use is by crop instead of by country. (It is also possible to analyse it by crop and country simultaneously but the reader who wishes to do so, at least for major crops, will need to consult original sources such as the *FAO Production Yearbooks*.) The range of crops is very large but only five are of major importance, occupying more than 2 million hectares each—rice, far and away the most important, followed by permanent crops such as rubber, oil palm, coconut, cocoa, coffee and tea, for which no comprehensive crop-by-crop data are available. Then come other arable crops, including maize, pulses—peas, beans, lentils—and sugar cane (see Table 7.4).

Rice is far and away the most important crop in the region. Recall that 'rice is food and food is rice'. It accounts for 38 per cent of all agricultural land, two-thirds of the arable (tilled) land. The proportion of arable occupied by rice is over half in every agricultural country in the region, ranging up to 129 per cent in Viet Nam, where a significant proportion of the rice land is cropped twice yearly. Most rice is grown in wet fields, about a third irrigated and highly productive, the rest rain-fed and less productive. Of the latter portion a small fraction is grown by shifting cultivation on sloping land, though yields are less reliable than on flat land as water supply varies considerably.

In addition to the other arable crops listed in Table 7.4 a number of others are of some significance or local importance. The ancient tubers, taro (*Colocasia*) and yam (*Dioscorea*), are now mostly kitchen-garden crops though sold in small quantities in most produce markets. They have been largely supplanted by 'American' tubers, the sweet potato, grown for its tasty leaves as well as for its tubers, and the cool-climate *Solanum* potato, miscalled 'Irish'. Tomatoes and chilli—more 'Americans'—are also widely grown. Much more localised are wheat and millet, grown in drier parts of Myanmar, and sorghum (*Sorgho* spp.), grown in Thailand, mostly as animal feed. Local crop specialisation is also seen in respect of a number of other arable crops. Two-fifths of the maize is grown in

Table 7.4 Agricultural land use by crop, 1998

Land use	Harvested area (mill. ha)	Proportion of regional total (%)	Proportion of global area (%)
Arable			
Rice	40.8	37.6	27.1
Maize	8.5	7.8	6.2
Pulses	3.2	2.9	4.8
Manioc	2.8	2.6	17.4
Sugar cane	2.1	1.9	11.0
Soya bean	1.6	1.5	2.3
Groundnuts	1.5	1.4	6.4
Sesame	0.9	0.8	13.1
Sweet potatoes	0.6	0.6	7.1
Cottonseed	0.2	0.2	0.6
Others	0.9	0.8	n.c.
Perennial crops			
Tea	0.3	0.3	11.2
Coffee	1.3	1.2	11.7
Cocoa	0.6	0.6	10.0
Others	25.6	23.6	n.c.
Perennial pasture (est.)	17.6	16.2	n.c.
Total	108.5	100.0	

Note: n.c. = not calculated
Source: *FAO Production Yearbook 1998*

Indonesia and another third in the Philippines, mainly the Visayas, some on sloping ploughland, some as a 'catch-crop' preceding, following, sometimes even accompanying rice.

Rice

Rice is grown in some quantity in every agricultural country of the region but not in proportion to each country's population. Thus Cambodia, with only 2 per cent of the region's people, has nearly 5 per cent of its rice land. Indonesia, with 41 per cent of the people, has only 28 per cent of the rice land; Malaysia 4 per cent of the people but only 1.5 per cent of the rice land, most of it in its northern peninsular states where a moderately marked dry season assists yields. The Philippines also has less rice land than its population might seem to warrant, while Myanmar and Thailand, major export producers (the former mostly in the past) have much more, Thailand especially. In part these disparities reflect climate and history. The strongly equatorial environment of most of Malaysia has never really favoured rice, especially as it was and is cheaper to import

Table 7.5 Rice and irrigated areas, production and yields, 1998

Country	Rice area (harv.) (000 ha)	Irrigated area (000 ha)[1]	Prop'n irrig. (%)	Production (000 tonnes)	Yields (tonnes/ha)
Cambodia	1 961	270	13.8	3 515	1.8
Indonesia	11 613	4 815	41.4	48 472	4.2
Laos	618	164	26.5	1 675	2.7
Malaysia	645	340	52.7	1 940	3.0
Myanmar	5 408	1 556	28.8	16 651	3.1
Philippines	3 170	1 550	48.9	8 555	2.7
Thailand	10 000	5 010	50.1	23 240	2.3
Viet Nam	7 362	2 300	31.2	29 142	4.0
Total	40 777	16 005	Av. 39.3	123 190	Av. 3.0

Note: [1] Data for 1997
Source: *FAO Production Yearbook 1998*

it from export-production areas in the lower Irrawaddy, Chao Phrya and Mekong valleys.

The disparities also reflect very different technological levels, for the last three decades have seen major increases in yields from the 1–1.5 tonnes of grain per hectare produced in the region for generations, probably millennia. The 'three-legged stool' of high-yielding varieties (HYVs), pesticides (plus herbicides) and irrigation has supported much higher yields from each hectare of land. Some countries still lag, notably Myanmar, Cambodia and Viet Nam. Thai yields are not particularly spectacular, partly because the country, since the mid-nineteenth century a producer of premium grades of rice for export, has chosen to some degree to sacrifice quantity for quality and the higher prices it brings. Table 7.5 sets out the country-by-country situation.

Perhaps the most extraordinary feat revealed by this table is Viet Nam's. Though less than a third of its rice land is irrigated, the country nevertheless manages to achieve a very respectable 4 tonnes of grain per hectare. It does this by managing to squeeze two crops each year from much of its rice land even though most is rain-fed, not irrigated. Elsewhere it is only irrigated land from which two crops a year are taken. In especially favoured areas—that around Yogyakarta in Java is one—continuous cropping of up to three rice-crops annually is possible. A field may be harvested in the morning as soon as the dew has dried off the panicles, immediately ploughed, harrowed, and the seedlings transplanted in the relative cool of late afternoon. Irrigation is crucial in another way. Because it is used both to supplement rainfall during the wet season as well as to provide the bulk of the crop's water needs in the dry season, yields are relatively stable and predictable from season to season. The main danger is flooding.

Export production of rice is dominated by Thailand, joined by southern Viet Nam in recent years. The proportion sent abroad by Myanmar is steadily diminishing. Grain goes to northern Viet Nam and to every other country in the region as well as beyond it. No other cereal crops are significant contributors to exports. Small quantities of other arable crops such as pulses and maize are exported internationally within the region, partly for animal food. By far the most important has been manioc, exported as chips, mainly from gently rolling terrain in northeast Thailand. This area is also the source of *kenaf—Hibiscus* fibre—exported as a substitute for jute.

Tree-crops

Much more important as export crops are the products of trees—rubber from the *Hevea* tree, kernels, kernel-oil and oil from the flesh of the oil palm, copra or oil from coconuts, and dried beans from the cacao shrub. Of these, only coconut products—oil for cooking and soap—are retained in any quantity in the region. All the rest are destined mainly for export outside Southeast Asia, a situation that has existed since the establishment of their cultivation.

For rubber this was in the very last years of the nineteenth century though the major expansion came in the twentieth, especially with the spread of pneumatic tyres in industrial countries, and with the development of vulcanisation which could transform rubber into one of the predecessors of plastics. From being a favourite crop of capitalists rubber was quickly taken up by smallholders, both planting hill lands which hitherto had been little used.

Most oil palm plantings date from after about 1952, a time of global shortage of vegetable oils. Palm oil is used in margarine, for cooking, in soap, in cosmetics and also as a lubricant in rolling steel plate.

Cocoa is even later, its planting having been much promoted by the government in Peninsular Malaysia in the 1960s. Since it grows happily under the shade of established coconut palms—to the mutual benefit of both—it is a means of increasing productivity, especially on better-quality coconut land.

As with many of the minor arable crops, production from tree-crops is highly localised, not only with respect to particular crops and to particular countries, but, with the partial exception of the ubiquitous coconut, to specific areas within producer countries. Production data also show the very considerable importance of the region's tree-crops in global output—78 per cent of the world's natural rubber, just over four-fifths of its palm oil, three-fifths of its coconuts, 12 per cent of its coffee, 11 per cent of its tea and cocoa, not to mention all of such Southeast Asian fruits as the rambutan, durian and mangosteen.

Two-thirds of the region's *Hevea* rubber is grown in just three countries, Thailand, Indonesia and Malaysia. Once the premier producer, Malaysia's ranking has fallen. Despite the technical efficiency of the industry's plantation sector especially, rubber is labour-intensive and is consequently highly sensitive to the cost of labour, which constitutes about four-fifths of production costs. As wages have risen with growing economic wealth, it has become more and more difficult to compete with lower-cost producers such as Thailand or Indonesia and especially with expanding production areas in southern Viet Nam where production has trebled over the last decade. Natural rubber is also highly sensitive to competition from synthetic rubber made from petroleum. For some purposes—motor-tyres is one—synthetic is superior to natural rubber. One of the few areas in which natural rubber, of the highest grades, enjoys a price premium over the synthetic version is for the production of condoms and other high-reliability dipped rubber goods.

Oil palms produce two kinds of oil, one from the fleshy pericarp, the other from the kernel. Southeast Asia is a global leader for the former, producing 82 per cent of the total. Half of the world's production comes from Malaysia, to the chagrin of some vegetable oil producers in temperate countries such as the US who have tried to keep palm oil out of their country. Production is almost entirely from large estates served by central processing plants and these are especially concentrated in the central and southern states of Peninsular Malaysia and in eastern Sabah.

Coconut has many uses, from palm thatch to toddy, from copra to high-grade charcoal. Its wide range of uses is one of the reasons why it grows in rural household gardens in all but the cooler parts of the region. Copra and oil, however, are the main commercial products, the former being simply the dried flesh of the coconut. Like rubber, it is a labour-intensive form of production, surviving in Malaysia as a commercial proposition only where grown in combination with cocoa or to meet the growing urban demand for young nuts for drinking or for fresh flesh for making curries. Low labour-cost producers, Indonesia and the Philippines, dominate commercial production as they have done for many decades.

Indonesia also dominates the production of tea and coffee, of which the whole region produces little more than the quantity needed to satisfy local markets. The coffee-drinking habit was introduced and promoted by the Dutch in Indonesia, the French in Viet Nam and by the Spanish and Americans in the Philippines so that to this day these are the main producer countries, accounting for 90 per cent of production.

The tea habit is of much longer standing. Indeed the tea plant is native to the region's northern margins. But the British—as great consumers—

decided against building an export-based tea industry in nineteenth-century Southeast Asia, preferring to develop it in Sri Lanka and India where extensive uplands of moderate slope but considerable elevation, plus cheap labour, fostered the production of premium qualities, some of which Southeast Asia imports.

Livestock

Given that almost 18 per cent of Southeast Asia's agriculturally used land is estimated to be in permanent pasture it may seem surprising that herds of animals are rather uncommon. Indeed, many of the kinds of animals grazed in herds and flocks in temperate lands are, in Southeast Asia, kept indoors in stalls and hand-fed with grass or wastes gathered wherever they can be. Dairy herds may be found near some large cities, some established in former times to provide fresh milk for colonials' teas and for their children, others kept by cattle-keepers of South Asian descent who almost alone amongst Southeast Asia's peoples have long been accustomed to the consumption of milk and milk products such as ghee (clarified butter) and curd.

Most buffaloes, which form 30 per cent of the 'large cattle' category, are kept for traction, pulling ploughs mostly, now rarely carts and sledges. Only in remoter areas with abundant land, notably in Thailand and Laos, are herds of these animals kept for slaughter—usually on festive occasions—or for training as adults in the gentle arts of tillage. Cattle also perform tractive tasks, especially in Myanmar and among the Cham peoples of southern Viet Nam who prefer them to buffaloes. Cattle are also herded but in no great number, often depending upon roadside and riverbank grazing while rice-fields are cropped, grazing their stubble in the dry season.

Pastures certainly exist. Some are abandoned rice-fields, as in central and southern parts of Peninsular Malaysia. Many are on hill slopes of grass and scrub maintained by annual burning to promote fresh new growth at the onset of the rains. All are of low to very low quality, rich in roughage, poor in fats, protein, even vitamins and minerals. Ironically, some of the region's best grasslands are on golf courses.

Of the smaller animals—goats and sheep (ovines), pigs (porcines)—the last are much the most important though a regional total of 54 million pigs is not especially large given the size of the human population. The number of pigs is just over 5 per cent of the world's total—a fair total given the predominance of Muslims in the region. Non-Muslim Viet Nam stands out with just over a third of the pig population, with a further fifth in the largely Christian Philippines. Though all countries have some pigs, in those with many Muslims sheep and goats provide a substitute, to the extent that they are often, especially in Java, kept in stalls like pigs and fed upon grass cut elsewhere and carried in. Some 70 per cent of the region's ovines are found in Indonesia, with another 20 per cent in the Philippines, where, however, they are usually kept in flocks.

In world terms, Southeast Asia's ovines are insignificant, making up less than 2 per cent of the total, only a third of the number of sheep in Australia. Its bovines are equally unimportant, at 3 per cent comprising only a fractionally higher proportion of the global total.

Little change in this situation can be envisaged, because cattle and buffaloes are less versatile as 'tractors' than small petrol motors. They get tired and have yet to master the arts of pumping irrigation water and drawing carts at highway speeds. There is little incentive to improve the quality of pastures or of meat from grazing animals—usually tough though tasty. It is almost as cheap for the urban middle classes to buy Australian or New Zealand steaks or chops from the supermarket rather than braving the dubious hygiene of local meat markets.

AGRICULTURAL SYSTEMS

Having thus dissected the primary sector—at least foraging and agriculture—it is necessary to reintegrate matters, for no segment exists in isolation from its physical, economic, cultural and social surroundings. Many different categorisations could be made, for while some categories of activities are clear—for example the large-scale production of palm oil—many are slippery.

Thus a family of shifting cultivators in Laos will depend upon a large range of activities for both subsistence and cash: collecting fungi, edible leaves, possibly insects and insect larvae from the forest; small game hunted from abandoned gardens, stream fish, pond fish; from a cultivated clearing, rice, maize, sweet potato, perhaps manioc as an emergency back-up food in a poor season; maybe some vegetables grown near the house, chilli especially; possibly occasional expeditions to sell handicrafts in a town.

Rice-growing in the lowlands may be a monoculture but food-getting may also involve digging a sump in a rice-field to which fish resort in the dry season, whence they are captured or excavated, especially by children, in occasional flurries of muddy delight. Equally, the wet season brings frogs by the million to be hunted by torchlight before the snakes get them. Smallholders who grow a variety of tree-crops may also grow a little rice or obtain some of their income from off-farm work.

By contrast, workers on rubber or palm oil plantations—rural proletarians these—work for wages and wages only, usually at a single, specialised task, tapping, weeding, pruning, driving a tractor or a locomotive hauling palm-fruits to a factory. In ecological terms the shifting cultivator and the rice-growing peasant are generalists, operating in a very complex system, partly natural, partly created, partly physical and biological, partly metaphysical, social and economic. By contrast the rural proletarian functions in a system that is biologically less complex—one crop, not many—that is driven by the market, formed by the cash nexus and the social structures necessary to the maintenance of veritable 'factories in the field'.

Keeping in mind the slipperiness of categories of activity, several major kinds can be distinguished on the basis of scale and economic orientation. Size or scale is really a matter of production economics rather than of areal extent. An intensive producer of vegetables with 5 hectares would be 'large'. A rubber smallholding of 5 hectares would be small. Nevertheless there is a clear gradation of scale from the many small 'peasant' farms, many now run only on a part-time basis, up to plantations of several thousand hectares producing rubber, palm oil or sugar. Fisheries see a similar gradation from the single operator of a dip-net up to large sea-going trawlers, like plantations representing large capital investments, often by companies rather than individuals. In economic orientation there is a similar gradation from production—whether foraging or farming—mainly for self-consumption, up to entirely commercial production where, at best, self-consumption is represented by a 'grace-and-favour' plot for plantation employees to grow a little food.

Shifting cultivation

Shifting cultivation, contrary to some opinions, is generally not a form of nomadism. Nowadays it is relatively uncommon for its practitioners to shift their long-houses or villages, for cultivators have often acquired sufficient of this world's goods to make such a migration a formidable undertaking. Rather it is characterised by the rotation of fields rather than of crops. This involves a year or two of cropping—usually of rice, maize and some tubers—followed by a period of fallow during which the natural vegetation regenerates.

At one time it was thought that the relatively short period of cultivation was explainable by the reduction in soil fertility that cropping entails. While this may be so for some very poor upland soils, it is more likely that it is the vigorous growth of weeds and the sprouting of cut stumps that cause so much competition with the growing crop after a couple of years that weeding is not feasible. What is certain is that fallow under grass is a very poor restorer of soil nutrients compared with fallow under resurgent woody vegetation. Once the stage of grass fallow is reached—usually *Imperata* grass—only a great deal of labour spent in tillage and weeding can keep it at bay and on poor soils abandonment is usually the best option.

Equally certain is the fact that hardly anywhere in the region do shifting cultivators now attack virgin forest, not only because there is little left but also because governments will not let them. A common pattern is for loggers to cut roads and drag-paths to remove millable timber. Cultivators then penetrate along these routes, temporarily initiating cultivation and shifting fields.

'Shifting-field' cultivation may also be practised in traditional tribal areas, providing an entire basis for life, spiritual and material. Such 'integral' shifting cultivators survive still in the mountains of the Indochinese cordillera, northern Thailand and much of upland Myanmar. Amongst such peoples land is 'owned' by local groups, with individual families holding rights to its use and its fruits. As often as not, such rights are not recognised by governments, leading sometimes to serious conflicts.

The family is the basic operational unit though amongst opium farmers labour is sometimes employed. Fields, some in cultivation, most in fallow at various stages of regeneration, are scattered and each family's lands may be interspersed with those of others, though sometimes a number of families will cooperate to clear—occasionally also to plant—an area of some tens of hectares. Usually a field in current cropping is 1–2 ha in size.

The annual cycle of cultivation is similar everywhere, dominated by the seasons. The secret lies in getting a good burn of the felled second-growth, for a good burn not only provides abundant ash to nourish growing crops but also slows the growth of competing vegetation. The late dry season is thus the time of flame and smoke, so much so that shifting cultivators are sometimes blamed for causing choking air pollution at this time. (The reality is that much of the burning is done by commercial operators seeking to establish tree-crops.) Once sufficient rain to germinate seeds is judged to have fallen seeds and, for tubers, slips, are planted directly into the soil rendered friable by burning. Tillage is rare, though some Shan people of mainland Southeast Asia use a light plough.

The crop combinations of shifting cultivators are often complex, certainly by comparison with the simple wet-rice monoculture of the plains. A range of crops, often planted higgledy-piggledy, has a number of advantages. Tall plants, such as bananas and maize, to some degree shelter lower ones such as pumpkins, ensuring good protection against erosive raindrop impact upon the soil, drawing nutrients from varying levels within it, providing a range of produce that spreads the risk of failure of any particular crop due to disease, pests or climatic misfortune and giving continuity to the food supply. Little weeding is done and the crops are left pretty much to their own devices until harvest-time approaches—

roughly three to four months after planting for maize, five or six for rice and a year or more for bananas and tubers.

Shifting cultivation is by no means the same everywhere. The traditional economy of Negrito groups in the interior of the Malay Peninsula was basically foraging, supplemented by limited cultivation of bananas and tubers, nowadays with collection of jungle produce, especially rattans, providing a cash income. Or shifting cultivation may be a more central part of the economy. Amongst the Palaung and peoples of the Assam border region of Myanmar, raising cattle, the famous *mithan*, is a supplementary activity. In parts of Laos, pond fish supplement shifting cultivation. It may also be a supplement to permanent wet-rice cultivation, or vice versa, the case especially where there is little flat land available.

Shifting cultivation is generally thought of as being confined to hills and mountains but in fact it may be practised on flat land in areas of low population density. There is good evidence that it was once much more widespread on flat terrain in the past, in parts of coastal Myanmar extending even to the agriculturally difficult mangrove ecosystem.

It is also thought of as being environmentally damaging. Colonial-period records are full of complaints about the prodigality of cultivators who would cut down valuable timber in order to produce a derisory amount of food. In fact forest-dwellers had little option, for forest can support only very small populations—perhaps a family per square kilometre at best—while shifting cultivation can provide for 20–30 people per square kilometre without long-term environmental damage other than rendering the forest useless for timber extraction. In a word, at low densities it is sustainable.

But in much of the region, 'death-control' has led to a growing population. This can readily initiate a downward spiral of damage. If unoccupied land is not available, population growth, via increased demand for food, leads to reduction of fallow under scrub. Though 90 per cent of soil nutrients are restored after a fallow of six to eight years, shorter fallows eventually lead to lower levels of nutrients. These in turn lead to lower crop yields, in turn again requiring the clearance of larger areas or even shorter fallows in order to sustain food production.

Or so the argument goes. In reality there is little adequate documentation of this process. Severely damaged lands are simply abandoned before the system breaks down entirely. Two things are likely. One is that the introduction of short-term cash crops, such as opium poppy, or its substitutes *Solanum* potatoes or cut flowers, does not necessarily lead to any real change to shifting cultivation. (Substitution is feasible only where easy transport to market is possible.) Second and more certain is that increasing population rarely, if ever, leads to wholesale terracing of hillsides and their conversion into 'vertical swamps' to grow wet rice. Rather, the general pattern is to intercalate trees among the temporary crops. Much of the rubber in Sarawak was introduced in this manner. In colonial Burma teak was grown on a 60 to 80 year cycle in areas of shifting cultivation. This provided cash—eventually—while the open canopy and deciduous character of the trees allowed intercropping with food crops to succeed. This *taungya* system was exported to Java, where it also survives.

However, 60 to 80 years is a very long time to wait for an economic return. For much of mainland Southeast Asia, as for the drier areas of the eastern Indonesian archipelago, the critical question remains—which crops can be fitted into systems of shifting cultivation that will give a good, short-run cash return, are capable of bearing the costs of transportation to market in difficult or fragmented terrain, are sustainable and not environmentally damaging? The answer at the moment is—probably nothing.

For some communities of shifting cultivators, those living in reasonably accessible locations, one answer is 'eco-tourism'. Their communities, their local environment, their jungle skills can be and are being sold. Examples include the Aeta minority group based at Mount Pinatubo, Luzon, long-house stays in Sarawak, and national park activities more widely in the region. The danger for local minorities is that they become performers in human zoos operated mainly for the benefit of others.

Peasant production

Scholars sometimes spend a deal of effort defining peasants (and the peasantry), but fundamentally they are small-scale farmers producing crops for their own and their family's survival—just like shifting cultivators. The major differences lie in social organisation, and to a lesser degree in stability of settlement. The region's peasant farmers are generally members of the dominant cultural group in a state—Burmans in Myanmar, *Dai Viet* or *Kinh* in Viet Nam. They are truly part of the state and have long been recognised to be so. By contrast, many shifting cultivators are tribal peoples, members of relatively simply structured societies in which 'all men are equal'—at least in principle, power and authority residing in a local chief or persons of dignity and standing. Peasants often own the land they farm, holding formal, government-recognised title. Most shifting cultivators do not, holding vague rights of use, readily extinguished by others with 'superior' claims—loggers, land developers, governments. Peasant farming, nowadays usually partly commercialised, once formed the economic and social core of every major political unit in the region. In some it does so still. Area-for-area, peasant farming is also much more productive than shifting cultivation. Most peasant producers can obtain 3 tonnes of rice per hectare whereas the shifting cultivator is lucky to obtain half that. This is a reflection of the fact that most peasants are lowland farmers. Most shifting cultivators are not. Only in peripheral areas and where narrow valleys alternate with hills does shifting cultivation or permanent tree-crop agriculture form part of the peasant enterprise.

Land, as the direct source of sustenance, was once regarded with almost mystical reverence, an attitude that still survives to some degree, for the 'gods' and spirits of the land and of the rice must still be kept happy. The 'spirit houses' of Thailand, Cambodia and Bali are evidence enough of that. Of land the average peasant has little enough. Compared with western countries the Southeast Asian peasant farm is somewhere between one hundred and a thousand times smaller—not to mention the fact that whole countries like Singapore and Brunei are only the size of one of Australia's larger cattle stations.

Most Southeast Asian peasant farms are one to three hectares in size, enough—just—to support a family with a great deal of effort. In areas of recent settlement, Mindanao for example, they tend to be larger and the same is true where soils are poor, as in northeast Thailand, much of it by geological origin the sandy bottom and shores of an ancient sea. (To travel in that region is to see still the salt glistening in roadside cuttings.)

Small though farms may be, many are fragmented into spatially separated plots, sometimes as a result of inheritance, sometimes as a result of land sales and purchases. Such fragmentation reduces the efficiency of production where large machines are used and this was once advanced as a political argument in favour of collectivisation, though in practice few large machines were ever used on large collective farms. (One of the 'classic' propaganda photographs of the Socialist Republic of Viet Nam shows a modern wheeled tractor in a rice-field. Close examination shows that the machine was hopelessly bogged.) Fragmentation is also a drain on time—thus money—where some degree of commercial production exists. But for this to be 'inefficient', as economists are wont to claim, there have to be real 'opportunity costs'. Needless to say, opportunities do not necessarily exist in the Vietnamese countryside, for instance. On the other hand, fragmentation of farm holdings may be a good thing, helping to spread the risk of crop failure from drought or flood, from sea-water incursion, pests and disease.

Since most peasant farms are rice farms, they are also subdivided into plots for operational reasons. The Louisiana rice-farmer may use laser-levelling to prepare the land to ensure optimal, even depth of flooding. His Southeast Asian counterpart must do it by eye or pay the price of reduced yields because of uneven water-depth. Minute subdivision of the land by low bunds assists the levelling process and aids water-control, despite the penalty of up to 10 per cent of the area being in bunds. In some areas, dry crops, even trees, may be planted on rice-field bunds to increase total production.

Where the land slopes terraces are essential, in areas of unstable soil requiring stone facing for support. However, it is only in areas of desperate need to ensure food or where soils are intrinsically at least fairly fertile that the large labour of making and maintaining terraces has been and is worthwhile. Such is the case in parts of the uplands of Sumatera, Java, Bali, and north-central Luzon especially. Most terraces are irrigated, for purely rain-fed rice terraces, though they exist, especially in parts of northern Myanmar and northern Viet Nam, are born of poverty and a high degree of self-sufficiency in food production.

Unlike the farms of most shifting cultivators, those of lowland peasants are ecologically relatively simple. Rice is usually the one important crop though supplemented by tree-crops such as coconuts and fruits around village houses. Vegetables may also be grown nearby and increasingly, especially near urban markets and of course where water supplies permit, they are grown in wet fields when these are not actually required for rice. Traditionally a large range of rice varieties was grown, the farmer's basic aim being to match the chosen varieties as nearly as possible to the micro-environments of his fields. Thus varieties maturing in about 120 days from transplanting were planted in areas that dried out more quickly as harvest-time approached, whilst higher-yielding varieties taking longer to mature would be planted in damper spots. Yet others could be planted where the water was expected to be a metre or two deep—the floating rices. Most were able to withstand a fair range of climatic eventualities, giving some sort of yield even when conditions were difficult. Since farmers were not weather prophets, they also planted a range of varieties in order to spread the risk of failure of any particular one, as well as using rices with particular desired grain characteristics—glutinous or non-glutinous, round grains or long, particular smell or cooking characteristics, even colour (black for desserts and ruby-red rice wine, red for auspicious occasions).

While increasing ecological complexity is represented by off-season cropping, the opposite tendency is also at work. The wide adoption of HYVs over the last 30 years has swept many of these complexities away and rice is no longer the revered—even worshipped—staff of life, but is now a commodity. Many varieties are no longer cultivated, surviving deep-frozen in the germ-plasm collection of the International Rice Research Institute at Los Baños, Philippines. Yields generally have doubled, sometimes more, but mainly in irrigated areas. The same or very similar HYVs are grown over large areas, raising the prospect of possible massive failure due to newly evolved rice diseases. That such a Doomsday scenario has not yet occurred partly reflects the fact that large quantities of pesticides keep pests and disease at bay and partly the fact that rice breeders have generally managed to keep at least half a step ahead of the 'nasties' that threaten the region's rices. But the price of control and of yield increases using chemicals is a steep one in terms of toxicity problems, affecting not just rice-field fish and other garnered food-sources, but people as well. The heavy fertiliser inputs necessary to optimise HYV yields have unquestionably led to significant eutrophication (excessive nutrient supply) in many fresh and near-shore waters.

These and other environmental impacts arising from the adoption of 'western' farming systems based upon large energy subsidies—herbicides, pesticides, fertilisers, machines, fuels—raise serious questions of sustainability. Using traditional methods, especially those involving organic manures and recycling, applied to traditional varieties, wet-rice yields of around 1.5 tonnes per hectare have been achieved for centuries. But without an enormous expansion of the cultivated area that level could not now feed the region's people, let alone provide a surplus for export. Such an expansion is beyond contemplation even were suitable land available, a highly doubtful assumption. Rice land costs around US$20 000 per hectare to develop and the prospective returns are simply not there.

Can dependence upon 'chemical rice-farming' be reduced without sacrificing current yields? Can biological diversity and the degree of protection it offers against natural disasters be enhanced? Can the consequences of droughts and floods be mitigated—for by many scenarios Southeast Asia will become warmer, possibly wetter and more stormy? These matters affect peasant rice-growers particularly, for they are many and relatively poor.

There is little doubt that over-use of chemicals is partly responsible for environmental problems. On-the-ground instruction is the remedy. Conservation and recycling of organic wastes are technically feasible but usually at the price of increased labour inputs. For example, the *Azolla Anabaena* complex—one a water-dwelling fern, the other a blue-green alga—can fix many kilograms of nitrogen per hectare from the air every wet season. It requires simple skills to manage its production in or near the rice-fields. But there is a significant labour cost and for many it is easier to buy a bag of urea. The genetic approach—to improve the rice-plant's response to fertiliser, increase its resistance to pests and reduce its vulnerability to the vagaries of the weather—is necessarily slow.

Here the region's major producer of new HYVs, the International Rice Research Institute, is making steady progress. The range of varieties available to farmers is much greater than 30 years ago though this is less true for rain-fed areas. Vulnerability to droughts and floods can be reduced by improved control of run-off in catchments feeding irrigation systems, by improving water storage, and by expanding irrigation.

But the real question is not whether these things can be done but whether it is worth doing so. The Malaysian case is instructive. Despite subsidies and large investments of public money in infrastructure to improve rice production, significant areas are no longer in production, even in the climatically more suitable northern states of the country. The main reason is that general economic growth has brought about a rise in the real cost of labour. This, coupled with the small size of rice-farm holdings, has made production to some degree uneconomic, a trend already clear in the 1960s when farmers in Melaka were sustaining their families by off-farm earnings. In some of the core rice areas, Kedah state for instance, production has been maintained, but only by decreasing labour inputs, notably by sowing seed broadcast instead of transplanting seedlings, by machine tillage, harvesting and threshing, in a word by increasing capital intensity. Production is substantially commercial. Farmers are no longer peasants.

Other small-scale farming systems

Other small-scale farmers are not peasants either, though sharing many of their characteristics including family-based operations, fairly high labour inputs, small holdings, usually low capital inputs and sometimes rather simple ecosystems. Small farmers growing vegetables for urban markets have long existed near towns and cities though the most complex and intensive systems of production may be those of Overseas Chinese.

In terms of areas occupied, however, more important are small producers of a single commercial crop. In the wetter, equatorial parts of the region that crop is usually *Hevea* rubber or coconuts, crops that are equally at home in the lower hills and on flat land, coconuts producing well even on free-draining coastal sands. Commercial small farmers in mainland Southeast Asia are more likely to be producers of arable crops—manioc, maize for animal feed, *kenaf* (*Hibiscus*) fibre.

They may also be specialist producers: of spices in Maluku (cloves, nutmeg and mace); in Peninsular Malaysia of rambutans, mangosteens or durians (though for most growers a range of perennial crops, often grown together in the same 'orchard', is the norm). As with other kinds of smallholdings, both environmental and market risks are spread, though at the expense of increasing transaction costs since very small quantities of produce are brought to market at any one time—a single jackfruit for instance. Some small farms specialise in animal production, especially poultry for the live bird trade and pigs on the outskirts of urban areas, often depending partly or wholly upon swill collected from townsfolk or institutions.

Market-gardeners

Market-gardening is by far the most labour-intensive system of agriculture in the region with inputs, in terms of area, at least double those of the most intensive forms of rice cultivation. This is partly a reflection of a rapid alternation of crops, usually six to eight every year. The list of crops is a long one but dominated by green vegetables such as the *Brassicas* (kale, cabbage, *choy sum*), the *Alliums* (onion, shallot, garlic), and lettuce (*Lactuca*). Gourds, especially cucumber, are common as are green beans of many kinds.

At one time, combining vegetable production with poultry, pigs and pond fish was usual. These systems were highly conservative of nutrients. Thus unsaleable vegetables fed not only the family but also pigs, and their excrement fed pond fish. Wastes were composted for use as garden fertiliser. Such systems required considerable inputs from outside, whether animal feed, wastes or fertilisers, but by recycling assiduously large returns were obtained. The average 1960s intensive mixed farm in Singapore annually produced 66 tonnes of vegetables, 75 pigs, 1500 chickens and 26 000 eggs—all from around 2 hectares of land.

Such systems require substantial labour to make them work and as labour costs have risen so specialisation upon a single activity—broiler chickens, pond fish, pigs, green vegetables—has grown, as have the environmental problems. 'Mucking-out' pig-sties is hard work even if the muck is good fertiliser. It is much easier to pump water from a pond or stream and flush it away, causing major problems downstream. Nevertheless, intensive vegetable and livestock smallholdings continue to flourish around the cities and towns of those parts of the region where labour costs are low, Viet Nam especially, though most have now gone from Singapore, overcome by higher labour costs and increasingly stringent anti-pollution regulations.

Perennial tree-crop smallholders

Perennial tree-crop smallholdings are much less labour-intensive than intensive market gardens, requiring around 175 person-days per hectare each year to produce 700–1000 kg of sheet and scrap rubber in the case of that kind of farm. This output represents less than 1 per cent of the biological 'standing crop' so that nutrient requirements are much lower and their turnover in the system is much slower than in more intensive forms of production. Much the same is true of coconut, pepper, cocoa and coffee production, the only major difference being that the economic life of pepper vines is about half that of the trees. All are conservative of nutrients, though pepper is much less so than the others. Their ecosystems are relatively simple, as with rice, the bulk of the standing crop being represented by a single species, sometimes two, as in parts of Malaysia where coconut and cocoa are grown together. Short-term crops such as soya-bean may also accompany coconuts because the fronds cast only light shade, enabling other crops to be grown to provide additional income.

By contrast, mature rubber casts deep shade to the extent that little will grow below it. This lack of a ground cover of vegetation, partly maintained by weeding, has led some observers to speculate that rubber, especially at the high density of 600 stems per hectare smallholders favour as a means of increasing yields, promotes serious soil erosion. There is no evidence for this from controlled scientific experimentation. Indeed, it has also been argued that perennial tree-crops to some degree mimic the rainforests they have widely replaced and so are environmentally conservative. The truth is that sediment yields from rubber areas are higher than from forests but not massively so, and are very much lower than from any form of upland cultivation involving tillage.

This form of cultivation is particularly characteristic of the wetter parts of insular Southeast Asia, including the peninsular parts of Myanmar and Thailand, with small but growing outliers in Cambodia and southern Viet Nam. Rubber, especially, is grown on basalt-derived soils in the latter two regions where the richness of the soils to some degree compensates for low dry-season yields. Climate controls seasonal rounds of work. On rubber smallholdings in equatorial areas the trees are tapped about 25 days per month, the rest usually being 'washed out' by rain. Early in the morning an incision is made into the bark of each *Hevea* tree, shaving off a thin layer and exposing new latex-carrying cells. Latex flows from the V-shaped incision into a small cup wired to the tree which holds about 200 ml. Given that each tree is visited twice on a tapping day and with 400–600 trees per hectare, it is easy to see that a good deal of fetching and carrying is needed, so that this form of perennial tree-cropping is the most labour-intensive amongst the various kinds. Pails of latex are carried to a central point, usually on the farm, where the latex is tipped into vats, formic or acetic acid being added to coagulate the rubber. This now has the consistency and appearance of bean-curd and after being cut into thick sheets these are compressed in a mangle and hung out on a line to dry like so much laundry. Where the latex is taken to a central processing plant the equipment is a little more sophisticated and instead of being dried in the sun the sheet rubber is smoked, the better to preserve it. Rubber smoke-houses emit such a distinctive smell that the nose may detect rubber-production areas before the eye does.

The rounds of work on coconut and cocoa smallholdings are less regular. Nuts are produced all the year round, though less vigorously when the palms are stressed, and are ripe enough for plucking at about a year to 18 months. The nuts are then usually cut free using a knife on the end of a bamboo, which is quicker and safer than having a worker climb the stem. Occasionally, in the Malay world, a trained monkey performs this step, necessary because the nuts do not always fall when ripe and otherwise may germinate on the palm. For the production of copra—the dried flesh—it is necessary only to split the nuts and to lay them out to dry, the meat then readily coming away from the shell. Oven drying, which produces a superior quality, is rare because the better price obtainable is usually insufficient to encourage the additional labour and expense involved.

In the region generally, very few of the coconut palm's many uses are actually realised. Its thatch is of rather poor quality, especially compared with *Nypa*. The coir requires considerable processing—for use as door-mats and rope—and this industry no longer survives. From its immature inflorescence sap may be tapped. This rapidly ferments into toddy, a cheap alcoholic refreshment much favoured by persons of South Indian origin in the region. Boiling this sap down produces a palm sugar but this is inferior to that from *Arenga* palms and palm sugar has been largely replaced by cane sugar throughout the region, surviving mainly for use in sweets such as the famed *gula melaka*, a concoction of sago, palm sugar and coconut milk. The last is a water extract from fresh coconut flesh and is widely used in regional cuisine. The milk is not to be confused with coconut water, which occupies the interior of the nuts and is consumed merely as a refreshing drink. Near towns only, transport costs being high, young nuts may be harvested for this purpose alone and there is even a small export of such nuts, shaved down to save transportation costs.

Cocoa seeds are borne in pods formed on the main branches and stem of the small tree *Theobroma cacao*. Given a fairly even distribution of rainfall during the year, the pods ripen at about six months after fertilisation of the flowers, though trees produce pods somewhat irregularly throughout the year. Each tree needs to be visited at intervals of 10 to 15 days to harvest the ripe pods, so that harvesting is much less intensive than for rubber but rather more than with coconuts. However opening pods, like splitting coconuts, is a tediously labour-intensive business. For every day spent gathering pods another is needed to open them, a process that cannot long be delayed. The seeds are then fermented, usually in heaps, a process essential to the development of the chocolate flavour. Sun-drying follows and the dried seeds are then bagged and sold. An established smallholding needs about 150 days of work per hectare. Two or three hectares is area enough to occupy a family's labour for a year, so that a cocoa smallholding is somewhat more labour-intensive than either a rubber or a coconut farm. Since *Theobroma cacao* is notably subject to pests and disease, it also demands a significant input of poisonous chemicals during growth, unlike either rubber or coconuts.

Other tree-crops are grown by commercially oriented small farmers as specialised monocultures (a single crop), or as polycultures (many crops together in promiscuous cultivation). Some require a long period to come into bearing—much longer than the three to five years characteristic of rubber, coconuts and cocoa. Such include durian, mangosteen, langsat (duku), fruits of *Artocarpus* species, jackfruit, breadfruit and several others, the palmyra palm (*Borassus* sp.) and the tamarind (*Tamarindus*).

These obviously require more initial capital to develop, quite apart from the fact that fruit seedlings are usually more costly. Mango, citrus, rambutan, carambola, guava, the sweet and sour sops, sapodilla, and rose-apple need three or four years to come into bearing.

However, for quick returns, the herbaceous crops—such as banana, papaya and pineapple—come into their own. Some of these fruits can be harvested at any time, just as soon as they mature. Examples include the coconut, carambola (star fruit) and guava amongst the tree-crops, as well as all the herbaceous crops, which fruit at a more or less fixed time from planting. The economic consequence for the grower is an even cash-flow.

By contrast many of the trees fruit seasonally, though not at the same time in the year. Even the same species may fruit at different times in different parts of the region, though why this is so is not fully understood. Thus the noble durian fruits mainly from October to February in Indonesia, in May and June in Peninsular Thailand and from June to August in Malaysia, though in a few places it can be persuaded to fruit year-round. For the smallholder the consequences are severe harvest-time anxiety and irregular cash income.

To some degree this can be overcome by growing many kinds of perennial crop together in the same plot, as most will cohabit quite happily. Risk is spread and so is income, but transaction costs rise because only small amounts can be sent to market at any one time. How extensive this mixed form of cultivation may be is basically anyone's guess; it is the agricultural census-taker's nightmare. Certainly most rural families grow perennials together in small house-plots but some also depend largely upon this form of production.

Fruit production is unquestionably expanding in step with rising real incomes, though not all of it comes from smallholdings. One decade-old estimate of annual production is for a regional total of 24 million tonnes and it cannot be less today. The Philippines was dominant with about 28 per cent of this, mostly of the short-term perennials pineapple and banana, some marketed under international brands such as Dole. Mindanao—a 'land below the wind' (typhoons)—is the main production area. As might be expected on the basis of its size, Indonesia produces close to a quarter of the region's fruits.

In step with production increases, some destined for overseas markets, has come increasing crop specialisation. This has long been characteristic of pineapple-growing, because pineapples can grow in environments uninhabitable by any other crop, in deforested blackwater swamps for instance. Monocropping simplifies agroecosystems, increases market risks as well as risks of pests and disease, but reduces transaction costs—it costs a lot less per fruit to move a lorry-load of pineapples than a bicycle-load. It also encourages specialist skills amongst growers, such as cloning, and raises product standards. In a word, it is fully commercial and in the long run is likely to carry the day despite its environmental and economic risks.

Commercial arable-crop producers

Most arable crops are grown in those parts of the region with seasonal climates. Sugar-cane, for example, requires warm, dry weather to push the sucrose content up to economic levels, though it will grow happily in all but the coolest parts of the region. Sesame, wheat, and millet are also crops that do best with a fair degree of dryness and are characteristic of parts of Myanmar's Dry Zone. Here irrigation is often available to make up for any shortfall in moisture, so that rice is also part of the local crop assemblage.

Arable cropping is by no means confined to flat lands. A century ago visitors in eastern Myanmar spoke of the 'handy Shan [i.e. Thai] plough' being used on quite steep hill slopes in a form of rotational farming in which temporarily abandoned lands in grass and herb fallow were grazed by cattle. This persists, though still only marginally commercialised. A similar but totally commercial form of arable production has emerged in the last three decades, notably in northeastern Thailand. On its plateau, slopes are moderate, such lands comprising about two-thirds of the area. (The rest is mainly in wet rice.) Three major crops have dominated the scene—manioc and maize for animal feed, much of it exported, and *Hibiscus* fibre, locally called *kenaf*, a dry-land jute. All are highly speculative, with areas fluctuating in line with international prices.

All are also environmentally damaging. In some areas fair-quality forest has been felled to make way for them, though most cleared land is of indifferent quality as forest. Soil nutrient levels are generally low, in part because the soils are generally sandy and free-draining. They can support no more than three successive crops, for the application of fertilisers is generally uneconomic. Large areas are therefore abandoned, forming rough grazing for cattle and buffaloes, of which there is an export to the Central Plains region. Rates of soil erosion are high because rainfall intensities peak during the short wet season in the middle of the year. What the downstream effects may be is not altogether clear since no one really knows how far and how fast eroded sediments travel and where they are deposited. The effects are unlikely to be negligible.

Growing sugar-cane on slopes has similar impacts but it is also a lowland crop, either way being extremely demanding of soil nutrients. This is one reason why its major production areas are on nutrient-rich basic volcanic soils and nearby alluvium in the Philippines.

Sugar

Sugar-growing is far and away the longest-established form of commercial arable-crop production, dating back to the Dutch colonial period in Java. Just how sugar-cane came to replace palm sugar—the traditional sweetener—is not known in detail but it seems likely that it was grown for chewing as much as for manufactured sugar. Prior to the late nineteenth century cane sugar was made in much the same way as palm sugar—by heating the extracted liquid to drive off much of the water, the remaining syrup then slowly crystallising to form a dark-coloured, somewhat sticky sugar. At the end of last century it was discovered that by spinning the syrup in a centrifuge much of the liquid could be removed, leaving light-coloured crystals which were then bleached to give our familiar white sugar.

This technique had a number of effects. It quickly drove old-fashioned 'clayed' sugar off the market. Production necessarily became concentrated around sugar 'centrals'—large enterprises which alone could afford the machines. In turn this meant that commercial production had to be located within economic cane-hauling distance of the central. To this day production is therefore highly localised and in the production area little else is grown. In the Philippines province of Negros Occidentale, for example, half of the total cultivated area is in cane.

A further aspect is that land ownership is also often concentrated, though in fact this is not a necessary condition of sugar production. In the Philippines' Visayas and central Luzon plains regions large holdings, owned by wealthy individuals or companies, are let out to individual growers on short-term cultivation contracts. Such permanent workers make up just under three-quarters of the total workforce of each *hacienda*—the large-scale farm owned or managed by the *hacendero*. (Both terms are Spanish and relate to the colonial days when such large estates raised cattle.) Around a further quarter of the workers are local casual workers daily-paid by management, while another 10–15 per cent are migrants employed only during the three or four months of harvest. This system of *metayage*—the word is French—results in a degree of insecurity of employment and poverty, because sugar production is still somewhat speculative and very much at the mercy of often-fluctuating global prices. To some degree this vulnerability stems from the fact that the region's sugar has to compete with highly subsidised, capital-intensive production from sugar-beet in Europe.

Growing cane is not particularly labour-intensive compared to other systems in the region, requiring about 120 person-days per hectare each year but with a very sharp peak in input at harvest. Roughly 70 per cent of the work is done at that time, so that compared with perennial tree-crop systems labour-use is much less labour-efficient.

The annual round of work is somewhat like that of one rice crop per year, though sugar takes 12–14 months from soil preparation to harvest. In Negros the first labour peak is in the period from October or November to January when it is relatively dry. The soil is tilled, usually by tractor-drawn plough, and sections of cane are cut ready for planting, a task usually completed by March. Weeding and fertiliser application occupy only a few days and by July the cane is sufficiently tall to suppress most weeds. In July, August and September little work on sugar is required. Cutting and loading out follows in the subsequent dry season, at which time tillage and other preparations for the next crop are also under way. On many farms a second spontaneously grown crop is taken from the originally planted root-stock. This 'ratoon' crop reduces tillage and planting costs, though requiring more weeding and at the further cost of a yield reduction by about one-third. Cane is carried to the centrals by lorry, by tractor-trailer, or on flat land by light railway. Harvest and transportation costs are often crucial in the system. Since these are higher for cane grown on steeper lands—up to about eight degrees of slope—these tend to go out of production when prices fall.

Sugar-cane is a highly nutrient-demanding crop, as it yields up to 40 tonnes per hectare. Most of the nutrients contained in the crop are 'exported' from the fields, only the leaves being slashed off at harvest and recycled. Crushing at the mill yields 10–12 per cent of sugar and the residue is usually either burnt in the mill's boilers or simply allowed to rot. Though this waste—called bagasse—will make useful particle-board, its manufacture is not common and the cost of returning it to the field is prohibitive, not to mention the fact that it could cause cultivation chaos by sprouting again.

Thus on all but the most fertile soils a substantial fertiliser input—almost always of artificials—is crucial to the system functioning. This input naturally leads to significant environmental problems, especially eutrophication, while repeated cropping with sugar leads eventually to loss of soil condition. On slopes the erosion risk is severe until the crop is mature, especially if ploughing and ridging are up and down the slope, cheaper processes than tilling on the contour. The consequences include substantial sediment generation—roughly three, sometimes four orders of magnitude higher than under protective, closed vegetation. However, the downstream consequences are not well studied. They can scarcely be less than significant.

Other 'factories-in-the fields'

One of the striking sights of parts of central and southern Peninsular Malaysia and parts of Malaysian Sabah are endless serried ranks of rubber trees or oil palms, intersected with laterite roads. Few settlements, few people. Settlements there are, of a very particular kind: the estate headquarters, home of management, often occupying fine houses set on a hill; home of technical staff, in less grand dwellings; and terrace houses or partitioned labour lines, home to the bulk of the workers. People there are, gathered into these 'company settlements', but engaged in field labour only in the cool of the day, tapping rubber, weeding, pruning palms, gathering fruits. Such plantations, some occupying several thousand hectares, are very characteristic of Malaysia because it is mainly there that this outgrowth of international capitalism was not attacked by the nationalistic economic policies that elsewhere quickly followed political independence after the Pacific War.

Tropical plantations, financed and managed by foreigners, have a long history, having begun—using slave labour—in the Americas. In Southeast Asia such plantations using tree-crops developed in the nineteenth century: in parts of Java mainly coffee, with rubber following in Peninsular Malaysia and Sumatera in the early years of the twentieth century. Small plantings of oil palm were made, mainly in Johor, prior to the Pacific War, but the major expansion came in the 1950s and 1960s.

The 1960s also saw the development of a hybrid form of plantation production in which the state, in the form of a land development authority, was the capitalist, organising workers much along plantation lines but ultimately giving them title to the blocks of land and trees they worked. The 1970s saw the substantial 'repatriation' of plantation ownership as private Malaysian individuals, and especially state-sponsored Malay organisations, bought shares in erstwhile foreign companies. The main effect of this on the ground has been the partial disappearance of white faces from plantation managements.

Plantations are to a degree 'worlds unto themselves', though much less so than formerly. For the workers, housing, education and health care are to a degree tied to employment. Since the capitalist owns all, there are few alternative forms of employment and plantations see a steady stream of permanent outmigration to urban areas as well as a good deal of commuting, especially by motorcycle, to off-plantation work. They also tend to be cultural microcosms as well; the bulk of the labour is likely to be Chinese, Tamil or, increasingly, Malay.

Within the plantation work is systematised, specialised and mind-numbingly boring—just like the landscape. On a rubber plantation work begins at around 5 a.m. with the daily muster, except when it is raining. Each group of tappers or weeders moves to its task section of the estate. Tapping has been described already, though on plantations tapping latex into a plastic bag containing an anti-coagulant is more common than on smallholdings, the objective being to reduce the frequency of latex collection and thus labour requirements. Rubber production is a labour-intensive business and in Malaysia costs can be contained only by producing premium grades of rubber and liquid latex as well as by employing, sometimes only semi-legally, recently immigrant labour, mainly from Indonesia.

Tasks on oil palm plantations differ to some degree, the main jobs being weeding, pruning the palms and harvesting the fruit. This must be swiftly followed by processing in the central factory, as the proportion of free fatty acids in the fruits quickly rises after cutting, reducing the quality of the oil expressed from them and thus its value. Margarine pays better than soap! In contrast to rubber, from which less than 1 per cent of biological production is removed for processing, with oil palm the annual output of fruits—around 30 tonnes per hectare—represents more than half of the palms' annual biological production. Since many soils on which the crop grows are modestly supplied with nutrients this loss has to be made good by fertiliser application.

In addition, the amount of waste arising during processing is very substantial. With rubber a quarter to a fifth of the latex is water, about a tenth of which is evaporated off as the sheets dry. The rest, laced with acid, certainly causes water pollution problems, especially near larger factories. But these are not to be compared, in kind or scale, with those created by oil palm processing. Of each ton of fruit processed, only about 220 kg is pure oil. The rest is waste—shells, fibre, sludge. Some can be burnt as fuel for steam boilers in the factory. Some cannot and its disposal is an endless headache for managers as well as for those affected by discharges. As with bagasse, return to the fields is technically and economically impracticable. Like sugar, but even more so by reason of the mediocre quality of most soils on which oil palm is grown, the production system requires very substantial energy subsidies to make it work, raising questions of long-term sustainability. Rubber also does better with the application of fertilisers and stimulants to promote the flow of latex, but because the nutrient export is only a small fraction of the total biological production it is much more sustainable.

Conclusion

In ecological terms the economic pressures are towards system simplification. Rice farms may produce just rice rather than being part of a complex system of raising food and obtaining cash. With land consolidation and thoroughgoing commercialisation rice farms can be expected to grow both in size and in capital intensity. In the wetter parts of insular Southeast Asia, the complexities of shifting cultivation have already been supplanted, partly or wholly, by the simplicities of perennial tree-crops. Except for home gardens where complexity will probably remain, fruit production is steadily becoming more specialised, with single crops—

durian, mango, rambutan, mangosteen—replacing multi-layered promiscuous cultivation. Increasing complexity is the exception rather than the norm, though the intercalation of cocoa or annuals such as soya-bean into coconut farms has been successful, reducing environmental and economic risk while raising land-use intensity and farmers' income. Intercalation is also beginning in wet-rice systems though the move up to two crops a year that usually accompanies irrigation development leaves little time in a year for much more than a crop of vegetables. An 'after-crop' of maize or vegetables is often feasible in one-rice-crop systems, especially as the use of old-fashioned 210-day rices is declining in the face of new varieties that mature more quickly. This shift is facilitated by the slowing in market demand, for as people's income rises so their consumption of the basic staple falls.

Combining livestock-raising with tree-crops—to mutual benefit in terms of nutrient cycling and conservation—is technically feasible on coconut and oil palm farms, though probably not so on rubber farms because the animals displace the latex cups. What is required is improvement of the cover crops and other ground-level vegetation so that herd animals 'get a decent bite'. Obviously a different system of management would be needed and this has so far received little attention, not least because of the difficulty of competing with meat imports.

Complexity in highly intensive vegetable production systems will to some degree remain for good agronomic reasons—crop rotation is a necessity. But integration with pigs, poultry and fish is clearly declining in the face of high labour costs as well as the relatively high transaction costs these integrated, nutrient-conserving systems imply.

Systems of shifting cultivation are likely to remain fairly complex in remoter areas where the costs of transportation and the weakness of marketing systems preclude anything other than a good measure of self-sufficiency. Nowhere is there in sight for mainland Southeast Asia the ecological and economic equivalent of rubber. Rather complexity is likely to continue to take another form, that of circular migration to urban areas, involving the production and sale of handcrafts as well as temporary wage-labour, as even the mountain peoples and minorities are being drawn into increasingly large and complex markets for all manner and kinds of goods and services.

EIGHT
GOODS AND SERVICES, MAKING AND PROVIDING

What 'goods' are is to some degree a matter of convention. A rice pudding is clearly a manufactured good but what about husked rice? Having had its hard coat removed, having been mechanically polished to make it white, having lost about a third of its weight in the process, isn't it a manufacture? The somewhat illogical answer is 'yes'—but not if it is husked by the producer and then consumed. Similarly with services. The provision of piped water is considered to be a kind of service even though the water may have undergone considerable processing to make it drinkable. Just how arbitrary these definitions may be can be shown by one of Southeast Asia's more remarkable statistical anomalies. Singapore 'consumes' some 60 million tonnes of petroleum annually. Actually it does nothing of the sort; it merely imports a large quantity of petroleum, turns it into petrol, fuel oil and a host of other petroleum-based products and then exports most of them.

The point is that, unlike primary economic activities such as agriculture and fishing, secondary activities—including manufacturing goods, construction, making energy and supplying water—are not so easily put into categories. This is even more true for tertiary activities—basically all the rest. These economic statisticians' conventions also ignore the fact that, unlike people in the west who generally have just one income source, people in Southeast Asia may have many income sources—a bit of rice-growing, some fishing to supply protein, a few months' work on a construction site, washing dishes in a restaurant, hawking hand-woven cloth on city streets, even sitting quietly at home for a time and living from children's earnings. Just how widespread 'multiple-sourcing' of income may be is simply not known though recent detailed studies suggest it is quite common, especially amongst rural people with little or no access to sufficient land to farm effectively. In this chapter, as earlier, the conventions are followed, for they have the advantage of consistency.

What features are shared by the secondary and tertiary sectors of the region's economies? As everywhere else they are spatially constricted. Agriculture is found 'most everywhere'. Not so manufacturing or services. Most are concentrated in areas that are substantially urban, though again what this means in particular cases is a matter of more-or-less arbitrary decision. Secondary and tertiary activities depend upon secondary sources of energy, not sunlight but gas and electricity, in Southeast Asia both mostly derived from fossil sources—coal and petroleum. Such activities are linked to ultimate sources of life—soil and water—by extremely complex pathways involving many intermediate linkages. They are mostly quite unlike primary activities, which for Southeast Asian subsistence farmers encompass production and consumption within the family. These linkages, as well as goods and services involved in them, exist in hierarchies based upon value—and these days value is mainly established in the marketplace. Thus in manufacturing, simple processes like moulding clay into bricks and tiles and baking them, or in retail trade hawking vegetables, are widespread. The skills needed are simple, the financial rewards small, the practitioners found almost everywhere. At the other end of the scale are complex processes like designing computer software or highly specialised skills like brain surgery. The incomes obtained by the few people who possess them are high. Only the largest and wealthiest cities can support them.

A further commonality is that in Southeast Asia it is only very recently that employment in the secondary and tertiary sectors has risen above the halfway mark. By 1997, 51 per cent of those employed were in these sectors, compared with 42 per cent ten years earlier. Manufacturing, plus construction, electricity, gas and water, accounted for 17 per cent of the workforce, services 34 per cent, up from 11 per cent and 31 per cent respectively in 1987.

THE ENERGY BASE

One base for this striking change is energy, largely from fossil sources. Not all of it is used in the production of goods and services. As economies become more wealthy an increasing proportion of the energy consumed is used for pleasant but not entirely necessary things like air-conditioning homes. Nevertheless energy consumption is a useful measure, especially electricity consumption, because little electricity is used in primary production. Table 8.1 gives country-by-country details.

Clearly electricity consumption is not related to size of country whether measured by area or population. Thailand, with 12 per cent of

Table 8.1 Consumption of electricity, 1987 and latest

Country	1987		1997		Increase since 1987 (%)	
	Total (bill. kwh)	Per person (kwh)	Total (bill. kwh)	Per person (kwh)	Total	Per person
Brunei (1996)	1.0	4 302	1.6	4 968	56	16
Cambodia (1996)	0.1	9	0.2	19	100	110
Indonesia (1996)	36.6	213	73.8	342	102	61
Laos (1996)	0.2	54	0.5	61	159	13
Malaysia (1997)	17.4	1 050	51.2	2 151	194	105
Myanmar (1996)	2.3	60	4.3	81	54	35
Philippines (1996)	22.6	394	34.8	467	54	19
Singapore (1998)	11.8	4 633	28.3	7 115	140	54
Thailand (1996)	30.4	569	92.2	1 391	203	145
Viet Nam (1998)	6.1	97	21.8	194	257	100

Source: Derived from UNESCAP *Statistical Yearbook for Asia and the Pacific 1999 (figures rounded)*

the population, consumes around 30 per cent of the power. Singapore, having only 0.6 per cent of the region's people nevertheless consumes 9 per cent of the electricity, all of it generated locally using imported fuel. Rather, consumption is related to wealth and to economic structure, with Singapore as a major consumer despite its contracting industrial workforce. The relatively poor, mainly agricultural countries consume rather little. (Laos is exceptional in that it consumes only a third of its mainly hydro-production, exporting most to Thailand.) Nevertheless all have secured good supplies. On a region-wide basis total consumption has more than doubled in the last decade and despite an overall increase of population by a fifth and a growth in the workforce by a quarter, per person consumption has increased dramatically, not least because urban areas have also grown. They are much cheaper to supply than rural areas because the unit costs of reticulation are lower.

These developments are underpinned by a regional surplus of fossil energy—coal, petroleum and natural gas—although for geological reasons there are considerable variations in supplies. Total production is substantial. Petroleum is the mainstay of the region's commercial energy sources with a production of close to 130 million tonnes yearly, more than enough to meet needs, substantially up from around 100 million tonnes a decade ago and enough to provide for export, much of it via Singapore's burgeoning refineries. Coal has seen something of a renaissance. At around 42 million tonnes a year compared with just under 9 million tonnes in 1987, production is now almost entirely directed towards coal-fired electricity generation where once it was burnt at the place where its energy was required, because electricity is by far the cleaner and more versatile fuel, saleable in large quantities or very small.

But the country-by-country picture is less rosy. Several countries have little or no fossil energy usable at current prices, obtainable with present-day technology. Or so it seems. Details of the location, size and nature of petroleum reserves, especially, are closely-guarded secrets. Laos appears to have little coal and neither oil nor gas—hence the vigorous development of hydroelectricity, mainly using Thai capital to ensure Thai supplies. Myanmar's go-it-alone policy may have led to falling petroleum production and the need to import about half of its requirements, because oil is said to be there still—in the ground. Thailand, Cambodia and Viet Nam have supplies, mostly offshore. Thailand, however, produces only 5 per cent of its needs. For Viet Nam the opposite is true. It consumes less than 1 per cent of its production and by substantially increasing coal production and hydroelectricity generation seems content to reap the foreign exchange benefits this situation brings. In insular Southeast Asia it is the Philippines that lacks fossil energy, especially petroleum, producing only 1 per cent of its consumption domestically. Little wonder that it seeks to realise its claimed resources thought to exist offshore. All the other countries have substantial exports, generally being expanded only slowly. Indonesia's, for example, increased by only 4 per cent in the decade from 1987 and Malaysia's by only 6.5 per cent over the same period.

The structure of the energy industry is not like that of the region's manufacturing, being dominated by large capital-intensive units, many wholly owned by foreign interests, especially in oil and gas where the investments required to explore and exploit them are very large and the time needed to repay them is measured in decades. Small coal-mines exist, as do small-scale geothermal plants, around Los Baños south of Manila for example. Micro and mini hydroelectric plants on the Chinese pattern do not exist, probably because of their substantial disadvantages in terms of economies of scale. (A fortunate corollary of the failure to adopt a localised approach is the near-universal adoption of 220 volts as the standard low-tension supply.) Small diesel generators are widespread, some as back-up in cities, especially in the Philippines, many as a prime source in small towns and rural areas, as generally speaking national distribution grids are incomplete. One ironical consequence is that villages along major high-tension lines may lack a low-tension supply.

In petroleum production ownership is substantially in foreign hands. All the major international companies, Elf-Aquitaine, Mobil-Exxon, Shell-BP and many others operate in the region, either alone or in joint ventures with local capital. The latter is represented mainly by government interests. In Indonesia Pertamina controls some of the refining and much of the distribution. It was originally formed from foreign companies nationalised during

Table 8.2 Energy-source profiles, selected countries, 1995

Country	Total primary energy (10^{10} kcal)	Source (%)					
		Coal	Oil	Gas	Hydro	Geothermal	Other
Indonesia	69 856	11	45	39	2	3	–
Malaysia	39 982	4	43	51	1	–	–
Philippines	15 516	7	33	25	15	14	6
Thailand	51 604	14	66	18	1	–	–

Source: APEC Energy Statistics 1995.

the Sukarno era. In Malaysia the national oil company Petronas fills much the same role, reflecting a government desire to control at least part of this sector—very much to its profit. Myanmar has stuck to total government control, suffering serious difficulties in developing this sector as a consequence. Cambodia and Viet Nam have opened up to foreign enterprise, in Cambodia to Petronas, amongst others. Regional multinationals may be the shape of things to come as ASEAN gains regional solidarity.

The ownership of other parts of the energy sector lies mostly in the hands of governments or government corporations, a major exception being substantial private ownership of electricity generation and distribution in the Philippines. In Singapore this sector is run by the Public Utilities Board. EGAT, the Electricity Generating Authority of Thailand, has been particularly effective in responding to demand. Similar boards run things in Malaysia.

Thermal generation dominates. Most of it is oil-fired and therefore located within short distances of major ports and near urban markets. As mentioned earlier, hydro-power is of major importance in mountainous Laos, where 95 per cent of its power comes from this source. Energy-source data are not available for all the countries in the region but selected profiles are given in Table 8.2. (The data include imports.)

These data confirm the great importance of fossil fuels, especially oil and gas. While the region as a whole has a commercial energy base sufficient for its immediate needs, there must be some question concerning long-term sustainability. Only Laos and the Philippines derive significant commercial energy from anything other than fossil fuels, so that restructuring is likely to be a major undertaking.

Manufacturing

Retrospect

Perhaps the most remarkable fact about manufacturing is the speed with which this sector has grown—in every country in the region. In 1960 the proportion of people engaged in manufacturing lay in the 5–7 per cent range, even in Singapore, then basically a trading post. In the region as a whole, three-quarters of the workforce was engaged in agriculture. Such manufacturing as existed was of three different kinds.

First were industries based upon agriculture such as rice and sugar milling, pineapple canning, palm and coconut oil extraction. Their objects were either to reduce bulk thus reducing transportation costs, to preserve perishables or to do both, and above all to supply foreign markets. These industries were partly foreign-owned, some by Overseas Chinese, virtually none by anyone else.

The second group of manufacturing industries comprised those set up to meet the needs of western expatriates and those which added bulk during manufacture. Such included brewing and aerated-water manufacture. 'Anchor' and 'Tiger' beer in Malaya, 'Anker' in Indonesia and '33' in Viet Nam date from this time. Tin cans (Metal Box Company), metal drums, even motor-vehicles (Ford) were others. Most were also foreign-owned or owned by Overseas Chinese.

The third group comprised those industries making low-value goods which could not readily withstand the costs of overland transportation. These included road metal, bricks and tiles, drainpipes. Even these had to compete with imports from Europe in port cities where older dwellings are to this day roofed with imported tiles. A few of these industries were also foreign-owned. Hume Pipes in Singapore was an example and many were owned and operated by Overseas Chinese.

Technically, many of the factories were extremely simple, often highly labour-intensive. For example, though a century ago steam-powered rice-mills existed at major export points like Rangoon, Bangkok and Saigon, even in the 1930s in Viet Nam some rice-mills still comprised hundreds of coolies husking rice by hand. Matchsticks were split by hand and dipped by hand into red phosphorus even in the 1960s. Cigars and cigarettes were rolled by hand. Not until the 1960s did Indonesian firms buy automatic machines, sold by Singaporeans, to make *kretek*, the widely popular clove-flavoured cigarettes.

Structure

Until recently almost all industrial units were small in size as well as using simple tools, workshops rather than factories. Smallness—whether measured by physical size, numbers employed or capital invested—has to a degree persisted to the present. In most countries the growth in the number of employees has been more rapid than the growth in the number of establishments (factories) so that the average size—measured in terms of number of employees—is steadily rising. According to latest statistics, averages range from around 90 workers per factory in Singapore and the

Philippines, up to around 190 in Indonesia's factories. But these figures hide a very large range. For example, on Penang Island in Peninsular Malaysia in the 1980s, 95 per cent of factories employed fewer than 50 workers, more than half employing fewer than five. Less than a fifth occupied more than 186 square metres. Since then the average number of employees per factory in Malaysia has apparently fallen dramatically after having previously risen. (The figures were 137 per factory in 1992, only 61 in 1995, though this may merely reflect a change in the basis of statistics.) Small factories persist throughout the region, while average size has tended to rise as a result of the setting up of large foreign-owned factories in most countries of the region. Cambodia is something of an exception, as some such are still not operating, having been abandoned around the time of the Pol Pot takeover in 1975.

Growth

Measuring the growth of production in manufacturing is not a simple matter, especially where money values are concerned. Economists therefore use index numbers relating to a base year. Unfortunately index numbers for the whole sector are available for very few countries. Taking 1990 as the base year (=100), the Philippines grew from 61 in 1985 to 200 by 1996. The corresponding figures for Singapore were 55 and 153, a slower growth-rate from a proportionately larger starting point. Sectoral index numbers are also available in a few cases and these too reflect strong growth. The category 'Electrical machinery', which includes electronics, showed an eightfold increase in Malaysia from 1985 to 1996, Singapore a 136 per cent increase. One sector that Singapore is losing is textiles, down from an index number of 100 in 1990 to only 43 in 1996, as labour costs have risen in comparison with neighbouring countries such as Malaysia and Indonesia. In this sector Malaysian production increased nearly threefold in the decade to 1996.

Overall growth in manufacturing can be measured in two other ways—by employment and by contribution to the Gross Domestic Product. Data for the whole region (excluding Cambodia and Laos) show a rise in the number of workers from around 16 million in 1987 to 26 million in 1997, a two-thirds increase. This is substantially more than the increase by 26 per cent of the whole workforce. The consequence, in structural terms, is increase in the proportion of workers in manufacturing from 9.4 per cent in 1987 to 12.2 per cent in 1997, still well below the 25–30 per cent characteristic of industrialised countries but a rapid and substantial advance all the same. Only Malaysia, with 30.5 per cent of its workers in manufacturing, and Singapore with 22.6 per cent approach that level. Myanmar, Philippines, Viet Nam, probably also Cambodia and Laos, are yet to have a tenth of their workers in manufacturing.

In money terms, manufacturing in the region is usually more productive than either the service sector or, especially, agriculture, at least so far as limited data allow such a judgement. Unfortunately relevant national accounts statistics are old and incomplete. For Thailand they show a marked change in the proportion of GDP derived from manufacturing from around 17 per cent (of 'Total industries') in 1970 to 31 per cent by 1993, even though only about 11 per cent of the workforce was employed in manufacturing. Similar data for Indonesia show an increase from 9 per cent in 1970 to 23 per cent by 1993, with about the same proportion of workers in manufacturing as Thailand.

Multinationals and growth

The involvement of multinational corporations in manufacturing is substantial. By the late 1970s four-fifths of the assets in Singapore's manufacturing were foreign-owned, about half of them in petroleum refining. (Singapore and Rotterdam are the world's largest refining centres.) Foreign-controlled companies already accounted for an even higher proportion of manufactured exports. Since then Singaporean enterprises have made headway, to the extent that Singapore is now an exporter of industrial capital and expertise, mostly within the region.

On the multinational side, three major reasons supported entry to the manufacturing sector. While some earlier-established industries saw entry as a means to retain or to expand market share in the face of tariff walls erected to protect nascent industries—Glaxo and Nestlé are examples—industries that came later saw the possibility of enlarged markets, especially as disposable incomes began to rise in the late 1960s. With the formation of ASEAN, one of whose avowed objectives was the eventual formation of a common market, this objective became more attractive, though the reality is that the dismantling of intra-ASEAN trade barriers has been remarkably slow.

A second reason was to take advantage of cheaper labour, especially at the most labour-intensive points in the production process. The advent of containerisation probably assisted this process by lowering, proportionately, the cost of transportation. The third objective was tariff avoidance. Under the international Generalised System of Preferences, exports from the region to the US, Canada and the European Community attracted substantially lower import tariffs because they came from 'developing countries'. It was much cheaper for a Japanese exporter, for example, to manufacture in Southeast Asia for export to Europe than to export directly from Japan because direct exports attracted higher tariffs. Finally, and more arguably, multinationals in the region were, and are, subject to much less stringent labour regulations, less union activity and to generally more liberal standards of environmental pollution control—sometimes none at all.

On the part of the receiving countries a further set of reasons promoted industrial investment though circumstances varied from country to country. First was the perception, realised very variously, that only through growth in manufacturing could overall growth be achieved. Export economies were narrowly based upon a few commodities—in Malaysia rubber and tin, in Thailand premium grades of rice, in the Philippines sugar. The international terms of trade for these commodities were steadily turning against them compared with manufactures. Second was acceptance of the idea that all growth was good growth and that questions of how it might be shared and controlled could be at least temporarily set aside—if government were firm enough. Underlying this was the notion that rapid growth and increasing wealth would draw the teeth of the political Left.

Singapore was early on the scene with the formation of the Economic Development Board in 1961 and the creation of the large Jurong industrial area to the southwest of the island. The country's partial loss of access to the larger Malaysian market following its secession in 1965, followed in 1968 by the withdrawal of the British garrison which had contributed about 11 per cent to Singapore's GDP, forced it to accept a high level of foreign control in manufacturing, especially as local investors were notably reluctant to provide the necessary venture capital. Government investment in infrastructure was very substantial. Land was reclaimed, roads, railway and other services provided along with standard fully serviced factory buildings that could be rented in whole or part and modified to suit tenants.

Malaysia's industrial development was less precipitate for it had an already-developed export-oriented agricultural sector, unlike Singapore. But government involvement was nevertheless substantial. Like Singapore it adopted fiscal incentives such as tax holidays, tax credit for investment in training staff, and tariff exemptions on production machinery and raw material imports. Every state in the Federation developed at least one serviced industrial area—near Kuala Lumpur along the Federal Highway linking the capital with Port Kelang, at Penang both near the airport at Bayan Lepas and on the adjoining mainland at Perai.

The main players on the Singapore scene have been from the US, Japan, the Netherlands, the UK and Germany, while in Malaysia Singapore has followed Japan as the major investor, with substantial contributions from the UK, US and Hong Kong. Hong Kong investors have been seeking cheaper labour just like their Singapore counterparts while also seeking to spread the risk associated with investment in China.

The characteristics of manufacturing to some degree reflect differing approaches by investors. Thus compared to many of the other countries' enterprises, those owned by Americans concentrate upon capital-intensive production, notably in electronic and electrical goods, are larger in size, have higher productivity and market their products better. Only the topmost management levels are staffed by Americans. By contrast, Japanese-owned factories are smaller, less capital-intensive, do not generally use state-of-the-art machinery and use more low-skill labour. Worker productivity is lower and virtually all higher managerial positions are filled by Japanese. Some characteristics are shared. Few firms carry out research and development locally. Some, especially in technologically simpler industries such as textiles, clothing and footwear, are notably footloose. As mentioned earlier, Singapore has lost most of this sector. Malaysia may soon follow as wage rates in Indonesia, Myanmar, Cambodia and Viet Nam are much lower.

For foreign investors to invest in manufacturing, six major requirements must be substantially met: political and fiscal stability, an educated workforce, few restrictions upon trade and the repatriation of profits, government and private integrity, good infrastructure, tax incentives. These conditions are by no means fully met everywhere in the region. The degree to which they are is reflected in both structure and location of manufacturing.

Structure: Singapore, Malaysia, Philippines

Industrial plants wholly or partly owned by foreigners have added a new dimension to the region's industrial structure. Though not particularly large by international standards many are large by those of the region, for establishments employing hundreds of workers are quite new. Thus by 1989, for example, Singapore's 557 wholly foreign-owned plants produced 61 per cent of the industrial output while employing 46 per cent of the sector's workers. By contrast, the republic's 2400 wholly locally owned establishments supplied 16 per cent of the output but employed 31 per cent of the workforce.

In terms of efficiency, foreign-owned firms produce about double the value-added compared with locally owned firms and their output per worker is nearly three times greater. This disparity is a reflection of the fact that foreign-owned firms produce for export markets. (Around four-fifths of manufactured exports are produced by wholly or partly foreign-owned firms.) In a high wage-cost situation—high in regional rather than western-country terms—capital intensity is high, in the petroleum industry very high, around a million US dollars per worker. Foreign firms must therefore be efficient to compete internationally and this they achieve partly through economies of scale, high capital intensity, good management and marketing.

Industrial structure is also very much concerned with what is made. The region's manufacturers probably do not turn out either the proverbial

Table 8.3 Manufacturing structure—Philippines (1995), Malaysia (1995), Singapore (1999) (per cent in each SITC category)

Factories and workers

SITC	No. of factories			No. of workers			Workers per factory		
category	Phil.	Mal.	Sing.	Phil.	Mal.	Sing.	Phil.	Mal.	Sing.
15, 16	25.6	15.9	8.0	21.7	8.5	4.2	76	33	45
17, 18, 19	23.9	20.1	5.1	24.5	8.5	3.2	91	26	54
20, 21	9.7	15.1	3.5	7.0	15.4	1.8	65	63	45
22	6.2	4.0	9.9	2.5	2.5	5.7	37	39	49
23	0.2	0.2	0.4	0.4	0.3	0.9	163	92	175
24	4.7	2.5	5.5	4.9	2.3	4.5	92	56	69
25	5.2	7.8	8.4	4.9	10.6	5.8	84	84	58
26	3.6	4.0	2.3	3.6	3.7	1.8	88	58	67
27	2.3	2.0	0.5	3.0	2.2	0.4	115	68	68
28	5.7	12.6	15.7	3.9	5.4	10.6	61	26	57
29	4.4	6.1	14.9	3.2	4.6	10.2	4164	46	57
30, 31, 32	3.0	4.0	11.0	14.8	30.6	37.6	439	469	289
33	2.5	2.2	7.8	2.7	3.7	10.7	100	101	116
34, 35	3.0	3.4	7.0	2.8	1.5	2.6	85	26	32
Total	100.0	100.0	100.0	99.9	99.8	100.0	Av. 89	61	84

Gross output and value added

SITC	Gross output			Value added		
category	Phil.	Mal.	Sing.	Phil.	Mal.	Sing.
15, 16	28.7	15.0	2.5	32.0	10.3	2.5
17, 18, 19	7.2	3.8	0.9	8.3	5.2	0.8
20, 21	3.6	7.0	0.8	3.3	8.9	1.2
22	1.3	1.4	2.2	1.4	2.8	4.0
23	12.5	2.5	10.1	10.5	3.2	4.4
24	9.8	5.9	10.2	11.7	8.0	18.1
25	3.1	6.5	2.0	3.2	8.5	2.4
26	3.5	3.3	1.2	4.6	5.5	1.3
27	7.0	4.5	0.4	5.2	2.4	0.6
28	1.9	3.5	4.6	1.6	4.2	5.0
29	2.1	4.7	4.2	2.0	5.0	5.0
30, 31, 32	12.7	36.0	55.6	11.3	30.1	48.2
33	6.0	5.3	4.3	4.0	5.0	5.7
34, 35	0.8	0.7	0.8	0.9	0.8	0.8
Total	100.2	99.9	99.8	100.0	99.9	100.0

Notes: Data for Philippines and Singapore refer to factories with 10 or more workers. Corresponding table for Malaysia bears no statement as to size of factories. Percentages rounded.

Key: 15, 16, Food, drink and tobacco; 17, 18, 19, Textiles, clothing, footwear; 20, 21, Wood, paper; 22, Printing, publishing, records & tapes; 23 Refined petroleum; 24, Chemicals; 25, Rubber and plastics; 26 Non-metallic mineral products; 27 Basic metals; 28, Fabricated metals, not machinery; 29, Machinery & equipment; 30, 31, 32, Electrical & electronic machines, appliances, instruments, time-pieces; 33, Transport equipment; 34, 35, Other manufactures, waste materials.

Sources: Derived from Philippines *Yearbook, 1999;* Malaysia, *Buku Tahunan Perangkaan, 1998;* Singapore, *Yearbook of Statistics, 2000*

needle or anchor on any scale but they do produce a very large range of goods, mostly final and intermediate consumer goods rather than basic manufactures such as iron and steel. (Attempts to sustain the latter at Malaysia's Malayawata smelter and Indonesia's Krakatau plant have not been notably successful, suffering from high costs and limited markets.) In part the diversity of products is a hangover from the days when, except in Singapore, tariff barriers against imports and other fiscal incentives were given to promote local development in manufactures. This protection is declining, except in Myanmar, but it remains to some degree in most other countries.

Diversity is also reflected in entirely new sectors, notably in electronic and electrical machines and parts, camera, watch and clock assembly, developed by foreign capital assisted by specific government policies to promote them. The range of products is too great to be captured by the primary categories used in Table 8.3 and the reader will need to consult the directories and census reports available for a few countries for more details. (Table 8.3 uses percentages rather than actual money values as percentages change less from year to year and avoid problems created by changing exchange rates.) Data are given for Singapore, as the region's major manufacturer and its wealthiest country, for Malaysia, an 'upper-middle' producer, now with a higher proportion of its workers in manufacturing; and the Philippines, as a 'lower-middle' producer. Some comparisons are then drawn with Viet Nam which is at an early stage of industrialisation though data for it are not shown in Table 8.3 because of differences in the categorisation of manufactures.

Table 8.3 is as complex as it is not only because of the many different kinds of goods that are made but also because there are several different ways in which industrial structure can be described and compared. The number of factories is not necessarily proportional to population. Nor is the number of workers. In each of the examples given, the Philippines and Singapore have on average about the same number of workers in each factory, Malaysia fewer. But Singapore has a factory for every 670 of its people, Malaysia, one for every 880 and the Philippines only one for every 6000 people, though workshops with less than 10 workers are not counted. On this basis Singapore and Malaysia are much more industrialised than the Philippines. Myanmar, Cambodia, Laos and Viet Nam would come out much lower in the ranking were data available.

A similar sort of pecking order emerges if the proportion of the total number of factories or of the number of workers in each category are examined (Table 8.3A). The 'traditional' sectors based upon primary production, Standard International Trade Classification (SITC) categories 15–21, are still very important in the Philippines and Malaysia, accounting for 59 per cent of the factories and 53 per cent of the workers in the former. By contrast, these sectors account for only 17 per cent of the factories and 9 per cent of the workers in Singapore. Singapore and Malaysia stand out with a high proportions of workers in electronics, electrical machines, cameras, clocks, watches and various kinds of instruments (SITC 30–32). Many of the factories in this sector are large, especially in Malaysia, at least partly foreign-owned and mainly directed towards export markets. The only other sectors with remotely comparable sizes of factories are petroleum (23) and transport equipment (33), mainly motor-vehicle assembly.

Two other ways of looking at the structure of manufacturing are via gross output and value added (Table 8.3B). These measures avoid the distortions brought about by the wide range in size of factory and output per worker, the latter being very large. For example, in the Philippines output per worker in the petroleum refining industry (23) is 100 times greater than in textiles, clothing and footwear (17–19), the former extremely capital-intensive, the latter very labour-intensive. As Table 8.3B shows, there is again a distinct pecking order in some sectors. In the Philippines, the older industries in sectors 15–21 account for two-fifths of gross output and slightly more of the value added to raw material inputs in the course of manufacture. By contrast the proportion of each in Singapore is only one-twentieth of each total and around a quarter in Malaysia.

Some sectors have a lower share of value added than of gross output. Petroleum refining (23) notably has roughly half the share of value added as compared to gross output—as well as rather few refineries and few workers. These are universal characteristics, reflecting large size, high capitalisation and technical levels as well as low inputs of labour. On the other hand, some sectors, not necessarily the same in each country, have a higher share of value added than of gross output. Rubber and plastics, chemicals and in Singapore transport equipment and the printing, publishing and records industries are examples. This situation may reflect efficiencies in production as well as high technical levels. Singapore, for instance, competes internationally in the printing industry whereas Malaysia and the Philippines do not. One striking feature is that the categories 30–32 group, which contributes so substantially to employment and output of manufactures in Malaysia and Singapore, has a distinctly lower share of value added than of total output. This reflects the position of these industries substantially as producers of intermediate goods, exported elsewhere in partly finished form for others to take advantage of further added value.

Structure: rest of the region

Available data do not permit a similarly detailed look at manufacturing in the rest of the region because they are either even more out of date, use different categories, or simply do not exist. Thailand's industrial structure is increasingly like that of Malaysia, though it retains a substantial yet modernising food sector. Such is the universal popularity of Thai cuisine that there is now a growing export market for the wherewithal to prepare it, such as sweet chilli sauce, curry pastes and coconut milk. Indonesia's structure is rather like that of the Philippines, not coincidentally because both continue to protect some of their older industries, partly for fear of the economic consequences of industrial restructuring and partly for fear of upsetting the politically powerful. Both have the advantage of substantial internal markets that permit some degree of market isolation, an option less open to smaller, poorer countries.

One poorer country is Viet Nam. Manufacturing is steadily expanding, especially from the already established base in and around Ho Chi Minh City, though to a degree hindered by bumbling bureaucracy and shortcomings in infrastructure. Its industrial structure has been statistically outlined in 1994 and although the categories used do not exactly coincide with those used in Table 8.3, enough do to make some comparisons.

Comparing Table 8.4 with Table 8.3B some striking differences emerge, even by comparison with the Philippines whose overall manufacturing sector is less advanced than Malaysia's and Singapore's. The food sector is notably unimportant but expectedly so, because most Vietnamese do not eat processed foods and many eat what they themselves produce. Textiles, clothing and leather goods are probably substantially for local use though there is some export of clothing, as there is of leather, thanks in part to German aid in improving quality to exportable levels. Wood, mainly sawn timber, is still important, as it is in Malaysia. (Logs, a significant export, do not count as manufactures.) Quite striking is the 'fuels' sector, though this probably includes coal, not considered a manufacture elsewhere. It certainly includes petroleum products and reflects a level of dependence upon this modern sector for exports proportionately much greater than wealthy Singapore and Malaysia. The relatively small

Table 8.4 Viet Nam: gross output of manufacturing by sector, 1994 (per cent)

Sector	Category	Proportion
Food, drink	15, 16	6.9
Textiles, clothing, leather	17, 18, 19	15.2
Wood & paper	20, 21	8.3
Printing	22	1.6
Fuels	23(?)	24.4
Chemicals, fertiliser, rubber	24, 25	13.0
Glass, earthenware	26	1.7
Basic metals	27	3.2
Other metal products	28	2.5
Equipment & machinery	29	5.5
Electric, electronic machines	30, 31	2.9
Construction materials	?	12.2
Others	?	2.7
Total		100.1

Source: Derived from *Viet Nam Statistical Yearbook, 1995*

proportion of output of basic metals may seem surprising in a post-'command' economy, but reflects the fact that the country was never seduced into following the Stalinist Soviet pattern of basing manufacturing upon heavy industry, even though alone in the region it had the fuel resources—coking coal—to do so. What is especially noteworthy is the very limited development thus far of categories 30, 31, 32, electrical and electronic machines, instruments and timepieces. Given the current openness, at least in principle, to foreign investment in this sector, it is likely that it will expand once bureaucratic channels are cleared and infrastructure, especially electricity supply, is improved.

Viet Nam's is probably the best placed of the 'least developed' economies in the region to develop its manufactures. It has fuels, is developing an integrated electricity grid—a matter of considerable expense and difficulty in such a mountainous, elongated country—and has a potentially large internal market. It is also seen as a place to invest, particularly by regional capitalists in Thailand, Malaysia and Singapore. Not so Myanmar, Cambodia and Laos. Myanmar has major fiscal problems. Its government has a poor image and is seen to be sitting on a potential political time-bomb. Cambodia, though open, is seen as insecure. Poor Laos has the worst of most worlds, with small, poor markets, weak infrastructure, except for hydroelectricity, and a transportation system that is very much subject to the whims and fancies of officials outside the country and at best difficult within it.

Location

Manufacturing, to state the obvious, is spatially concentrated. This is so at most levels—within countries, within states and provinces, often even within the towns and cities in which it almost entirely exists. This is so also within those countries which once attempted to follow a socialist blueprint. Though Communist theorists pointed to the need to ensure broad equality of income amongst regions, the lack of infrastructure and the costs of providing it were too great for precept to be put into practice. Thus most manufacturing in Myanmar is in Yangon, in Cambodia Phnom Penh, in Laos Vientiane. Amongst these former socialist countries only Viet Nam breaks this pattern of capital-city dominance but Saigon/Ho Chi Minh City was the capital of the capitalist South Vietnam when its industrial base was laid. On a gross output basis that includes electricity, Ho Chi Minh City produces 26 per cent of the country's manufactures, with another 17 per cent from the neighbouring Ba Ria – Vung Tau region, compared with only 9 per cent from Ha Noi and Hai Phong—the long-standing production centres in the North. Manufacturing is not necessarily a concomitant of urban concentration. Hué, a medium-sized city, produces only a thousandth of Viet Nam's manufactures—amongst them 'Hu Da', the region's best beer.

As might be expected, a high degree of industrial localisation is characteristic of the long-term capitalist countries, but the degree to which manufacturing is spatially concentrated has probably increased over the last several decades, paralleling the change away from the colonial situation in which agricultural and forestry processing industries were not necessarily located in metropolitan and other major cities.

Thus in the Philippines, four-fifths of all manufacturing is within 40 km of downtown Manila, despite legislation to slow concentration. In that case a spatial limit was imposed, to which the industrialists' response was to build factories just beyond the limit, at Calamba for example. Indonesia shows similar concentration in the Jakarta and Bandung metropolitan regions of West Java where some two-thirds of the country's approved foreign investments in manufacturing have been made, plus half of its domestic investments. Industrial concentration in Malaysia is marginally less marked, perhaps reflecting some degree of devolution of political power to the states. But some two-thirds of manufacturing has been in only three states: in Selangor (including the federal capital), especially the Klang Valley; Penang, especially Sebarang Perai; and Johor. The so-called 'Borneo territories'—significant term—are notably lacking in much manufacturing beyond the processing of primary materials. Greater Bangkok is also the scene of major industrial expansion—west to Don Muang and Rangsit, north towards Ayuthia, east and south along the coast as far as Rayong. Bangkok dominates Thailand's manufacturing, with at least 65 per cent of total output.

Two contradictory processes are clearly at work so far as changes in location are concerned—concentration and its opposite. The forces driving concentration are extremely powerful. The major cities already contain most of the manufacturing. Although new entrants to the sector may have to compete with already-established firms, there is some developed infrastructure however inadequate it may be in the poorer countries. This not only includes basic needs such as roads, power, water and other necessary support but also a workforce that is more or less skilled and accustomed to the disciplines of the manufacturing process. Where export production is the major objective, location near a port or, increasingly, for reasonably low-bulk, high-value goods, near an airport, is essential. This is where many export processing zones—essentially free-trade enclaves not subject to the usual Customs restrictions—are located, as in Kuala Lumpur's Kelang Valley, feeding Port Kelang. In addition cities are centres of wealth by comparison with the countryside, so that production for local markets needs to be located near the major markets and these are in the cities.

But even in the major cities there are countervailing forces: high land rents, traffic congestion which increases transport costs, pollution, and high labour costs. All reduce the competitive advantage of the cities but obviously not to the extent that there has been any significant shift to smaller towns and the countryside. Clearly, primary-based manufacturing has some advantage in the countryside, especially if it involves reduction of bulk and significant value added, or if it is highly polluting. Oil palm processing is a good example. Any other industries that choose small towns or the countryside in which to locate factories generally need more than cheap land and other basics. Good access and a supply of cheap labour is obviously attractive to labour-intensive manufacturing such as clothing, or assembly of electrical and electronic components, especially where economies of scale are not too important. Thus in Melaka state, Malaysia, both of these kinds of industries are significant even in predominantly rural areas, which contain many hitherto underemployed young women.

Governments have also encouraged this kind of spatial dispersal, not least because there are significant private and social costs in relocating people to cities with all the social, even psychological dislocation this causes. Thailand, for instance, has a specific smaller towns development plan aimed at encouraging manufacturing by providing infrastructure, even start-up loans. Overall, though, the forces of centralisation within major urban agglomerations have prevailed.

More generally, a broad pattern of structural change in manufacturing is discernible. Not only is the sector expanding absolutely and relative to other sectors of the region's economies, but its internal structure is changing. Amongst the poorer countries most manufacturing is still like that of colonial times, albeit now locally owned—small in scale, typified by workshops rather than factories, using simple tools, producing commodities for local markets, or if larger then largely based upon primary production and/or substantially directed towards exports. Food, wood and paper, textiles, clothing, footwear, and non-metal products are examples. To these have been added petroleum refining—also primary-based—a sector much expanded since colonial times with Singapore, Malaysia, Thailand and the Philippines adding this capital-intensive, technically quite advanced sector to earlier-established plants in Myanmar and Indonesia.

At the other end of the income spectrum Singapore and Malaysia are fully industrialised though both lack the whole gamut of manufactures characteristic of larger, higher labour-cost economies. Singapore has moved up the technical ladder, exporting its capital and expertise in 'bottom-end' manufacturing, such as textiles, clothing, even assembly of the more labour-intensive kinds, to other countries in the region, as it swings back to being a provider of services. In between are ranged the other countries. Viet Nam is just beginning to add foreign-owned manufacturing, some of it funded from Thailand, Malaysia and Singapore. On a smaller scale and rather uncertainly, so is Cambodia. The Philippines has advanced further down that road but is to some degree constrained by popular objection to wholly foreign-owned enterprises and by government reluctance fully to open internal markets. Indonesia is in a somewhat similar situation, made more uncertain by political instability.

Services

Structural change has led to considerable growth in this the tertiary sector, both relative to the other two sectors and absolutely as reflected in both employment and GDP. This growth partly reflects growing economic complexity with lengthening linkages between producers and consumers. Simple economies in which producers and consumers are members of the same family of peasants or tribal people still exist, notably in the countries of mainland Southeast Asia except Thailand, in the eastern Indonesian Archipelago including Timor, and remoter areas of much of the rest of the region. But even where life is simple the service sector exists: traders to buy jungle produce, opium, surplus rice and other non-perishable commodities, priests and teachers to minister to the spirit, health workers to care for the body, police and other civil servants to administer and keep a general eye on things.

While the service sector has long existed in the countryside it is in towns and cities that it comes into its own. Although derided as parasitic in socialist practice in the region, much of it is essential to the proper functioning of complex societies and economies—banking and finance, wholesale and retail trade, education, health. Modern economies survive perfectly well without tourism but the drive to see other places and 'experience life' is a deep-seated one even in traditional societies. Consider the *berjalai* of Borneo's Dayak people, a sometimes years-long journey outside the home territory undertaken by young men as a rite of passage to marriage and adulthood. Antiquities and other life-styles attract visitors to the extent that local and even national economies become dependent upon the tourist dollar—witness Bali, Bangkok and Chiang Mai, Siem Riep (Angkor) and Yogyakarta (Borobudur).

Goods, services and consumption

Unlike most developed countries, the countries of Southeast Asia do not usually conduct national surveys of wholesale and retail trade or, generally, of the movement of goods within their national boundaries. The same is even more true of trade in services. Data are therefore very patchy so that the best that can be done is to make some broad observations about regional patterns.

As with income, size and many other measures there is a very large range in size of wholesale and especially retail business amongst Southeast Asia's component countries. At one end of the retail spectrum are tiny businesses operated by single individuals. In every village there are stalls selling cigarettes—often one at a time—matches, salt, sugar, plastic containers, biscuits and other very basic goods. There may be a stall selling tea and coffee, or bowls of noodles—as much a social meeting point as a real business, with tiny stocks and minuscule turnover, often operated as an adjunct to other activities. Some traders are itinerants, these days generally on a bicycle or motorcycle. Some sell. Some buy. Some do both, penetrating to the remotest settlement, for even dwellers in deepest rainforest have things to sell: rattans and bamboos to be bundled into rafts and floated downriver; in more accessible villages handcrafts for sale to tourists—blow-pipes, palm-leaf, hats, bamboo, combs, a little deliciously-fragrant hill-grown rice surplus to family needs; in parts of mainland Southeast Asia, lumps of crude opium. At the other end of the spectrum lie air-conditioned shopping malls and department stores, perhaps run by international retail firms, some Japanese, selling internationally known brands, genuine or fake—Sony, National, Louis Vuitton, Rolex, Givenchy and a host of others. Such high-order goods are to be found only in the larger and wealthier towns and cities, of course, for only these are fully integrated into the global economy that produces them. As anywhere there are clearly hierarchies of goods and of settlements in which they are sold, though what these may be in each country is not known in detail.

The key factor is disposable income and this is substantially higher in

Table 8.5 Regional indicators of consumer durable consumption (articles per 100 urban households)

	Air-conditioners			Cameras	
Highest	Singapore	35	Highest	Singapore	72
	Malaysia	8		Philippines	34
Lowest	Viet Nam	3	Lowest	Thailand	15
	Indonesia	2		Indonesia	14
	Cars			**Motorcycles**	
Highest	Malaysia	44	Highest	Malaysia	61
	Singapore	36		Thailand	49
Lowest	Philippines	7	Lowest	Indonesia	24
	Viet Nam	1		Singapore	5
	Radios			**Refrigerators**	
Highest	Singapore	97	Highest	Singapore	99
	Malaysia	92		Malaysia	92
Lowest	Indonesia	74	Lowest	Philippines	42
	Thailand	70		Indonesia	20

Source: Economist Intelligence Unit 1994, *Asian Consumer Markets Atlas*

the cities. This is reflected in what people buy. As income increases less is spent upon food, clothing and other basic needs and more is spent upon consumer durables like air-conditioners, cameras, cars and motorcycles, radios and refrigerators, all readily available in most major towns. As with many other characteristics there is a striking range as a 1990s survey of urban consumption indicated. (See Table 8.5. The survey excluded Myanmar, Cambodia, Laos and Brunei.)

Although comprehensive data are lacking, Table 8.5 gives some clues as to the nature of wholesale and retail trade in the various countries listed. Clearly it reflects income levels. It also shows that there is little to be expected by way of further growth in internal markets for some durables in some countries. Most people have a radio and a refrigerator in Singapore, for example, whereas few in Indonesia or Viet Nam have these 'positional goods'—items that reflect social status rather than being essentials. Had the survey included international brands of watches, luggage, footwear and clothing it is likely that a similar pattern would have emerged; likewise international air travel or dining in high-class restaurants or visiting holiday resorts on the services side.

Consumer durables, though, are only a small part of family budgets and again the kinds of things people buy—and thus trade—reflect income. Food is a major component amongst poorer families for whom a soft drink or a cigarette is a luxury item. As incomes rise more is spent on other things such as entertainment and education or travel. Table 8.6 shows the

Table 8.6 Consumption by sector (urban areas only)(%)

Consumption sector	Indonesia	Malaysia	Philippines	Singapore	Thailand	HCM City
Food	47	23	51	19	30	72
Alcohol & tobacco	4	n.a.	3	n.a.	3	n.a.
Housing	20	9	18	10	24	4
Footwear & clothing	6	4	4	7	5	3
Transportation	n.a.	19	5	15	18	4
Education & entertainment	2[1]	7[2]	3	15	5	5
Consumer durables	3	n.a.	5	9	9	n.a.
Other goods & services	18	38	11	32	6	12
Total	100	100	100	100	100	100

Notes: n.a. = not available; [1] entertainment only; [2] education only
Source: Economist Intelligence Unit, 1994, *Asian Consumer Atlas*

situation for middle and upper-income countries and Ho Chi Minh City, probably Viet Nam's wealthiest centre.

Income is not the only factor influencing the nature of trade in goods and services. Another is age structure, which affects the kinds of goods and services demanded. While much remains to be learned in this area some general conclusions can be drawn. In countries with fairly high birth rates and young populations—all the countries of mainland Southeast Asia except Thailand, parts of Malaysia, the Philippines and Indonesia—there is a considerable demand for obstetrical services, baby food, primary education and health care. Where birth rates have fallen recently—most of the rest of the region, except Singapore—rates of family formation are high, so there is a heavy demand for employment. This is substantially met by the expanding manufacturing sector, and leads to needs for housing, transportation, especially to and from work, clothing and footwear, consumer durables and, at higher income levels, recreation and entertainment. Obviously the demands for these kinds of goods and services are much enhanced by migration to the cities, for it is typically young adults who move.

Where birth rates fell several decades ago—mainly Singapore at the national level but also including Overseas Chinese groups elsewhere—the populations are ageing. Consumer demands change again towards health care, entertainment, travel and recreation for the fit. For the wealthy a second home becomes desirable. Clearly these demographic changes underly the changes in consumption brought about by increasing wealth as well as those brought about by the generally increasing range of family incomes. The last has the effect of creating a largely urban underclass, lacking even the basics of adequate food, shelter and health care.

Trade

Internal trade

Very little is known, directly, of the structure of internal trade—the size and complexity of networks, the commodities that flow along them—except where port and railway administrations create data. But since most goods and people travel by road on journeys largely unrecorded by any authority it is difficult to paint a picture of internal trade patterns. What is unquestionable is that trade networks are much more complexly linked than even 50 years ago. Strictly local, cellular market areas are confined to low-value, bulky goods like sand and gravel or, in unroaded areas, basic foods such as rice. As the value of goods relative to bulk—and hence transportation costs—increases, so too does the market area, other things being equal. The same thing happens where, as a result of improved transportation, the cost of moving goods as a proportion of their total cost falls.

Thus where 150 years ago only such rare and valuable commodities as pepper and other spices, salt, scented woods, embroidered cloths and substances used in medicine were at all widely traded, now the range is truly enormous, as a glance at a *Yearbook of International Trade Statistics* will show. The quantity of goods moving has also increased, recently at rates far outstripping population growth. In the Philippines, for example, the value of goods moved internally by water, rail and air jumped 30 per cent from 1994 to 1995. Whether the trade networks involved in any particular single commodity have also become more complex is debatable, for past limitations of transportation, including the need of territorial chiefs to derive a revenue from the transit of goods, resulted in goods passing through many hands from producer to consumer. For some commodities at least—tea is an example—it seems likely that networks are now simpler than in the past.

One exception to the general lack of data on internal trade is the Philippines, where the circumstance of its insular character means that many goods pass through ports and are thus enumerated. Given the industrial structure described earlier, it is no surprise that in terms of value, food, drink and tobacco make up about 30 per cent of the commodities carried. Given the concentration of manufacturing in and around Manila and its major port function, it is equally unsurprising that the national capital has by far the highest outflow of goods of any region in the country, around a quarter of the total by water, rail and air. In terms of regional commodity inflows, Mindanao and the Visayas dominate each with 40 per cent of total inflows. Consequently they have large trade deficits—much more flows in than out. What the commodity-flow patterns might be within other countries can only guessed at, but given the dominance of capital city regions in manufacturing and mostly as ports, it seems likely that all have positive trade balances. The same would doubtless apply to the trade in services.

At the local level retail marketing takes various forms ranging from air-conditioned shopping malls and department stores in the wealthier cities, through 'traditional' open markets to itinerant purveyors of food, clothing and knick-knacks. Malls, department stores, indeed glass-fronted shops, are very much the product of the colonial era. Robinsons and Cold Storage are two names that survive from that time.

Open markets survive, many now under a simple roof, with 'wet' sections selling vegetables, fish and meat, while dry sections sell cloth, utensils and dry provisions. These colourful markets are a feature of every size of town down to the smallest, some major urban ones becoming tourist attractions. Phnom Penh's, housed in a Corbusier-style building, is one example. Bangkok's floating market is another.

Systems of 'rotating' or periodical markets are widespread in rural areas and small market towns. Itinerant merchants move from one market to another on a regular pattern, usually selling goods other than daily necessities, such as clothing or utensils. Periodical markets are slightly different in that the sellers do not move from one location to another, being usually the producers of the goods they sell. Some are held in the countryside, others in an appropriate open space in a small town, usually on a fixed day each week. Notable are the *tamu* of Sabah, Malaysia, where one can buy everything from local fruits and vegetables to jars and gongs, the local 'positional' goods. Though periodical markets are often spoken of as 'traditional', many were, in fact, started by colonial administrators.

International trade

If trade is the 'life-blood of the nation', then for the poorer countries and regions the blood runs slowly and is remarkably thin. Compare Laos and Singapore. In the former the value of international trade is only a few dollars per person. In the latter it is many thousands, reflecting its roles as a manufacturer, a trade entrepot and provider of services to the region.

The first basic question concerning international trade is how much is traded. Once again, in terms of value there are huge contrasts. Singapore's life-blood truly is trade. With just over 3 million people in 1998 its total trade was nearly two-fifths larger than that of the next in line, Malaysia,

Table 8.7 Value of trade nationally (million US$) and per person (US$) proportion by country

Country	Imports (US$ mill.)	%	Exports (US$ mill.)	%	Total (US$ mill.)	%	Trade per person (US$)
Brunei	1 764	0.6	2 337	0.7	4 101	0.7	13 019
Indonesia	27 337	9.8	48 847	15.0	76 184	12.6	374
Malaysia	57 895	20.7	73 304	23.8	131 199	21.7	5 910
Myanmar	2 669	1.0	1 076	0.3	3 745	0.6	83
Philippines	30 705	11.0	27 703	8.5	58 408	9.7	778
Singapore	104 711	37.5	109 906	33.8	214 617	35.5	67 068
Thailand	42 968	15.4	54 433	16.8	97 401	16.1	1 594
Viet Nam (1996)	11 144	4.0	7 255	2.2	18 399	3.0	237
Total	279 193	100.0	324 861	100.0	604 054	99.9	Av. 1199

Source: International Trade Statistics Yearbook, 1996

with 21 million people. Thailand's trade is substantially greater than that of Indonesia, while Myanmar and Viet Nam (and Cambodia and Laos if data were available) scrape along at the bottom. In terms of value of trade per person, the contrasts are even more extreme, with Myanmar's value being less than 1 per cent that of Singapore and that of Viet Nam.

As Table 8.7 shows the regional pecking order for trade is quite the reverse of that of either physical size or population though matching GDP fairly well (see Table 6.6). Singapore is obviously the major player but the other specialist producer, Brunei, is cut down to size as a relatively minor trader despite its high level on a per person basis. Since the early 1970s, Singapore has increased its share of the region's trade, as have Malaysia and Thailand. Every other country's share has dropped so that the spread amongst traders has increased as the dominance of Singapore, Malaysia and Thailand has increased. It seems likely that this pattern of dominance is related to the expansion of export-oriented manufacturing coupled, in Singapore's case, with overall growth in the republic's entrepot function.

The ongoing economic downturn in the region has done several things to trade. First, it has substantially cut total trade—by about 14 per cent overall from 1995 to 1998, imports dropping rather more than exports. In all likelihood this occurred because consumption was curtailed and capital expenditures were reduced, while the drop in the value of many regional currencies—baht, ringgit, rupiah, even the Singapore dollar—actually enhanced competitiveness, so that the value of exports dropped less markedly. The rises in the international price of petroleum undoubtedly assisted producers, especially Brunei. Singapore's dominance has not been significantly challenged. Minor players such as Myanmar and especially Viet Nam, have seen substantial growth in trade, for their economies are much less globalised and thus less affected by the Asian crisis.

The region's visible trade balance—basically the difference between the value of exports and of imports—is negative. Only Indonesia, Brunei and Malaysia are 'in the black'. So were Singapore and Thailand in 1998, the only year in which this has been reflected in statistics back to 1963. For some countries being in the red is of no particular account. Singapore easily balances its books by having a massive surplus of 'invisibles'—the value of services provided, income from investments and other earnings abroad. The Philippines manages, in part, by remittances from overseas workers. Thailand and Malaysia benefit from capital inflows, though these change quickly from year to year. (Malaysia moved quickly to control prospective capital outflows in the late 1990s.) Others run chronic deficits, in part made good by unrecorded trade—otherwise the black market—or by foreign aid. Cambodia's economy, for example, is basically supported by both of these. One thing is certain: those countries significantly dependent upon agricultural exports, notably Myanmar, have suffered from a global long-term adverse change in the terms of trade. (Basically this means that prices of most agricultural commodities have risen more slowly than those of manufactures.) This, of course, is one of the major motives for promoting export manufacturing, as described earlier.

In global terms, the region fares reasonably well. With about 8.5 per cent of the world's population, it accounts for around 7 per cent of its international trade. But this may not be very meaningful for all international trade is to some degree an artifact of the global division into nations of very varied size so that a large country like Indonesia or the US will have less international trade—other things being equal—than a small country such as Singapore. To make a 'real' comparison it would be necessary to compare Singapore with, say, Tanjung Priok, Indonesia's main port.

Much more important is the question of what is traded. The days when the region was regarded by outsiders solely as the source of exotica such as pepper, nutmeg, cloves, rare woods and gold have long gone, the gold and diamonds locked in vaults or boudoirs, the rare woods and spices still traded but totally insignificant in the face of small floods of palm oil and rubber, of clothing and footwear, clocks and computers. True the old colonial economy survives—rice from Thailand, rubber from Indonesia, southern Thailand and Malaysia, palm oil from Malaysia, petroleum and gas from Brunei and Indonesia. But imported manufactures now largely come from Japan or from within the region rather than from metropolitan countries, though these remain sources of investment, of 'high-tech' machinery and high-value consumer goods, for their western origin has snob value.

Table 8.8 Commodity structure of international trade, 1998 (%)

Commodity Group	Brunei (1994) Imp.	Brunei (1994) Exp.	Indonesia Imp.	Indonesia Exp.	Malaysia Imp.	Malaysia Exp.	Myanmar (1996) Imp.	Myanmar (1996) Exp.
0, 1	12.8	–	9.9	8.1	4.9	2.5	3.1	46.2
2	32.7	–	8.6	7.6	2.5	3.2	2.0	31.0
3	0.4	95.3	10.1	19.3	3.2	6.2	4.4	0.5
4	21.4	–	–	3.1	0.5	7.5	3.5	–
5	14.6	3.4	14.7	4.3	6.9	3.4	8.6	–
6	17.8	–	17.1	18.1	11.2	8.4	20.0	3.2
7	–	–	36.2	9.5	62.8	59.2	27.0	1.1
8	–	1.3	2.8	13.5	5.3	8.7	2.1	8.1
9	0.3	–	0.4	16.4	2.6	1.0	29.2	9.8
Total	100.0	100.0	99.8	99.9	99.9	100.1	99.9	99.9

	Philippines Imp.	Philippines Exp.	Singapore Imp.	Singapore Exp.	Thailand Imp.	Thailand Exp.
0, 1	8.3	4.3	4.0	3.1	4.2	18.2
2	3.1	1.4	0.8	1.0	4.3	4.5
3	7.1	0.5	8.1	7.5	9.3	2.4
4	–	2.4	0.3	0.3	–	–
5	7.7	1.1	5.9	6.3	9.6	4.2
6	11.2	3.7	9.0	4.6	17.1	11.9
7	57.5	72.1	60.3	66.4	46.9	38.3
8	4.6	13.5	10.1	8.2	5.9	16.8
9	0.3	0.7	1.5	2.6	2.4	3.6
Total	99.8	99.7	100.0	100.0	99.7	99.9

Key: 0 Food & live animals; 1 Beverages & tobacco; 2 Raw materials, excl. fuels; 3 Mineral fuels; 4 Fats & oil; 5 Chemicals; 6 Basic manufactures; 7 Machines & transport equipment; 8 Miscellaneous manufactures; 9 Other

Source: *International Trade Statistics Yearbook, 1998*

As Table 8.8 shows, the poorer countries still depend largely upon raw material exports or relatively easily produced manufactures such as textiles, footwear and clothing. The wealthier countries have export structures that, at the basic level of commodity classification, are quite similar to those of their imports. In fact, a substantial proportion of these industrial goods are only semi-finished, the most labour-intensive part of the manufacturing process having been set up in the region to lower costs, to circumvent trade barriers or to reduce tax and other liabilities.

Brunei lives on oil and gas exports (50 and 45 per cent respectively), though increasingly also upon income from oil-generated investments. But much the same could be said of other places—Banjermasin in southeastern Kalimantan, Pekanbaru in Sumatera, Seria in Sarawak. It just happens that this tiny entity is an independent nation. Myanmar also depends largely upon a single commodity group—food—which accounts for half of its exports, mainly rice and other agricultural products plus rubber. Having followed largely autarkic economic policies since independence in 1947, its trade is insignificant, retaining every characteristic of the old colonial economy except private ownership of trade organisations. The export economies of Cambodia and Laos are somewhat similar to that of Myanmar. All are very minor participants in regional trade.

At the other end of the commodity spectrum are Singapore, the Philippines and Malaysia with 66, 72 and 59 per cent respectively of exports falling into Category 7. In the first, 'office machines', which includes computers, and 'electrical machines' together make up more than half of all exports, the corresponding proportions for the Philippines and Malaysia being about one-third. In between lie Thailand and Indonesia. Thailand has about a quarter of its exports in Category 7 but also is a substantial exporter of clothing. While Indonesia still has a substantial export of raw materials, mainly oil and gas—which the Philippines and Thailand do not, because they possess little—it still has significant old-style exports. Categories 0–2 through Category 7 are growing, since the country's infrastructure for the production of export manufactures is reasonably good, especially in Java, and wages are low.

Direction of trade

Who trades with whom internationally is far from being entirely a matter of free-market economics. Although the days when the dominant link was with a metropolitan country are long past, each former imperialist power has sought to retain at least something of its former trade and some still figure amongst the 'Top Ten' listings. Blood is thicker than the glue of money alone so that price and propinquity alone probably do not explain the existence of Hong Kong and China amongst most countries' 'Top Ten', because trade, especially foreign trade, still substantially involves Overseas Chinese. But money also talks, so that Asia's economic giant, Japan, necessarily appears high in the listings, particularly in its role as a source of multinational-company trade, a function shared to a fair degree with the US.

Trade patterns reflect both past historical links as well as present economic and political realities. Thus Viet Nam still trades to some degree with France, Malaysia, Brunei and Singapore with Britain and Indonesia with the Netherlands, though less than 5 per cent of the trade of each is towards the former metropolitan countries. Perhaps the most striking case of continuance of a colonial-period link is that between the Philippines

Table 8.9 Imports and exports by region of origin and destination, 1998 (%)

	Other SE Asia	East Asia	North & Central America	Europe	West & South Asia	Australia & NZ
Brunei						
Imports	49.0	12.4	13.9	14.2	1.2	3.7
Exports	15.0	71.2	9.2	2.2	–	0.3
Indonesia						
Imports	16.4	25.6	16.6	23.2	4.6	7.3
Exports	18.9	31.5	15.3	16.9	5.8	3.5
Malaysia						
Imports	22.8	31.5	20.4	13.3	1.5	2.7
Exports	24.3	20.2	22.4	16.9	6.1	2.7
Myanmar (1997)						
Imports	52.9	32.8	2.3	4.8	4.8	0.7
Exports	29.9	21.1	3.8	6.5	32.1	0.5
Philippines						
Imports	14.9	36.0	22.6	10.8	5.8	3.1
Exports	12.9	21.7	35.2	20.8	0.7	0.7
Singapore						
Imports	23.2	27.3	19.0	15.7	6.9	1.5
Exports	23.9	21.0	20.4	17.8	5.1	3.6
Thailand (1997)						
Imports	12.4	34.1	14.6	17.2	7.7	2.6
Exports	21.5	25.7	20.7	17.9	3.7	1.9
Viet Nam (1995)						
Imports	29.2	36.0	1.9	11.5	0.8	1.3
Exports	20.4	42.5	4.2	15.5	1.2	1.0

Source: International Trade Statistics Yearbook, 1998

and the US, especially in respect of exports. The European share of trade is in the 15 to 23 per cent range for most countries. Trade links between the region's once-socialist countries and the rest of the former socialist bloc also survive although the actual amounts of trade are very small. Thus Viet Nam, Cambodia and Laos still trade with Russia, the Ukraine and former Soviet bloc countries in central and eastern Europe. Viet Nam's export to North and Central America in the mid-1990s was actually almost entirely to Cuba, though that has now changed.

The East Asian region, as a trading partner, is dominated by Japan. Part of its dominance is explainable by its export-oriented investment—as with the US—partly by aggressive marketing and trade development, partly by propinquity. Trade with Hong Kong is especially significant because it is close by, has a reputation of reliability and has Overseas Chinese links.

Within Southeast Asia itself trade links are not as strong as might be expected given ASEAN's long commitment to work towards regional free trade. That work has progressed rather slowly, in part because of fears that free entry of goods from Singapore, Malaysia and Thailand will swamp partly-protected markets elsewhere. Another limitation is that countries are to a degree competitors producing much the same commodities—rubber in Indonesia, Thailand and Malaysia, clothing and footwear in Thailand and the Philippines, electrical and electronic machines in Singapore, Malaysia and Thailand.

To some degree the current level of intra-regional trade—around 18 per cent of the total—reflects the lack of developed international trading links, even of actual facilities. Thus Myanmar, Viet Nam and Cambodia trade via Bangkok or Singapore because they lack the knowledge and expertise to be international players and the quantities involved are too small or of too low a quality to attract the attention of major traders. Laos, being landlocked, trades via Bangkok or to a lesser degree via Vinh in northern Viet Nam, and some of its consignments may appear in the statistics of those countries.

In addition the region also has significant unrecorded trade the amount of which can only be guessed. Mindanao and the Sulu Archipelago trade with Malaysian Sabah. There is small-vessel trade from east Sumateran rivers to Malaysia and Singapore, not necessarily recorded at both ends or at all. Substantial amounts of Myanmar's timber exports are not recorded and the same is said to be true for Cambodia, Laos and Viet Nam, as well as remoter areas in Indonesia. Myanmar and Viet Nam also have vigorous trade across the land borders with China, to the extent that Vietnamese manufacturers are seriously concerned about competition from Chinese goods bartered or otherwise traded across the land border. As well there is significant trade into that country by lorry across Cambodia. If lack of records were the only consideration such trade would be a trivial matter. The fact that governments lose revenue from Customs dues is not.

Trade in services

Every country trades in services as well as goods. Goods move through transportation networks abroad and these may be owned locally or by foreigners. Tourists arrive and spend money on services, not all of them legal. People also travel abroad for pleasure or business and if, as is usually the case, income from the services with which they are provided accrues to foreigners, that is a cost to the home country's economy—one good reason why countries short of foreign exchange restrict overseas

Table 8.10 Current account income and expenditure, goods and services, 1998 (US$ million)

	Goods		Services		Balance		
	Income	Exp.	Income	Exp.	Goods	Services	Both
Cambodia	705	1 097	110	189	–392	–79	–471
Indonesia	50 371	31 942	4 479	11 813	18 429	–7 334	11 095
Laos	342	507	145	96	–165	49	–116
Malaysia (1997)	77 881	74 005	15 016	17 516	3 876	–2 500	1 376
Myanmar	1 171	2 455	543	445	–1 284	98	–1 186
Philippines	29 496	29 524	7 477	10 107	–28	–2 630	–2 625
Singapore	110 379	95 702	18 327	17 997	14 677	330	15 007
Thailand	52 747	36 513	13 156	11 998	16 234	1 158	17 392

Note: No data for Brunei, Viet Nam.
Source: IMF *Balance of Payments Statistics Yearbook, 1999*

travel. On the other hand, money flows into national exchequers from services provided abroad, such as national shipping and airlines, remittances from overseas workers, repatriated profits from investments, income from consultants' fees and a host of other sources.

In the region generally, countries receive more for providing services to foreigners than they pay for services to others, though the position on the current account can vary considerably from year to year. (The current account basically sets out, for any year, the income from the supply of goods and services. For each there is either a positive or a negative balance as well as an overall balance. See Table 8.10.) This situation is substantially different from 20 years ago when only Singapore made a profit from services. In 1997 Indonesia made a substantial profit, mainly from tourism, though that disappeared a year later. Singapore gains on the provision of services, reflecting its regional investments and its growing status as a provider of services. The Philippines usually stands out as a major loser in the trade in goods and, despite the large number of its nationals living abroad sending money home, usually ends up with a large deficit, a position reversed in 1998. Small, poor economies such as those of Myanmar, Cambodia and Laos have chronic balance-of-payments problems, especially in respect of services, substantially provided—at a cost—by others. Table 8.10 sets out the recent position.

Tourism

Tourism makes a substantial contribution to the region's balance of payments and to foreign exchange earnings though it is not always easy to disentangle it from other contributions. To some degree, capturing the tourist dollar is a matter of reputation and of organisation. Thus Myanmar, though possessing stunning scenery, pristine beaches and marvellous antiquities at Bagan and elsewhere, has been unable to combat its image as fiercely authoritarian, disorganised, backward and dirty. Like some other countries in the region it has so little confidence in its own cultural integrity that it seeks to insulate the tourist from its own realities for fear of the social and political consequences of catering for large numbers of foreigners, some of whom will do what authority would wish they would not do. Others have seen the tourist as a cow to be milked, preferably for the benefit of the ruling elite and their cronies—as in the Marcos-era Philippines, Sukarno-era Indonesia—rather than as a means of bettering the livelihoods of local people in their own places, to which tourists resort from interest in seeing them as they are.

The region is one of extraordinarily varied and rich culture—music, dance, philosophy, religion and cuisine. It is rich, too, in history and in physical beauty whether on the seashore, in fields and forests or among historic monuments. Consider Balinese rice terraces, classical dances from the *Ramayana* at Prambanan by the light of the full moon, or dawn over Angkor Wat. But even modern cities have their attractions—not just the fleshpots of Bangkok's Patpong and Soi Cowboy, Manila's Pasay City or Makati, but also Bangkok's bustling *klongs* (canals), the Pasteur Institute where snakes are milked for their venom, or Singapore's splendid zoo and superbly varied cuisine.

Singapore, Malaysia and Thailand have felt the tourist dollar worth vigorous chasing. All have international airlines serving prospective areas of customer origin. They are regarded as clean, safe and offering value for money. Their main transportation hubs, especially Bangkok and Singapore, are such as to attract tourist business solely by reason of that function. Every country in mainland Southeast Asia other than Thailand can be accessed from outside the region virtually only via Bangkok, Singapore or Hong Kong. Singapore is also a major hub for Indonesia, eastern Malaysia and Brunei, though both Jakarta and Manila are reasonably well served from outside even if their international airlines do not rate as highly with international travellers as those of Singapore, Thailand, Malaysia, or, outside the region, Hong Kong or Australia.

Tourism is not solely an international economic activity. As wealth has increased in Singapore, Malaysia and Thailand, especially, so has local tourism, though Singapore, being so small, has virtually no internal tourism unless visiting offshore islands or the zoo be so considered. In the mid-1990s, for example, Malaysia's domestic tourist receipts were estimated to be rising at around 15 per cent annually.

Increasing disposable income both within and without the region is only part of the reason for tourism's growth. Unlike commodity trade, international tourism is much less subject to tariffs and quotas, though subject to some degree to limitations upon foreign ownership of businesses and land. It is a large employer of people, though requiring new skills. Large quantities of foreign currency are generated. Angkor Wat, for example, is thought to be Cambodia's largest single earner. Natural assets such as scenery or antiquities have small costs to generate income, the major ones being transportation infrastructure, accommodation, and for some countries provision of adequate and accustomed food and drink. Some of these result in significant 'leakage' of foreign exchange earnings.

Another aspect of the socio-economic downside is that tourism may be an 'enclave' activity with foreign ownership and management, limited transfer of skills and employment of locals only in relatively unskilled and menial positions. Tourism's environmental impact is also questioned: hotels may discharge sewage onto adjoining beaches (for example, at Pattaya), or they may cause serious traffic congestion and pollution (as at Kuta). On the other hand, tourism may provide the financial support for national parks, for the protection and preservation of antiquities (for instance Angkor, and Borobudur), as well as the continuance of traditional ways of life. The dance and *gamelan* troupes of Bali could scarcely survive without tourist demand. However, benefits like these are place-specific. Someone on another island benefits not at all—the situation existing until recent developments on Lombok, Bali's neighbour. Even on Bali, villages accessible only by motorcycle are partly cut off from access to the tourist honeypot, sometimes by choice.

One way of assessing the economic importance of tourism in each country is to compare the receipts from inbound tourists with commodity exports or total income from services (Table 8.11). This shows that tourism is a major earner only in Cambodia, Indonesia, Laos, the Philippines and Thailand. In all the others receipts are less than one-tenth of the amounts earned from exporting goods. Amongst these Singapore has a fairly high level, presumably as a result of its role as a major transportation hub while returning Filipinos, *balikbayan*, contribute significantly in the Philippines.

Though comprehensive data are lacking, the wealthier countries generate considerable out-bound tourism. Thus Malaysia's income from tourists coming in is only about 20 per cent more than its own out-bound tourists spend elsewhere, while Singaporean tourists spend abroad the equivalent of nearly half of the tourist income the city-state earns. By contrast poorer countries and those which limit foreign travel by their nationals, such as Myanmar, spend little on out-bound tourism. Out-bound Filipinos spend only a twentieth of what is gained from inbound travellers, while in Myanmar the corresponding fraction is one-eighth.

On the whole the industry is a nice little earner, but very much affected by changing consumer preferences. Between 1996 and 1997, for example, regional tourist receipts dropped by 23 per cent, led by Indonesia and Singapore. Since the latter is a hub for regional tourism rather than a

Table 8.11 Tourism receipts (US$ million) and ratio (%) of tourism receipts to income from commodity exports and from total services, 1997

Country	Tourism receipts	Per cent of total receipts	Exports ratio	Services
Brunei	39	0.2	1.8	n.a.
Cambodia	143	0.6	19.4	89.4
Indonesia	5 437	21.5	9.7	78.3
Laos	73	0.3	23.0	68.9
Malaysia	2 703	10.7	3.5	18.0
Myanmar	34	0.1	3.5	6.5
Philippines	2 831	11.2	11.2	18.7
Singapore	6 843	27.1	5.4	22.4
Thailand	7 048	27.9	12.4	44.7
Viet Nam (1996)	88	0.3	1.2	n.a.
Total	25 239	99.9	Av. 9.2	n.c.

Note: n.a. = not available; n.c. = not calculated.
Sources: *Yearbook of Tourism Statistics, 1999; Balance of Payments Yearbooks, 1998, 1999*

destination in its own right, it suffered especially from the large drop in Indonesia. To some degree their losses have been compensated by solid rises in income accruing to Laos and Cambodia, with 66 and 21 per cent rises over one year, albeit from very small bases.

Tourism makes a modest contribution to the total income from the provision of services in Singapore and Malaysia, reflecting their already well-developed service sectors. At the other extreme are Cambodia, Indonesia, Laos, and to a lesser degree Thailand, whose service sector is weakly developed so that tourism makes a major contribution to total income from it. It is not clear why tourism plays such a minor role in Myanmar's service sector, nor indeed why its income from services is considerable, for this comprises a third of the country's income from both exports and services.

Transportation

In the region generally there is little doubt that the circulation of goods and people has increased substantially in the last several decades, though finding data to prove this is difficult. Carriage by pack animals (horses and cattle) still survives in the mountainous borderlands of Myanmar, Thailand, Laos and Viet Nam, often with tortuous links with southwestern

China. The ubiquitous motorcycle and pickup truck now penetrate once-isolated villages. On the rivers rafts and canoes still move goods and people, the latter now propelled by outboard motors. At sea sailing vessels survive in Indonesian waters, trading to Jakarta's old port, to Ujung Pandang (Sulawesi), up the rivers of Borneo and Sumatera, across the beaches of southern Java and the Eastern Archipelago, but now diesel engines supplement sail. Twin-outrigger *banka*s still ply the waters of the Sulu Sea, now propelled by multiple outboard motors, and sometimes crewed by hard-eyed men carrying revolvers and automatic rifles, because smuggling and piracy continue.

Shipping

Most bulky commodities travel by sea within and beyond the region. Only high-value goods such as electronic components and computers go by air, though the relative costs of sea and air are converging steadily, especially for small consignments. The region as a whole is not particularly well supplied with natural harbours, especially those accessible to modern bulk carriers and container vessels. A number of established ports have become less important as vessels on major international routes have become larger. Yangon (Rangoon), up the Irrawaddy, Bangkok up the Chao Phrya, Phnom Penh up the Mekong, can handle vessels up to around 8000 tonnes, Yangon a little more.

The overall pattern is of a hierarchy of hubs from which routes radiate to small ports or even across-the-beach loading points, the latter even serving international log-carriers bound for Japan, Hong Kong and Korea. Singapore's six ports, all operated by the Port of Singapore Authority, comprise far and away the single dominant hub, though Hong Kong is also a hub for secondary ports in the northern waters of the South China Sea. Singapore handles about three-fifths of the region's total container traffic, including four-fifths of Indonesia's containers and a fifth of Malaysia's. Jakarta's port, Tanjung Priok, and Kuala Lumpur's Port Kelang do handle some cargo traffic direct to ports outside the region but most of the secondary ports operate only feeder container services. Thereby they can offer transit times only a couple of days longer than from a major hub. A further, lower level of ports—most possessing very limited facilities for container cargoes—feeds these secondary hubs. Examples would include river ports such as Palembang in southern Sumatera, Kuching in Sarawak or Bandar Seri Begawan in Brunei, though most dry cargoes to Brunei go via the container port at Muara.

Specialist cargoes may have specialist ports or none at all. Indonesia's Dumai (northeastern Sumatera), for instance, handles a large proportion of the country's total cargo. Singapore's many refineries are directly served

Table 8.12 Merchant fleets, 1998: number and displacement (million tonnes)

Country	Number	Weight
Cambodia	195	0.62
Indonesia	2 359	3.25
Laos	1	*
Malaysia	828	5.21
Myanmar	124	0.49
Philippines	1 726	8.51
Singapore	1 677	20.37
Thailand	552	2.00
Viet Nam	629	0.78
Total	8 091	41.23

Note: * less than 0.01 mill. t.
Sources: *Europa World Yearbook, 2000*

by dedicated wharves or mooring points. Miri in Sarawak, Lumut in Brunei and Batangas in Luzon are other examples of petroleum ports.

The degree to which Southeast Asian countries use their own vessels to carry their own goods is hard to establish due to lack of data, though having to use ships owned by others is a fruitful source of 'leakage' of payments for services. The region as whole owns only about 4 per cent of the world's registered ships over 1000 tonnes deadweight, so that a significant proportion of its trade is carried by ships flying foreign flags.

The region's leading countries of ownership decided to sponsor their own national lines in the 1960s, Indonesia having nationalised its previously Dutch-owned fleet following independence. These national lines have survived in a highly competitive business. Singapore leads with about 49 per cent of the region's shipping (Table 8.12). Its fleet, like that of Malaysia, is truly deep-sea in scale with the size of their vessels averaging around the 20 000-tonne mark. The Filipino fleet is mixed deep-sea and coastal, as might be expected in an archipelagic nation. The same is even more true for Indonesia. Both fleets include significant numbers of passenger vessels. By contrast, the Vietnamese fleet is almost entirely coastal, its vessels averaging only 1300 tonnes.

Air transport

Air transportation networks share two major features with shipping networks. They focus mainly upon a number of hubs, from which services radiate like spokes on a wheel, and there is also a hierarchy of hubs. A few airports have many services. Most airports have few services each

Table 8.13 Outward direct air flights (per week): selected cities, late 1998

City	International	Domestic
Bangkok	1 142	516
Singapore	1 370	–
Manila	323	529
Jakarta	206	589
Kuala Lumpur	533	648
Den Pasar	167	221
Kota Kinabalu	51	268
Miri	–	286
Surabaya	24	251
Penang	54	133
Bandar Seri Begawan	161	–
Cebu	21	129

Source: *ABC Airways Guide*

day. (Flight frequency is not a very good measure of capacity for, like ships, aeroplanes vary widely in size, though not so much as ships. However, it is the only readily available measure.) The busiest hubs, in terms of scheduled aircraft movements, are, expectedly, capital cities in relatively wealthy countries: Bangkok, Singapore, Manila, Jakarta, Kuala Lumpur. These all have 50 or more direct connections with each other or with other centres. Globally they rank highly in terms of passengers carried: the Kuala Lumpur–Singapore link is the world's fourth busiest air route, while seven of the world's 20 busiest international links are located in the region, five of them from Singapore. By contrast, the capitals of the poorer countries have limited linkages even within their own territory. Cities with 150–400 direct outward flights weekly are all important secondary cities in insular Southeast Asia, some with international traffic (see Table 8.13).

The hierarchical nature of airline nodality is very clear from Table 8.13, although the measure is again a direct flight, not passengers and freight carried. At the top are the five major centres just mentioned, while at the bottom is a host of small aerodromes with limited services, usually with grass strips and limited navigational aids, served by small aircraft. In between are intermediate centres, some with international services. Examples include Kuching, with services to Bandar Seri Begawan, Singapore, Pontianak, Manila, even Perth, and the capitals of poorer mainland countries. Yangon has 50 direct services a week to other centres in the region outside Myanmar—and none outside Asia. Much the same is true of the other capitals.

Networks are highly centralised upon the hubs, reflecting in part the

Table 8.14 Air service nodality direct connections, late 1998

Connections	No. of Nodes
1–2	72
3–9	46
10–19	10
20–49	5
50+	5
	Total airports 138

Note: Cities with more than one airport, e.g. Jakarta, totals aggregated.
'Connections' are direct and outward only.
Source: Compiled from *ABC Airways Guide*

fact that the airline business in the region is highly nationalistic and fragmented. Each country has its own major airline, most partly or entirely owned by government. Several compete favourably on the international market, in part because labour costs are substantially lower than amongst major European, North American and Australasian carriers such as British Airways, Lufthansa, United, Qantas and Air New Zealand. All these make the 'Top 30' global airlines in terms of passengers carried as do Singapore, Thai and Malaysian.

The region's carriers are centred operationally upon the national capital. Thus in Thailand the network is centred on Bangkok's Don Muang airport. Myanmar has a secondary network centred upon Mandalay, the Philippines upon Cebu (Mactan) and Indonesia has minor networks centred on Den Pasar, Balikpapan and Ujung Pandang. Given high levels of centrality it is not surprising that circular routings are extremely limited. One linking the 'Big Five' airports is possible, but little else is, with very limited links across the northern part of the South China Sea, except via Hong Kong. International links amongst minor airports are expanding, however, especially across the Straits of Melaka. (The town of Melaka itself is possibly unique in having a service to Pekan Baru, Sumatera, but not one domestically.) Gaps remain, especially from the southern Philippines, while services east and south from points east of Den Pasar (Bali) are extremely limited. Indirect international routings via the smaller centres are not encouraged by the lack of inter-line cooperation in setting through-fares. 'Change airlines and pay through the nose' seems to be a global motto.

The use of smaller airports has, however, been encouraged by the development of international tourism. Thus Phuket has direct services to Hong Kong, Kuala Lumpur, Penang, Singapore and Taipei while Siem Riep (for Angkor) has same-aircraft services to Saigon and Bangkok. Singapore has direct services to the Malaysian tourist islands of Langkawi and Tioman. Many such services are operated by firms other than national carriers. Bangkok Air is an example. One particular new development is of services to southern Chinese airports other than Hong Kong. Chengdu, Macau, Kunming, Xiamen and Shenzhen have direct though limited services, reflecting China's new entrepreneurial spirit. At the same time, long-distance links with Eastern European destinations have also expanded with services to Warsaw, Vienna, Sofia and Budapest. However, direct one-aircraft links to Central and South America do not exist and some services to main North American entry-points require a change.

Railways

Like ships and larger aircraft, railways carry freight but almost universally in the region this function has been losing ground relative to road transport, in part because of the costs of transhipping goods from one transport mode to another (e.g. lorry to railway freight car). This cost is reduced, relatively, as the length of journey and size of consignment increase or as containers are used. But most railway systems are fragmented and short and are not necessarily set up to handle containers. Java has the densest network also largely used by passengers. Thailand and Peninsular Malaysia are well linked and are gearing up to improve container handling. An as yet unrestored link also exists southeast from Bangkok to Phnom Penh via Arunyaprathet and Poipet but then there is a further gap, never filled, to Saigon. The rail then extends to the China border at Lao Kai on the Hanoi–Kunming route and near Lang Son on the Hanoi–Nanning route. On both there is a change of gauge necessitating transhipment and it is doubtful that much cargo moves on through bills of lading.

As with most airlines, the railways are government owned and operated. All are in need, in whole or in part, of upgrading in terms of track-bed, signalling and rolling stock. Most are receiving some funding for this but all are limited in capacity by being, mostly, metre-gauge, needing larger tunnels and rolling stock to take containers, and better organisation all round.

With the rapid expansion of cities has come the realisation that the railway is also a highly efficient, non-polluting means of moving large numbers of people. However, urban systems are extremely expensive to construct and to avoid creating traffic congestion require the removal of level crossings where rights-of-way exist, or going into the air or underground where they do not. Singapore can readily afford its MRT system, though its routing is less than optimal, as is the spacing of its stations. (The university is not directly served and nor are its international airport and railway station.) Bangkok, Manila and Kuala Lumpur are all beginning to turn to urban rail services to solve pressing problems of long transit times, congestion and pollution, as is the Jakarta region as part of planning for the huge 'Jabotabek' conurbation, expected to hold 30 million people within 10 years.

One other area for railway development that is worth mentioning is tourism by rail. Some of the region's lines traverse landscapes of stunning beauty and interest, for example, Jakarta to Surabaya, Hanoi to Saigon, Mandalay to Lashio. Yet existing services are uncomfortable and usually impossible to book from abroad. The better services may operate at night, as on the Bangkok–Chiang Mai route, while it may be difficult to interrupt journeys to visit places of interest en route. Only the Orient Express, expensive but luxurious, has thus far tapped into this market on the Bangkok–Singapore route.

Roads and inland waterways

Road was not the usual way for goods to be moved in early times. True there were well-worn paths along which people and pack animals—horses, cattle, elephants—moved high-value, low-bulk goods. Salt, cloth, tea, medicaments, opium and ceramics were carried on routes such as those east from Bhamo to 'Yunnan-fu', now Kunming, or between Moulmein and Chiang Mai, a route also used to drove cattle, like many of the routes across the Malay Peninsula. One of the few major cart routes ran northeast across the Korat Plateau to Vientiane and that, like the others, for the most part was a dry-weather traverse. As mentioned earlier, the railways, built by colonial governments, formed quite limited networks and while some administrations—notably the British in Malaya (Peninsular Malaysia) and the Dutch in Java—pushed the construction of cart-roads, many areas remained unserved until the last half-century. Many parts of upland Myanmar, Laos, Viet Nam, interior Sumatera, Borneo and West Irian still remain essentially unroaded, being served by river and path just as they were centuries ago—except that outboard and diesel engines have revolutionised travel times by water.

Inland waterways are still of some significance in continental Southeast Asia and on the larger islands where the sheer size of the landmasses has permitted the development of rivers long and deep enough to carry traffic. On the Irrawaddy system, for example, state-owned vessels carried nearly 25 million passengers and 3 million tonnes of cargo in the mid-1990s. The lower Chao Phrya, linked with an extensive system of canals, many cut in the nineteenth century to carry rice to Bangkok for export, still carry barges laden with rice, sand and other bulk freight. Parts of the Mekong also move goods and people. Ocean-going vessels are able to reach Phnom Penh, though few now do because its port cannot handle containers. Also, as Milton Osborne so eloquently describes, the river has never become a major artery because its hinterland produces too little to justify what would be the enormous cost of engineering works to overcome such natural barriers to its flow as the Khône Falls. On the island of Borneo the Kapuas, the Kahayan and the Barito give access to the interior but like all the region's rivers flow is seasonably variable so that towards the upper reaches settlements may be reached by a particular size of vessel during the wet season but not in the dry. The essence of good transportation is dependability and, despite difficulties of terrain and costs of overcoming them, here is where the road scores, despite its higher costs, tonne for tonne, than waterways.

Road networks are quite unlike those of other forms of transport which are usually very simple, often a single hub with a few routes radiating from it. Road networks in the lowland areas tend to be quite circular, linking many nodal points, permitting indirect journeys. Thus in the Malay Peninsula the traveller by road up the east coast from Johor Baru can head west across the peninsula by many routes before heading south again to close the circuit whereas by rail only one circular route exists, the only one in the continental part of the region—Johor Baru – Gemas – Tumpat – Haadyai – Perai – Johor Baru—and that would involve several changes of train. The result is a generally high degree of connectivity by road though segments of road unconnected to others still exist, especially where rivers are still a major means of transportation, because crossing major rivers is expensive. For example, the Lao road system has only recently been connected, by the largely Australian-funded Friendship Bridge, to the Thai system. The Myanmar system has very limited connections to Thailand. External road links are also very limited and though in principle it might be possible to drive from Singapore to Beijing or to New Delhi, bureaucratic obstacles make this impossible. Even where direct cross-border roads exist these obstacles generally require goods and people to transfer, though a few hardy motorists succeed in making long-distance journeys.

With just under 1 million kilometres of road of any description it cannot be said that the region as a whole is well roaded though there is fifty times more road than railway. (Table 8.15 gives details.) Accessibility by road is indicated by the length of road available, on average, to serve each square kilometre of land. On this basis, urban Singapore, expectedly, comes out well, as do Peninsular Malaysia and the Philippines. In fact most developed lowland areas have fair to good networks though undeveloped swamplands notably lack roads, which are difficult and expensive to construct in this terrain, common on the eastern coast of Sumatera, the coastlands of Borneo and West Irian.

Most upland areas are quite another matter, except in Peninsular Malaysia where the terrain is generally not too severe and, since much is planted to economic crops, the land produces enough to support a good system. Indeed, the many thousands of kilometres of laterite-surfaced private roads, not counted in official statistics, are crucial to the very

Table 8.15 Length of road, average length of road per square kilometre of land and proportion sealed, mid-1990s

	Length (000 km)	Length per km² (m)	Proportion sealed (%)
Brunei	2.7	467	62
Cambodia	35.7	198	8
Indonesia	378.0	198	45
Laos	18.1	100	14
Malaysia	106.8	–	–
Peninsular	93.0	707	75
Sabah	9.8	133	26
Sarawak	4.0	32	n.a.
Myanmar	27.6	41	12
Philippines	204.2	681	22
Singapore	3.0	4 630	97
Thailand	62.0	121	97
Viet Nam	106.0	320	26
	944.1	Av. 211	

Sources: Europa World Yearbook, 2000; World Road Statistics, 1997

existence of such crops. In most upland areas roads are few and of generally poor quality, construction and maintenance hindered by steep slopes, unstable, deep-weathered rock, lack of adequate design, even sheer peculation. One illustration of the last is the mountain highway northeast from Baguio to Bontoc and Banaue. True, engineers have to cope with landslides, sometimes triggered by earthquakes, heavy rain and other environmental problems but it is significant that those sections built by Japanese contractors are in better shape than others. The motto seems to be: 'Why build a really good road when a poor one will require periodical rebuilding and, being essential, will forever be a "cash cow"?'

Quality of roads is a key issue and in many parts of the region the proportion of dry-weather roads is high. In Laos, for example, 57 per cent of the roads are classed as 'dirt track'; in Myanmar 62 per cent do not have all-weather surfaces. Laterite is widespread outside alluvial lowlands and volcanic areas and is an admirable material for cheap roads carrying light traffic, though it cuts up under heavy vehicles in the wet. Malaysia and Thailand use both laterite and gravel effectively to build all-weather roads. Others are obsessed with expensive 'black-top' or concrete highways, which, where they deteriorate through lack of maintenance—a common occurrence—provide a surface inferior to that of well-maintained laterite or gravel. The clear key to rural betterment is access to markets and a dry-weather road is of limited utility because the dry season is exactly when farmers have little produce to sell.

Table 8.16 Mass and private communications (no. of persons per receiver), mid-1990s

Country	Radio	Television	Telephone (mainlines)
Brunei	1	1	4
Cambodia	8	109	1 968
Indonesia	7	14	47
Laos	7	98	244
Malaysia	2	6	5
Myanmar	11	179	260
Philippines	6	19	50
Singapore	9	4	2
Thailand	4	14	14
Viet Nam	9	21	23
Average	6	12	29

Source: *Europa World Yearbook, 2000* (figures rounded)

Communications

No modern economy can function adequately without adequate communications but within the region there are very large differences in the levels of provision. In Singapore a personal computer linked to cyberspace is a commonplace. Every child at school uses one. Laos has very few and then only in the hands of government and the wealthiest, linked tenuously to the rest of the world. Large areas have very limited telephone access. Indeed, in remoter areas those who can afford it need to employ global satellite systems. Ironically, in most countries access to the radio is better than to the telephone, not least because it is cheap and literally wire-less. As Table 8.16 shows, most people have access to a radio even in the poorest countries, while only in Cambodia, Laos and Myanmar are people to be numbered in the hundreds per television set. In these countries, and in Viet Nam, a set is a community rather than a personal good. The same is true for most rural parts of the Philippines and Indonesia where the village headman, the police and the shopkeeper are customarily telephone subscribers. Curiously, Singapore has more registered televisions than radios.

In most countries radio, television and the telephone systems are government-owned, though private radio and television exist in Thailand, Indonesia and the Philippines. The latter's telephones are also privately owned, though not notably efficient. What is broadcast is thus completely or partly controlled. But, whatever the level of control, it is very clear that the mass media—including newspapers, which are mostly privately owned—have powerful social and economic consequences, though the extent to which this is so must be to some degree a matter of personal judgement.

The kind of images and concerns presented by the media are strongly urban and middle-class in character. Advertising is very much consumer-oriented so that the place to be is seen to be in town where one may 'consume' everything from soya or fish sauce through flavoured toothpaste to durables such as fans, refrigerators and motorcycles. Towns are places, if not literally of milk and honey, then of an endless variety of consumer goodies, seemingly available to all. Towns are the locus of wealth, of political power, of education and upward social mobility.

NINE
'THE CITIES ARE WHERE IT'S AT'

In a sense cities have been 'where it's at' since cities have been cities. Traditionally they were the heart of the state—home of the ruler, focus of powers spiritual and temporal, the mystic epitome of Khmer, Thai, Burman, Vietnamese and Malay cultures. To a degree they remain so today. Both the Thai and Cambodian royal courts house 'Brahmin priests', responsible, with the King, for the spiritual health of the nation and for the ceremonies designed to maintain it. The city, especially the capital, was thus and remains an icon, not merely a nodal point for the interchange of goods and services but the place to be for anyone who is anyone or who wants to be someone.

The iconic function carries across into the structure of cities, even the smaller ones, focusing upon palaces, temples, mosques, government buildings more or less imposing as the circumstances of their building allows. Some are genuinely old, like Hanoi's 'scholars' temple'. Most arenot, like the royal enclosure at Phnom Penh, Bangkok's royal palaces and temples, Hué's early nineteenth-century reproduction of Beijing's Forbidden City. Some are colonial—Hanoi's opera house, Singapore's government complex partly surrounding the *padang* (a green open space modelled on the colonial Indian *maidan*), replicated on a smaller scale, partly with pseudo-Arab architecture, in Kuala Lumpur. Some are post-colonial—Sukarno's grandiose National Mosque and Merdeka Square, Ho Chi Minh's mausoleum and the grand boulevard before it so clearly modelled on Lenin's tomb and Red Square. (Ho's house, simple and refined, is also preserved, a much more appropriate memorial.) Of the capitals, only Manila does not have a real iconic core unless it is the cathedral and the archbishop's palace, because the Spanish capital, Intramuros, was devastated during the Pacific War and remains a partly restored historic relic.

Retrospect

Capitals were and are 'pivots of the four quarters' to use Paul Wheatley's happy phrase, though nowadays they preside over more or less well defined territorial states rather than congeries of peoples. The capitals are prime seats of power, power that also resides in part with the common people who claim, at least in part, the right to make and unmake governments. But political and spiritual power are only part of the story for the capitals are literally the capitals of capital. Here is centred the financial apparatus of the nations, its banks and financial houses, its borrowers and lenders, as well as the recent major outgrowth of capital—manufacturing industry.

Trading cities had long existed, of course: Melaka and Palembang, now-insignificant Hoi An or Bantey Mas, the latter once a city-state founded on the site of modern Ha Tien by a Cantonese adventurer surnamed Mak, elevated now to god-like status. (His figure is in a local temple.)

But trade did not necessarily imply a permanent settlement. 'Dumb barter', which eschews face-to-face contact, as between Malays and aborigines, survived well into the twentieth century and to this day periodical markets are held in rural areas of Borneo without a permanent settlement being established. Foreign trade was often a royal prerogative, as it is a government one in armaments in today's Singapore, or as the trade in salt was until fairly recently in parts of mainland Southeast Asia. To be sure, local potentates were supported by 'their people' on whom local taxes were levied but even then it is doubtful that many intermediate-sized cities existed, for as late as the nineteenth century—the state of Perak is an example—some rulers travelled from one place to another, the royal court consuming part of the agricultural surplus on the spot.

It seems likely that the dominance of a single large city within each polity is a phenomenon of long standing. Today's nation-states are not those of the past, of course, and where they incorporate former partly or wholly independent entities it is no coincidence that primate-city dominance was once less marked than it is today, even into the 1960s. This was certainly the case for Malaya, now Peninsular Malaysia, where Kuala Lumpur in the 1950s was little larger than Penang or Ipoh, though some would argue that Kuala Lumpur was just one second-rank city in an urban system dominated by Singapore. But consider Indonesia. Until quite recently Jakarta was not very much larger than other large centres such as Surabaya and Yogyakarta. To generalise very broadly, it seems that most pre-colonial polities were dominated by a single, usually royal city amongst whose functions trade plus the manufacture of arms and luxury goods were part.

The colonial period saw the spatial aggregation of polities into the much larger units which mostly continue until today. Many once-royal capitals survived, indeed flourished, such as Yogyakarta, Aceh, Ujung Pandang (Makassar) in Indonesia. Others have faded away, like Oudong in Cambodia, Amarapura and Ava in Myanmar, and Sri Menanti in Peninsular Malaysia. To the survivors were added hosts of colonial-period settlements both large and small, many swelling from earlier village settlements as district administrations were set up, each in turn attracting local trade. Third-ranking towns of Peninsular Malaysia—second after state capitals—are very much of this nature as are the *hyun* 'capitals' of Viet Nam, ranking below the provinces.

To these may be added brand new colonial ports and mining centres on 'green-field' sites: Penang established by Francis Light who went on to found Adelaide, South Australia, is an example. Singapore, not quite 'green-field' because Malay *kampung* were well established, is said by Singaporeans officially to have been founded by a British adventurer, Thomas Stamford Raffles. Kuala Lumpur was established at the muddy junction of the Kelang and Gombak rivers by a Hakka Chinese tin-miner, one Yap Ah Loy. A considerable number of smaller urban centres in the 'Tin Belt' of western Peninsular Malaysia also began as Chinese mining towns, most surviving as rural service centres after the tin-mining industry declined and was replaced by perennial tree-crops as the economic base.

Two other colonial-era developments impinged upon the urban structure. Colonialists found the tropical heat enervating and sought cooler, highland sites for sanitoria for relief from it, beyond the reach of malarial mosquitoes. Examples include Maymyo in Myanmar, Da Lat and Tam Dao in Viet Nam, Maxwell's Hill and the Cameron Highlands in Peninsular Malaysia, Bogor and Puncak near Jakarta. Baguio was founded as a 'summer capital' to which most of the apparatus of colonial government once migrated in much the same way as the Government of India moved up to Simla from New Delhi. These 'hill stations' have generally flourished, adding the growing of temperate vegetables in their vicinities to their initial restorative functions.

The other development affecting the emerging urban structure came late in the piece as a result of Communist 'insurgency'. In Peninsular Malaysia the creation, during the 'Emergency', of more than 500 'New Villages' occupied by a million people added a large number of small units to the urban hierarchy as they quickly added urban functions. Attempts to copy this strategy in southern Viet Nam failed and had little lasting impact on the hierarchy. However, during the Viet Nam War, large numbers of refugees sought security in the towns and cities of the South. Although many moved back to villages following reunification in 1976 some did not, thereby contributing to rapid urban growth characteristic of every country in the region since the Pacific War.

Recent urbanisation

When looking at matters urban it is as well to be reminded that the notion of 'urban' is very much a matter of who is making definitions and for what purpose. Certainly there is no exact consensus from country to country, even within each country. For some 'urban' is a functional concept. An urban area is one in which people involved in secondary and tertiary economic activities predominate. That is not wholly satisfactory, for people may move from one economic sector to another in the space of a few months—even days. For others it is a matter of population density—many people in an area equals 'urban'. But that overlooks the fact that in some places—on some of the best volcanic soils of Java, for example—purely agricultural densities may be as high or higher than in the garden suburbs of cities, Petaling Jaya in suburban Kuala Lumpur to give just one example.

Or one can deny the utility of 'urban' and 'rural' altogether and simply see them as ends of a continuum with the distinction being quite arbitrary but somewhere towards the middle. In practice this is what really happens. Administrators decide that the urban boundary—usually an administrative one—is to be pushed out. The effects of this on the figures can be quite dramatic. For example, it has been suggested that in Peninsular Malaysia roughly a third of urban population growth arises from natural increase—a third from rural–urban migration and another third from boundary redefinition. The matter is not helped by the fact that several countries—such as Thailand, Indonesia and the Philippines—take *de jure* censuses, not *de facto*. This means that people are enumerated as where they should be—in their home village, for example—rather than where they actually are at census time. Enumerations of this kind tend to underestimate urban populations just as countries in which officials are slow to expand city boundaries do. To add to these shortcomings are real problems with data. Many relate to the last round of censuses in 1991 and much has happened in a decade.

Half a century ago, Southeast Asia, notwithstanding its long urban tradition, was not much urbanised. Only Africa south of the Sahara and South Asia had a lower proportion of people living in towns. Even in 1960 barely a tenth of our region's people was urban, compared with over half in North America, northern Europe, Australia and New Zealand—and these figures are only for people in towns of over 100 000 people. But, as Table 9.1 shows, by 1997 most countries—using their own definition of 'urban'—had at least a fifth of their population in towns. (Singapore has considered all its people to be urban for the last half century, though in fact there are still a few thousand engaged in rural pursuits.)

Debate still continues as to whether Southeast Asian urbanisation is like the urbanisation that accompanied the Industrial Revolution. Thirty

Figure 9.1 Major urban centres classified by size

years ago some scholars spoke of 'pseudo-urbanisation', partly on the ground that its initial phases were not accompanied by rapid industrialisation. The city was a magnet for its own sake. In it anyone could make a living of some kind even if it were as a member of an underclass living rough in the interstices of the urban fabric. This fact continues to attract migrants. Industrialisation quickly followed, though of a kind unlike that of the Industrial Revolution in that much was and is based upon multinational corporations and foreign capital, as well as being technically quite different.

What is indisputable is the extraordinary rapidity of urbanisation and its recency, as Table 9.1 shows. But patterns within the region are quite contrasting. In Singapore probably 95 per cent of the population could properly have been described as 'urban' by 1950, the city's statisticians

Table 9.1 Urban population, 1960, 1980, 1997–98, number (million) and proportion (%)

	1960		1980		Increase 1960–1980	1997		Increase 1980 to 1997–98
Country	No.	%	No.	%	(% p.a.)	No.	%	(% p.a.)
Brunei	–	43	–	50	12.9	–	67	3.2
Cambodia	0.5	10	1.0	14	5.0	1.8	16	4.4
Indonesia	14.0	15	32.9	22	6.8	74.8	37	7.5
Laos	0.2	9	0.4	13	5.0	1.1	22	6.5
Malaysia	3.0	37	5.8	42	4.7	11.9	55	6.2
Myanmar	3.2	14	8.1	24	7.7	11.7	27	2.6
Philippines	5.9	21	18.1	37	10.4	41.1	56	7.5
Singapore	1.6	100	2.3	100	2.2	3.1	100	2.1
Thailand	3.0	11	7.9	17	8.2	12.5	21	3.4
Viet Nam	5.2	20	10.3	19	4.9	15.0	20	2.7
Total	36.6	Av. 17	86.8	Av. 23	Av. 6.9	173.0	Av. 34	Av. 5.8

Notes: 'Urban' as defined nationally. Brunei's urban population was, respectively 36, 129 and 200 thousand in 1960, 1980, 1997. Average rates of increase are simple, not compound.

Sources: *World Urbanization, 1950–1970; World Development Report, 1999–00; General Population Census of Cambodia, 1998*

notwithstanding, and certainly by 1960. Brunei's urban population, mainly in the capital now termed Bandar Seri Begawan—earlier simply Brunei Town—and in Seria the main oil-field centre, in fact probably comprised around half of the total as early as 1950, because boundaries did not keep pace with the realities of employment and residence. For the rest, most had urban populations comprising between 10 and 20 per cent of their national totals.

By the 1960s growth in manufacturing had begun in the socialist countries as the means of strengthening the national economic base. In the others this sector grew as political independence was increasingly worked out in economic independence, in policy terms expressed mainly as import substitution. But no great progress had been made though industrial estates such as Petaling Jaya, outside Kuala Lumpur, such as Jurong in Singapore and others on the outskirts of Manila, had begun.

Many rural–urban migrants entered the tertiary sector, especially personal services, hawking and other forms of petty trading or transportation, as it grew to meet the needs of spatially expanding cities. This was the era when most middle-class families kept a menage—people to guard the gate, to drive the car, to wash clothes, to clean the house and to cook. A dozen or twenty servants and their dependants living in a separate quarter was not unusual. Government bureaucracies also tended to expand though this usually took up people who were already urban, except for men entering the armed forces. Underemployment and unemployment were substantial though commonly underestimated in statistics. Manila's pattern of 14 per cent unemployed in the mid-1950s was not unusual.

In what were or became socialist cities things were quite otherwise. Rural–urban migration was controlled. In northern Viet Nam as the war developed, strategic considerations led to the spatial dispersal of manufacturing, much of it directed towards armaments, and with it people.

In the south the opposite happened as refugees flooded the towns, some moving spontaneously, some being herded into what were essentially concentration camps to create 'free-fire zones' for RVN and US troops. Between 1961 and 1969 it has been estimated that one-third of the south's population passed through government hands as refugees. Most ended up in urban areas. By the mid-1970s Da Nang—in part a major US military base—had grown from a modest town of 25 000 people to nearly 350 000. Saigon grew to over 2 million.

The spread of conflict to Cambodia also displaced large numbers and by 1975 nearly 1.5 million refugees were settled in and around Phnom Penh, most if not all, along with the established residents, being forced out by the Pol Pot regime in that year. Relatively large numbers also moved in Laos both as a means of depriving the Pathet Lao—the Communist alternative government—of support and to escape bombing. Perhaps 700 000 moved in the eight years from 1962, about half to provincial capitals where many remained. While many moved back to their original places of residence following the progressive establishment of peace from the mid-1970s, some did not.

At the same time it seems likely that in southern Viet Nam many who were 'decanted' into the countryside in the late 1970s—some genuine refugees, some supporters of the old puppet regime, some caught up willy-nilly—had drifted back to the cities. They have also been joined, especially in the north, by city-folk rusticated to ill-planned and badly supported land development schemes in various parts of the nation, notably the Central Highlands where the once-tiny administrative centre of Buon Me Thuot is now an agglomeration of more than 300 000 people.

Control of movement has been less stringent in Myanmar though again insecurity in parts of the countryside has contributed to urban growth to some degree. These events, coupled with slow growth of their economies—though not of population—have resulted in overall levels of urbanisation lower than elsewhere in the region. They are catching up. Ha Noi now has people living under plastic sheets on its streets just as Jakarta has.

By 1980 only Singapore, Malaysia and Brunei, already substantially urban, had not seen close to a doubling or more of their urban population since 1960. Just under a quarter of the region's population was urban by 1980 having increased from 17 per cent in 1960. This involved very substantial numbers and high rates of growth, mainly as a result of starting from a fairly low base. By 1997 a third of the population was urban, though in most countries the rates had fallen from their previously high levels. One major exception was Indonesia, with 43 per cent of the region's urban people, but the last two decades have also seen substantial growth in Malaysia and the Philippines which already were quite urbanised by 1980.

Whether the recent economic downturn has had any effect upon rates of urban growth is not known but in the face of the massive numbers involved it seems unlikely that there has been a significant impact. Indeed, the re-emergence of insecurity in small towns in Ambon and elsewhere may push people to larger, safer places. Certainly, the fact that life-support for refugees in Timor is most readily obtained in towns, even though the rural insurgency has ceased, may very well pull people there.

The Indonesian case

This leads to the question of where urban growth has taken place. Detailed data are not available for all major cities at the same time, so that comparisons are difficult. Indonesia had 30 towns with populations of 100 000 or more in the early 1980s and these held about 20 million people, some 12 per cent of the national population. By the mid-1990s, cities of this size totalled 49 and contained 33.5 million people, representing a little over 17 per cent of the whole population. Table 9.4 shows that much of the increase was actually in the smaller towns. Table 9.2 indicates that the proportion of urban people in the republic who lived in Jakarta, the primate city, fell between 1980 and 1995. Lest this be thought to be a statistical aberration, the same thing shows up in most other countries, except Myanmar, though unfortunately there are limited data for Brunei, Laos and Cambodia. For Cambodia, recent census data suggest that 32 per cent of the urban population is in Phnom Penh.

On the whole, rates of growth in the larger towns seem to have been slowing, especially in the primate city and despite outwards boundary changes in some cases. But patterns are probably quite uneven within countries. An analysis of the 30 Indonesian towns that had at least 100 000 people in 1980 is instructive (Table 9.3), though it should be recalled that where urban boundaries are not moved outwards to reflect population characteristics 'growth' is less than it otherwise would be.

Growth in the largest cities—those with half a million or more in 1980—was consistently by between one-third and two-thirds. Patterns were much less consistent in the smaller cities. Old Javanese cities like Surakarta and Yogyakarta grew very little; Madiun and Mangelang, also

Table 9.2 Proportion of total urban population in primate city (%), 1980 and 1995

	1980	1995
Indonesia (Jakarta)	18	13
Malaysia (Kuala Lumpur)	16	11
Myanmar (Yangon)	27	35
Philippines (Manila)	33	24
Singapore	100	100
Thailand (Bangkok)	59	55
Viet Nam (HCM City)	27	25

Source: World Development Report, 1999–2000

in Central Java, grew not at all. On the other hand the twin north coastal cities of the same region, Pekalongan and Tegal grew rapidly, as did Pekanbaru in Sumatera's Riau province. A further 15 towns had reached the 100 000 population threshold by 1995, most ending up in the 100 000–200 000 range. A few were larger, notably Tangerang, just west of Jakarta, with 1.2 million in an overspill settlement from the capital. Den Pasar, which has greatly benefited from the tourist industry on Bali, and Mataram the capital of the nearby island of Lombok, join the group with roughly 450 000 and 300 000 people respectively. But these—plus Ambon in the Moluccas—are exceptional. On most of the other islands urban centres are very small, reflecting the small, often impoverished character of their economic hinterlands. One significant exception is Batam, on the island of that name just south of Singapore, which has become part of a major growth triangle with Singapore and Johor.

Do similar patterns exist in other parts of the region? Without readily accessible data-bases it is difficult to be sure. What is sure is that rates of growth in the primate cities, like those of cities generally, are mostly falling though the numbers of people involved are still very large. The reasons for this are partly demographic. Rural people, having moved to the towns, quickly abandon high-fertility reproductive behaviours, often in less than a generation, though whether this applies with more strength in large towns than smaller ones is unclear. In part it seems likely that the diseconomies and discomforts of life in the largest cities may be having some effect. To continue the Indonesian example: in 1993 the average daily travel time to work in Jakarta was 82 minutes. In Bandung, Medan, Semarang and Surabaya—all 'million cities' offering virtually everything that Jakarta does—the average times ranged between 20 and 30 minutes.

So far as the reasons for fairly consistent rates of growth in large towns and very varying rates in the smaller ones are concerned, only specific detailed knowledge of each case could provide the answers. Larger towns have their own economic momentum. Smaller ones more rapidly

Table 9.3 Urban growth and structure in Indonesia, 1980 and 1995 (000s)

	Pop'n 1980	Pop'n 1995	Increase (%)
Jakarta	6 503	9 161	41
Surabaya	2 028	2 701	33
Bandung	1 463	2 368	62
Medan	1 379	1 910	39
Semarang	1 027	1 367	33
Palembang	786	1 352	72
Ujung Pandang	709	1 092	54
Malang	512	763	49
Padang	481	722	50
Surakarta	470	517	10
Yogyakarta	399	420	5
Banjarmasin	381	535	40
Pontianak	305	449	47
Tanjung Karang[1]	284	832	193
Balikpapan	280	416	48
Samarinda	265	536	103
Bogor	247	286	16
Jambi	230	410	78
Cirebon	224	262	17
Kediri	222	261	18
Manado	218	399	83
Ambon	209	313	50
Pekanbaru	186	558	200
Madiun	151	107	–29
Permatang Siantar	150	231	54
Pekalongan	133	341	158
Tegal	131	314	138
Mangelang	124	123	0
Sukabumi	110	125	14
Probolinggo	100	190	90
Total	19 707	28 229	Av. 43

Note: [1] The combined centres of Tanjung Karang and Teluk Betung were renamed Banda Lampung.

Source: *UN Demographic Yearbook, 1997.*

reflect changes locally and in their immediate hinterland. A couple of new factories in Jakarta make little difference. Two similar ones in, say, Probolinggo would make a lot. The opening of a mine may create a settlement where none existed. Tembagapura is an Indonesian example. The expansion of government bureaucracies in small towns and some degree of economic growth in their rural hinterlands have also played a part.

Equally, rural decline also exists, as in parts of northern and north-eastern Thailand or in parts of Peninsular Malaysia, where agricultural disintensification is occurring. This feeds through to affect the small rural service centres. These are also affected by improvements in transportation, which, coupled with larger incomes, in part derived from outside the farm sector, results in a lower relative cost of travel. Small centres offering a limited range of goods and services are thus bypassed in favour of the larger ones. A significant part of migration to the larger towns is from small towns and if not made good by rural migration must also result in decline of the smaller centres. Much of the detail of these processes and their effects yet remains to be filled in by field studies. It seems likely that improved mobility will have significant effects, especially upon the smaller centres.

Spatial growth and density

While growth in urban population has universally been accompanied by expansion of the built-up area, the degree to which this is so has never been comprehensively studied, though the means to do it—in the form of remote-sensed imagery—has long existed. A number of processes, some contradictory, are at work and these have led to rather varying patterns of urban and suburban transformation.

All the towns and cities of the region have seen substantial peripheral growth. This is of two basic kinds, contiguous, and non-contiguous, the latter resulting in the growth of largely-dormitory suburbs, usually around a pre-existing node each linked to the city centre by one or more highways, sometimes a railway, with intervening agricultural areas. There are hundreds of examples: Bogor, Tanggerang and Bekasi in Greater Jakarta or 'Jabotabek' as it is increasingly known. Southeast of Kuala Lumpur, Kajang, once a rural service centre renowned for its *satay*, Seremban, and even Melaka Town have become functionally part of Kuala Lumpur, as Rangsit has for Bangkok. Smaller towns such as Kota Kinabalu have expanded in the same way, that centre now incorporating a string of small once-rural service centres along the main road to Tuaran, some 30 kilometres away. Contiguous growth has been fostered by the development of planned industrial areas complete with their own housing though these have not necessarily been successful in reducing commuting, one of the planners' stated aims. In some cases—Singapore's Jurong is one—what now appears as continuous built-up area began as non-contiguous growth with subsequent 'back-filling' towards the city centre.

Most of the region's cities may also have experienced internal growth in the form of rising population densities, seen most obviously in high-rise residential construction as in Singapore's many public housing estates. Appearances can be deceptive, though. Areas of low-rise informal housing that once characterised the rapid-growth phase of primate cities—Singapore's Henderson Road and Kuala Lumpur's Kampung Baru are examples—were so crowded that they held more or less the same number of people as the high-rise housing which replaced them. The same is probably true today. Much of the rise in city population densities comes about simply by more people occupying the same space, whether it be people living under bridges, in canal-side shacks or in the crowded servants' quarters, as in the middle-class suburb of Menteng, Jakarta.

In western cities there continues to be a long-established 'flight to the suburbs', for as wealth increases so does the ability to purchase larger personal living space. Eventually this leads to the well-known 'doughnut phenomenon'—very few people in the centre of the city. To what degree a similar process exists in Southeast Asian cities is not clear. Certainly middle-class people are well able to afford the enhanced costs of transportation a move to the suburbs brings. The morning and evening peaks of congestion on major roads would seem to suggest that their numbers are substantial. This in turn suggests that while densities may have risen in some cities and in parts of cities, in others they have fallen as spread has continued at the periphery. Declining urban densities seem to have begun long ago, in Rangoon (now Yangon) falling from 770 people per hectare in 1931 to 460, 20 years later.

So far as the region's urban population densities are concerned data are fragmentary. On the whole densities are not particularly high. In 1994, for example, the 8.6 million people of Manila's urban agglomeration occupied most of an area of 614 km^2 to give an average of 140 people per hectare, much less than the average density of Hong Kong's built-up area, which is around 650 people per ha and far below Paris's peak density of 1850 people per ha in 1931. In the Greater Manila of 1994, densities in its major components ranged from only 101 (Quezon City) to 277 people per hectare (Pasay). Bangkok has an even lower average density. The *UN Demographic Yearbook* in 1990 recorded some 5.8 million people in an area of 1565 km^2 to give an average density of only 38 persons per ha, not much above the figure for all Thai cities with more than 100 000 population—34 per ha. In fact many Filippino cities appear to have average densities below that of some of the more densely populated rural areas of Java—8 to 10 per ha—but that may merely reflect cases of 'over-bounding', meaning that administrative, thus enumerative, boundaries extend into the surrounding countryside. Such low average densities compare with many suburban areas in Australia. (An average of three persons on a tenth-acre plot gives a density of 75 per ha.)

Little is known of the spatial pattern of urban densities except that they are highly variable within cities, reflecting their land-use zonation. Thus the royal or presidential precincts, government and western-style business zones have low to very low densities while areas of informal housing (squatter areas in many cases) may have rather high densities. More generally there seems to be a fairly regular decrease in densities outwards from the inner city. Though very old, data for Greater Bangkok illustrate this. The five innermost districts averaged 263 people per ha, many of them incidentally of Chinese origin. The ring formed by the next five districts averaged 112 people per ha. These rings are both commercial and residential. A third largely residential ring had a density of only 27 people per ha while the outermost ring, a small portion residential, some agricultural, some being land held for speculative purposes, the average density was only 4 per ha.

These low densities also have important implications for the internal structure of Southeast Asian cities—in particular the survival of some forms of agriculture in them, and especially for the provision of services such as piped water, electricity, sewerage and transportation. Conceptually they have implications for the continued usefulness of notions of what is 'urban' and what is not.

Urban structure

This term is sometimes used to refer to the internal structure of cities but more correctly refers to numbers (or kinds) of cities in a defined territory. One universal characteristic is that urban centres form a hierarchy—many small ones, few big ones. Other things being equal—and they rarely are—big ones are further apart than small ones. In addition big ones provide a wider range of goods and services, since the demand for the more expensive kinds is less. (Brain surgery is available in Bangkok but not in Haadyai or Kalasin. Food is on sale everywhere even in small villages.) These principles are basic to Central Place Theory worked out long ago by the German economist Christaller on the basis of his study of part of Germany. Unfortunately they have not been systematically tested in Southeast Asia.

One requirement of Central Place Theory is that any particular 'defined territory' be reasonable large—and of course have urban centres in it, a requirement that rules out substantial areas of interior Borneo and West Irian for instance. This requirement also rules out Brunei and Singapore. The former has two major centres, Bandar Seri Begawan and Seria, as well as a number of smaller centres such as Limbang, Tutong and Kuala Belait, but the state is so small that most really form part of a single small but extended urban complex. This problem of definition arises again on a much larger scale when great urban complexes such as 'Jabotabek', centred upon Jakarta, or 'Greater Manila' are concerned. Singapore is clearly a 'central place' for much more than its own territory, a situation not considered by Christaller.

Primacy

Data do not permit the comparison of the urban structures of all the major territorial states in the region but they are sufficient to compare one upper-middle-income area—Peninsular Malaysia—one middle-income country—Thailand—a lower-middle-income country—Indonesia and poor Viet Nam, all at about the same time, in the early 1990s. (Data are as set out in the sources and are not wholly reliable.)

Dominance of a single large city in size and economy is a particular characteristic of small to medium size countries and of some large ones. In general though, other things being more or less equal, the gap in size between the largest city and the next to largest tends to be somewhat less than where a country is small. The costs of overcoming the friction of distance are significant so that a large country often supports a number of cities of more or less similar sizes. Australia is a case in point. The US is another. In Southeast Asia distances are not so great so the tendency is for there to be one large primate city holding economic power and, usually, political power. The exception is Ha Noi, capital but only second-ranked in Viet Nam. The shape of a country may possibly influence a country's urban structure too. Bangkok and other cities are fairly accessible from most directions. By contrast, most of Viet Nam's cities are accessible for any significant distance only from the north or from the south, except in the Mekong and Red River deltas, being hemmed in by mountains on the west and the sea on the east. Is this a reason why Viet Nam has so many more towns over 100 000 population than nearby Thailand?

Although the degree of primacy of the region's largest cities has been declining—at least as measured conventionally—the question of why primacy remains. At the national level—leaving aside Singapore and Brunei—Thailand shows the highest level of primacy though much depends upon which set of statistics is used. Bangkok may be around 20 times larger than Chiang Mai. According to the World Bank, the capital holds 55 per cent of the total urban population (Table 9.2). Myanmar also ranks high, with Yangon being the only primate city to increase its share of the total urban population since 1980. By contrast Malaysia's Kuala Lumpur is notably low in the dominance pecking order with Manila and Ho Chi Minh City, probably also Phnom Penh and Vientiane ranging somewhere in between. Jakarta's dominance is said to be on the low side but this may be doubted for it is only part of an extended metropolitan region extending at least to Tangerang on the west, a 'million city' on its own, to Bogor on the south and Bekasi to the east. In 1990 this region contained some 17 million people, 13 million of them urban, almost double the number given in United Nations statistics. For the moment discussion will continue to be based upon the latter data set.

The reasons for dominance by a single city—or single urban complex—are multifarious. Economically, a town grows if its hinterland also grows either spatially or in terms of production. (A hinterland of a town can grow spatially, for instance, by capturing part of another town's hinterland, by diverting rural production through the building of a new road or by providing services a competing town lacks.) Over the last several decades hinterlands have grown in absolute terms in most of the region though it is unquestionable that some areas have lost ground, for example rice-growing in Malaysia outside those areas—Kedah, Perlis and Kelantan—designated as such by the government. More recently hinterlands based upon tin, whose market has almost disappeared, and those growing rubber, whose market is depressed, have clearly suffered economically. So too have many of the rural centres servicing them. But overall many hinterlands have improved their economic position and so have the towns. Some of that growth has fed through up the urban hierarchy, not least because urban investments have generally proved more remunerative than rural ones, aided also by government subventions to rural areas some of which has found its way back to towns.

Towns also grow economically when they add new sectors, especially in manufacturing. There is no question but that this has been a potent driver of growth. Cities are larger markets than towns other things being equal. Often things are not. Even though transportation, food and housing costs may be higher, incomes are often higher still. In the mid-1990s, for example, average household incomes in Jakarta were half as much again as those in nearby Bandung. Growth can thus feed on itself more readily in larger cities, so long as the economy in general remains buoyant.

The political dimension in primacy is also important, as is recent history. The Thai state has long been highly centralised. To this day civil servants in the provinces complain that 'everything' has to be referred to Bangkok for action. While this is obviously not exactly true, it is true is that remarkably trivial matters do go to the capital to be dealt with by a small army of functionaries. By contrast, Malaysia is a federal country. Though there has been a strong tendency to centralise power in Kuala Lumpur over the last several decades, the constituent states still remain powerful, especially as land matters are constitutionally reserved to them. At the same time, though, it is clear that states that happen to elect assemblies not controlled by the ruling Alliance Party are partly, perhaps substantially, cut off from federal government capital spending and this too feeds through the economy to the towns.

Another factor in the Malaysian case is the recency of Kuala Lumpur's establishment as the Federal capital. When Malaysia's predecessor, Malaya, became independent in 1957 Kuala Lumpur was a small town of less than 200 000 people, little larger than other towns like Ipoh and Georgetown (Penang). Economic power essentially still resided in

Singapore, from which the British had ruled the peninsula since the late nineteenth century. Only after 1965 when Singapore left Malaysia did Kuala Lumpur come into its own, rapidly becoming a clearly primate city.

Elsewhere capitals have had that status for much longer periods. In Viet Nam it seems possible that Ha Noi might have grown to be the primate city but for partition in 1957 but the present situation in which Saigon (Ho Chi Minh City) is the economic centre and Ha Noi is the focus of political power remains from colonial times. Much the same is true elsewhere. All the primate cities were colonial capitals—Saigon of the relatively wealthy Cochinchina rather than the whole of Viet Nam, it is true.

Another dimension of primacy is that at the sub-national level. Here dominance is by a single town, almost invariably the provincial capital. In Viet Nam, for example, every town below the half-million mark is a provincial capital and within each province each accounts for upwards of two-thirds of the provincial urban population. Much the same is true in Thailand at both provincial and 'county' (*muang*) levels. In small sub-national territorial units a single town may account for virtually all of the urban population. For instance Kangar, capital of Perlis state, northwest Peninsular Malaysia, accounts for around 92 per cent of the state's population and effectively all of its urban population. Again size of territorial and administrative unit comes into play. Malaysia's eastern states of Sabah and Sarawak have quite regular urban hierarchies topped by the once-colonial capitals Kota Kinabalu and Kuching. Each state contains an array of only somewhat smaller towns—Miri, Sibu, Bintulu in Sarawak, Sandakan, Tawau, Lahad Datu, Kota Belud and Kudat in Sabah.

Other aspects of structure

While primacy is an important aspect of urban structure other aspects are also significant, always bearing in mind the quite arbitrary way in which statisticians and administrators determine what is urban. Table 9.4 summarises the situation in the four countries taken as examples, with data for Indonesia in 1980 and 1995 to add an evolutionary perspective.

The dominance of large towns has been made much of by many observers, especially in respect of Thailand. That case is clearly a statistical artifact. But even if the (1990) population of Chiang Mai is taken as 800 000, that drops Bangkok's share of Thailand's urban population by only two percentage points. Unless all of Thailand's urban centres are consistently underbounded—leading to people being counted as 'rural' when they are 'urban'—and that is a possibility, then Thailand indeed stands out as being dominated by Bangkok. Conversely, it has relatively few people in towns of less than 100 000 people.

Table 9.4 Examples of urban structure: Indonesia, 1980 and 1995, Peninsular Malaysia, Thailand, Viet Nam, early 1990s

	Indonesia		Peninsular Malaysia	Thailand	Viet Nam
	1980	**1995**	**1991**	**1990**	**1992**
Total population (million)	162.5	194.4	14.8	56.0	69.4
Urban population					
No. (mill.)	32.9	81.6	7.5	10.5	13.4
Prop'n total (%)	20	42	51	19	19
Population in largest town					
No. (mill.)	6.5	9.2	1.2	5.9	3.0
Prop'n urban (%)	20	11	16	55	23
Population in five largest towns					
No. (mill.)	12.4	17.5	2.6	6.8	5.5
Prop'n urban (%)	38	21	35	65	41
Population in towns >500 000					
No. of towns	8	15	1	1	3
No. (mill.)	14.4	25.6	1.2	5.9	4.8
Prop'n urban (%)	44	31	16	55	36
Population in towns >200 000					
No. of towns	22	32	8	5	7
No. (mill.)	18.6	31.1	3.0	6.8	6.2
Prop'n urban (%)	57	38	40	65	47
Population in towns >100 000					
No. of towns	30	49	10	11	21
No. (mill.)	19.6	33.5	3.6	7.7	7.7
Prop'n urban (%)	60	41	48	73	58
Population in towns <100 000					
No. (mill.)	13.3	48.1	3.9	2.8	5.7
Prop'n urban (%)	40	59	52	27	42

Notes: No data are available for number of towns <100 000. Figures rounded. Percentages calculated from unrounded totals. 'Proportion urban' from World Bank *World Development Reports, 1982, 1997.* Urban populations from *UN Demographic Yearbook.* This source is clearly in error in giving the population of Chiang Mai, Thailand's second city, as only 167 000 in 1990, when its true population was nearer 800 000.

Much more important is the fact that many urban people live in towns of less than 100 000. In the cases of Indonesia and Peninsular Malaysia most do, while in Viet Nam more than two-fifths do. Equally striking is the large increase in the proportion of Indonesia's smaller towns between 1980 and 1995 paralleled by a drop in the proportion—though not the number—of people in the various categories of larger cities. It is a fair guess that the next round of censuses, due in 2001, will show similar patterns elsewhere in the region. The era of rapid large-city growth is probably over except perhaps in Myanmar, Cambodia and Laos, which could be experiencing the kind of growth that occurred elsewhere in the region in the 1960s. For the rest the pattern is rising numbers but falling proportions.

Can other regularities in urban structure be discerned? So far as the total urban population is concerned it seems quite anomalous that a moderately wealthy country such as Thailand should be, apparently, as little urbanised as a poor one—Viet Nam. This may indeed be a statistical artifact of the kind just described, made more obvious by the fact that Thailand conducts *de jure* censuses. On the face of it, given average income levels, one would expect an urban structure somewhat like that of Indonesia or Peninsular Malaysia, making due allowance for differing levels of government centralism, especially in respect of the latter.

One possible reason for the differences—observable in all the urban categories set out in Table 9.4—is the very different character of Thailand's agricultural sector. This comprises a substantial proportion of the workforce but contributes relatively little to the economy. Since most small towns are essentially rural service centres their size (and number?) directly reflects the state of the rural, almost entirely agricultural, hinterland. In neither Peninsular Malaysia nor Indonesia, on average, is this sector so relatively poor as in Thailand. Moreover, it seems likely that, for Thai, Bangkok is seen to be the only place to be whereas elsewhere a medium city or a small town will do almost as well. Indeed detailed studies of migration in Indonesia and Malaysia suggest that step-wise movement up through the urban hierarchy—rural to small town, to big town and so on—is quite common. In a word, it is not just the primate city that is 'where it's at', other cities are too.

In particular it is in cities with more than 200 000 people, except in Thailand, that some uniformity is seen. The range is only 7 per cent of the total urban population, from 38 per cent in Indonesia (1995) to 47 per cent in Viet Nam (1992). Unfortunately insufficient data now exist to do more than speculate upon future trends. At some point the trend of both absolute and relative growth of towns in the less than 100 000 people category observable in Indonesia is likely to change.

In the west smaller towns have experienced severe difficulties in retaining population in the face of a relative decline in agriculture, their major support, as well as lower relative costs of transportation. They are often too small or too remote or otherwise insufficiently attractive to pull in investment. Slowly they die unless near enough to an expanding mega-urban region to become incorporated within it as the pre-existing core of a new, largely commuter-based settlement.

Brookfield and his colleagues have described just such a process around Kuala Lumpur. Beyond this commuter zone substantial working age-group depopulation has occurred resulting in a degree of economic decline in small towns. The degree to which small-town decline is occurring and the extent to which it affects different sizes of towns is largely conjectural at this point. The contrary process has to some degree been stimulated by direct government intervention. The Thai intermediate cities policy, for example, has clearly helped the growth of towns such as Khon Kaen and Korat.

In the never-ending interplay of centrifugal and centripetal forces one particular feature of urban structure in the region has survived. These are the many traditional centres of political power and trade, some thriving: Marawi, on Lake Lanao, Mindanao, Jolo in the Sulu Archipelago, Yogyakarta, Surakarta (Solo), Cirebon and many others on Java, Ubud on Bali to this day housing Puri Saren, home of the local Agung (King). Johor Baru, Kuala Trengganu, Kuala Kangsar, Pekan and several other towns are royal capitals in Peninsular Malaysia, the first two also being state administrative capitals. Mainland Southeast Asia has not seen quite the same phenomenon. Royal rule extended much more widely. Bangkok and Phnom Penh are royal towns but have not been so for particularly long. While Ayutthia has reconstituted itself close to its original site, the old Khmer capital at Oudong is not a town at all, the site marked only by stupas wherein are buried the ashes of royalty and by two important monasteries, one in ruins as a result, it is said, of an American bomb.

Ritual centres survive scarcely at all, except as ruins, though that function survives. Angkor Wat, for example, is still a favoured place for novice monks to have their heads shaved. Every town in the Buddhist lands has one or more active monasteries so that the ritual function continues, but it is no longer an exclusive function even in Tay Ninh, southern Viet Nam, a small-scale 'Vatican' for the syncretist Cao Dai religion.

Metropolitan regions

Villages, paradoxically, have often become parts of urban regions in many parts of Southeast Asia. Their layout and external appearance may be much the same as they were 20 or more years ago—a somewhat random or linear scattering of thatch and timber houses at the foot of a slope or along a road. Infilling of open space between once-rural homes occurs, of course, reflecting a partial or total change of function from rural and agricultural to urban. Home-gardens and in most lowland areas intensive market-gardening, sometimes rice production, continue though such rural activities may occupy a minority of people all the time or most people some of the time. In a word, the city now encompasses the countryside surrounding it, for buses, lorries, pickups and light motorcycles permit a wide separation of home and work. No longer are households dependent upon a single source of income. It is entirely feasible for many to keep one foot in the country and another in town, a situation strengthened by the persistence of extended family and other kin ties.

The evolution, especially in the last two decades and only in parts of the capitalist economic realm, of extended metropolitan regions does not invalidate the general description of the Southeast Asian city, but merely modifies it. Singapore, for example, has lost much of its shop-house-dominated commercial zone, partly by internal transformation represented by urban redevelopment into public housing and amenity centres, partly by expansion of the western-style Central Business District. It has also lost its areas of informal housing, while its intensive market-gardening—once a feature of districts like Toa Payoh, Tampenis and Choa Chu Kang—scarcely survives. Arguably, its metropolitan region has expanded into Malaysian Johor to the north and, offshore, to Indonesian Batam to the south, funded largely by Singaporean capital, to form one of Asia's new 'growth triangles'.

Such a transnational spread is quite unusual, though the development of such 'extended metropolitan regions' is not. Such regions are sometimes referred to, incorrectly, as *kotadesasi,* from the Indonesian word *kota,* 'town'—literally 'fort'—and *desa*, 'village'. *Kotadesasi* refers to the process of metropolitan-region formation, not to the regions themselves which can correctly be called '*kotadesasi* zones' or better, '*kotadesa*'.

They are characterised by large increases in non-agricultural activities in areas formerly agricultural, by more intensive use of the remaining agricultural areas, where this is technically feasible—usually involving a shift to market-gardening from rice, or maintenance of agriculture as a part-time activity, often at lower land-use intensities—orchards not paddy-fields—or by abandonment.

Other characteristics include extreme spatial and temporal mobility of labour—doing the same job in different places or different jobs in the same place or both—a complex mixture of land uses and of circulation. A series of urban nodes is characteristic with open, agricultural land between. Each node tends to spread outwards, often in step-wise or leap-frog fashion with later infilling of built-up areas so that land uses change over short distances in a seemingly or actually chaotic fashion.

Kotadesa regions

One well-studied *kotadesasi* zone—in fact the first to have this term applied to it—is Jabotabek, an acronym for the capital, *Ja*karta, together with the surrounding *kabupaten* (districts) of *Bo*gor, *Ta*ngerang and *Bek*asi, together with their district capitals of the same name. In 1990 this region contained 17.1 million people, 4 million of them classified as 'rural', up from a total of 7.4 million—4.5 million rural—in 1980. By now the total is probably in the 20–25 million range, rivalling Tokyo. The decade 1980–90 saw relatively slow growth in Jakarta itself—only an annual average of 2.7 per cent—while growth in Bogor city was just under 1 per cent.

By contrast rates in the Bogor, Tangerang and Bekasi districts ranged from 5 to 8.5 per cent. The results of such rapid growth are several-fold. Farmers are displaced by new housing and industrial developments at a rate of 4–6 people per ha. Few are absorbed into new activities. Pollution from these sources causes falling production on the remaining agricultural land which is then abandoned and eventually sold, not necessarily by the occupier. A substantial part of the expansion is onto sloping land, creating major problems of erosion, accelerated run-off and flooding. Private investors face lack of infrastructure, especially electricity and telephones. Commuting is a serious difficulty with long journey times and congestion extending until late in the evening. The management of solid and liquid wastes is a herculean task. Indeed all kinds of management tasks are seriously difficult, in part because of relatively low urban population densities.

Similar *kotadesa* regions have emerged in other parts of the region although with some differences in detail. Kuala Lumpur has expanded onto relatively sparsely populated rubber land rather than a highly productive rice plain so that the agricultural component of this much smaller *kotadesa* is much less important than in Manila or Bangkok.

The direction of growth has clearly been influenced by (as well as influencing) major transportation axes. For Jabotabek this is particularly the 200-km Jakarta–Bogor–Bandung axis, rapidly growing at both ends, squeezing largely rural Cianjur in the middle.

For Kuala Lumpur initial development was along the Federal Highway linking the city with its port at Kelang. This is now largely built-up and the spread continues south to Sepang, southeast to Seremban and to Rawang and Serendah to the northwest. Manila's spread has very much followed the trunk highways, certainly as far as San Fernando (Pampanga) in the north and Los Baños in the south. For Greater Bangkok, as elsewhere, just where the real, as distinct from the administrative boundary of the extended metropolis might lie is debatable but it arguably includes Nakhon Pathom to the west, Ayutthia to the north and Chonburi to the east.

Even Ho Chi Minh City is showing signs of an emerging metropolitan region, extending from My Tho—in 1992 a town of 108 000—to Bien

Hoa, somewhat over double that size. In the north Ha Noi is beginning to spill over into the countryside and in Viet Nam as a whole most settlements have spread markedly in the last five years. As elsewhere, much of this is onto superior-quality agricultural land which is thus 'sterilised' for ever, a serious matter where the people/agricultural land ratio is so high.

But too much should not be made of the emergence of extended metropolitan regions. A substantial portion of the urban population resides in medium and small towns. Most of these conform to the general model described earlier. They are growing substantially but centripetal forces are still stronger than centrifugal ones. Inner cities and towns are where the jobs are, where there are offices, shops and markets, bus terminals and railway stations. In Baguio, for example, a large town with close to 200 000 people, there are virtually no suburban shopping centres. Neither do hawkers carry daily necessities into suburban streets as they would in Indonesian towns. The result is a very large central market, a high degree of centralisation and a pattern still very much characteristic of Filipino towns. Some intermediate cities are certainly likely to become part of large metropolitan regions. In Viet Nam for instance, an obvious growth axis lies between Ha Noi and Hai Phong. The Penang axis is topographically constrained on Penang Island but growth on the mainland is steadily proceeding both north and south from the 1970s core at Butterworth and Perai, incorporating small towns as it goes.

Clearly there are, at least in principle, limits to the expansion of metropolitan regions. At which point diseconomies, including dirt, noise and congestion, begin to kick in will be basically a matter to be determined by the market, for planners and administrators have little control. (Former Jakarta Governor Ali Sidikin tried to limit the city's growth by keeping people out. This was a notable failure.) Capital feeds on itself. Southeast Asia's metropolitan regions contain much of their country's wealth. In Indonesia 70 per cent is in Jakarta. But the returns from real estate development, to a lesser degree from investment in manufacturing, are so high that funds also flow substantially from other regions. In the rural areas, technological change, driven in part by rising costs of labour, is tending to displace farmers, not all of whom balance their budgets by off-farm, part-time work. Many leave farming altogether, hundreds of thousands driven off the land though not necessarily out of their homes, by the process of urban spread.

Internal structure

To the first-time visitor from outside the region any one of Southeast Asia's cities is an initially bewildering kaleidoscope of rapidly changing cityscapes. Distinguished colonial-era buildings, hawker stalls mobile and fixed, 'Chinese' shop-houses, glass-sheathed skyscrapers, thatched huts, genteel residences, workshops spilling onto the street, air-conditioned assembly plants, container port, traditional sailing vessels, cargo lighters with painted eyes, buses, lorries, handcarts and trishaws are mixed in a seeming infinity of heterogeneous, colourful patterns. Land uses may change over a few metres. Squatters live on bridges or under them protected from the elements only by a sheet of plastic, cooking done on the simplest of stoves just centimetres from a sleeping mat to be unrolled to soften the hardness of plank or pavement. Juxtapose this with the ordered calm of a royal or government quarter. Superimpose upon the kaleidoscope the recency of most parts of most cities and the result is chaos.

Or is it? Perhaps the most common regularity is irregularity. That given, much depends upon the scale of analysis. One useful approach is to conceive of two polar 'systems' or 'sectors': one large-scale, capitalistic, impersonal, the other small-scale, 'peasant-like', in that the prime economic consideration is family survival, personal and face-to-face. Scholars refer to these systems as the 'formal sector' (or 'upper circuit') and the 'informal sector' (or 'lower circuit'). Each is linked to the other by flows of materials, such as food from the countryside to hawker and market stall, and services, especially labour. Each is a world unto itself, yet paradoxically not entirely so for each is linked by occupational and spatial mobility. Each serves and is served by the other. Each is reflected in distinctive townscapes: colourful 'wet markets' and air-conditioned shopping malls; cooked-food centres, noodle sellers and international restaurants; pawnshops, tontines and banks; street theatres and cinemas; signboards in the vernacular, signs in English; thatched hut and western-style bungalow or apartment block.

Spatially and functionally these systems interdigitate at very varying scales. Western-style suburbs or high-rise public housing may extend for kilometres but nevertheless may be penetrated by petty traders—bread-sellers crying their wares, purveyors of snack foods and gewgaws for children, laundry people, tailors, itinerant traders in a dozen commodities, all part of a small-scale trading system that has its historical origin in the cities of centuries ago. Inside a royal precinct—Phnom Penh's is one such—all is decorum and order. Outside it are representatives of the urban underclass, the halt and maimed, in the city for bare survival's sake. In the noisome slums of Klong Toey (Bangkok) or Tondo (Manila), the formal sector nevertheless penetrates—Coca-Cola, 555 cigarettes and Wrigley's chewing gum, though at one remove via local dealers. Too much should not be made of this formal/informal distinction. They are fuzzy categories and to some degree grade into each other.

These distinctions are nevertheless reflected in the internal structure of towns and cities in various ways. Government, with its ordered structures of bureaucratic organs, is clearly part of the formal sector. Every city and most towns, even quite small ones, have a government zone, in the capital comprising a people's assembly of some kind—even under authoritarian regimes—government offices, in former colonial cities a large church or cathedral, in former British territories often grouped around open space modelled on the Anglo-Indian *maidan*. Nearby is a royal or presidential quarter.

Adjacent to these is usually a western-style commercial zone. Here are the offices of banks and insurance companies, of major trading companies together with western-style shops, arcades and malls. Buildings are tall and built in an international style of architecture that owes little or nothing to its host culture. In a word it is the Central Business District—but only of one kind of business, not necessarily foreign-owned but certainly at least partly foreign-oriented. Here are hotels and western restaurants, foreign-language bookshops, international brands of clothing and jewellery.

Sometimes adjoining this zone, sometimes separated from it by zones of mixed land uses, is a further zone that originated as a part of the city once set aside for resident aliens, in most cities Overseas Chinese. Even Singapore, predominantly a Chinese city, has its Chinatown though through redevelopment it has lost much of its earlier character. Virtually every other large town in the region has a similar zone. Here the ubiquitous shop-house reigns supreme: two- or three-storey buildings with ground-floor commercial, sometimes with small-scale industrial functions, living quarters above, built in brick and timber with highly distinctive architectural features. In a few cities—Singapore is again an example—one or more small Indian quarters may exist, their presence signalled more by the people than by the architecture. (Singapore's small city-centre Indian quarter centred on Chulia Street—'Indian moneylender street'—has now virtually disappeared though a larger, more distant one centred upon Lower Serangoon Road, thrives.) Where the western-style business zone 'dies' at night, animated only by round-the-clock operations of international finance houses, the Chinatowns are still up and running. Want shoes repaired or a ready-made shirt at midnight? No problem! This activity is, of course, partly a reflection of relative poverty. Ends are made to meet by opening very long hours, for family labour is costed at close to zero.

Manufacturing zones form a further element in the urban fabric. While workshop enterprises may be scattered in many parts of the city—cycle repairs, tinsmiths and other metalworkers—larger industrial undertakings occupy distinct zones. Older industries, established in colonial times, are often located near the railway or port area. Later-established factories tend to occupy distinct zones along main highways. (Singapore's pre-1960s industries ranged along the main axis leading to the Causeway and nearby

Johor.) Or they may be largely confined to more recently developed industrial estates (for example Singapore's Jurong, many times extended west and south by further land reclamation; the Kelang Valley clustered along the Federal Highway leading from Kuala Lumpur to Port Kelang). One further favoured location is near a major airport. While significant manufacturing has yet to show up near Singapore's Changi Airport, it has certainly done so near Bangkok's Don Muang and Penang's Bayan Lepas airports. (In Singapore road access is quick and easy so there is less reason for such a strategic location being used.)

Most major cities have a port area, because most originated as colonial-era *points d'appui*, albeit usually based upon a pre-existing settlement core, as at Raja Suleiman's Manila, the Temenggong's Singapore, Jakarta's fishing village. In some cases there are several port zones, one for smaller, local craft, another for larger vessels. Singapore's Kallang Basin was thus long a port for Bugis (Makassarese) vessels from Indonesia and for local 'bum-boats' (lighters) which once thronged the Singapore River, their cargoes being manhandled across Boat Quay and into adjoining *godowns* (warehouses). Keppel Harbour, to the west, was the colonial port for large steamers. Around this a major ship-repair facility developed. By the 1970s outports on the southern islands, serving mainly the petroleum refineries, had come into existence with a complete new port at Jurong handling general cargo, a little of it still handled by lighters, moved out of the Singapore River as part of a general clean-up of the area. Most cargo, however, is moved by container, for which Singapore is the major regional trans-shipment point.

Residential areas, as in most cities, are of widely varying types, the main variable—money—being reflected in their location, and the size and style of their buildings. Traditionally the upper classes in Asian cities have tended to live near the city centre, a fact represented in some Southeast Asian cities—Bangkok and Phnom Penh are examples—by the survival of royal quarters in the inner city. But the poorest also need access to the inner city, because here are the best prospects of scraping a living. Thus the seaward side of Roxas Boulevard, a major thoroughfare in Manila, was long and still to some degree remains home to the urban underclass.

Older upper-class residential areas still adjoin inner-city commercial zones. Singapore's Orchard Road is backed by Nassim and Dalvey Roads—large detached bungalows of the 1930s–1950s set in extensive grounds shaded by mature trees. In some cases this kind of zone is related to the topography, as in Kuala Lumpur where Kenny Hill to the west of the inner city—once the home of the colonial elite—the Ampang Road – Court Hill area, developed in the 1960s, and the heights of Petaling Jaya attract much higher rents than the adjoining suburban flatlands. Another example is Forbes Park, set off from the rest of Manila by security controls, its luxurious homes surrounded by high walls topped with razor wire or shards of glass, overseen by the eyes of closed circuit television.

Middle-class housing, like upper-class housing, has generally been left to private enterprise to provide, except in Singapore, where four-fifths of all housing was constructed at government initiative. Characteristically this provision takes the form of private housing estates, mostly constructed on 'green-field' sites as the cities have expanded. They form dormitory suburbs par excellence, provided with their own markets and shopping centres but little else by way of employment. House lots are small with enough room to park a car and grow a few flowers. Homes are usually semi-detached, two-storeyed or single-storey terrace houses. Densities are moderately low and these suburbs are consequently extremely expensive to service. Many rely upon septic-tank sewage disposal but are otherwise fully serviced. Suburbs of this kind sprawl around Kuala Lumpur, linked to the city centre by four-lane highways choked with traffic at peak hours. Similar housing also surrounds much of Bangkok, though the pattern of growth has been less controlled resulting in a wide urban fringe zone in which agricultural land, some of it abandoned, and housing estates form an irregular patchwork of land uses. Infilling of the remaining patches then follows to consolidate suburban land use.

One exception to this pattern is Singapore, where most middle- and working-class housing is high-rise, though there are also significant areas of middle-class low-rise housing. Much has been constructed at government initiative though many tenants have subsequently purchased the homes they occupy. Control of use and activities in these estates is tight, residents being supplied with a long list of dos and don'ts, but apart from noise these places are clean and comfortable—unlike the informal housing they initially replaced. In the design and administration of such estates little notice has been taken of cultural preferences and they are seen by some as a means of breaking up and preventing the formation of ethnic enclaves such as characterised parts of 1960s Singapore—the Malay concentration in Geylang Serai for instance. Malays have had to overcome their repugnance of people living above them. (Interestingly, public high-rise housing in Kuala Lumpur is occupied by scarcely any Malays and it is sometimes argued that its suburban sprawl is partly to be accounted for by this cultural factor.)

No other city has seen government intervention in housing on the scale of Singapore. No other city can afford it. The notion of 'new towns' has been taken on board by city planners, though implemented with varying degrees of success. Essentially, new towns are planned to combine residence, places of work and recreation in local more or less self-contained communities, the objective being not only to improve housing and living conditions generally but also to avoid long journeys to work. Kuala Lumpur's satellite, Petaling Jaya, and Singapore's Jurong are examples.

Like many of their British counterparts they were from the outset and have remained essentially dormitory suburbs for the reason that the mere provision of employment in local factories and offices cannot ensure that nearby residents will take it up. Consequently in both satellites no more than about a third of their labour resides locally and the commuter problems they were designed to avoid remain. The spatial separation of residence and workplace has become general. Cheap housing is generally distant housing. The continuing public and private costs of sprawl are unabated, in part because powerful private interests see—until very recently, correctly—the opportunity to make substantial capital gains from the ownership of land and urban expansion.

Working-class people, many of them recent rural–urban migrants, have had and mostly continue to have serious difficulties in providing themselves with housing. The very poorest—the urban underclass—pick up a living from scavenging, begging and casual work if they can get it. No one knows how many they may be but there are significant numbers in most of the major cities except Singapore and Brunei. For these 'home' is likely to be a doorway, a patch of shrubbery under a bridge, or a plastic sheet attached to a wall. Even 'socialist' Ha Noi has them, though their numbers are much greater in Manila and Jakarta.

More numerous are occupants of 'informal housing'. Some are truly squatters—illegally occupying land owned by others—but many pay landowners for the privilege of erecting a shack of cardboard, plywood or corrugated iron and other 'waste' materials, often scavenged from dumps or stolen. Recognising the serious health risks that such areas pose, city authorities have generally endeavoured to provide very basic services such as latrines and water from public stand-pipes, though in some areas even the former are lacking, scavenging being done by pigs and scrofulous dogs. Electricity is sometimes provided, sometimes not, and if provided the supply is often illegally tapped. Sullage and often sewage flow where they may.

Densities are quite variable. Inner-city areas are extremely crowded. Those further out are not. In both, forms of 'agriculture' may survive. Pigs are common scavengers fed on collected food-waste when scavenging does not suffice. Many families keep chickens, also scavengers fed on domestic food waste as at Payatas, Quezon City. Even dairy cattle may be kept, in stalls or allowed to wander, as was once the case in Singapore's Potong Pasir and Queenstown.

The location of areas of informal housing varies from city to city. Singapore scarcely has any, unless employer-provided quarters on construction sites be so considered. (In the 1960s, however, there were substantial areas, notably Red Hill and Potong Pasir.) Some informal housing areas are or were close to city centres, like Kampung Baru in Kuala Lumpur, Klong Toey in Bangkok, parts of Tondo and Pestaño in

Greater Manila. Others are more distant. Some once-rural villages on the urban fringe contain informal housing interspersed with rural-type homes.

Akin to these areas, but less obvious to the casual eye, are inner-city tenements—the region's Harlems and East Ends. Crowding is endemic, with densities upwards of 400 per hectare in some places. While basic sanitary services exist they are often unclean and poorly maintained. Characteristic are three- or four-storey walk-ups, often subdivided into cubicles, with facilities partly or wholly shared. Examples include Samphanthawong in Bangkok, the old Dutch town of Jakarta, and Binondo and parts of Ermita in Manila. Much of Singapore's Chinatown and Kallang have now been redeveloped.

Just how many people live—and often work—in areas of informal housing and deteriorating inner-city tenements is basically anyone's guess, partly because there are as many definitions of 'deteriorated' as there are people writing about it. In the early 1960s it was estimated that around a quarter of the people in Jakarta, Kuala Lumpur, Manila and Singapore were living in informal, largely self-built housing, with between a further quarter and a half of the total population living in poor-quality inner-city tenements. Singapore has largely transformed both of these kinds of areas. While informal, squatter settlements still exist in Greater Kuala Lumpur, housing mainly illegal immigrants, many of those of the 1960s have either been swept away by urban improvement schemes or have been substantially upgraded. Crowded tenement areas still exist, however, for example in Brickfields. In Metro Manila half the population of a major component, Quezon City, was said to be living in informal housing at the end of the 1980s and at that time the urban poor—living in informal housing and in slums—made up nearly half of the total population.

Official attitudes to both kinds of settlements of the poor have been quite variable both from city to city and within cities from time to time. Only in Singapore has the thrust to sweep them away been largely successful, so that 86 per cent of the population lives in what is or was public housing. Beginning in the 1960s its Housing and Development Board has been ruthlessly effective to the extent that a minority of urban conservationists were, by the 1990s, calling it the 'Housing and Destruction Board', regarding its offshoot the Urban Renewal Authority as an agency for totally replacing old, established shop-house areas with 'soulless' high-rises. (In the event, the conservationists had their way. Refurbishment—'gentrification'—is now part of official policy.) Kuala Lumpur has also rebuilt or upgraded many of its informal housing areas. Newcomers to the city have been housed, in part, in dozens of once-rural *kampungs* (villages) surrounding the capital.

Decanting the urban poor into peripheral settlements has also been attempted, especially on the outskirts of Yangon and also Marcos-era Manila. (One of the curious sights at Carmen, south of Manila, was rows of government 'utility cores'—water and sanitation—around which slum-dwellers were expected to build their own homes. Most were never occupied.) Such attempts have universally failed. Suburban lots were too small to grow more than a fraction of the resettled family's food and too far from existing employment in the inner city for the poor to afford to commute to work, particularly as obtaining casual employment depended on established personal networks and being available for work at short notice.

Except in Singapore, rebuilding has generally been slow given high inner-city land values, requiring very large subsidies from local governments that most have been unable to meet. Consequently some schemes failed to provide housing for those for whom they were ostensibly designed because rents were too high. An extreme Marcos-era case was Manila's BLISS project, which resulted in the construction of pleasant homes so expensive that only 10 per cent of the city's families could afford them. (Most seem to have ended up in the hands of Marcos supporters, while much of the public money to build them allegedly found its way into the hands of cronies.)

Urban slums of whatever description are seen by many of their occupants as stepping-stones towards a secure and permanent place in the metropolis. To be sure they are also the temporary home of circular migrants who move into the city for a few months' work. Most succeed in finding such a place, however dismal it may be in terms of living conditions. Flows of capital from within cities themselves, from the countryside and, as a result of globalisation, from abroad, generate increasingly severe competition for land while at the same time demanding cheap labour. That labour has had to find affordable living space, preferably near employment in order to minimise transportation costs in cities in which place of work and place of residence are increasingly divorced. Crowded, poor-quality housing is an inevitable result. Except where rapid and sustained growth of the economy as a whole exists—as it has in Singapore—such areas are likely to persist.

The urban fabric

Houses of cardboard, plywood and corrugated iron are very much part of most Southeast Asian cities. So too are sprawling suburbs, many of them much like their western counterparts in design—rows of rectangular boxes—and in materials—brick, concrete and tile. However inelegant, they represent a truly international architectural style. Informal housing parallels the *bustees* of India and the *favelas* of Latin America; inner-city tenements equate to the back-to-back houses of industrial Britain; sprawling suburbs are similar to thousands in Europe and North America. Only institutional buildings like temples and mosques, palm trees in the yards, the commodities in some of the shops and the smells of cooking indicate other cultures.

In the western-style central business districts not even these last indicate 'otherness'. Only people's faces and clothing, sometimes building signs and advertisements, distinguish Southeast Asia from Europe or North America. High-rise buildings of steel framing clad in concrete and glass owe little or nothing to their national cultural milieux, though often designed locally. They are truly the concrete outgrowths of international capitalism. Only exceptionally do commercial buildings consciously reflect local cultures. One striking example is Phnom Penh's riverside Hotel Cambodiana just a few hundred metres downriver from the city's royal compound whose architecture it partly reflects. Another is the Singapore Chinese Chamber of Commerce building—a western high-rise office block wearing an incongruous Chinese tiled roof.

Government and other civic buildings tend to be replaced much less frequently than commercial ones, so that the region's cities contain some splendid examples both of western colonial architecture—not, in fact, confined to former colonial cities—and of syncretic architecture, the latter also encompassing the 'alien commercial zones' where the 'Chinese' shop-house reigns supreme, as well as civic buildings more closely following Chinese models.

Civic buildings

Notable amongst colonial-era civic buildings are those of Ha Noi. Painted in yellow ochre, encompassing a range of styles—including Palladian, Louis XIV and broadly 'nineteenth-century French civic'—they form a distinctive part of the city's landscape. Notable are the Opera House, the former governor's residence and the Town Hall. Large detached houses, once occupied by high colonial officials and wealthy merchants, some Chinese or Sino-Vietnamese, also survive, some as office buildings, others as restaurants and small hotels. One of the few concessions to Asian-ness and the climate is the use of shutters rather than glass windows, but even the shutters use Mediterranean-type fixed and movable louvres rather than being solid wood on traditional lines.

One particular feature of colonial-period civic buildings is their use of classical elements—heavy pediments and Greek pillars—and of domes to enclose large spaces. Singapore's Victoria Theatre, Supreme Court and (former) City Hall, as well as Saigon's National Theatre are good examples of this reflection of a need to emphasise solidity, stability—a need for *impressement* to overawe 'the natives'. Most are in stone—a material entirely abandoned in favour of ferro-concrete in post-colonial times. Ferro-concrete is strikingly used in one of the few Modernist civic buildings in the region, the Corbusier-style Central Market in Phnom Penh. This uses a high roof, narrow windows and air vents to promote cross-ventilation in a predominantly hot and humid environment. However, building for the climate in most larger colonial-period buildings was not particularly successful for the structures heat up during the day and remain hot throughout the afternoon and evening so that surviving examples of those times are nowadays mostly air-conditioned.

Churches are also a reflection of imperial *impressement.* Some are small and quite charming, like Singapore's Armenian church and Kuala Lumpur's St Margaret's. Others impress by sheer solidity. Most of the Spanish-era churches in the Philippines, some of which go back to the seventeenth century, to some degree follow Spanish stylistic models, especially in their interiors. St Augustine's in Intramuros, Manila, is an example. 'Colonial gothic' is well represented, for instance in Singapore's St Andrew's Cathedral and in Saigon's Roman Catholic cathedral, a somewhat nondescript structure, unusually in brick.

Political détente between the former socialist states of Indochina and Communist powers is not generally reflected architecturally though Phnom Penh, for example, retains street names reflecting Soviet influence. A major example is Ho Chi Minh's mausoleum in Ha Noi, clearly modelled on Lenin's tomb in Moscow's Red Square.

Civic buildings that solely reflect indigenous culture scarcely exist, for most are syncretic in style, in manner of construction or both. Some of the survivors from early times include Angkor Wat, still in use for religious purposes, and Melaka's seventeenth-century Cheng Hoon Teng temple, said to be the oldest surviving Chinese temple outside China itself. Hué's former Imperial City, built in the early nineteenth century, is a scaled-down version of Beijing's Forbidden City. It survives in part, though now merely a tourist spot. Certain of its stylistic elements are Vietnamese, though the use of 'Chinese' and 'Vietnamese' as cultural categories is an uncertain proceeding. The (mostly) rather earlier Scholar's Temple in Ha Noi is still in use as a temple, though thronged with tourists.

Stylistic mixtures of indigenous and imported do not necessarily solely involve 'the west'. In Kuala Lumpur the block of buildings comprising the railway station, the railway administration building and the former colonial offices were designed by a British architect in vaguely Saracenic (Arab) style, complete with arches and domes, even fake minarets—on the railway station, these in vaguely Mughal style—and a large British-style town clock in its own domed tower. Laughable perhaps, but adding distinctiveness. Much more successful is the city's post-colonial National Museum. Though in ferro-concrete and brick it incorporates Minangkabau stylistic elements quite convincingly. The National Mosque, designed by a British consortium, contains little that is specifically Malay but is a thoroughly pleasing modern Islamic building. Both reflect the fact that in much of insular Southeast Asia indigenous architecture tiles and thatch, hardly appropriate to modern urban conte laterite, stone and brick were part of the constructional re major pre-colonial cities of mainland Southeast Asia, as well of Sri Vijaya, now Palembang, southern Sumatera, and in c Another charming colonial-era attempt to interpret indigenous Phnom Penh's National Museum. The degree to which it is 'inc genous' must be open to some debate for Khmer culture is to some degree derived from Thai, in architecture as in dance, but no Thai would ever paint such a building in the strikingly appropriate deep red of this Khmer building.

The Khmer royal quarter nearby is, perhaps, more clearly of Thai—perhaps partly Chinese—inspiration. Roofs are in terracotta and green glazed tiles decorated with finials in the Thai or Chinese manner but also supported—not structurally—by Hinduistic *garudas* such as are to be found throughout much of the region. Western elements include an iron pavilion built for the Empress Eugénie, ceilings with western-style allegorical painted panels, formal hedges and flowerbeds, curtains and light-fixtures. Similar eclecticism is to be found in the Royal Palace complex around the Temple of the Emerald Buddha in Bangkok, and in the *kraton* (royal compound) of the Sultans of Yogyakarta, all mainly of nineteenth-century and early twentieth-century construction. Topiary, pavilions and lamp-standards of Victorian England may seem incongruous. Yet there were no indigenous alternatives in permanent materials, so how could it be otherwise, for Southeast Asian cultures have long been inclusive rather than exclusive.

Domestic architecture

This inclusiveness is also expressed in domestic architecture of two kinds, one the homes of indigenous elites and the other in the ubiquitous 'Chinese' shop-house. (To a very limited degree, notably in Singapore, these categories overlap as inner-city shop-houses have been gentrified.) As Lee Kip Lin describes, the colonial-period Singapore elite, Chinese and westerners alike, built homes containing a variety of influences: pseudo-Tudor 'black-and-white' half-timbering, classical Greek orders of columns and pediments decorating elaborate carriage porches, 'Portuguese' tiled stairways, carved and painted Chinese-style swing-doors, Chinese roof styles with half-round tiles, finials, sometimes even a roof-dragon, deep verandahs and external bamboo blinds—'chicks'—on Indian lines, even, in early examples, Malay-style palm-thatch roofs. The whole structure, of one or two storeys, was raised on brick pillars in the Malay 'stilt-house' manner. In the days before air-conditioning these were very well adapted to the climate—much more so than many modern 'concrete boxes'. Post-independence domestic architecture for the wealthy throughout the region has sought deliberately to incorporate indigenous cultural elements, especially in Malaysia, Singapore (where William Lim is a noted exponent), Thailand and Indonesia. (Powell's misnamed book *The Asian House*—actually on the Southeast Asian house—gives details.) The result is some stunning designs though only a minority of architects have attempted this kind of syncretic approach.

Professional architects had nothing to do with the design and construction of the region's 'Chinese' shop-house—'Chinese' in the sense that they were designed and built by and for Chinese. Shop-houses are typically of rectangular plan in row- or terrace-house form, each house occupying the whole plot of land. Two or three storeys are invariable, usually with an internal light-well providing light and ventilation as a small outdoor but enclosed space wherein there is usually a well with the kitchen nearby. The rest of the ground floor is given over to business. The facade facing the street is highly elaborate, often including pseudo-classical pilasters, plaster panels and friezes with floral or geometrical designs. The main door is double, usually a set of swinging half-doors plus a set of stout timber doors padlocked at night for security, the ensemble guarded by two animal statues—lions or dogs—surmounted by a large sign bearing the owner's name.

The origins of this widespread form are obscure. Many of the original migrants to the Malay Peninsula, Singapore, Thailand and Indonesia came from China's Fujian province yet, seemingly, no 'original' shop-houses survive there. Perhaps the earliest type survives at Hoi An, central Viet Nam, where the ground floor facade can be opened out completely by removing thick horizontal planks set in grooves to create an open-fronted store. On the upper floors of most shop-houses louvred shutters may extend from the floor level almost to the ceiling, a balustrade protecting the lower portion of the opening. This feature occurs in many older residences in Portugal, as does decorative tiling, and it is possible that these elements represent a borrowing from that source just as the tiled *tangga* (stairway) of Melaka Malay village houses seems to be.

Reflections

Villages remain part of expanding cities, transformed from within as they come to house urban people, their agricultural lands likewise converted into dormitory suburbs or, if they survive in productive use, being converted into high-yielding fish-ponds and market-gardens. The result is large urban regions containing a great mixture of land uses over short distances. Dormitory settlements, shopping centres, workshops and factories are linked—inadequately—by roads congested beyond belief at all hours except in the middle of the night. Basic urban services may be quite limited, especially in lower-income areas. Such urban complexes may well be the shape of things to come even for the intermediate cities of the present time.

Extended urban regions would not exist but for two basic facts: high demand, pushed by growing wealth and a speculative spirit; and such rapidity of expansion as to prevent the imposition of any but the most rudimentary forms of planning and control. The internal structure of such agglomerations is loose and irregular, fully deserving of the phrase 'suburbs in search of the urbs' once applied to Los Angeles, and other low-density American cities. Like Los Angeles, Southeast Asia's growing extended metropolitan regions are founded upon considerable personal mobility, albeit more upon motorcycles, buses, and mini-buses than upon cars.

Such cities are inherently inefficient and will long remain so. While it is true that services—piped water supply, sewerage, drainage, electricity, gas, telephones—can be provided progressively as incomes rise, low densities must mean high overall unit costs. A Hong Kong housing estate of 100 000 residents might have three kilometres of road, about the same length of trunk sewer, high-voltage power cable and water-main. It would support several bus routes with frequent services, perhaps a rail-transit station. A similar estate in a typical Southeast Asian city would require anywhere from double these distances up to ten times more. Yet apart from labour and tax virtually everything else costs the same—water and drainpipes, cables, tarmac, vehicles, fuel. The costs to the community of such dispersal in space are not easy to establish but they cannot be less than considerable. They must also include the cost of replacing—somewhere—the high-value agricultural land that surrounds many lowland cities.

But to argue for the benefits of spatial concentration on purely economic grounds is to miss the point. 'House-and-garden', as still in Japan, Australasia, much of Europe and virtually all of the United States and Canada, is very much to be desired, an icon as powerful as the city itself. Most urban people are only a generation removed from the paddy-field, if that, so to recreate something, however limited, of the rural ambience is very much to be desired. Land speculation by the rich and powerful, abetted by the growing middle class, is also seen as a road to more money, besides conferring the social cachet that still accompanies land ownership. Land, whether urban or rural, is still wealth.

The intermediate cities and the towns do not necessarily share the growth of the metropolitan regions. Some of the smaller rural service centres, suffer from stagnation, even economic regression in their hinterlands. Some, along major development axes, have yet to be incorporated into larger agglomerations. Yet others still have productive hinterlands and are too far from expanding metropolises ever to be incorporated within them. These may form the nuclei for future growth. Indeed, as the diseconomies of very large urban complexes take hold, such intermediate cities will become increasingly well placed to grow. Many have begun to do so already. They too will increasingly become 'where it's at'.

TEN
WHITHER SOUTHEAST ASIA?

The tension between forces tending towards the continued expansion of large metropolitan regions and those in a contrary direction are a microcosm of broader tensions within the region as a whole. It would be as vain to seek a permanent resolution of these tensions in Southeast Asia as it would in Australia, where conflict, of a peaceful kind, is even inherent in the nation's constitution. But in Southeast Asia the parties to conflicts tend to have guns and to seek political support from abroad for their particular view of how its polities should be ordered. Crystal-ball-gazing is an inherently risky occupation. What follows is therefore very much a personal view.

ECONOMIC AND POLITICAL FORCES

Centripetal—centralising—forces can be distinguished on several planes. All the countries of the region are now members of the Association of Southeast Asian Nations (ASEAN), except newly formed East Timor, though it too has expressed the wish to join, as well as seeking membership of the South Pacific Commission. From the outset, one of ASEAN's major objectives has been economic—the ultimate formation of a free-trade bloc on the lines of the European Community or North American Free Trade Area (NAFTA). Progress in this direction has been slow, not least because of huge disparities in income levels and standards of living amongst the member states. There is a real fear that aggressive Singaporean, Malaysian and Thai capital—which further suffers from the perception that it is 'actually Chinese'—will undercut the position of economic (and political) elites in other member countries. Both the

Philippines and Indonesia have been notably reluctant to permit the setting up of businesses that are wholly foreign-owned. Both are labour-surplus countries. Neither is permitted—legally—to allow large-scale imports of labour. On the other hand Malaysia, with perhaps a million illegal migrants, and Thailand, with perhaps a million more are, with Singapore, net importers of labour. In fact, something of a regional labour market, has already emerged to parallel the regional capital market, though neither is free.

Economic forces

Real economic integration would see the emergence of a single major regional airline, for example. (Consider how potent a combination of Thai, Malaysian and Singapore airlines might be on the international scene, but Singapore Airlines is much more interested in partnership outside the region.) Economic integration would see a single major shipping line charged with the carriage of the region's produce in its own bottoms. It would see free trade in services, notably finance and banking, as well as in commodities. Some progress has been made towards free trade in commodities, though it has been slow. Present plans call for a reduction of duties to a maximum of 5 per cent by 2010—but only amongst the original members of ASEAN. Free trade in services has scarcely been considered. Part of the problem clearly lies in the perception that free trade to some degree implies loss of sovereignty, certainly loss of direct control over major sectors of the economy. Yet paradoxically such loss of control has to some degree already occurred. Foreign-owned multinationals, mostly American and Japanese, control significant parts of the electronics sector, for example. Is Singaporean capital less to be trusted than US or Japanese?

Against economic centralisation two sets of forces operate, one international, the other national. ASEAN states are also members of the Asian Free Trade Area (AFTA) and of the World Trade Organisation (WTO), both bodies working towards free trade. But it is by no means clear that national economic interests are best served by ASEAN vis-a-vis AFTA and WTO. Take the electronics sector as an example again. It is much more important that ASEAN producers such as Singapore, Malaysia and, increasingly, Thailand have free access to markets outside ASEAN than to markets within it. Outside markets are larger and still show capacity for growth. Earnings arise in solid Deutschmarks, pounds sterling and US dollars rather than kip, riels and kyats. Consumers in these wealthier ASEAN countries are also happy to buy prestige goods imported from the countries to which electronics are exported.

These ASEAN countries are already basically part of the global economy, so why should they bother with their other ASEAN partners?

Is there really sufficient identity of economic interest with the others to make it worthwhile developing links and taking the risks necessary to their realisation and making the economic compromises required? The answer is clearly a qualified 'yes'—qualified mainly because the risks of investing in ASEAN partner countries are seen to require the inducement of substantial profits. The Philippines is clearly antipathetic towards wholly foreign-owned businesses, as street demonstrations against them testify. Indonesia is concerned that mountains of debt will lead to loss of control to foreign interests at 'fire-sale' prices, a concern shared with Thailand, which nevertheless sees its own important investment opportunities in Laos, Cambodia and Viet Nam. Myanmar is easing controls on foreign investment but is fiscally (and politically) chaotic. A great deal of business in the ASEAN region is small-scale. Many of the larger business entities are of quite recent evolution. The means to develop transnational business within ASEAN is thus twice limited, once by the fact that large-scale enterprises are relatively few in number and again by the fact that a region-wide cadre of businesspeople with decades of international experience scarcely exists other than amongst Overseas Chinese and other 'immigrant' communities.

A tension between centripetal and centrifugal economic forces also exists within countries. The existence of extended metropolitan regions testifies to the strength of centralising forces. Wealth, in open economies, tends to flow to locations giving the greatest returns consonant with perceived risks. Concentrations of capital tend to become self-sustaining—unless and until diseconomies kick in. The latter include costs of land and labour—though usually not capital which costs pretty much the same anywhere in a state. They also include political risks, for urban work-forces—perhaps also urban administrations—have the nasty habit of becoming politicised. Peripheral locations can become attractive. Land is cheaper. So is labour. Officialdom may be a little more accommodating, especially when the environmental impacts of industry are considered. Small towns and even rural areas may then have significant advantages, especially if infrastructure is adequate and costs of transportation of both raw materials and finished products are easily met. Thus Thai capital is flowing into parts of Cambodia and Laos, more recently into areas close to the Myanmar border, employing cheaper labour.

Political forces

Centripetal and centrifugal forces are also at work at the political level. The mere fact that ASEAN now incorporates all but one of the region's states is itself a reflection of centralising forces, a measure of perceptions of commonality of interests vis-a-vis outsiders. For those countries that have most recently joined—Myanmar, Laos, Cambodia, earlier Viet

Nam—there is clearly a lessened risk of total political and economic marginalisation. The ASEAN policy of non-interference in each member's internal affairs is seen as a sufficient safeguard of national sovereignty, though given the significant numbers of each other's nationals in each other's countries there must always be difficulties involving such people. Engagement rather than confrontation is seen as the proper 'Asian way' towards the amelioration of some of the harsher attitudes and actions of governments towards their own people.

At the same time there is a need for regional solidarity in the face of perceived political and economic threats from outside. These include Chinese claims to the South China Sea, its islands, its sea-floor and its waters. Despite the fact that there are overlapping and competing territorial claims amongst ASEAN countries, they have nevertheless presented a single position to China which for long has argued that the South China Sea has been inalienably part of China for centuries past and that any discussions on the issue could only be conducted on a bilateral basis. China has now agreed to multilateral discussions while still reserving its position on the matter of sovereignty.

It is also evident that ASEAN is prepared to take a unified position against both the EC and NAFTA in relation to trade matters should the need arise. Less solidly it has also taken a position in the 'Asian values' debate. It has also shown itself willing to hold—at least for a time—a unified position on the question of international sanctions and other action in the face of human rights abuses. Nothing whatever was done, initially, in exerting diplomatic pressure upon Indonesian 'scorched earth' action in East Timor though both Malaysia and the Philippines offered to help 'pick up the pieces'.

Forces in ASEAN

This raises thorny issues of centripetal and centrifugal forces amongst and within the countries of ASEAN. The region's history shows that, in principle, cultural and physical diversity are not hindrances to the exercise of central authority. The empires of Sri Vijaya and Majapahit, like Mughal India, were large states by any reckoning. But their administration was necessarily decentralised in days of slow communications. Like their colonial successors, they were kept together basically by force or the threat of it. But, like the congeries of small states into which they split, rule was personal not territorial. Only colonial times saw the emergence of a new kind of state, one with defined boundaries, fixed and immutable at least in the short run. The region's modern states, successors to the colonial states before them, have proved to be remarkably resilient. Throughout the colonial period territorial agglomeration prevailed. The many small states of the Malay Peninsula, for example, had, by independence in 1957, been welded into a single unit, Malaya, which expanded again in 1962 to include Sabah, Sarawak and Singapore to form Malaysia. (Singapore left this federation in 1965.)

But history has left a number of actual and potential points of conflict between the region's nations. While Indonesia's 'Confrontation'—actually a minor war—with Malaysia was wound down with the replacement of Sukarno by Suharto as president, other points of tension remain. One is the Philippines' claim to Sabah. This is based upon the view that the Sultan of Sulu—to whose authority the Republic of the Philippines is successor—did not cede Sabah to what became the British North Borneo Company—to which Malaysia was the ultimate successor—but only leased it. The issue is very much on the back burner but the Philippines has never renounced its claim.

In some Peninsular Thai quarters the cession of the now-Malaysian states of Kedah, Perlis, Kelantan and Trengganu to the British has never been accepted. The 1970s saw an active separatist movement in that area aimed at combining these predominantly Malay states with other similar provinces on the Thai side to form a new Islamic state. Similarly there remain well-hidden fears that Thailand may at some future time attempt to reconstitute its ancient territory by incorporating all or most of Laos and Cambodia.

But the only overt territorial takeover, by Indonesia of East Timor, ultimately failed in the face of sustained diplomatic pressure from outside the region and a festering independence struggle on the land itself.

A number of other tension points were created by the whole question of who owns what and who has exclusive rights of use offshore, an issue never considered during colonial times. In addition to China's overarching claim in the South China Sea there are many others involving two or more ASEAN parties: between Myanmar and Thailand in the Andaman Sea, between Thailand and Malaysia in the northwestern part of the South China Sea, between Malaysia and Indonesia in the Celebes Sea, between Viet Nam and Cambodia in the Gulf of Thailand and many others. (See the collection of essays in Hill, Owen and Roberts, *Fishing in Troubled Waters* for details.)

Some have already been resolved by direct negotiation, as for instance Thailand's offshore boundary with Malaysia. Here a satisfactory compromise has been reached, including agreement that part of the Exclusive Economic Zone be exploited for mutual benefit. Less tractable is the case of the Spratley Islands and their vicinity, where there are multiple claims and military garrisons occupy different islands. Few of these claims are trivial, because there is every likelihood that offshore waters cover significant natural resources, including petroleum. For the moment there is agreement to 'make haste slowly' and to present a united front against claims from 'outside', that is both versions of the Chinese government.

So far as the territorial integrity of each country within the region is concerned the 'colonial glue' has stuck remarkably firmly. To be sure Singapore split from Malaysia but that was peacefully accomplished, the British in particular having exerted strong diplomatic pressure upon the Malaysian central government to ensure that the 'recalcitrant' Lee Kwan Yew and his colleagues were not brought to heel by force. No such pressure was initially exerted against Indonesia following its military invasion of East Timor in 1975 but United Nations pressure ultimately prevailed, permitting independence in 1999.

As in the colonial period the ultimate sanction in preserving the integrity of the state is force and this, or its threat, has been widely used in post-independence times. While local interests have sought to obtain a degree of independence from central governments using moral suasion alone, most have taken up arms. In Myanmar, for example, the central government has at no time since independence in 1947 controlled the whole of the national territory. In the south the Mon moved against the government while in the north Shan and Kachin continue resistance, in the case of the former still in an armed struggle. Whether a federal state structure would have satisfied these irredentists is a moot question, for at the very outset a centralised unitary state, in fact dominated by Burmans, was determined upon.

In contrast, Indonesia, by recognising local interests and a high degree of cultural diversity started out as a federal state—the United States of Indonesia—but quickly moved to a unitary structure, accepting the notion that federalism was an invitation to secession. That move has not been sufficient to forestall separatist movements, some still active. The 'Republic of the South Moluccas' has long had a 'government' in exile in the Netherlands. Aceh, once an independent kingdom, fought the Dutch and is now fighting the central government. The 'Free Papua' movement continues in West Irian.

Laos, Cambodia and Viet Nam fought serious civil wars that quickly became bound up with Cold War politics and so were internationalised. Conflict was not so much about the formation of new states but more about who should control undivided states. Loss of life was very substantial—4 million dead in Viet Nam alone. So was loss of infrastructure and the enormously wasteful diversion of resources into war.

By the late 1990s, however, none continued to experience civil conflict except Indonesia. In Thailand the Patani Liberation Front and other separatist movements have degenerated into occasional banditry rather than being cohesive organisations. The Communist insurrection that so seriously threatened Malaya (Peninsular Malaysia) has faded away in step with the decline of Communist states and the appeal of the ideology upon which they were founded. On the whole, politicians have succeeded in diverting the masses' attention away from questions of how nations' economic cakes should be divided to issues of how to ensure the cakes' growth.

This is not to suggest that internal conflicts have been fully resolved or that new points of tension will not emerge. Certainly there is little evidence of strong class-based political action. Although the proletariat is growing apace as the result of structural transformation of the economies there is no appealing mass ideology, no strong mass organisation. The oligarchs and the growing middle class are happy to see that situation continue. Whether strong, democratic trades unions will emerge to force governments to confront issues of social and economic equity is doubtful. Most governments, even authoritarian ones, have sufficient concern for their own survival to ensure that a modicum of worker welfare accompanies the growth in wealth. There is evidence that incomes are becoming more unequal—Malaysia is a case in point—but growth is so large and so recent that inequities are not a major issue. Employment is an issue but it too is becoming less pervasive in the face of continued—or revived—growth, and in many countries outside Indochina the demographic reality of a decreasing proportion of the population seeking to enter the workforce.

Regionalism and ethnicity

If class is not the area in which points of tension are likely to emerge or to continue, which are? While regionalism and ethnicity—broadly construed to include religious affiliation—do not necessarily combine to provide points of disagreement and political action, in Southeast Asia they coincide sufficiently often for both to be considered together. Regional income disparities are not easy to document, as many countries do not prepare estimates of regional Gross Domestic Product or of income. In this context perceptions are at least as important as realities, for both may lead to action.

There is little doubt that some of Indonesia's provinces—Aceh is most definitely one—see the centre as exploitative, grabbing 'their' wealth and giving little in return. In the Acehnese case, as in nearby Riau, the wealth is petroleum. In both cases, only a tiny fraction of the revenue they generate finds its way back from the central government. In other cases the wealth is land. There is little doubt that the taking of land, often with little or no compensation, for settlement purposes has been a fruitful source of tension—in southern and central Sumatera and in Kalimantan, for instance. Inland from Pontianak, western Kalimantan, Madurese settlers have been killed in considerable numbers by Dayaks whose traditional lands were occupied. This led to retaliation by Madurese and deaths on both sides at the hands of the military seeking to restore public order. There is little doubt that the settlement of thousands of Indonesians in East Timor was a potent factor in the civil war there, while similar settlements in West Irian continue to provoke a 'Papuan' reaction from peoples who are culturally, linguistically and physically very different. In that case the fact that virtually all of the government revenue generated by mining flows to Jakarta exacerbates tensions.

On the other hand, land seems not to be a major issue in conflicts in the Moluccas and Halmahera. These are partly religious—Christian versus Muslim—reinforced by prejudice against newcomers seen to be supported by the powers of the state. In the cities ethnic tension takes a different form. Business was and to some degree still is dominated by an alliance of Suharto family and cronies and Indonesian Chinese. (Some sources suggest that they owned or controlled four-fifths of all business activity, though this seems to be rather unlikely.) Here class and ethnicity coincide to form a potentially explosive mixture. It is not yet clear whether the new government has the political will to develop—let alone enforce—some form of affirmative action, perhaps something along the lines of Malaysia's New Economic Policy of 1969 which drew the Malay community more firmly into the modern economy and has put greater wealth into its hands. Equally it is unclear whether the oligarchs would accept such action or would react by sequestering even more of their wealth offshore.

Local grievances have played important roles in other parts of insular Southeast Asia though for the moment they are quiescent rather than active. The anti-government guerilla war in parts of upland Luzon has now, hopefully, been largely defused by the grant of a measure of political autonomy. Again a major issue was control of land, with the then government happy to commandeer land for hydroelectric schemes that would mainly benefit lowland capitalist interests or to grant the same interests large concessions for mining. A larger conflict in Mindanao, again over land but reinforced by Christian–Muslim differences, flares up periodically. There remain those who still seek the setting up of an independent Islamic state. Just how this might be done on the ground, given the complex interdigitation of Muslim and Christian areas, is highly problematic.

In Peninsular Malaysia the proponents of a new Islamic state incorporating the four northernmost Malay-dominant states are few and inactive. Both the central Alliance government and the opposition-controlled Islamic-oriented state governments are fortunate that the latter have never openly flirted with secession. Across the South China Sea, though, secessionist sentiment still exists amongst Chinese and Kadazans in Sabah where, in the early 1970s under Tun Mustapha, there was a real prospect of action in that direction, forestalled by a substantial reinforcement of the army. (The 'cover story' was an increase of tension with the Philippines. In private Mustapha, Sabah's Chief Minister, made no secret of his ambition to reconstitute a Sulu state incorporating Sabah on one side and the Sulu Archipelago on the other. He was also using his personal aircraft to smuggle arms into the Philippines. Mustapha was a Suluk.)

Given past events it would be a very brave person who would forecast widespread sweetness and light for the future. Though Southeast Asians have necessarily had many centuries' practice in coping with pluralism, both governments and individuals obviously still have serious difficulties in so doing. Many seem to adhere to a crude form of Social Darwinism by which some forms of society—Burman, Thai, Vietnamese (*Kinh*), and many others—are seen to be inherently superior to others—Mon, Shan, Kachin, Miao, Meo, Cham, Rhadé and dozens of others. Consequently social policies are overtly or covertly assimilationist. A 'real Thai' or a 'real Khmer' must therefore be Buddhist, for Buddhism is the state religion. A 'real Filipino' must be a Roman Catholic, though perhaps not as former President Ramos is a Protestant. (Southeast Asia is not alone in this, of course. Neither Australia nor New Zealand has ever had a 'native' Prime Minister.) Only in Malaysia and Singapore is there a deliberate policy of ensuring minority representation at the highest levels of government, though they and all other governments have yet to take the same affirmative step with respect to women—to a degree both legally and in practice a disadvantaged group throughout the region.

The politics of gender remain strongly patriarchal throughout the region, although there have long been women members of parliament where such a body exists and their number has been slowly increasing. In Thailand's 1996 election, for example, there were 360 women candidates, about 18.5 per cent, up from 10 per cent in the early 1990s. But none has had real power, not even Corazon Aquino, the former Philippines President, who was essentially the creature of one faction within that country's ruling group. Women ministers tend to be relegated to 'caring' ministries such as health, welfare and 'women's affairs'. The subordinate position of women is demonstrated in both precept and practice. For example, women do not universally have the right to inherit property equally with men, to retain their maiden name following marriage, to determine the place of family residence, or to initiate divorce proceedings. Should they marry a foreigner he may have serious difficulty obtaining a residence permit. While access to education is in principle open to both sexes, practice may be rather different, with disproportionately large numbers of males at the higher levels, especially at university, where male faculty still predominate. The same situation exists in business, where the 'glass ceiling' is particularly thick and women are often paid less than men for doing the same job.

Personalism and government

It is sometimes argued, especially in the west, that Asia, including Southeast Asia, has yet to move fully to truly civil forms of government, that is to say to states in which the rule of law prevails rather than the rule of persons. Earlier it was suggested that the traditional state in the region was based upon people, not territory. Even today it is clear that patron–client relationships play a major role both in the structuring of its societies and in the political process, certainly to a greater degree than in most western countries. In this context two major questions arise: 'To what degree is this so?' and 'Does it really matter?'

Though the sociology of ruling elites is not a particularly well developed field in the region it is nevertheless possible to discern some outlines, especially so far as the political process is concerned. As is well known, the military plays a significant role in several countries and it is clear that cliques, based in part upon relationships developed in military academies, can become politically important, as they have done in Myanmar, the Philippines and in Thailand. Whether the same is true in Singapore, where certain military officers hold Cabinet rank, is debatable but more than once in the last several decades there have been rumours of a military-backed coup. One such allegedly was to replace Lee Kwan Yew, then Prime Minister, by his then Finance Minister, Goh Keng Swee. Suharto in Indonesia also relied heavily upon his generals and the military has been substantially involved in business. Myanmar, of course, is essentially governed by a military clique. The military, because it lacks strong checks and balances to power, can readily become a playground for patrons and clients.

But the civil sphere is by no means immune. It is sometimes claimed that the Philippines, since independence, has been ruled successively by various factions within an oligarchy based upon a series of partly interlocking systems of patronage—interlocking in part because of intermarriage amongst the families concerned. Ferdinand Marcos and his 'Ilocos gang' were to a degree interlopers in this cosy arrangement, though his rule perfectly illustrates the strength of patronage networks at the highest levels. Suharto, with his family and favoured associates, is another example. Opponents of Malaysian Prime Minister Mahathir claim that he is the centre of a similar network, one in which, they claim, public position is used for private gain.

There seems to be little doubt that cronyism is alive and well in much of the region. The more important consideration is the degree to which it has aided or hindered economic growth. Here some judgements can be made, though necessarily on the basis of incomplete evidence for investigative finality is far from having been reached. Nevertheless it is clear that the Marcos clique systematically plundered the Filippino treasury as well as diverting large sums to economically useless prestige projects. The latter part of its 'reign' was a low-growth or no-growth period during which hundreds of millions of dollars were sequestered abroad. The Suharto family is alleged to have stashed similar sums abroad. This kind of action is economically particularly damaging. With some justification it can be argued that corruption does not matter greatly because there are limits to personal consumption and 'dirty money' is as good as clean money when it comes to productive investment. But where, as in these cases, money is lodged abroad in large quantities the effects are considerable. Local currencies weaken and potentially productive capital is lost.

The social and political effects of patronage networks are more debatable. Upward mobility can be achieved by 'hitching your wagon to a rising star'. But ability tends to be devalued in this circumstance. One great attraction of Communism in the region was that it encouraged the mobilisation of effort from all levels of society and allowed ability to emerge through the party ranks—provided that its basic precepts were accepted. Can it truly be said that present-day social structures achieve such objectives? Throughout the region, except perhaps in Myanmar, political oppositions are disunited and weak, lacking both broad support and a solid ideological base. Unlike the parliamentary democracies of the Asia–Pacific region they do not, generally, form a credible alternative government.

Democracies and autocracies

Southeast Asia's parliamentary democracies, if that they be, are clearly of a particular kind. Malaysia and Singapore have had the same party in control since independence, the Alliance in the former and the People's Action Party in the latter. Both parties have manoeuvred to retain power by holding out financial inducements to opposition politicians, by taking up planks from their political platforms, by threatening and administering 'punishment' to such segments of the political structure as have the temerity to vote against the ruling parties. Such 'punishment' commonly takes the form of restricted government expenditures in the recalcitrant state. Recourse has also been had to administrative detention or to other legal action. By contrast Thailand has seen a series of 'revolving governments'. In none of these cases can it be convincingly argued that the political process has seriously damaged economic prospects, though the effects of Malaysia's imposition of controls on foreign capital have yet to be seen fully. The governments of Malaysia and Singapore, of course, argue that their brands of political stability have been essential to growth.

Authoritarianism, however, has not been notably successful in promoting economic growth. True Myanmar has begun to attract limited foreign investment, much of it from other ASEAN countries, but successive authoritarian regimes have not been notably successful in stimulating the economy. Viet Nam is also opening its economy under a socialist form of authoritarian government and is enjoying modest growth, much of it eaten up by a burgeoning population. Laos and Cambodia, also authoritarian, labour under serious structural difficulties. Laos adds environmental problems. It is difficult to see what their future might be. For Indonesia, the Suharto era was one of substantial structural change and, despite 'the family' having skimmed off a great deal of cream, also one of growth, especially on Java, much less so in some of the Outer Islands. But failure to secure the political succession—the fatal flaw of many authoritarian regimes—as well as inadequate fiscal control have clearly led to a substantial frittering away of past gains. International venture capital is extremely footloose and perceptions of political instability can lead to rapid changes in capital flows. The nations no longer have the degree of economic, even political, autonomy they may once have possessed. Others are calling at least some of the shots in an increasingly linked world.

Globalisation, growth and structural transitions

Cores and peripheries

Increasing international linkages are only one part of the globalisation process. They are clearly 'space-specific' in that particular parts of countries, as well as particular kinds and manners of people, are very differently affected. The economic cores of the region's wealthier countries are already very much part of the global economy. Participants, if they have the money, can jump on a plane and be in any global centre within a day. Yet peripheral regions within countries can often be reached only after several days' travel. Their global links are quite limited. Such areas are simply irrelevant in the new global order. In some parts of the world, the Pacific Islands is one, it would be a matter of no concern to anyone other than those directly involved if whole countries disappeared. (Nauru is a case in point. So is Tuvalu.) A similar situation exists in Southeast Asia's peripheral areas. It would be a matter of complete indifference to global capital if Laos and much of its adjoining hill country, most parts of Nusatenggara, all of West Irian, most of Borneo, sank into the sea. Such areas are also politically unimportant—unless they threaten the territorial integrity of the state by threatening secession, as some have already. Thus far the responses from the centre have been mixed, repression usually prevailing over conciliation. It can be argued that increasing gradients of wealth between cores and peripheries within countries will eventually be diminished by the action of free market forces and by people simply transferring themselves to cores, such cores expanding spatially as wealth increases. It can also be held that failure of peripheral regions to participate proportionately in the benefits of growth is an inadequate basis for schismatic political activity.

But relative poverty is very far from being the only characteristic of marginal regions, for it is often paralleled by major cultural divisions. Existing national boundaries by no means reflect cultural realities. Myanmar is acutely aware of the substantial cultural commonalties between Shan and Thai and clearly sees membership of ASEAN as a means of forestalling possible Thai expansion into its northeast.

Given the great disparities of population, power and wealth between Thailand and Laos it would be ridiculous to foresee a 'Greater Lao' state incorporating Thailand's northeastern Isan region, which is culturally and linguistically at least as much Lao as it is Thai. But the converse is not so fanciful. Laos is a state put together by the French, politically isolated, weak, poor. Again it seems entirely plausible that in ASEAN membership it sees a bulwark against becoming a bone of contention between Thailand on one side and a resurgent Viet Nam on the other.

Cambodia, although larger, is a similar case. Historically it is a well-nibbled bone between Thailand and Viet Nam. (Its three northwestern provinces were restored to it, from Thailand, less than a century ago.) Two decades ago it seemed that the Cambodians were bent upon self-destruction. Whether that calamity is postponed indefinitely or not remains to be seen but again, as a politically and economically weak state, it must be vulnerable to external pressure, as it is to internal pressures, some arising from sharp differences in levels of wealth, some from political factionalism, some from the question of the royal succession.

Insular Southeast Asia also has a weak state: East Timor. By most measures it is desperately poor, somewhat more so than the rest of the island for much of its urban infrastructure—such as it was—has been destroyed by Indonesian forces and militias. It has serious longstanding problems of environmental degradation in the interior, has little active agricultural export (mainly coffee) and, potentially, the hostility of its neighbour. Offshore petroleum resources exist but it will require huge investments to exploit them. It will clearly require support if it is to survive. Australia may provide some of it though if it does it will likely be seen as 'neo-colonialist' by Indonesia. A delicate political balancing act is clearly in store.

Growth

Most Southeast Asian economies suffered a downturn in the late 1990s both resulting from and resulting in some loss of business confidence.

Those which were less involved in the global economy weathered the 'Asian Crisis' better than the others since they retain substantial economic autonomy. Poverty has its rewards! To what degree fiscal mismanagement, including high levels of both internal and external debt, especially the latter, and other deeper structural causes played a role in triggering that crisis will have to await detailed post-mortems. It may be doubted that the crisis is over, though by 2000 Thailand, Malaysia, Singapore and to a lesser degree the Philippines were showing signs of resurgence. The Indonesian economy is very much in the balance, largely because of continuing political uncertainties. Singapore, as the region's major creditor, may be taking this as an opportunity to expand ownership of the region's businesses by buying struggling companies at fire-sale prices, but it is not yet clear that this is so.

Much will depend upon growth in the global economy and upon investors' perceptions of this as expressed in the major stock exchanges. What is likely is that rates of growth will slow amongst the region's wealthier countries, because in a period of overall growth wealthy countries invariably grow at lower rates than poor ones. Sustained annual growth rates in excess of 5 per cent annually from a low base are not difficult to contemplate. Such rates may be more difficult to achieve in the wealthier countries. However, the demand for services could be expanding more rapidly than the demand for commodities, manufactured or otherwise. If this is the case Singapore, Malaysia, even Thailand to some degree, should be well placed to meet demand. Thailand, for example, is aggressively marketing medical services in the region.

So far, Singapore alone has moved to a post-industrial economy. While the others still move into this stage it will be well placed to benefit both from offshore investment in middle- and lower-end manufacturing and in service provision. Although post-industrial Europe is moving some of its manufacturing eastwards and North America is doing the same southwards, manufacturing in Southeast Asia's less developed countries is still likely to remain competitive despite greater distances. (In fact distance is steadily becoming less crucial as transportation costs relative to total costs continue to fall—though vulnerable to rises in the prices of fuels.)

The region's competitive edge lies largely in labour costs and, for some countries, in bureaucratic efficiency. This edge will not last forever. For one thing, the proportion and numbers of entrants to the workforce have already begun to fall, especially in Singapore, Malaysia and Thailand. This trend will certainly spread as fertility rates fall throughout the region. While this demographic process tends to push up the cost of labour in any country a countervailing remedy is 'temporarily' to import labour. This avoids the cost of closing plants locally and setting up again in a lower labour-cost area. It tends to push down the cost of competing labour drawn from local sources and has the significant advantage that people can be sent home to become someone else's concern in the event of an economic downturn. Both Malaysia and Singapore use this strategy, while Thailand seems to be responding in part by developing a new industrial base in its border area with Myanmar so as to draw upon cheap labour.

The political implications of the international movement of labour are less clear. For Malaysia importation from Indonesia and Muslim areas of the southern Philippines has the effect of strengthening *bumiputeras* against 'immigrant races', not that the latter can do much about it. But with migration may come settlement. Singapore's location and the power of its bureaucracy can effectively prevent the latter. But elsewhere borders are porous and governments are not necessarily able to send newcomers home even if they want to. With settlement may come demands for political rights and it is by no means clear that these could be denied.

One possible scenario of structural change is that some countries in the region will either not develop fully fledged manufacturing economies or will very quickly move through that stage to become 'post-industrial' in short order. A possible candidate is Malaysia, already a capital exporter. Until the Asian crisis it seemed possible that it could suffer the consequences of high labour costs and be forced, like Singapore, to develop 'high-end' manufacturing and to shift to services. Such, in fact is still planned for the environs of Kuala Lumpur, though given the imposition of controls on capital repatriation and the country's high level of debt it is a little difficult to see how this might proceed at the rate envisaged. (The Malaysian economy has been kept afloat in part because of a massive devaluation of its currency.) Malaysia's economy has long been exposed to global economic risks, especially when it was basically a primary producer. Perhaps this has conditioned its leaders to take risks and to 'roll with the blow' that a high level of international exposure entails.

Assessing region-wide risk of economic decline is necessarily subjective. The pace of structural change makes it even more difficult. The past is relatively easy. Subsistence agriculture, especially unirrigated cropping, is subject to the vagaries of nature. Irrigation clearly reduces risk. In insular Southeast Asia the risk of declines in the production of crops like rubber, oil palm, cocoa and coconut from natural causes is insignificant though locally the two last, especially, are subject to disease and pests. Such commercial crops are much more vulnerable to price fluctuations on the international markets (because producer countries are price-takers, not price-makers), to rises in the cost of labour and to adverse changes in terms of trade. But poor, substantially self-supporting economies like those of Myanmar and remoter parts of the region generally are to a degree insulated from global markets and are thus more secure.

Exposure to global markets has unquestionably brought large increases in wealth, a number of countries sustaining annual growth rates in excess of 5 per cent over extended periods. Has the price of this been increased vulnerability? For the fortunate possessors of petroleum and gas the answer is probably negative, though only in respect of those commodities, since through OPEC (Organisation of Petroleum Exporting Countries) they are indeed price-makers. One of the early hopes of ASEAN was that its concerted action would result in the setting of export prices for a number of the primary commodities in which the region specialised. One such was tin. Yet the market collapsed, partly as a result of a swing away from tin-plate to aluminium cans, leaving substantial debt. Other attempts to corner the market and set prices have never got off the ground.

The region's export economies are clearly vulnerable to international markets. They are also vulnerable to protectionist sentiment. While the world's largest economy, the US, has espoused the cause of freeing up international trade, abolishing quotas, reducing tariffs, in reality its government has shown itself very ready to do exactly the opposite where the interests of some American producers are seen to be threatened. This, of course, is an ongoing complaint by the Cairns Group of primary producers, including Australia and New Zealand. If sanctions can be invoked against them why not others? Were Silicon Valley seriously to be threatened by Southeast Asian chip producers would the US not act to keep out their goods? (During the Carter administration a move initiated by US peanut growers to keep out palm oil came close to success.) One countervailing fact is that US- European- and Japanese-owned multinationals derive considerable profits from producing offshore in Southeast Asia and might consequently be expected to oppose restriction of imports from Southeast Asia of the goods they produce.

Education, health and economic growth

Education

Education is obviously one of the many keys to economic growth, as anywhere. The precise nature of the payoffs derived from investment in education are very much dependent upon a matching of demand with supply, a particularly difficult matter given that education involves a lead-time—from investment to pay-off—of a decade or more. To over-educate people is wasteful. To under-educate them is to see lack of appropriate education become a constraint to growth.

In the region generally, the proportion of the population being educated ranges between 17 per cent (Myanmar) and 27 per cent (Philippines). What is particularly striking is that all of the poorer countries—Myanmar, Laos, Cambodia, Viet Nam—have a relatively low proportion of their people at school even though they have large numbers of young people, in fact 17, 18, 20 and 21 per cent of the total population respectively. Singapore and Thailand have a relatively low proportion of people of school age (roughly

5–19 years), Malaysia and the Philippines rather more, for they are at an earlier stage in the demographic transition. Thailand, for example, has about 70 per cent of the people in this age-group at school. Viet Nam has only 60 per cent. More striking are the proportions of tertiary-level students: Thailand 2.7 per cent of students at this level, Viet Nam only 0.8 per cent. This is not to argue that GNP and the proportion of students in tertiary education are necessarily directly related. Malaysia is substantially more wealthy than the Philippines yet only 2 per cent of its people are in tertiary-level education compared with 11 per cent in the Philippines. By contrast, Singapore has 17 per cent of its students at this level. Yet all the poorer countries have less than 4 per cent of their students in tertiary education.

The judgement as to what constitutes 'over-' or 'under-' education is necessarily subjective. The Philippines arguably over-educates. Tens if not hundreds of thousands of its overseas workers, mostly employed in low-grade tasks such as domestic servants, have tertiary-level diplomas. By contrast Thailand, and perhaps Malaysia, under-educate. Certainly, informed opinion holds that Thailand's future growth is likely to be hindered by lack of adequate skills. Here emerges the knotty problem of making judgements as to relative quality of education. Arguably, secondary education in Malaysia is better than in Thailand or in the Philippines. Certainly there have been few complaints about inadequacies at this level though some about inadequate skills in English at tertiary level. What is also certain is that basic literacy and numeracy are likely to be insufficient to support rapid economic growth, especially the jump up from low-skilled tasks such as demanded by clothing and footwear manufacturing, to high-skilled computer-based manufacturing and services. In Singapore, for example, every student at both secondary and tertiary level is computer-literate. Virtually everyone has access to a computer. Even primary students use computers and many own one. The 'soft infrastructure' basis for its future growth is thus firmly laid.

In the poorer countries a particular issue is the degree to which abandonment of socialist principles and individualisation of production is leading to children being withdrawn from school in order to increase the availability of family labour and thus family production. There is good evidence that this is happening in Laos and Cambodia, for example. Some would argue that in a labour-surplus situation this may not matter too much. There are, nevertheless, important implications for education as a route to social mobility and for future growth as structural change and demands for higher levels of skills are, barring total economic collapse, inevitable.

Health

As might be expected where levels of income have such a large range as in the region, the provision of health services and levels of health vary greatly in the region, especially spatially. Urban areas are generally adequately supplied with doctors and hospital beds, though whether all who need them necessarily have access to them is quite another matter. The average ratio of doctors to people is around one to 600–1000 people. In the countryside, especially remoter areas, matters may be quite otherwise with one doctor to 40 000 people being not uncommon in parts of Myanmar, Cambodia, Laos, of Nusatenggara and West Irian. The rural areas of the wealthier countries are reasonably well provided for by fixed or travelling clinics staffed by paramedics and some provision exists for the more seriously ill to be passed up the chain of medical care. Community medicine and maternal care, including family planning, are particular concerns of such clinics. The result has been substantial falls in death rates, especially maternal and neonatal death rates, though overall these are still somewhat higher in rural than in urban areas.

In most towns and cities basic services such as reasonably clean water and latrines exist, though everyone does not necessarily use them. Even where water is not potable most are aware of the need to boil it. Consequently, levels of gastro-intestinal disorders are fairly low though parts of the region, even those best served, still occasionally experience epidemics of cholera. The cleanest cities—and the dirtiest—are also subject to 'people-encouraged' maladies such as dengue fever and sexually transmitted diseases, including HIV/AIDS. The former is mosquito-borne—mostly by *Aedes* species—and these breed freely in urban detritus such as cans, old tyres and anything else that can hold water. The latter include gonorrhoea, rampant in some areas, as well as HIV/AIDS.

HIV/AIDS is not yet having quite the devastating demographic effects that it is creating in parts of Africa such as Rwanda though, as in Africa, the poorer parts of the region lack the financial means to pay for drugs to control it. There is considerable scope for growing numbers of cases; in Thailand, to take one example, surveys have indicated high proportions of carriers amongst prostitutes and high levels of men using their services, though both are now falling. In the region generally, Thailand and Cambodia comprise the epicentre, with around one person in 80 being an HIV carrier. Nearby Myanmar has just over one carrier in 100 and Malaysia roughly one in 300. Outside these Singapore, Brunei and Viet Nam have one carrier in 800–1000 and the other countries one in 3000–4000. There seems little doubt that this has sparked a trade in 'untouched' women from Myanmar, Laos, even southwestern China. It is also triggering a change in male behaviours, though sexual promiscuity throughout much of the region is fostered by labour mobility resulting in men being away from their homes for often extended periods.

Both male and female migrant workers often live and work in less than satisfactory conditions, as do many rural–urban migrants. Crowding, poor ventilation and insanitary behaviours have led to a significant resurgence in tuberculosis, very much a working-class disease. Ironically its spread partly relates to success in controlling it. Patients under treatment initially feel so much better that they may not complete it and this aids the development of antibiotic-resistant strains of the bacillus.

Rural areas have also seen a resurgence in another old enemy, malaria, which like dengue is mosquito-borne, this one by *Anopheles* species. The great expansion of rice agriculture in the nineteenth and twentieth centuries probably reduced the incidence of the disease. Though *Anopheles* breed in wet rice-fields, fish are great predators of larvae, keeping levels moderate. On sloping lands cleared for agriculture, provided that temperatures are above about 20°C, below which the malarial parasite dies. Mosquitoes, especially *Anopheles maculatus*, breed abundantly in sunlit streams. But while land clearance clearly assists the resurgence of malaria, foolish use of prophylactics—substances ingested to make the blood poisonous to the parasite—makes matters worse by fostering the emergence of resistant strains. The area around Pailin in western Cambodia is notorious. It is clear that in terms of control, science is barely half a step ahead of both the tuberculosis bacillus and *Plasmodium,* the malarial parasite.

Biological vulnerability is not merely confined to human disease. Most *Hevea* rubber is clonal, meaning that all trees from one original clone are genetically identical. Single varieties of rice are used over very large areas. As plant breeders put new varieties onto the market so too do disease-causing organisms evolve. In rice, for example, tungro virus and the brown plant-hopper were once relatively unimportant but are now seriously damaging. Modern genetic technology can 'engineer' ways out of these dilemmas, for example by inserting 'foreign' genes into plants to achieve the desired characteristics whether higher yields, better keeping qualities, disease resistance or whatever. Southeast Asian farmers have improved their crops for centuries but what is being seen here is totally new. The danger is of economic dependence upon genetically modified crops which then are wiped out by the unforeseen evolution of pests and diseases. Genetic uniformity is risky. Diversity spreads risk.

Environmental issues

The maintenance of diversity is one of the considerations at the base of forest preservation, one of the more actively supported environmental issues in the region. While many of the arguments in favour of conservation are couched in moralistic terms, there are good practical reasons for it. Southeast Asian forests are one of the globe's remaining storehouses of hugely diverse genetic resources—both plant and animal. Yet despite centuries of biological work the nature and extent of this storehouse is only marginally known, because most biologists work in temperate lands. At the end of the 1980s the forest area comprised around 49 per cent of the total area of Southeast Asia, down from 66 per cent at the end of the 1960s, and falling by around 1 per cent each year. Viet Nam, the Philippines and Thailand had notably low percentages of forest cover, respectively 17, 22 and 29 per cent. Java and Bali had less than 10 per cent of forest cover. In Sumatera, 70 per cent of lowland forests had gone by the end of the 1980s. By contrast Kalimantan was still 74 per cent forested, rising to 84 per cent in West Irian.

These data are for forest cover—not for loggable commercial forests. What may be the proportion of the remaining cover that has already been logged is simply not known. Indeed the whole issue of 'deforestation' is seriously confused, because some writers refer to selectively logged areas as 'deforested', which manifestly they are not. What is clear is that even selective logging damages genetic resources—quite apart from its immediate, severe though short-lived effects. Harvesting 'commercial species'—now several times more numerous than they were 50 years ago—constitutes a form of selection pressure upon such species, favouring non-commercial species—in loggers' terms 'rubbish trees'. What this may mean in terms of habitat loss, changes in the balance amongst species and genetic loss is yet scarcely understood.

In terms of loss of total biomass there is firmer knowledge. No agricultural crop has a biomass approaching that of mature forest, not even oil palm or rubber, so that the replacement of forests by crops results in a fall to around one-third where tree-crops replace forest with a decline to around 1–2 per cent where annual crops replace the forest. In global terms this severely reduces the ability of the vegetation to sequester carbon dioxide (CO_2) leading to increases in the level of this gas in the atmosphere. (The relationship of vegetation loss to CO_2 uptake may not be linear since higher levels of CO_2 may lead to increased levels of its uptake.) As everyone knows, enhanced CO_2 is thought to lead to higher temperatures.

If this is so, then the continuing scale of forest removals in the region must have significant global effects. The present levels will not continue indefinitely for two important reasons. First and obviously the remaining forest is a finite resource. Second, the value of what remains will rise as the quantity reduces. The rate at which this happens will depend not only upon the global market for tropical hardwoods but also demand for particular Southeast Asian species and the degree to which they can be substituted by species from as yet only partly exploited sources such as Amazonia. The basic fact is, however, that many of Southeast Asia's hardwoods are too cheap. Consequently much is used for low-grade purposes such as shuttering in concrete construction. But timber exploitation, both legal and illegal, is intimately linked with the politically powerful and there is simply little political will significantly to reduce the annual cut, though Thailand is a noteworthy exception.

Deforestation brings in its train two noteworthy consequences, one clear-cut, one less so. While end-of-dry-season clearance and firing have existed amongst traditional shifting cultivators for millennia, they now have little or no impact on mature forests because the areas they cultivate are virtually all in secondary forest, scrub, even grassland. More serious is damage by landless lowland farmers who often follow the roads cut by loggers, there to develop smallholdings, many of them impermanent. World Bank estimates in 1990 for Indonesia suggest that around half of all clearance was by such small farmers with another 30 per cent or so being cleared under land development projects. The scale of such clearances is so large that significant air pollution results from the smoke they generate, disrupting aerial navigation and road traffic, and causing increases in asthmas and other respiratory disorders in the susceptible. These effects extend to neighbouring Singapore and Malaysia.

More debatable is the effect of forest removals on the fabric of the land. As mentioned earlier, conventional wisdom holds that deforestation results in accelerated erosion, more frequent and more intense flooding, rapid siltation of dams and reservoirs and many other sequelae. It cannot be denied that these exist, sometimes causing serious economic loss. The real difficulty is distinguishing between what would happen anyway and what is induced by human activity. Thus cutting vegetation does not itself generate sediment on slopes for it actually adds large quantities of branches and foliage to the forest ecosystem thus protecting the soil. True tree roots die, possibly decreasing slope stability, increasing landslide risk but selective logging takes only a few stems per hectare so the effects cannot be large. Rather it is cutting roads—without consolidation of cut material—that leads to loss of soil permeability by soil compression using heavy machines. Traditional extraction methods, using animal power, are much less damaging but much more expensive, at least in terms of direct costs to loggers. Using them would erode the region's competitive position, which is economically and politically intolerable, so they will not be used.

Mention was made earlier of the role the region's forests have in acting as a 'sink' for the 'greenhouse' gas CO_2. This naturally leads to the question of possible effects of global warming and of a possible rise in global sea levels. Warming is commonly modelled statistically in Global Circulation Models (GCMs). Unfortunately the region is a poor source of data for the construction of GCMs. Only at a very few stations have temperature records been kept for more than a century. (The Bogor Botanic Garden is one place they have.) Many are located in cities where the development of the urban heat island has been especially rapid since the 1960s both as urban areas have expanded, trapping heat, especially at night, in their very fabric, and also as air-conditioners, pumping out heat, have come into general use. In any case the spatial resolution of GCMs—grids of about 4 degrees of latitude by 5 degrees of longitude—is quite inadequate so that fronts, cyclones, even Hadley cell circulation are very poorly represented. So are the diversities of land use.

The cynic might suggest that by the time the climate changes significantly there will be too little forest left to worry about its effects. In fact these are virtually unknown. Warming would probably result in some species—such as the Dipterocarps—colonising higher elevations, though whether all the vegetation zones would simply march upslope and into higher latitudes is highly conjectural. Much of the equatorial zone would also become wetter and cloudier, reducing evaporation. This would certainly encourage the growth of epiphytes coupled with greater warmth, and might result in faster growth rates and higher levels of phytomass, especially at higher altitudes. Should a rise in sea level occur an expansion of mangrove, probably mainly at the expense of freshwater swamp forest, would be expected.

In urban areas and around high-value agricultural land the major response to higher sea levels would likely be embanking, though its costs are substantial. As is shown by work on coastal areas already suffering from marine encroachment along parts of the western coast of Peninsular Malaysia, the most cost-effective tactic is abandonment, though in those parts of the region more dependent upon agriculture compensatory development elsewhere would be required.

Rather more important may be questions of the impact of climatic change upon crops. Crude though they be, current GCMs predict an increase in rainfall as well as of temperature. Combined with the yield-enhancing effects of higher levels of carbon dioxide, many crops would increase production. But the effects would be far from uniform. Increased cloudiness in low-latitude areas would lead to reduced yields of rice, maize and rubber mainly in the range of 10–15 per cent, though oil palm would show an increase. Higher latitudes would see significantly higher yields of rice, by as much as a third in Myanmar. To some degree management strategies may compensate for climatic changes, for example by planting annual crops earlier. But this might not be feasible. In Luzon, for example, earlier planting of rice would lead to its grain-filling growth stage coinciding with strong seasonal winds, leading to loss.

One of the predictions of current GCMs is that atmospheric circulation would become more vigorous—more wind, more of the time. The economic consequences of this in the typhoon zone—roughly within 100 kilometres of the sea, north of about 8°N latitude—would probably be very substantial. The Philippines already loses about 1–2 per cent of its GDP to natural disasters—mainly tropical cyclones—every year. This amount would probably increase. More vigorous circulation would see an intensification of the ENSO (El Niño Southern Oscillation), one effect of which would be more intense drought. The El Niño of 1990–91, for example, caused a loss of over US$750 million in the Philippines, a figure likely to be augmented if droughts are longer, more intense or more frequent. Forecasting rice yields in Java indicates that yield declines in El Niño years would be greater than in normal years. There is good evidence that the frequency of El Niño is increasing.

Vulnerability to other kinds of natural disasters will probably decline in the years ahead, not because most are amenable to control—though soil conservation is effective—but because improved communications and better preparedness will mitigate their worst effects. The two keys are wealth and will. Most rural homes and many urban ones are built of cheap, light materials, vulnerable to wind, flood and volcanic ash-fall. As wealth increases this situation will improve though it would be unfortunate if the indigenous 'stilt-house' style of architecture were to be abandoned, at least in flood-prone areas. The political will to prepare for calamities is another matter; there is little political mileage to be gained from preparing for uncertain eventualities. Likewise making good calamitous damage is often piecemeal and grudging, too often seen as an opportunity for the enrichment of the corrupt.

The response of governments to environmental insecurities raises a broader issue, that of insecurity generally. It cannot be said that personal freedom and property are entirely secure anywhere in the region. Even Singapore, its 'national socialist' paradise—the phrase is Dr Goh Keng Swee's—has its small list of those disaffected with government who so fear persecution that they find it politic to live in exile. Both Singapore and neighbouring Malaysia retain colonial-era legal powers of arrest and detention for reasons other than criminal. Other jurisdictions—Myanmar is one, Cambodia another—on occasion dispense with the legal formalities. The ordinary person-in-the-street has something to fear from the arbitrary exercise of government power. He or she may also have rather more to fear from the arbitrary exercise of personal power, sometimes at the point of a gun. Parts of the region may be insecure at times, as is much of northeastern Myanmar, parts of Laos, recently the highway linking Vientiane and the royal capital Luang Prabang, the Sulu Sea—home to pirates for centuries—and, increasingly, parts of Indonesia.

Cities, though, are reasonably secure (Phnom Penh at night is not). They have quite other problems. Amongst them only Singapore—because it can afford it—has succeeded in moving beyond the 'grow now, clean up later' phase. However much the foreign press may play up the petty restrictions upon smoking and chewing gum—not to mention endless exhortations against such mildly antisocial behaviour as failing to flush the toilet—the city mostly lives up to its sedulously fostered 'clean and green' image, though its air can still be filthy. (City authorities prefer to keep quiet about the problems experienced in keeping some species alive at the Jurong Bird Park surrounded on all sides by its major industrial area.)

Most other cities and towns continue to experience major environmental problems. Solid waste is not necessarily collected and where it is it may be simply dumped in stinking heaps there to be worked over by armies of scavengers. What such may be like is vividly described in Mochtar Lubis's *Twilight in Djakarta*.

Disposal of liquid wastes, including sewage, also leaves much to be desired. In the very worst slums what pigs and dogs do not scavenge runs whither it may into noisome ponds, streams and estuaries, blackening the water, fouling the air.

Industrial wastes are often simply dumped near the factories that produce them or, if liquid, discharged with limited treatment—sometimes none—into nearby waterways, some of which are also used for irrigation and even domestic water. Discharges from industrial estates in urban fringe areas are a potent cause of farmers giving up cultivation. In rural areas they are a fruitful source of conflict with agriculturalists and fisherfolk, even householders who depend upon rivers for domestic supply.

Finale

These are problems of growth. Should growth continue they will eventually be resolved. But will growth continue? There seems little doubt that so much of the region's economy is bound up with the global capitalist system that growth of one entails the growth of the other. But is any part of the region's economies 'vital' to other, larger economies?

The answer must be a resounding 'No'. The days when Britain's interest in Malaya as its major source of foreign currency, when the 'Free World' depended upon vital strategic commodities such as rubber and tin, are long gone. The capitalist world does not owe Southeast Asia a living. For the moment the region has a comparative advantage in a number of areas: electronics and other types of assembly, clothing, premium grades of rice, palm oil, rubber for specialist purposes. But not much else.

To be sure, foreign investors would stand to make substantial losses were the region to 'go down the tube'. But in terms of total external investment by these investors, the commitment in the region is insubstantial. Japanese investment in the US is much greater, for example.

Despite current moves towards the removal of encumbrances to world trade there remains significant opposition to total freedom—and not only from countries like Indonesia and the Philippines who fear for the competitiveness of their manufacturing industries in a total free-market situation. The European Community, although enlarged, remains a bastion of protectionism. A few specialised, mainly agricultural, commodities that cannot be produced outside the tropics will always obtain free entry. It prefers to channel benefits to its own relatively low-cost producers such as Portugal and Poland.

Japan will probably cope with its own drastic changes in demographic structure—a rapidly-ageing population—and in its economy by continuing to shift offshore those parts of its manufacturing capacity in which productivity cannot be enhanced by further capital investment. It will do this because it is unwilling to import labour in quantity sufficient to compensate for the decline in its own labour-force, for it has serious difficulties with multiculturalism.

Southeast Asia is obviously an economic adjunct to Japan, as it is to the global economy generally. But a vital adjunct? No. There are too many alternatives elsewhere.

Might Southeast Asia become a semi-autonomous regional economy, much as the European Community and the US are? Would one of its major sources of wealth become the supply of capital and entrepreneurial know-how to other, less-developed regions? By 2005 Southeast Asia will have about 550–560 million people, roughly 8.5 per cent of humankind. This is double that of the US and around half or a bit less of the population of India or China. While much less wealthy than the former, it is much more wealthy than the two latter to the extent that it is a capital exporter as well as a capital importer. Consequently it is to some degree capable of self-sustained growth both in respect of potential markets and investment. Labour and land it has but technology will necessarily have mostly to be imported, as the region's own research and development capacity is very limited at present.

If the region were really on the way to becoming a semi-autonomous regional economy it might be expected that the proportion of intra-regional trade to total trade would have grown. This has not happened. Nor will it until its internal legal barriers, especially in respect of the trade in services, are substantially dismantled. Long-term security of investments is not necessarily assured. In some cases even sovereign risk is high, for instance in Myanmar and Cambodia. Investors thus require high returns and quick repayment to compensate. The fields in which these can be obtained are quite limited, so that a great deal of internal putting of houses in order will be needed both to keep locally generated capital and to attract it from sources internal to the region, let alone from outside. The recent Asian financial crisis, by no means over, is a warning that there is no substitute for sound financial management at all levels from government down. It is clear that such management is not yet fully sound, that the financial cowboys have not necessarily been reined in, that business confidence has not yet been fully restored. While the region may at some date develop a prosperous semi-autonomous economy on European or North American lines, that time is far off.

Or is the alternative a long-continued state of semi-dependence? Dependence upon the west for markets, capital and know-how may continue in parallel with dependence upon investment inside the region where returns are safe and reasonably high as well as outside in the large but still relatively poor economies of China and South Asia. Those Southeast Asian countries with Overseas Chinese and South Asian populations will be well placed to participate, if only for practical reasons of communication.

Cultural diversity is thus an advantage in the marketplace. Is it an advantage in other spheres? Will it continue even as the constituent cultures interact and in interacting change themselves, as through history they have done? In respect of the first question the answer must depend upon which spheres. A great deal of the politics of the region is ethnically based. Thai politics is dominated by Central Thai, themselves by no means a totally cohesive group. Malaysian politics is dominated by Malays. The multicultural parties—Penang's Gerakan is one—are weak and small. The governing Alliance is founded upon separate but unequal parties, one each for Malays, Chinese and Indians. In Myanmar and in Viet Nam the political process is dominated by Burmans and *Kinh* respectively. Could it be otherwise given their proportion in the population? Much the same is true of Chinese in Singapore and Javanese in Indonesia.

The Philippines' situation is different, because the dominant power is religious—Christian rather than ethnic. Ilocanos, Pampangans, Visayans and many others make common political cause despite regional, cultural and linguistic differences. Whether some sections of the Muslim minority will settle permanently for the modicum of internal autonomy it now has is another matter.

The Indonesian situation is potentially explosive. The country has been held together since its foundation basically by the exercise of firm control from the centre. That control has now slipped. Centrifugal forces prevail and unless the grievances of the outer provinces are addressed—and quickly—there is real prospect of serious conflict possibly leading to secession. Those grievances, however, are only partly related to ethnicity and religion. Aceh is dominated by Acehnese, many of whom observe the tenets of Islam more strictly than other Indonesians. Parts of Maluku are controlled by Christians, but economic factors play a part. Nevertheless, the fear of being a 'minority in one's own land' is real. It exists amongst Dayaks vis-a-vis recently immigrant Madurese in western Kalimantan, as amongst indigenous Lampung people in southern Sumatera or West Irian's 'Papuans' in relation to Javanese and other migrant groups whose presence was hastened and often paid for by previous regimes. The possible cost in lives and political turmoil of decades of 'transmigration'—government-sponsored settlement—is only now becoming apparent. Land was often simply seized with little or no compensation for its traditional owners, most of whom the government did not recognise as such.

But Indonesia, paradoxically, offers an example of the way in which cultural differences can be contained within a single polity. At the time of the nation's foundation there was no dominant 'Indonesian culture' within which others could be subsumed, to which others could be assimilated. A crucial decision was to develop a single national language—in fact based upon 'trade Malay' and Minangkabau, the former the *lingua franca* of trade throughout much of the coastal parts of insular Southeast Asia. Bahasa Indonesia is the universal language of education, business and administration, nowadays for many their only language. Cultural differences are widely recognised and accepted in people's day-to-day dealings with each other. Bataks may glory in their cannibal past, Javanese in their past cultural achievements. But they see themselves first and foremost as Indonesians. Time will tell if that self-view is glue sufficiently strong to hold the nation together.

By contrast, in many of the countries dominated by a single more or less unified group—Burmans, Thai, Khmer, *Kinh* (Vietnamese)—policies and practice tend to be overtly or covertly assimilationist. Dominant groups tend to write their own agendas so it is no surprise, for example, that some purported histories of Thailand omit all mention of peoples such as the Mon and the Khmer—descendants of advanced civilisations—who happened to occupy substantial portions of what later became Thailand. Minorities in that land, until recently, have been subjected to worse indignities than having their history ignored. Some were not citizens of Thailand, because to be a citizen it was necessary to speak Thai. During the time of the dictator Pibul, Thai Muslims were persecuted. In nearby Malaysia, inland aboriginal peoples were the subject of slave raids well into the nineteenth century and are today, like Chinese and others, the subject of Muslim missionary activity, for Islam is the state religion. This is not to suggest that assimilation is 'forced', for there are many kinds and degrees of pressure.

The retention of cultural identity is obviously a two-way process. Minorities must wish and act to retain it. Schools propagate a majority culture, usually the majority language. Minorities without a written language are severely disadvantaged, because to become literate is to become literate only in the language of others. But possession of a written language is no guarantee of cultural continuity if there is no initiative to use it. Thus for the Chams of southern Viet Nam, speakers of an ancient Malayo-Polynesian tongue, there are virtually no books and no newspapers available. Schools generally do not teach Cham. By contrast, in Sabah and Sarawak, there is a fair range of materials in local languages. Some daily newspapers are trilingual in Malay, English and a local language. Local languages—Dayak, Iban (similar tongues), and Kadazan—are used in radio broadcasts. For larger, wealthier groups such aids to cultural continuity are economically viable. Other, smaller groups—the Rhadé of the central highlands of Viet Nam are an example—are culturally so vigorous that they clearly will survive. The future of others is doubtful: the Orang Kanaq of Johor, Peninsular Malaysia; the Penan, foragers in deep jungle in Sarawak, and dozens of others.

Culture is not static. Nor can it be readily imposed from above. Culture contact continues to lead to the evolution of new forms. Especially in 'intellectual culture', in music, art and literature, cross-fertilisation is leading to exciting new forms. The patterns of people, land and economy in Southeast Asia have always been rich and variegated. As the wheel of time turns so the kaleidoscope will fall into yet more shapes incorporating old and new from within and without.

SERIOUS WORKS FOR SERIOUS SCHOLARS

Neither this nor the list that follows is exhaustive. The main focus is 'change through time'.

Acharya, Amitav, 2000, *The quest for identity,* Oxford University Press, Singapore.

Arakawa, H. (ed.), 1969, *Climates of northern and eastern Asia,* Elsevier, Amsterdam, chapters 3 and 4 on the Philippines and Indonesia respectively.

Boomgaard, P., 1998, 'Environmental impact of the European presence in Southeast Asia, 17th–19th centuries', *Illes i imperis,* 1, 21–35.

Brookfield, H.C., Abdul Samad Hadi and Zaharah Mahmud, 1991, *The city in the village*, Oxford University Press, Singapore. Emergence of the Kuala Lumpur urban region.

Brookfield, H., Potter, L. and Byron, Y., 1995, *In place of the forest,* UNUP, Tokyo. Social, economic and environmental consequences of deforestation.

Burkill, I.H., 1966, *A dictionary of the economic products of the Malay Peninsula,* Kuala Lumpur. Covers most of region. Very detailed.

Chandler, D.P. and Steinberg, D.J., 1987, *In search of Southeast Asia,* University of Hawaii Press, Honolulu. Revised edition of a major history.

Corbet, G.B. and Hill, J.E., 1992, *The mammals of the Indomalayan region,* Oxford University Press, Oxford. Based on taxa though with a brief synthesis in its introduction.

Dutt, A.K. (ed.), 1996, *Southeast Asia: a ten nation region,* Kluwer, Dordrecht.

Fisher, Charles, 1964, *South-East Asia,* Methuen, London. Old but still of interest. 'Classic' geography.

Fontanel, J. and Chantefort, A., 1978, *Bioclimats du monde indonésien,* Institut Français, Pondichery. Excellent maps and diagrams and an extended summary in English.

Forbes, Dean, 1996, *Asian metropolis, urbanisation and the Southeast Asian city,* Oxford University Press, Melbourne. Short introduction.

Geertz, Clifford, 1971, *Agricultural involution,* University of California Press, Berkeley.

Ginsberg, Norton, Kopell, Bruce and McGee, T.G. (eds), 1991, *The extended metropolis,* University of Hawaii Press, Honolulu. Chapters 1–4, 12–13.

Hanks, L., 1972, *Rice and man, agricultural ecology in Southeast Asia,* Aldine Publishing Co., Chicago.

Hickey, Gerald C., 1982, *Free in the forest* and *Sons of the mountains.* Classic studies of minorities in Viet Nam's Central Highlands.

Hitchcock, M., King, V. T. and Parnwell, M. (eds), 1993, *Tourism in South-east Asia,* Routledge, London. Studies of a rapidly growing service sector.

Hill, R.D. (ed.), 1979, *South-East Asia, a systematic geography,* Oxford University Press, Kuala Lumpur. Dated but still contains much of interest.

Hill, R.D., 1982, *Agriculture in the Malaysian region,* Akadémiai Kiadó, Budapest. A major clearing in the jungle.

Hill, R.D., 1998, 'Stasis and change in forty years of Southeast Asian agriculture', *Singapore journal of tropical geography*, 19(1), 1–25. Review of agricultural change in the region.

Hill, R.D., Owen, Norman G. and Roberts, E.V. (eds), *Fishing in troubled waters*, Centre of Asian Studies, University of Hong Kong, Hong Kong.

Hirose, L. and Walker, B.H. (eds), 1996, *Global change and terrestrial ecosystems in monsoon Asia*, Kluwer, Dordrecht, Chapters 1, 4, 5. State of the art analysis.

Jumsai, Sumet, 1997, *NAGA: cultural origins in Siam and the West Pacific*, Chalermnit Press and DD Books, Bangkok.

Kunstadter, P., Chapman, E.C. and Sanga Sabhasri (eds), 1978, *Farmers in the forest*, University Press of Hawaii, Honolulu. Realities of shifting cultivation.

Lee Kip Lin, 1988, *The Singapore house*, Times Editions, Singapore. Lavishly illustrated.

Leinbach, T.R. and Ulack, R. (eds), 1998, *Southeast Asia: diversity and development*, Prentice-Hall, Upper Saddle River, NJ.

Lim Heng Kow, 1978, *The evolution of the urban system in Malaya*, Penerbit Universiti Malaya, Kuala Lumpur. A pioneer study never repeated in other countries.

McGee, T.G., 1967, *The Southeast Asian city*, Bell, London. Pioneer work.

McGee, T.G. and Robinson, Ira M. (eds), 1995, *The mega-urban regions of Southeast Asia*, University of British Columbia Press, Vancouver. Important study.

Nieuwolt, S., 1981, 'The climates of continental Southeast Asia', in K. Takahashi and H. Arakawa (eds), *Climates of Southern and Western Asia*, Elsevier Scientific, Amsterdam.

Nieuwolt, S., 1982, 'Agroclimatic zones in Peninsular Malaysia;, *Climatological notes*, 30, 14–19. Local study worthy of replication throughout the region.

Nolan, Marcus, 1990, *Pacific basin developing countries, prospects for the future*, Institute for International Economics, Washington DC. Somewhat dated prophecy but much of interest.

O'Connor, A., 1983, *A theory of indigenous Southeast Asia urbanism*, Institute of Southeast Asian Studies, Singapore.

Oppenheimer, S., 1998, *Eden in the East*, Weidenfeld and Nicolson, London.

Ormeling, F.J., 1957, *The Timor problem*, J.B. Wolters, Djakarta. Classic study. Why East Timor has a difficult road ahead.

Osborne, Milton E., 1990, *Southeast Asia, an illustrated introductory history*, Allen & Unwin, Sydney. Long the standard work. Engagingly written.

Osborne, Milton E., 2000, *The Mekong: turbulent past, uncertain future*, Allen & Unwin, Sydney. Latest in series of excellent historical studies of Indochina.

Parnwell, M.J.G. and Bryant, R.L., 1996, *Environmental change in South-East Asia*, Routledge, London and New York.

Perry, Martin, Kong, Lily and Yeoh, Brenda, 1997, *Singapore, a developmental city state*, J. Wiley, Chichester.

Popkin, S.L., 1979, *The rational peasant*, University of California Press, Berkeley.

Powell, Robert, 1993, *The Asian house*, Select Books, Singapore. Actually on Southeast Asia.

Powell, Robert, 1998, *The tropical Asian house*, Select Books, Singapore. Both lavishly illustrated.

Rigg, J., 1997, *Southeast Asia: the human landscapes of modernization and development*, Routledge, London.

Rodan, G., Hewison, K. and Robinson, R. (eds), 1997, *The political economy of South-East Asia*, Oxford University Press, Melbourne.

Scott, J.C., 1979, *The moral economy of the peasant*, Yale University Press, New Haven.

Skeldon, Ronald, 1990, *Population mobility in developing countries*, Belhaven Press, London.

Skeldon, Ronald, 1997, *Migration and development: a global perspective*, Longman, Harlow. Both contain much of relevance to Southeast Asia.

Takeuchi, K., Jayawardena, A.W. and Takahasi Y. (compilers), 1995, *Catalogue of rivers for Southeast Asia and the Pacific*, UNESCO-IHP, Hong Kong. Basic data.

United Nations Centre for Human Settlements (Habitat) (eds), 1996, *The management of secondary cities in Southeast Asia*, UNCHS (Habitat), Nairobi.

Vatikiotis, M.R.J., 1996, *Political change in Southeast Asia*, Routledge, London.

Wallace, Alfred R., 1893 but reprinted many times. *The Malay archipelago*. The pioneer work in natural history, still unrivalled.

Watters, R.F. and McGee, T.G. (eds), 1997, *Asia Pacific, new geographies of the Pacific Rim*, Hurst, London. Essays, many on Southeast Asia.

Wheatley, Paul, 1983, *Nagara and commandery,* University of Chicago, Chicago. Origins of Southeast Asian urbanism.

Whitmore, T.C., 1998, *An introduction to tropical rain forests*, Oxford University Press, Oxford. Not just on Southeast Asia but strongly oriented to it.

Wu, David Y.H., McQueen, Humphrey and Yamamoto Yasushi (eds), 1997, *Emerging pluralism in Asia and the Pacific*, Hong Kong Institute of Asia-Pacific Studies, Hong Kong. Chapters 3–5, 8.

Yeoh, Brenda S.A., 1996, *Contesting space*, Oxford University Press, Kuala Lumpur. Singapore as a colonial 'contested space'.

LIGHTER READING

Much of the flavour of the region can be gained from travel literature and fiction. Some titles are dated. All are interesting and enjoyable.

Banomyong [Phanomyong] Pridi, *The king of the white elephant*, reprinted 1990. Thammasat Association, Los Angeles.

Baum, Vicki, *A tale from Bali*, reprinted 1999, Periplus, Hong Kong. Historical novel.

Bird, Isabella M., *The Golden Khersonese and the way thither*, reprinted 1967, Oxford University Press, Kuala Lumpur. Travels in Malaya in the 1870s.

Boontawe Kampoon, *Child of the Northeast*, trans. 1991, Editions Duang Kamol, Bangkok.

Boule, Pierre, *Sacrilege in Malaya*, trans. 1983, Oxford University Press, Kuala Lumpur.

Collis, Maurice, *Land of the great image*, 1943, Faber and Faber, London; *Lords of the sunset*, reprint 1996, AVA Publishing House, Bangkok; *She was a queen*, reprint 1991, New Directions, New York: *Siamese White*, 1951, Faber and Faber, London.

Conrad Joseph, *Almayer's folly*, 1895; *An outcast of the islands*, 1896; *Lord Jim*, 1900. All reprinted by Penguin Books.

Colquhoun, Archibald, *Across Chryse*, 1883, Low, Marston, Searle and Rivington, London; *Amongst the Shans*, 1885, Field & Tuer, London.

D'Alpuget, Blanche, *Monkeys in the dark*, 1980, Penguin Books, Ringwood, Vic.; *Turtle beach*, 1992, Penguin Books, London.

Dooley, Tom, *Deliver us from evil*, 1956, New American Library, New York; Viet Nam memoirs. *The edge of tomorrow*, 1958, Farrar, Strauss and Giroux, New York; Memoir of Laos.

Duong Thu Hong, *Novel without a name*, 1995, W. Morrow, New York, Viet Nam war.

Duras, Marguerite, *The lover*, 1986, Flamingo, London, Viet Nam.

Emerson, Gloria, *Winners and losers*, 1976, W.W. Norton, New York. Viet Nam War.

Enright, D.J., *Memoirs of a mendicant professor*, 1969, Chatto and Windus, London.

Farrell, J.G., *The Singapore grip*, 1978, Weidenfeld and Nicholson, London.

Fauconnier, H., *The soul of Malaya*, 1932, Elkin Matthews and Marrot, London.

Fernando, Lloyd (ed.), *Twenty-two Malaysian stories*, 1968, Heinemann Educational Books (Asia), Singapore.

Geddes, W.R., *Nine Dayak nights*, 1957, Oxford University Press, Melbourne. Ethnography that reads like a novel.

Goh Poh Seng, *Eyewitness*; 1976, Heinemann Educational Books (Asia), Singapore; *The Immolation*, 1977, Heinemann Educational Books (Asia), Singapore.

Gonzalez, N.V.M., *The bamboo dancers*, 1993 Bookmark, Makati; *Children of the ash-covered loam*, 1954, Benipayo Press, Manila; *Mindoro and beyond*, 1979, University of the Philippines Press, Quezon City. Short stories.

Greene, Graham, *The quiet American*, 1955, Heinemann, London. Viet Nam classic.

Han Suyin, . . . *And the rain my drink*, 1956, Cape, London. Malayan Emergency.

Huynh Sang Thong (ed.), *To be made over*, 1988, Yale Center for International and Area Studies, New Haven. Socialist Viet Nam.

Jeyaretnam, Philip, *Raffles Place ragtime*, 1988, Times Books, Singapore.

José, F. Sionil, *Po-on, Tree, My brother, my executioner, The pretenders, Mass, Ermita, Three Filipino women, Viajero, Sin, The god-stealer and other stories, Waywaya, Platinum.* Novels and stories set in the Philippines. Various dates, all published by Solidaridad, Manila.

Keith, Agnes, *Three came home*, reprinted 1985, Eland Books, London; *Land below the wind*, 1939, Michael Joseph, London. North Borneo memoirs.

Khamsing Srinawk, *The politician and other stories*, 1973, Oxford University Press, Kuala Lumpur.

Lewis, Norman, *A dragon apparent: travels in Indochina*, 1951, Cape, London.

Lim, Catherine, *The serpent's tooth*, 1982, Times Books, Singapore.

Lubis, Mochtar, *The outlaw and other stories*, 1987, Oxford University Press, Singapore; *A road with no end*, 1968, Hutchinson, London; *Twilight in Djakarta*, 1964, Vanguard Press, New York.

Lulofs, Madelon, *Rubber*, 1991, Oxford University Press, Singapore; *Coolie*, 1992, Oxford University Press, Kuala Lumpur. Dutch East Indies.

Mathews, Anna, *The night of Purnama*, 1963, Cape, London. Bali.

May, Someth, *Cambodian witness*, 1986, Faber, London.

'Multatuli' [Edward Douwes Dekker], *Max Havelaar*, in Dutch, 1860. 'Succès de scandale', trans. 1967 and 1984, Nijhoff, Leyden.

Ngo Vinh Long, *Before the revolution*, 1973, MIT Press, Cambridge, Mass. Viet Nam peasantry.

Orwell, George, *Burmese days*, 1950, Harcourt Brace, New York.

Pomeroy, William J., *The forest: a personal history of the Huk guerilla struggle in the Philippines*, 1965, International Publishers, New York.

Pramoedya Ananta Toer, *Awakenings*, 1991, Penguin, Harmondsworth; *The fugitive*, 1975, Heinemann, Hong Kong; *This earth of mankind*, 1982, Penguin

Books, Canberra; *Child of all nations*, 1984, Penguin, Harmondsworth; *House of glass*, 1996, W. Morrow, New York. Indonesian novels.

Pramoj Kukrit, *Red bamboo*, 1968, Progress Publishing, Bangkok; *Si Phaendin (Four reigns)*, Duang Kamol, Bangkok, Thailand.

Rizal, José, *The lost Eden*, 1987, University of Hawaii Press, Honolulu; *The subversive*, 1968, Norton, New York.

Santos, Bienvenido N., *Memory's fictions*, 1993, New Day, Quezon City, memoirs; *The volcano*, 1965, New Day, Manila; *You lovely people*, 1955, Bookmark, Makati; *Brother, my brother*, 1990, Bookmark, Makati; *The day the dancers came*, 1991, Bookmark, Makati.

Schanberg, Sydney, 1985, *The life and death of Dith Pran,* Penguin, New York. Cambodia under Khmer Rouge.

Seagrave, Sterling, *The Marcos dynasty*, 1988, Harper & Row, New York.

Sesser, Stan, *The lands of charm and cruelty: travels in Southeast Asia*, 1994, Picador, London.

Shahnon Ahmad, *No harvest but a thorn*, 1972, Oxford University Press, Kuala Lumpur; *Rope of ash*, 1979, Oxford University Press, Kuala Lumpur. Malayan novels.

Tan Kok Seng, *Son of Singapore*, 1972, University Education Press, Singapore; *Man of Malaysia*, 1974, Heinemann, Kuala Lumpur; *Eye on the world*, 1975, Heinemann, Kuala Lumpur. Autobiography.

Tran Tu Binh, *The red earth*, 1985, Center for International Studies, Ohio University, Athens, Ohio. Memoir of Viet Nam rubber plantation life.

Truong Nhu Tang, *Journal of a Viet Cong*, 1986, Cape, Lonon.

West, Morris, *The ambassador*, 1965, Dell, New York. Viet Nam novel.

Wintle, Justin, *Romancing Vietnam: inside the boat country*, 1991, Viking, New York. Travel.

Wood, W.A.R., *Consul in paradise: sixty-nine years in Siam*, 1965, Souvenir Press, London. Memoirs.

Wurlitzer, Rudolph, *Hard travel to sacred places*, 1994, Shambhala, Boston. Mainland Southeast Asia.

INDEX